Introducing Investments

Pearson Education

We work with leading authors to develop the strongest educational materials in finance, bringing cutting-edge thinking and best learning practice to a global market.

Under a range of well-known imprints, including Financial Times Prentice Hall, we craft high quality print and electronic publications which help readers to understand and apply their content, whether studying or at work.

To find out more about the complete range of our publishing, please visit us on the World Wide Web at: www.pearsoneduc.com

Introducing Investments
A personal finance approach

Keith Redhead

FT Prentice Hall
FINANCIAL TIMES

An imprint of **Pearson Education**

Harlow, England • London • New York • Boston • San Francisco • Toronto • Sydney • Singapore • Hong Kong
Tokyo • Seoul • Taipei • New Delhi • Cape Town • Madrid • Mexico City • Amsterdam • Munich • Paris • Milan

Pearson Education Limited

Edinburgh Gate
Harlow
Essex CM20 2JE

and Associated Companies around the world

Visit us on the World Wide Web at:
www.pearsoneduc.com

——————————————

ISBN 0 273 67305 X

British Library Cataloguing-in-Publication Data
A catalogue record for this book is available from the British Library

Library of Congress Cataloging-in-Publication Data

Redhead, Keith, 1949–
    Introducing investments: a personal finance approach / Keith Redhead.
        p. cm.
    Includes index.
    ISBN 0–273–67305–X (pbk.)
    1. Investments. 2. Portfolio management. 3. Finance, Personal. I. Title.

HG4521 .R364 2002
332,63'2—dc21

                                            2002070246

10 9 8 7 6 5 4 3 2 1
06 05 04 03

Typeset by 3 in 10/13pt Sabon
Printed and bound by Ashford Colour Press Ltd., Gosport

Contents

Preface

Financial investment is now one of the essential decisions taken by a large proportion, possibly a majority, of the adult populations of developed countries. Although the direct holding of stocks and bonds remains a minority (albeit a significant minority) activity, many more people have collective investments in forms such as pension funds and insurance funds. With demographic trends increasing the proportion of pensioners in the population, governments are signalling their reduced future provision of state pensions. Reduced state provision requires increased investment by individuals in their preparations for retirement.

Books on investment tend to fall into two categories. Those aimed at the general reader are usually descriptive and mainly list the types of investment available. The other category is aimed at an academic readership. These are highly analytical and often appear to lack direct relevance to practical decision making by individuals. Their level of theoretical and mathematical rigour can render them inaccessible to many readers.

This book attempts to bridge that divide. The aim is to provide a readable overview of investment alternatives together with an introduction to the relevant analysis. It aims to describe the investments available to individuals and to provide the analytical concepts for the evaluation of those alternatives without resort to heavy mathematics.

The potential readership of this book is broad. It should be suitable for non-specialist undergraduate and MBA students. In particular business students, for whom investment is a part rather than the main focus of their courses, are likely to find that this text meets their needs. People studying for qualification as financial advisers will find that this book covers a vital component of their courses of study. The book should also be of interest to readers whose concern is not with the acquisition of formal qualifications but with acquiring the knowledge required for informed decision making in relation to investment.

The chapters can be seen as dividing into themes. Chapters 2 to 6 focus on retail investments, particularly collective investments. Chapters 7 to 9 relate to the operation of financial markets. Chapters 10 to 14 deal with financial derivatives. Chapters 15 to 18 are concerned with capital market theory. Chapters 19 to 23 focus on methods of investment analysis and their usefulness. Chapters 24 to 26 focus on the construction and management of investment portfolios. Chapters 27 to 30 focus on investment in bonds.

For Susan, with love

Acknowledgements

We are grateful to the following for permission to reproduce copyright material:

Figure 1: 'Performance of GMIA against the DJIA (1997–2001)' from the *Financial Times, Mastering Investment Supplement*, Part 8, July 2 2001, p. 4 by Ritchie Lowry, reproduced with the permission of Good Money (http://www.goodmoney.com).

'Sandler addresses information but not psychology' from *Company Accountant*, Issue 170, October, published by The Institute of Company Accountants (Redhead, K. 2002); 'Enron, Worldcom and lemons' from *Company Accountant*, Issue 169, August, published by The Institute of Company Accountants (Redhead, K. 2002); 'Business as usual after boom and bust' from the *Financial Times, Mastering Investment Supplement*, Part 9, July 9 2001, pp. 2–4 by Amar Bhidé © Amar Bhidé; 'The coming of the single financial regulator' from the *Financial Times, Mastering Investment Supplement*, Part 10, July 16 2001, pp. 8, 10 by Howard Davies © Howard Davies; 'The perils for investors of human nature' from the *Financial Times, Mastering Investment Supplement*, Part 6, June 18 2001, pp. 6–7 by Simon Gervais and Terrance Odean © Simon Gervais and Terrance Odean; 'The curious case of Palm and 3Com' from the *Financial Times, Mastering Investment Supplement*, Part 6, June 18 2001, pp. 8, 10 by Owen Lamont © Owen Lamont; 'The logic that lies behind overseas diversification' from the *Financial Times, Mastering Investment Supplement*, Part 3, May 28 2001, pp. 6–7 by Robert Hodrick © Robert Hodrick; 'A model weighting game in estimating expected returns' from the *Financial Times, Mastering Investment Supplement*, Part 2, May 21 2001, pp. 6–7 by Ľuboš Pástor © Ľuboš Pástor; 'Markets and the business cycle' from the *Financial Times, Mastering Investment Supplement*, Part 2, May 21 2001, pp. 8, 10 by Jeremy Siegel © Jeremy Siegel; 'Investors seek lessons in thinking' from the *Financial Times, Mastering Investment Supplement*, Part 6, June 18 2001, pp. 2–4 by Nicholas Barberis © Nicholas Barberis; 'The bottom line to a social conscience' from the *Financial Times, Mastering Investment Supplement*, Part 8, July 2 2001, pp. 2–4 by Geoffrey Heal © Geoffrey Heal; 'Room for improvement in protecting investors' from the *Financial Times, Mastering Investment Supplement*, Part 8, July 2 2001, pp. 12–13 by David Beim © David Beim.

In some instances we have been unable to trace the owners of copyright material, and we would appreciate any information that would enable us to do so.

Chapter 1

Introduction

People save and invest for various purposes: for holidays, home improvements, cars, deposits for house purchase, children's education, old age and general security. Some of these are short-term objectives and others long-term. The single biggest long-term objective is usually the provision of a retirement income. The time horizon of the investment will influence the nature of the investment. Savings for a holiday are unlikely to be put into a risky investment such as shares, while saving for a pension is unlikely to be in low-return investments such as bank or building society accounts.

The largest investment item for many people is their pension fund. At an annuity rate of 8% p.a., a pension of £20,000 a year requires a pension fund of £250,000. Whether a pension is being provided by an employer or is being funded by the employee, a substantial sum of money needs to be accumulated. So successful investing is vital.

The need to invest for retirement is becoming increasingly important as governments progressively back away from promising adequate state pensions. In Europe and North America, as well as elsewhere in the world, the proportion of retired people in the population is increasing rapidly. This is often called the demographic timebomb. Life expectancy is increasing steadily, and with it the average period of life in retirement. The result is a rising ratio of pensioners to workers. It is often seen to be unrealistic to expect those of working age to pay the increasingly high taxes needed to pay good pensions to members of the retired population. One answer is to encourage people to provide for their own pensions by accumulating pension funds during their working lives (another approach is to raise the retirement age).

According to the US Census Bureau (1999), in Western Europe (the members of the European Union as of 1999) the ratio of people of retirement age (65+) to those of working age (20–64) was about 0.15 in 1950. By 2000 it had nearly doubled to 0.29. It is projected to approximately double again, to about 0.64, by 2050. The ratio of pensioners to people of working age would have risen from about 1:6 in 1950, to around 4:6 in 2050. It is clearly unrealistic to expect those of working age to be able, and willing, to pay sufficient taxation to provide so many retirees with adequate pensions.

There is also the issue of how to invest. Many people see stock market investments, particularly shares, as too risky. However, historically shares have massively outperformed other forms of investment such as bank deposits. The issue of relative risk needs to be seen in relation to an investor's time horizon. The picture from a 40-year perspective is very different from that of a one-month perspective. Investments in shares can benefit from time diversification; over long periods of time good periods can balance out bad periods. Also from a long-term perspective, the accumulated income from investments becomes more important in determining the final sum accumulated. For example, £1,000 invested at 4% over forty years will grow to £4,801 whereas at 8% it would grow to £21,725. The income receipts from stock market investments may be more stable than the interest receipts on bank or building society deposits.

According to the Barclays Capital Equity-Gilt study (1999), £100 invested in a balanced portfolio of UK shares in 1918 would have grown to nearly £420,000 by 1998 (with dividends, net of basic rate tax, being reinvested). An investment of £100 in Treasury bills over the same period would have grown to less than £2,500 (the Treasury Bill rate of return is roughly equivalent to premium bank or building society deposits). These represent rates of return of approximately 11% and 4% respectively. When allowance is made for the effects of inflation on the purchasing power of money, the average rate of return from bank and building society deposits has not been far above zero. The message seems to be that the accumulation of wealth over long time periods, such as the periods typically required for the accumulation of pension funds, requires investments to be made in stock markets.

Investors and borrowers

The financial system serves the function of transferring money from those wanting to invest to those wishing to borrow (the term borrower is being used loosely here since firms that raise capital by issuing shares are, strictly speaking, not borrowing but selling equity in their enterprises). The cash flows are illustrated by Figure 1.1. Savers invest by depositing money in banks (or building societies), by buying bonds, or by buying shares. The borrowers may be individuals who obtain bank loans or mortgages, governments that sell bonds, or private companies that raise money by both of these means plus the sale of shares. The money passes from investors to borrowers through the intermediation of banks or stock exchanges.

Most stock market investment by individuals is through the medium of institutional investments such as pension funds, insurance funds, unit trusts and investment trusts. The financial system cash flows where stock market investment is carried out through institutional investments are illustrated by Figure 1.2.

Personal financial planning

Personal financial planning is the process of planning one's spending, financing and investing so as to optimise one's financial situation. A personal financial plan

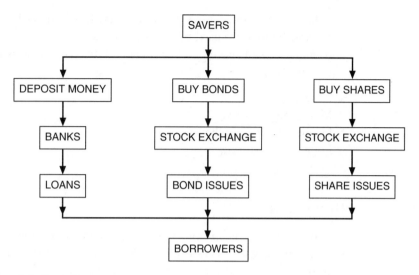

Figure 1.1 Cash flows

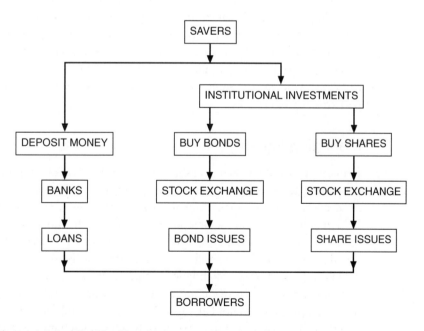

Figure 1.2 Institutional investments

specifies one's financial aims and objectives. It also describes the saving, financing and investing that are used to achieve these goals.

A financial plan should contain personal finance decisions related to the following components:

1 Budgeting.
2 Managing liquidity.
3 Financing large purchases.
4 Long-term investing.
5 Insurance.

Budgeting

The budgeting decision concerns the division of income between spending and saving. Saving will increase one's assets and/or reduce one's debts. If spending exceeds income (i.e. there is negative saving), assets will be reduced and/or liabilities increased. The excess of assets over liabilities is one's net worth. Saving increases net worth (negative saving reduces it).

Some saving might be very short term, for example keeping some of this month's salary to finance spending next month. Very short-term saving is part of the process of managing liquidity. Other saving is medium term; saving for a holiday, a car or a deposit on a house are examples. Such saving is for the purpose of financing large purchases. Long-term saving can have an investment horizon of 40 years or more. The most important long-term saving for many people is saving for a pension to provide an income in retirement. Other purposes of long-term saving include the financing of children's education and building up an estate to pass to one's heirs.

Long-term saving for a pension will feel much more important when the investor is 55 than when that investor is 25. However early saving is far more productive than later saving. For example, £1,000 invested for ten years at 8% p.a. will grow to £2,159 whereas the same sum invested at the same rate of return for forty years will grow to £21,725.

Managing liquidity

Liquidity is readily available cash, or other means of making purchases. Liquidity is needed for items such as day-to-day shopping and meeting unexpected expenses such as repair bills. Money management involves decisions regarding how much money to hold in liquid form and the precise forms in which the money is to be held. Generally the more liquid an asset is, the lower the return to be expected from it. The most liquid assets are banknotes and money in chequeable bank accounts. These assets provide little or no interest. Slightly less liquid assets, such as deposit accounts in banks or building societies, provide more interest but are slightly less accessible. It is normally inappropriate to hold all of one's wealth in liquid form since assets that are less liquid (such as bonds and shares) generally offer much higher expected rates of return.

The alternative to using one's own liquidity might be to borrow, for example by using a credit card. Credit management is concerned with decisions as to how much and what sources of credit to use. While credit is a source of additional liquidity, it has the disadvantage that interest has to be paid – and often at a high rate.

Financing large purchases

The finance for large purchases may be generated by saving or by borrowing. Savings need not be in highly liquid form (until the purchase is made) but should not be in a risky form. Such savings would be expected to yield more interest than liquid cash but a lower return than should be available from risky assets such as shares and long-term bonds.

The accumulation of money for an expenditure in one, two or three years might be in the form of bank deposits or other short-maturity money market investments. Over such a timescale, the risk of capital loss from investment in shares or long-term bonds might be seen as excessive relative to the potential extra return from such investments. As a general rule, the value of stock market investments increases more than in proportion to time while risk increases less than proportionately to the passage of time. Such relationships make stock market investments unsuitable for short-term saving but very suitable for the long-term accumulation of wealth.

The types of large expenditure for which saving or borrowing are likely to be used include holidays, car purchase, higher education and house purchase. Large expenditures, such as house purchase, are likely to be financed partly by borrowing (for example by means of mortgages). Short-timescale expenditures such as holidays are more likely to be financed by saving. The credit management involved when borrowing requires consideration of factors such as the number of years required for repayment and the affordability of the monthly repayments. For a particular size of debt, reducing the monthly payments will entail increasing the number of years for which repayments will be made. Consideration should also be given to the potential variability of regular payments. For example, mortgage borrowing typically carries the risk that interest rates, and hence monthly repayments, will rise.

Long-term investing

Although there may be some other reasons for long-term saving, such as funding children's education or provision of a legacy to pass on to one's heirs, the most important is the provision of a retirement income. To appreciate the scale of what is involved for an individual, consider the case of someone expecting to fund 20 years' retirement income from 40 years' work. Suppose that the aim is to maintain the standard of living at the level achieved during the working life. In the absence of a prospective real rate of return on investments, one-third of the income received while working needs to be saved in order to provide the retirement income.

The need to save one-third of one's income is based on a zero real net rate of return on investments (the real net rate of return is the return after taking account of inflation and taxation). Historically the real net rates of return on bank and building society accounts have been only a little above zero, on average. The achievement of high real net rates of return has required investment in shares. So the attainment of good investment returns has necessitated acceptance of the risk associated with investment in shares. However, that risk needs to be seen from a long-term perspective. Figure 1.3 (a and b) illustrates the behaviour of expected asset value and risk in relation to the passage of time.

The shape of the curve in Figure 1.3a can be explained as being similar to the effect of compound interest. The shape of the curve in Figure 1.3b might be explained in terms of the effects of time diversification; over a long timespan good periods tend to offset bad periods. The two figures illustrate why stock market investments should be used for long-term rather than short-term savings. In the short term shares provide high risk relative to return, while in the long term they tend to produce high return relative to risk.

Insurance

Insurance entails making payments to an insurer for financial protection. There is property insurance, which provides compensation in the event of damage to, or loss of, property such as houses and cars. Life assurance pays money to dependants in the event of one's death. A range of other eventualities can be insured against. For example, it is possible to take out insurance to cover health care expenses or loss of income.

Sometimes insurance is combined with a savings scheme. This is the case with life assurance products such as endowment policies and whole-of-life policies. Someone considering such schemes should give thought to the question of whether it might be advantageous to keep insurance policies and savings schemes separate.

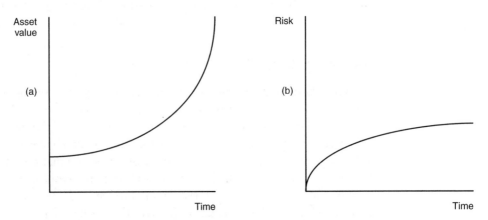

Figure 1.3 Expected asset value and risk in relation to time

● ● ● ● The nature of investment risk

When people think of risk they often focus on capital risk. Capital risk is the risk that the value of the investment might fall. Stock market investments, shares and bonds, are subject to capital risk since the prices of such investments can fall. However, this may not be the most important source of risk for an investor. Two other risks, which are often overlooked, are inflation risk and income risk.

Inflation risk is the risk that the purchasing power value of assets can be eroded by inflation. To give an idea of the potential effect of inflation, consider the impact of 2.5% p.a. inflation over 40 years. The purchasing power of £1 would fall to 37p. At an inflation rate of 5%, the real value of the £1 would fall to 14p. Over the last half century, a period during which UK inflation rates have at times exceeded 20% p.a., inflation has inflicted severe damage on the wealth of people with investments in deposits and bonds. This is a major reason for the fact that real net interest rates from banks and building societies have averaged little more than zero. The interest has largely been negated by inflation. There have been periods when real net interest rates have been negative (investments in banks and building societies have declined in real value even after reinvestment of interest).

The apparent risk-free nature of bank and building society deposits is called further into doubt when income risk is considered. This is a particular problem for investors who want an immediate income from their investments. Income risk is the risk that income payments from an investment (interest or dividends) can fall. Interest rates on bank and building society deposits fluctuate with variations in the economy's short-term interest rates. For example, during 2001 interest rates on premium accounts in the UK fell from around 6% p.a. to about 4% p.a., and in the USA the fall was from about 6% p.a. to less than 2% p.a. Someone who depends on interest to provide an income would have found such falls to be very problematical.

Bank and building society accounts are not the only investments that suffer from inflation risk and income risk. Conventional annuities, which are guaranteed fixed incomes bought at retirement using money in pension funds, also suffer from such risks. Inflation reduces the purchasing power of fixed incomes, and the level of the fixed incomes depends on long-term interest rates at the time of retirement (for example, the annual income bought for a particular sum in 2001 was about half the income bought with the same sum ten years earlier). As a result there is a move towards annuities that are based on investment in shares. Although investment in shares has high capital risk, it has relatively low inflation risk and income risk.

Chapter 2

Money market investments

After studying this chapter, readers should be able to:

- *distinguish between simple interest and compound interest*
- *understand the nature of variable and fixed interest rates*
- *be familiar with the convention for quoting interest rates on an annualised basis*
- *distinguish between nominal and real interest rates*
- *calculate interest rates and discount rates*
- *distinguish between interest yield and total return*
- *identify and evaluate money market investments*
- *understand the implications of holding foreign currency deposits.*

Money market investments tend to be short term (maturities of a year or less) and low risk, in the sense that their values are not strongly subject to market fluctuations. The most common form of money market investment is the deposit, although there are other forms such as bills and commercial paper. The return on deposits is in the form of interest. There are a number of features of interest rates and interest payments of which investors should be aware.

Simple interest and compound interest

When considering deposits with interest payable more frequently than once a year, the effective interest rate (annual percentage rate, APR) is higher than the simple rate. Increased frequency of compounding raises the effective rate. For example, an investment of £100 at an interest rate of 6% payable annually leads to the receipt of £106 at the end of the year. If the interest were payable six monthly, the value of the investment at the end of the year would be £100 × (1.03) × (1.03) = £106.09. There is interest on interest since the £3 interest from the first six months is reinvested for the second six months. If the interest were payable three monthly, the value of the investment at the end of the year would be £100 × (1.015) ×

$(1.015) \times (1.015) \times (1.015) = £106.14$. A high frequency of interest payment entails more interest on interest and hence a greater value at the end of the year.

When considering deposits covering periods of more than one year, simple annual returns are based on dividing the return over the period by the number of years in the period. Such an approach ignores the reinvestment of interest returns during the period of investment. The compound rate of interest is based on receipts being reinvested and producing their own returns. For example, if a deposit produces returns of 0%, 10% and 20% in successive years, the average simple rate of interest would be 10%. The average compound rate of interest would be $(1.0 \times 1.1 \times 1.2)^{1/3} - 1 = 0.097$, i.e. 9.7% p.a. When compounding (interest on interest) is allowed for, the interest rate required for the realisation of a particular sum of money is lower (in this case 9.7% p.a. rather than 10% p.a.).

Variable and fixed interest rates

A deposit at a variable interest rate is subject to interest rate variations as rates in the money markets change. Typically the change can be made by the bank at any time with little or no notice. Such deposits are subject to income risk. Income risk relates to the uncertainty as to the level of income that an investor derives from a deposit. A fall in interest rates entails a fall in income receipts.

A fixed rate deposit guarantees the interest rate for a specified period. For example, a five-year fixed rate deposit will pay the specified interest rate for the full five years, irrespective of what happens to interest rates in the money markets.

Both of these types of deposit typically pay, or accumulate, interest on an annual basis. The compounding of interest is normally on a predetermined date, typically the anniversary of the deposit.

An intermediate investment between these two is a deposit on which the interest is fixed for a period, after which it is revised. A typical example would be a six-month roll-over deposit on which the interest rate is fixed for six months, after which it is changed in line with money market rates. There would be a succession of six-month periods, with the interest rate fixed during each period. At the end of each period the interest rate would be reset and the new rate is fixed for the following six months. In such a case interest is payable, or accumulates, twice a year. Compounding would be six monthly.

Convention for quoting interest rates

Interest rates are always quoted on a per annum (i.e. per year) basis. Whatever the period of the investment, the interest rate is quoted per annum. If the investment period, or frequency of compounding, is less than a year, the annual interest rate is multiplied by the fraction of the year. For example, a six-month deposit with an interest rate of 5% p.a. pays interest of half 5%, i.e. 2.5%, over the six months.

Likewise for a deposit that pays interest every six months. If the period is three months and the rate is 6% p.a., the interest paid each three months is a quarter of 6%, i.e. 1.5%. In such cases the effective annual rate is greater than the quoted rate because of compounding.

If the investment period is longer than a year, interest rates are regarded as compounded annually (unless a shorter period is specified). For example, a three-year investment at 7% p.a. is treated as paying interest annually at 7%. So at the end of three years an investment of £100 would be worth £100 × 1.07 × 1.07 × 1.07 = £122.50.

● ● ● ● Nominal and real rates of interest

If inflation is expected, some interest is required simply to compensate for the rise in prices. The real interest is the yield net of compensation for inflation. The real interest rate measures the returns from an investment in terms of enhanced purchasing power. For example, if the rate of interest is 3% p.a., a deposit of £100 will grow to £103 over a year. If prices rise by 3% over the year, £103 at the end of the year will buy the same amount as £100 bought at the beginning of the year. The investor makes no real gain from the deposit. The real interest rate is zero.

The real interest rate is given by the expression:

$$Rr = (1 + Rn)/(1 + i) - 1$$

Exercise 2.1

(a) A bank deposit pays 8% p.a. one year and 10% p.a. the next. Calculate the average compound rate of return on the basis of annual interest payments.

(b) If the interest in (a) were paid on a six-month basis, what would be the average annual compound rate of return?

(c) Suppose that the rates in (a) are nominal interest rates and that inflation in the two years was 5% and 8% respectively. Calculate the average compound real rate of return.

(d) What would be the nominal and real values of an investment of £100 at the rates in (c) at the end of the two years?

Answers

(a) $\sqrt{(1.08)(1.1)} - 1 = \sqrt{1.188} - 1 = 1.09 - 1 = 0.09$ as a decimal, which is 9% p.a. as a percentage.

(b) $\sqrt{(1.04)(1.04)(1.05)(1.05)} - 1 = \sqrt{1.1925} - 1 = 1.092 - 1 = 0.092$ as a decimal, which is 9.2% p.a. as a percentage.

(c) $\sqrt{(1.08/1.05)(1.1/1.08)} - 1 = \sqrt{(1.0286)(1.0185)} - 1 = \sqrt{1.0476} - 1 = 1.0235 - 1 = 0.0235$ as a decimal, which is 2.35% as a percentage.

(d) The nominal value would be £100 × (1.08) × (1.1) = £118.80. The real value would be £100 × (1.08/1.05) × (1.1/1.08) = £104.76.

where Rr is the real interest rate, Rn is the nominal interest rate and i is the rate of inflation. The nominal interest rate (alternatively known as the money interest rate) is the rate quoted by banks, building societies and other deposit takers.

In the previous example the real rate of interest can be calculated as:

$$Rr = (1.03)/(1.03) - 1 = 0$$

i.e. the real rate of interest is zero. If the nominal rate of interest were 7%, the real interest rate would be:

$$Rr = (1.07)/(1.03) - 1 = 0.039, \text{ i.e. } 3.9\% \text{ p.a.}$$

Note that in this case simply subtracting the rate of inflation from the nominal rate of interest gives a close approximation to the real rate of interest. It should also be remembered that, when evaluating prospective investments, it is the rate of inflation expected to occur during the period of the investment that should be used in the calculation of the real rate of interest.

Exercise 2.2

(a) If nominal one-year interest rates over the next five years are expected to be 5% p.a., 6% p.a., 6% p.a., 5% p.a. and 4% p.a., what should a £100 investment grow to over the five years? What would be the average compound nominal rate of return?

(b) If £1 invested now is expected to be worth £1.50 in five years, what is the average compound nominal rate of return? If inflation is expected to be 2% p.a., what would the expected average compound real rate of return be?

(c) If £100 invested now is expected to be worth £140 in five years, what is the expected average compound nominal rate of return?

Answers

(a) $1.05 \times 1.06 \times 1.06 \times 1.05 \times 1.04 = 1.2883$

So £100 would grow to £128.83 over the five years.

The average compound nominal rate of return is:

$(\sqrt[5]{1.2883}) - 1 = 1.052 - 1 = 0.052$ i.e. 5.2% p.a.

(b) $(\sqrt[5]{1.50}) - 1 = 1.08447 - 1 = 0.08447$ i.e. 8.45% p.a. (to 2 decimal places)

The average compound nominal rate of return would be 8.45% p.a.

To keep pace with inflation the pound needs to rise to:

$£1.02^5 = £1.10408$ over the five years.

In real terms, after five years, £1.50 would be worth £1.50/1.10408 = £1.3586.

The average compound real rate of return would be:

$(\sqrt[5]{1.3586}) - 1 = 1.06321 - 1 = 0.06321$ i.e. 6.32% p.a. (to 2 decimal places)

(c) £140/£100 = 1.40

$(\sqrt[5]{1.40}) - 1 = 1.06961 - 1 = 0.06961$ i.e. 6.96% p.a. (to 2 decimal places)

Exercise 2.3

An investor, who pays income tax at 40%, has a bank deposit that pays 3%, 3.5%, 4%, 4% and 4.5% p.a. before tax in five successive years. Inflation is 2%, 2.5%, 2.5%, 3% and 3% p.a. respectively in the five years.

(a) What is the pre-tax average nominal rate of return?
(b) What is the pre-tax average real rate of return?
(c) What is the post-tax average real rate of return?

Answers

(a) $[(1.03)(1.035)(1.04)(1.04)(1.045)]^{0.2} - 1 = 0.038$ i.e. 3.8% p.a.
(b) Over the five years the price level rises at an average rate of:
$[(1.02)(1.025)(1.025)(1.03)(1.03)]^{0.2} - 1 = 0.026$ i.e. 2.6% p.a.
The average real rate of return is:
$(1.038/1.026) - 1 = 0.0117$ i.e. 1.17% p.a.
Alternatively:
$[(1.03/1.02)(1.035/1.025)(1.04/1.025)(1.04/1.03)(1.045/1.03)]^{0.2} - 1$
$= [1.0098 \times 1.0098 \times 1.0146 \times 1.0097 \times 1.0146]^{0.2} - 1$
$= 0.0117$ i.e. 1.17% p.a.
(c) The after-tax rates of return are: 1.8%, 2.1%, 2.4%, 2.4%, and 2.7% p.a.
The average after-tax nominal rate of return is:
$[(1.018)(1.021)(1.024)(1.024)(1.027)]^{0.2} - 1 = 0.0228$ i.e. 2.28% p.a.
The average after-tax real rate of return is: $(1.0228/1.026) - 1 = -0.0031$ i.e. −0.31% p.a. In real terms, after tax, the value of the investment falls.

● ● ● ● Rates of interest versus rates of discount

Some investments, such as Treasury bills, pay no interest. Capital gain is the only source of return. Bills promise the payment of a specific sum of money at maturity and provide a return to investors by selling at a lower price. The price difference is known as the discount. The percentage rate of discount on bills is expressed relative to the sum payable at maturity whereas the interest on deposits is expressed relative to the sum invested. As a result a particular rate of discount is worth more than the rate of interest of the same percentage.

As an illustration consider a discount rate of 10% and an interest rate of 10%. If the maturity value of the bill is £100, a discount rate of 10% implies a current price of £90. The 10% discount is applied to the £100 maturity value and is worth £10. An interest rate of 10% would be applied to the current price and is therefore worth £9. A discount rate of 10% is equivalent to an interest rate of (£10/£90) × 100 = 11.1%.

● ● ● ● Interest yield and total return

When money is deposited in a bank account it leads to a flow of interest payments and these payments are the only source of return on the deposit. Other investments

Exercise 2.4

If the current rate of discount on Treasury bills is 11% p.a., calculate the price of a £50,000 91-day bill with 60 days to redemption. What would its price be in four weeks' time if interest rates remain unchanged?

Answer
The 60-day rate of discount is:
  $(60/365) \times 11\% = 1.81\%$
So the price of the Treasury bill is:
  $[(100 - 1.81)/100] \times £50,000 = £49,096$
After four weeks there would be $60 - 28 = 32$ days to redemption. The 32-day rate of discount is:
  $(32/365) \times 11\% = 0.96\%$
So the price of the Treasury bill would be:
  $[(100 - 0.96)/100] \times £50,000 = £49,518$

have two sources of return: not only are there income flows such as interest payments, there are also capital gains or losses. In the case of deposits there are no capital gains or losses, but investments such as bonds are subject to price fluctuations and gains/losses resulting from them.

The interest yield on a bond is calculated as the annual coupon divided by the current bond price. The coupon is the periodic payment to the investor where the period is typically either six months or a year. The total return on a bond is known as the redemption yield. The redemption yield incorporates both the interest yield and the prospective capital gain.

Consider a bond that pays a coupon of £4 every six months (and hence £8 per year), is currently priced at £97 and matures in one year, at which point the investor will be paid £100 by the issuer of the bond. The interest yield is:

  $£8/£97 = 0.0825$ i.e. 8.25% p.a.

In addition there will be a capital gain of $£100 - £97 = £3$. As a rate of return the capital gain is $£3/£97 = 0.0309$, i.e. 3.09% p.a. The redemption yield (total return) is $8.25\% + 3.09\% = 11.34\%$ p.a.

Short maturity (money market) investments

A variation on the normal deposit is the certificate of deposit (CD). A bank receiving a deposit may issue a CD to the depositor stating that at maturity (which is frequently three months from issue) the deposit plus interest will be paid to the holder (bearer) of the CD. An advantage of a certificate of deposit to the investor, as compared with a normal time deposit, is that it can be sold and hence is more liquid. This enhanced liquidity leads investors to the acceptance of rates of interest below the rates for ordinary deposits of the same maturity. Banks are thus able to borrow at lower interest rates than would otherwise be applicable to the period of the deposit.

Certificates of deposit are used in the wholesale rather than the retail money markets. As a result investors tend to be corporates, banks and other financial institutions. Retail investors would normally have access to such instruments through collective investment vehicles such as unit trusts or insurance funds.

Another form of short-term investment is the bill. Bills are instruments that can be sold in the money market prior to maturity. Unlike deposits, bills do not have an interest yield. The return that a bill provides to its holder arises from the fact that it is bought at a discount. The issuer of a bill promises to pay a specified sum of money at its maturity date. An investor buying the bill will pay a smaller sum for it and thus obtains a return in the form of a capital gain.

Bills may be issued by central government, in which case they are often known as Treasury bills (e.g. in the UK and the US) and typically have a maturity of three or six months. Treasury bills are sold by auction (tender). There are two forms of auction used. In a bid price auction investors pay the price that they bid. In a striking price auction all successful bidders pay the same price. In both cases the bills are sold to the highest bidders. The bid price auction is probably the most frequent type.

Bills may also be issued by firms as a means of short-term borrowing, normally with maturities of 12 months or less. Such private sector bills include bills of exchange, which are used for trade credit. The buyer of the goods signs a bill drawn up by the seller. The buyer thereby promises to pay the holder of the bill for the goods at the end of a specified time period. If the payment is guaranteed by a bank (against default by the trade signatory), the bill is known as a bank bill and is seen as having a lower risk of default. These bills can be sold, at a discount, in the money markets. In this way the suppliers of goods can receive money immediately while the buyers defer payment.

Commercial paper is similar to a bill of exchange, except that it is issued by corporate borrowers for general borrowing rather than for financing a specific trade transaction. An issuer of commercial paper will set up a programme with a specified time period (for example five years) and a stated borrowing ceiling (for example £500 million). The firm would not normally borrow up to the ceiling immediately but would issue commercial paper over time as the need arose. Periodically paper would be sold, or repaid, subject to the borrowing ceiling not being exceeded. A bank (or several banks) would be appointed to deal with issues. The bank dealers contact potential investors in order to place the commercial paper. The market is wholesale, with minimum denominations that put it out of reach of most individual investors. Retail investors wishing to access this market would normally do so by means of institutional investments such as unit trust money market funds.

● ● ● ● Foreign currency deposits

An alternative to a deposit in an investor's national currency is a deposit in a foreign currency. This alternative may seem attractive if the foreign currency interest rate is high relative to the home currency interest rate. However, investors should be wary of such an alternative, for two reasons.

The first is based on what is known as the *International Fisher Effect*, according to which high foreign currency interest rates tend to be offset by a fall in the value of the foreign currency. Although the difference between domestic and foreign interest rates is unlikely to be exactly matched by exchange rate movements, deviations in one direction are as likely as deviations in the other. The expected interest rate, net of the effects of currency movements, should on average equal the rate available on domestic currency deposits.

The second reason for being wary of foreign currency deposits is the uncertainty of exchange rate movements. The net rate of return from a foreign currency deposit could turn out to be either above or below the rate on a domestic currency deposit, depending upon how the exchange rate moves. Since it is impossible to predict exchange rate movements, there is risk involved. So foreign currency deposits provide risk without any expectation of a higher rate of return.

The same reasoning applies to borrowing in foreign currencies. This was highlighted in the 1980s when some UK residents took out mortgages in Swiss francs on the grounds that the Swiss franc interest rate was lower than the pound sterling interest rate. Unfortunately for those borrowers, the Swiss franc strengthened against the pound. The result was a dramatic increase in the value of the mortgage debts, when measured in terms of pounds.

It may seem tempting to try to control the exchange rate risk by taking out forward contracts to guarantee future exchange rates. While this reduces the currency risk, it does not ensure the benefits of a higher foreign currency interest rate. Forward exchange rates embody the currency price changes suggested by the International Fisher Effect. An interest rate advantage would be precisely offset by a forward discount. The forward exchange rate guarantees that the currency price movement offsets the interest rate difference with the effect that the interest rate on the foreign currency is rendered identical to the rate on the domestic currency. This is known as *interest rate parity* and is a relationship that holds very closely among the major currencies.

Chapter 3

Institutional (collective) investments

After studying this chapter readers should be able to evaluate:

- *life assurance, including term assurance, whole-of-life policies, endowment policies and investment bonds*

- *mutual funds, including unit trusts, investment trusts, and OEICs*

- *the effects of fund charges on investment performance*

- *the economic and social significance of institutional investors*

- *the implications of the psychology of decision making for personal finance.*

In most developed economies the dominant form of investment is indirect. Indirect investment involves individuals putting money in a fund which then uses that money to buy stocks or other securities. Typically most of the shares issued within an economy are held indirectly through various types of fund. These funds are known as institutional, or collective, investments. Direct shareholding by individuals accounts for a minority of the total number of shares held.

In many countries, pension funds are the main form of institutional investment. These funds are built up during the working life of the investor and then used to finance an income during retirement. They may be operated by the company for which the person works. The company invests over time to build up a fund that is used to provide a retirement income for its employees. Alternatively the employees invest in a fund of their choosing with a view to building up a sum of money that can be used to buy an annuity (guaranteed stream of income) at retirement. The most important assets within the portfolios of pension funds tend to be stock market investments in the form of shares and bonds. However, other assets are frequently held, particularly deposits and property. Some funds have even been known to hold alternative investments such as works of art.

Pension funds can be divided into defined benefit and defined contribution funds. Defined benefit funds are virtually always company pension funds provided by firms for their employees. They stipulate a particular level of income in retirement, normally based on final salary and length of service. Defined contribution pension funds do not involve a prescribed income in retirement, instead they prescribe levels of contribution to the fund prior to retirement. The retirement income obtained through a defined contribution scheme depends upon the growth rate of the fund and the annuity rates available at the time of retirement.

Another important form of institutional investment is the insurance fund (or life assurance fund). These funds typically aim to provide a sum of money at a point of time in the future (or at death if that occurs earlier). They incorporate an element of life insurance. Commonly they require the investor to make a constant stream of contributions to the fund over the period covered by the policy. However, some allow for lump sum contributions or for variable periodic payments. Life assurance investments subdivide into whole-of-life policies, endowments and investment bonds.

life assurances

● ● ● ● Life assurance

Life assurance policies pay out a sum of money upon the death of the insured person. They subdivide into term assurance and whole-of-life policies.

Term assurance

Variable Term

Payments of benefits

Convert/ Renewable (+10% cost)

Term assurance provides a pay-out in the event of death occurring before the expiry date of the policy. The term involved may range from a few weeks to cover a foreign trip to 25 years to cover a mortgage. Normally the client pays a regular monthly sum for the duration of the policy. The sum assured could be constant, increasing or decreasing. The payment in the event of death may be a lump sum or a stream of income payments (the income alternative is known as family income benefit).

Renewable term assurance allows the client to extend the term assurance when, or before, the original policy reaches its expiry date. Convertible term assurance policies allow the client to convert to a permanent life assurance within the term of the original policy. These options to renew or convert guarantee future insurability for an additional cost of around 10% of the premium payments.

Whole-of-life policies

Whole-of-life assurance policies are permanent: they pay out upon death. Since pay-outs are inevitable, whole-of-life policies are more expensive than term assurance policies. The life office's need to build an investment reserve to pay benefits on policies means that the policies acquire a surrender value. The policyholder may cancel the policy and take its cash value. However, the cost of the life assurance renders such policies unsuitable for someone whose concern is simply to accumulate savings.

Without-profit policies invest solely in fixed income securities such as bonds. With-profits policies invest in shares and property as well as fixed income securities. In consequence, with-profits policies entail more potential for growth in the value of the investment. Unit-linked whole-of-life policies (which are usually invested in unit trusts) provide even greater growth potential, but at the cost of greater risk. Unit-linked policies often allow the client to vary the relative levels of insurance cover and investment over time. For example, when family commitments are high the life assurance cover may be raised at the expense of the rate of accumulation of units in the investment funds.

Endowment policies   *(equities)*

Endowment policies can be likened to savings plans with attached life assurance. They typically specify a period of time, such as 10 or 25 years, during which regular monthly payments are made. These monthly premiums finance the cost of insurance cover and contributions to an investment fund. At the end of the policy term, the accumulated value of the investment fund is paid to the policyholder. If the holder dies before the end of the term, the policy beneficiaries receive the higher of the value of the investment fund or the guaranteed sum assured. The guaranteed sum assured is the amount for which the person's life is insured.

An endowment policy can be used to pay off a mortgage debt. Throughout the term of the mortgage, interest is paid on the debt. In addition, regular payments are made into an endowment fund. At the end of the mortgage term the sum of money accumulated in the endowment fund is used to pay off the mortgage debt. For example, if returns on an endowment are 10% p.a., an annual payment of £16,380 into an endowment will be worth £100,000 in five years. This can be used to repay a £100,000 debt. An endowment mortgage involves paying interest on the £100,000 debt each year. If interest rates are 10% p.a., this amounts to £10,000 p.a. So the total annual payment is £16,380 + £10,000 = £26,380.

The main alternative to an endowment mortgage is a repayment mortgage. Repayment mortgages involve amortising the debt (gradually paying it off). A repayment mortgage is illustrated by Table 3.1. The repayment mortgage entails a constant payment of £26,380 each year, which is identical to the annual sum paid in the above case of an endowment mortgage. This identity of payments arises because the assumed annual return on the endowment fund equals the assumed rate of interest.

However, endowment funds are normally largely invested in equities (shares). Over long periods, such as the typical term of a mortgage, equity investments have

Table 3.1 Mortgage repayment schedule on a £100,000 five-year debt with interest fixed at 10% p.a.

Year	Interest	Repayment	Remaining debt
1	£10,000	£16,380	£83,620
2	£8,362	£18,018	£65,602
3	£6,561	£19,819	£45,783
4	£4,579	£21,801	£23,981
5	£2,399	£23,981	£0

provided average returns that exceed interest rates. This excess return means that the endowment fund not only pays off the mortgage but also produces a lump sum for the policyholder. Alternatively the prospective excess return allows for reduced payments into the endowment fund, but with the risk that equity returns turn out to be less than anticipated so that there is insufficient to pay off the mortgage. In the event of the policyholder dying before the policy matures, the insurance component of the policy will provide a sum of money to pay off the mortgage debt.

Investment bonds *(aka single prem. bonds)*

Investment bonds, alternatively known as single premium bonds, are investment products with a nominal amount of life assurance cover. Typically life cover is 1% of the value of the investment. Investment bonds may be unit-linked or with-profits.

An investor in a unit-linked bond normally has a choice of funds. These include managed, general, fixed interest and specialist funds. Managed funds are invested in a spread of shares, bonds, property and deposits. These funds invest in a diversified portfolio of shares, which may or may not include shares in foreign companies. These funds might aim to meet the investment objective of capital growth or high income, or a balance of the two. General funds can take the form of tracker funds that seek to parallel the performance of an index such as the FT All-Share Index. Fixed interest funds invest primarily in bonds, often with a high proportion of government bonds. Some insurance companies offer guaranteed equity bonds that are based on a stock market but which use options to guarantee that the value of the fund will not fall below a minimum level.

Specialist funds can have various types of specialisation. This might be geographic, for example focusing on Europe, North America or Japan, or there may be an industry focus, such as high technology or financials. The orientation could be related to firm size or situation, for example smaller company or recovery funds. Other funds often made available to investors include property, money market and with-profits funds. Property funds invest in industrial and commercial property. Money market funds invest in bank deposits and other money market instruments such as Treasury bills and commercial paper. With-profits funds are often unitised – investors acquire units in a with-profits fund.

Specialist funds are the most risky, particularly since they involve non-systematic (specific) risk as well as systematic (market) risk. General equity funds are next in order of riskiness, although they avoid much of the non-systematic risk if they are well diversified. Managed funds and with-profits funds are less risky than pure equity funds since they mix shares with less risky assets such as bonds and deposits. Money market funds are the least risky in the sense of uncertainty of capital value. Historically the average annual returns are related to the proportion of shares in the fund – the higher this proportion, the higher the returns over the long term.

Investment bonds usually allow the bondholder to switch between investment funds at any time. However, there may be a charge for a switch. Investment bonds *different policies*

CGT paid at source

are often segmented into a number of separate policies, perhaps five or ten. Each policy within the bond is usually identical. The advantage of the segmentation is that each policy can be surrendered (that is encashed) at a different point in time.

One disadvantage of investment bonds relative to unit trusts, investment trusts and open-ended investment companies (OEICs) arises from their capital gains tax treatment. In the case of unit trusts, investment trusts and OEICs, a capital gains tax liability arises only if the individual investor has gains above the exemption limit. In contrast, investment bonds pay capital gains tax within the fund, so that investors suffer the effects of capital gains tax irrespective of whether they, as individuals, fall below or above the threshold at which capital gains tax becomes payable.

Mutual funds

A third form of institutional investment is the mutual fund. These come in many varieties. In the United Kingdom there are three broad types: investment trusts, unit trusts and OEICs. Similar instruments exist in other countries, but often with different names. These forms of collective investment have both similarities and differences.

All forms of mutual fund allow investors to have a spread of investments for a small financial outlay. For example, £1,000 can buy part of a fund which contains more than 100 different shareholdings. In this way small investors can enjoy the risk-reduction benefits of a well-diversified portfolio. Stockbroker commission costs would render the acquisition of a large number of different shareholdings impractical for small investors.

Mutual funds offer other advantages to investors. They provide administration of the investments – for example, dividends could be automatically reinvested on their behalf. They remove the need for investors to ascertain which shares or bonds to buy – the choice is made by professional fund managers. However, these services have to be paid for with annual fees taken from the dividends (or from the capital of the fund) and there is some controversy over whether professional fund managers' investment choices are, on average, superior to random stock selections.

Mutual funds permit a choice of investment strategy. There are general, high-income and growth funds. There are funds that focus on asset classes, for example funds that invest exclusively in bonds. Many funds allow for particular geographical orientations (Europe funds, North America funds, Far East funds, etc.).

Differences between unit trusts, investment trusts and OEICs

A unit trust is a fund managed by a bank, insurance company or investment company. Individual investors buy units in the fund. An investment trust is a company whose purpose is to invest in other companies. Individual investors buy shares in the company. An OEIC is a company whose purpose is to invest in other companies (like an investment trust). Individual investors buy shares in funds operated by the OEICs, but these shares are similar to the units sold by unit trusts.

A unit trust is constituted by a trust deed. The unit trust manager is responsible for the day-to-day operation of the fund, and each unit trust fund has a trustee which must be independent of the manager. The role of trustee is normally taken by a bank or insurance company. The trustee is custodian of the assets (e.g. it holds the share certificates), maintains a register of unitholders, and generally oversees the management of the trust fund. The trustee has the role of protecting the interests of unitholders and ensuring that the managers do not stray from their stated objectives. The managers are able to advertise and market unit trusts directly to the public. The funds are exempt from capital gains tax; instead such taxes are payable by unitholders whose individual capital gains exceed the personal exemption limit. UK-authorised unit trusts investing in equities can hold no more than 10% of the fund in any one company and no more than 10% of the issued capital of a company can be held.

Unit trusts are open ended. The purchase or sale of units by individual investors causes the fund to expand or contract. Likewise the number of units increases or decreases. The transactions are carried out with the investment manager. OEICs are similar to unit trusts in these respects. Investment trusts are closed funds. The purchase or sale of shares by individual investors has no effect on the size of the fund. An unchanged number of shares changes hands. Transactions are carried out with other investors through the medium of a stock exchange.

Since sales of shares in investment trusts do not require the fund manager to sell any of the assets, the manager need not be concerned about the liquidity of the assets. However, the sale of unit trusts and OEICs involves the liquidation of part of the fund. Assets need to be sold so that the investment manager can redeem units. For this reason the managers of unit trusts and OEICs need to hold part of the fund in liquid assets. In particular part of the fund might be held on deposit so as to avoid the sale of securities in the event of units being redeemed. This is likely to reduce the expected rate of return on the fund. If there is a substantial volume of sales by investors, the fund manager will be forced to sell securities. If the markets for those securities are not liquid, the sales could be at unfavourable prices. The problem is compounded by the possibility that redemptions will peak during times of market uncertainty.

In the case of unit trusts, the value of a unit is based directly on the value of the investments in the fund. The total value of the units equals the total value of the investments in the fund. OEICs are similar to unit trusts in this respect. In the case of investment trusts, the total value of the shares normally differs from the total value of the investments in the fund. The prices of investment trust shares are determined by demand and supply, and these forces can pull the value of an investment trust company away from the value of the investments that it holds. Net asset value is the market value of all the assets in the fund (net of liabilities) divided by the number of investment trust shares issued. If the price of the investment trust shares is less than the net asset value, those shares are said to trade at a discount to net asset value. If the price of the shares exceeds the net asset value, they are said to trade at a premium. In other words, if the total value of the shares in an investment trust is less than the value of the investments (net of any debts) held by the trust, the price of the shares in the investment trust is said to be at a discount to net asset value; in the opposite situation the shares are said to be trading at a premium to net asset value.

Unit trusts typically involve a difference between the buying (offer) price and the selling (bid) price. Frequently buying prices are 5–7% higher than selling prices (buying from the unit trust manager and selling back to the manager). Investment trusts and OEICs have a single price, although the seller of an OEIC may have to pay an exit charge. In the case of investment trusts, transaction costs are incurred through commission payments to brokers rather than via a spread between buying and selling prices.

Unit trusts and OEICs are bought from the investment manager and are redeemed by being sold back to the investment manager. In the case of investment trusts, shares are bought and sold through the stock market. One feature that distinguishes OEICs from unit and investment trusts is the fact that they are umbrella funds. There are several different funds within an OEIC. Investors are able to switch between funds within an OEIC without incurring a capital gains tax liability. In the case of unit trusts and investment trusts, such a switch involves selling units or shares with capital gains being liable to tax.

Another difference between investment trusts on one hand and unit trusts and OEICs on the other concerns the ability to borrow. Investment trusts have extensive borrowing powers and can thereby increase their exposure to stocks by using the borrowed money to buy shares. This increase in market exposure can render investment trust prices more volatile than those of unit trusts and OEICs, which are able to borrow only up to 10% of the fund. Another factor that can cause investment trust prices to be more volatile than those of unit trusts and OEICs is the existence of discounts and premiums. Investment trust prices can change as a result of variations in discounts and premiums, whereas unit trusts and OEICs do not have this source of price volatility.

Some investment trusts are split-capital trusts, which means they are split into income shares and capital shares. The holders of the income shares receive the dividends from the investment trust plus a predetermined return of capital. The holders of the capital shares receive the capital gains. Split-capital trusts have a winding-up date on which the assets are sold and the proceeds are distributed to the holders of the investment trust shares. Some split-capital trusts issue zero-dividend preference shares, alternatively known as zeros. Zero-dividend preference shares pay nothing to the investor until the share matures. The return to the investor arises from the fact that the shares are bought at a discount to (a lower price than) the sum to be paid at maturity.

With unit trusts, investment trusts and OEICs the ultimate investor is taxed in almost exactly the same way as if he or she held the underlying assets directly. It is the unitholder or shareholder who is liable to tax, not the fund. In order to be exempt from capital gains tax, an investment trust must satisfy the following conditions:

- The company's income is derived at least 70% from securities.
- No single holding can exceed 15% of the fund.
- The investment trust's shares are quoted on the London Stock Exchange.
- The company must not distribute realised capital gains as dividends.
- It does not retain more than 15% of the income it receives from investment in securities.

[handwritten margin note: Inv. trust no CGT]

Exchange-traded funds (ETFs)

Exchange-traded funds are a recent innovation on stock exchanges. They are shares that replicate stock indices such as the FTSE 100. In other words they are index tracker funds. They are not unit trusts, investment trusts or OEICs. Relative to unit trusts and OEICs, exchange-traded funds have the advantage of being tradable at prices that continuously reflect the current value of the relevant index, whereas unit trusts and OEICs are bought and sold at prices that are established just once a day. Relative to investment trusts, ETFs have the advantage of not being subject to discounts and premiums to net asset value. This is because ETFs are open-ended (like unit trusts and OEICs). The fact that trades can be settled using the underlying shares rather than cash also serves to prevent the emergence of discounts and premiums. Shares in exchange-traded funds can be bought and sold through stockbrokers in the same way as any other shares. Traded index securities (TRAINS) are similar to exchange-traded funds.

[handwritten margin note: continuos price adjust]

[handwritten margin note: payment with v. shares.]

The effects of fund charges

The charges levied by fund managers vary considerably. In relation to unit trusts the cheapest tend to be tracker funds (which aim to parallel a stock index). Tracker funds typically have no front-end or exit charge and annual charges of as little as 0.25% or 0.5%. Conversely, actively managed funds tend to have initial charges of 5–7% and annual charges of up to (and sometimes exceeding) 1.5% p.a. These differences in management charges can have considerable effects on investment returns over time.

Consider the investment of £1,000 in each of two funds, A and B. Suppose that the investments in both funds grow at an average of 7% p.a. in real terms (that is, in excess of what is needed to compensate for inflation). This growth rate is in line with historical experience of equity funds and incorporates both capital gains and net dividend income. The figure of 7% p.a. does not take account of management charges.

Suppose that A is a tracker fund with no front-end charge and an annual management fee of 0.5%. All of the investors' money is invested and the charge reduces the average annual return to 6.5%. Suppose that B is an actively managed fund with a front-end charge of 6% and an annual management fee of 1.5%. Such a fund would also experience transaction costs from share dealing. If half the fund is traded each year at an average bid-offer spread of 1%, annual costs would increase by a further 0.5% to a total of 2%. An investor in B would find that only £940 is invested and that average annual returns, net of costs, are 5%. Table 3.2 shows the expected value of the two funds over various time periods.

Exercise 3.1

A pension fund has a prospective average growth rate of 8% p.a. over the next 35 years. Estimate the fund value at the end of the 35 years arising from a £10,000 investment in the fund with (a) no initial charge and a 0.5% annual charge, (b) no initial charge and a 1.5% annual charge, and (c) a 5% initial charge and a 1.5% annual charge.

Answer
(a) £10,000 × $(1.075)^{35}$ = £125,689
    (The figure of 1.075 is used because the net rate of return is expected to be 8% − 0.5% = 7.5% p.a. The value of $(1.075)^{35}$ can be calculated using the power function of a hand calculator.)
(b) £10,000 × $(1.065)^{35}$ = £90,623
(c) £9,500 × $(1.065)^{35}$ = £86,091

Pound cost averaging

Pound cost averaging refers to an advantage of buying unit trusts (or other institutional investments) on a regular basis. More units are bought at low prices than at high prices so that the average purchase price is less than the average price of units.

Suppose that a monthly investment of £150 is made for three months, during which the price per unit is 75p for one month, 100p for one month, and 125p for one month. When the price is 75p, 150/0.75 = 200 units are bought. At 100p, 150/1 = 150 units are acquired. At 125p, 120 are received. The total is 470 units. If the whole £450 were spent on units at the average price of 100p, 450 units would be acquired. Monthly investing led to 20 more units.

When compared with investing an initial lump sum, the gain from pound cost averaging has to be weighed against the returns from the unit trust over the relevant period. Monthly investment involves a delay in investing that entails foregoing some of the returns from the units.

Table 3.2 Expected value of funds A and B

Investment horizon	A	B
5 years	£1,370	£1,200
10 years	£1,877	£1,531
15 years	£2,572	£1,954
20 years	£3,524	£2,494
25 years	£4,828	£3,183
30 years	£6,614	£4,063

Mutual funds and the provision of liquidity

Mutual funds provide investors with liquidity since it is easy to acquire, and dispose of, portfolios of shares by means of buying and selling mutual funds. If investors were to create or liquidate portfolios directly, they would be involved in high costs in terms of time, effort and money. By using mutual funds they avoid the expenditure of time and effort. In the case of index tracking funds, where initial charges are usually zero, they also avoid the financial costs. In the case of investment trusts, the financial costs are greatly reduced since only one purchase or sale transaction is involved.

However, there are costs to the mutual funds of providing such liquidity. These arise from fund managers being forced to trade in shares when their retail investors choose to buy or sell rather than when the fund managers would choose to trade. Since investment trusts (closed-end funds) are not affected by retail trades in this way, they do not bear these costs.

Retail investors tend to buy into mutual funds (e.g. buying units in a unit trust) when markets are rising and sell when markets are falling. The immediate effect of retail investment is an addition to the cash held in the fund, and the immediate effect of retail sales is a reduction of the cash held. A result of this is that mutual fund managers have a relatively large proportion of their funds in cash during rising markets (just when the funds should have a relatively large proportion in shares) and a low proportion in cash during falling markets (when a high proportion in cash would be preferable). Even during stable markets the transactions of retail investors will force fund managers into trades that they would otherwise not choose to make.

In these ways the provision of liquidity, by mutual funds, to retail investors can adversely impact on the performance of the funds. This would suggest a case for initial and/or withdrawal charges that are payable into the fund. In this way frequent transactors in unit trust units, or OEIC shares, would compensate long-term investors for their negative impact on fund performance. This could be seen as payment, by frequent transactors, for the liquidity provided by the funds.

● ● ● ● Pension funds

Pensions may be personal or occupational. Personal pensions are arranged by individuals in order to provide incomes for their retirement, whereas occupational pensions are arranged by their employers. Occupational pensions may be final salary or money purchase. Occupational schemes involve contributions to the pension fund by the employer only (non-contributory schemes), or by both employer and employee.

Final-salary pension schemes link the size of the pension income to the employee's salary at retirement, and to the number of years worked for the employer. Such schemes are also known as defined-benefit schemes. The pension benefits are specified, in part by Inland Revenue rules, rather than the means of financing them.

Money-purchase schemes entail payments into a pension fund. At retirement the pension fund is usually used to buy an annuity, which is an income guaranteed for the life of the recipient. The retirement income depends upon the performance of the pension fund up to the retirement date and upon the annuity rates available at the retirement date. Money-purchase schemes are also known as defined-contribution schemes since the contributions to the scheme are prescribed by rules, not the size of the pension income.

Personal pensions are always of the money-purchase type. Personal Pension Plans and Stakeholder Pensions are variants, distinguished by the relatively low charges and more liberal conditions attaching to the latter. Stakeholder Pensions can even be taken out by people without employment incomes, and by people who are members of occupational schemes. They are restricted to people whose incomes fall below a specified level. Additional Voluntary Contributions (AVCs) are a form of personal pension that aims to top up occupational schemes. They may be contributions into a pension fund arranged by the employer, or into an independently operated fund in which case they are known as Free Standing Additional Voluntary Contributions (FSAVCs).

Most of the money in pension funds is invested in stock markets. In consequence there is a high degree of uncertainty concerning the future value of the pension fund. In the case of money-purchase schemes, it is the recipient of the pension who bears this risk. The recipient also bears the risk that annuity rates, and hence the retirement income that can be purchased, will be low at retirement. Since annuities are based on government bonds (gilts), this risk relates to the possibility that rates of yield on government bonds will be low at the time of retirement.

In the case of final-salary schemes, the employer bears the risks. A combination of poor investment performance, low bond yields and high rates of salary growth can result in pension funds being insufficient to meet the pension commitments. In such a case the employer must replenish the pension fund out of that employer's business revenues.

The accumulation of pension funds

Tables 3.3 and 3.4 illustrate the result of investing £1,000 a year in a pension fund. They show how pension funds accumulate over differing periods and at varying

Table 3.3 Pension funds accumulated from £1,000 per year without management charges

	3%	6%	9%
10	£11,464	£13,181	£15,193
20	£26,870	£36,785	£51,159
30	£47,575	£79,057	£136,305
40	£75,400	£154,758	£337,872

Table 3.4 Pension funds accumulated from £1,000 per year with management charges of 2% p.a.

	3%	6%	9%
10	£10,462	£12,006	£13,816
20	£22,019	£29,778	£40,995
30	£34,784	£56,084	£94,459
40	£48,885	£95,024	£199,630

rates of growth of the pension fund. The number of years is shown vertically and the average rates of investment growth, as percentages per annum, are shown horizontally. It can be seen that the effects of increased periods, and increased rates of growth, are dramatic. The combination of a long period with a high rate of growth is particularly striking. The tables also demonstrate the effects of management charges. A charge by the fund manager of 2% p.a. may not sound much, but it has a huge effect on the final value of the fund. The effect of the management charge becomes increasingly dramatic with long periods and high rates of growth.

The sensitivity of the final outcome, to the period of time over which pension contributions are paid, indicates the desirability of starting pension contributions early in life. For example, in Table 3.3 it can be seen that with 6% growth, someone starting contributions 20 years late (e.g. at 45 rather than 25) will need to pay in more than £4,000 a year to achieve the same pension.

The sensitivity of the final pension fund to differences in growth rates shows the level of uncertainty involved. It also indicates the risk taken by companies offering final salary schemes. A lower than expected rate of growth can leave the company with a substantial shortfall to make up. This helps to explain why so many employers are closing final salary pension schemes to new employees, and replacing them with money-purchase schemes. With money-purchase pension schemes, it is the employee rather than the employer who runs the risk of low investment returns.

The importance and significance of institutional investors

Institutional investors have come to dominate securities markets. For example, it has been estimated that around three-quarters of UK shares are held through institutional investments, as opposed to being held directly by individuals. There has been a steady increase in this relative importance of institutional investments over time – it has been estimated that in 1957 less than one-fifth of UK shares were held by institutional investors.

The trend towards increased importance of institutional investors is likely to continue, particularly with regard to pension funds. A major factor behind this expectation is the phenomenon often referred to as the demographic time bomb. The ratio of pensioners to workers is rising relentlessly. It has been estimated that by 2020 a ratio of just three workers for every pensioner is likely to be typical in developed countries (compared, for example, with more than five workers per pensioner in 1990). It is projected that the ratio will continue to fall as life expectancy increases. The question arises as to whether members of the workforce will be able (and willing) to pay the taxes required to support such a large number of pensioners. It is likely that the current (and future) workforce will need to accumulate substantial pension fund investments in order to avoid poverty in retirement or the need to continue working beyond present retirement ages (an often suggested partial solution to the problem is an increase in the age at which state pensions become payable).

One social implication of the growth in the relative importance of institutional investments is the disappearance of the distinction between workers and owners. In aggregate, workers (in large part) own the companies for which they work. The term 'in aggregate' is important here since it is not a direct ownership of the specific companies for which they work. Each worker through rights in pension funds, life assurance policies and other institutional investments, owns a slice of the aggregate of firms that have issued marketable securities.

The growing importance of institutional investors, in terms of their holding an increasing proportion of the total number of shares issued, has implications for corporate governance. Corporate governance concerns the way in which companies are controlled. Until the 1970s 'managerial capitalism' was dominant, a feature of which was that shareholding was fragmented. A company's shares were held by thousands of different shareholders. As a result shareholders could not easily co-ordinate to influence the management of companies. In consequence the managers of firms often operated them for their own benefit rather than for the benefit of shareholders.

The concentration of shareholdings in the hands of a relatively small number of institutions has made it possible for those shareholders to exert influence over the management of companies. Shareholders have voting rights at annual general meetings and those voting rights include elections for the board of directors. Institutional shareholders can now force managements to give priority to 'shareholder value' – in other words, the interests of shareholders now take precedence over the interests of managers. In the last resort institutional investors can replace directors. However, that possibility may be enough to ensure compliance by managers.

There are other methods available, for example putting investors on the board of directors as non-executive directors, or introducing share option schemes in order to give the managers a personal interest in the value of the shares.

The psychology of personal finance

Many retail investments are stock market related. These include pension funds, ISAs (individual savings accounts), unit trusts and investment bonds. It is desirable that decisions relating to stock market-related investments should be made rationally. Psychological research has indicated that there are biases in decision making. These biases have implications for the decision as to whether to invest in stock market-related products, the extent of such investment and the nature of these investments, and could cause investors to make poor decisions or financial advisers to give poor advice.

There is evidence from psychological studies that there are systematic biases in the way people think. One bias, suggested by Prospect Theory, is the tendency for people to weigh prospective losses around twice as heavily as prospective gains. Financial economics treats upside and downside risk as being equally weighted, whereas Prospect Theory suggests that people are more concerned with the downside. This relatively large fear of loss, known as loss aversion, will tend to deter retail investors from stock market-related investments.

Psychological research has found a number of other systematic biases that affect investors. These include overconfidence, representativeness, conservatism, narrow framing and ambiguity aversion. All of these biases interfere with the process of rational decision making.

Overconfidence arises partly from self-attribution bias. This is a tendency on the part of investors to regard successes as arising from their expertise while putting failures down to bad luck or the actions of others. This leads to excessive confidence in one's powers of forecasting and explains a number of types of apparently irrational behaviour. For example, it can explain why some investors hold poorly diversified portfolios – if investors are highly confident about their selection abilities, they will not feel the need to reduce risk by means of diversification. It could also explain why some investors trade very frequently, to the point where transaction costs cause their investment behaviour to be loss making. Overconfidence can explain why some investors churn their portfolios, that is persistently sell and buy. This behaviour entails a new set of initial charges each time, with the effect that the investors lose. This churning may be recommended by overconfident financial advisers (who incidentally receive a new set of commission payments each time the churning occurs).

To the extent that some investors attribute profits from rising markets to their own talents, rising markets could be self-perpetuating. Overconfident investors may be encouraged to invest further and thereby reinforce an upward movement in stock prices. Conversely, a falling market reduces confidence and investing. This is consistent with the view that markets exhibit over-reaction: they rise too high and fall too low (known as the over-reaction hypothesis). It also helps to explain why small investors tend to buy following market rises and sell following falls.

Representativeness helps to explain why many investors seem to extrapolate price movements. Many investors appear to believe that if prices have been rising in the past, they will continue to rise, and conversely with falling prices. The concept of representativeness suggests that this is because those investors see an investment with recent price increases as representative of longer-term successful investments, and conversely with price falls.

The concept of conservatism suggests that investors are slow to change their views following the receipt of new information. This may help to explain why small investors often delay investing until the market has risen for a period of time. It has been observed that small investors often invest just before the market peaks and sell just before it troughs.

Narrow framing refers to the tendency of investors to focus too narrowly. One aspect is focus on the constituents of a portfolio rather than on the portfolio as a whole. Since individual investments tend to be more volatile than the investor's portfolio as a whole, such narrow framing causes investors to overestimate price volatility. This could cause people to invest too little.

Another dimension of narrow framing is the focus on the short term even when the investment horizon is long term. It is not rational for an investor accumulating assets for retirement 25 years hence to be concerned about the week-to-week performance of the portfolio. Yet long-term investors do focus on short-term volatility. Studies have shown that when, in experimental situations, people have been presented with monthly distributions of returns, they are less likely to invest than when they are shown annual distributions (with the annualised volatility being the same in both cases). The implication is that focus on short-term volatility deters investment. It appears that people do not appreciate the effects of time diversification. By time diversification is meant the tendency for good periods to offset bad periods with the effect that the dispersion of investment returns does not increase proportionately with the period of the investment. Investors who focus too much on short-term fluctuations over-estimate stock market risk and allocate too little of their money to stock market investment.

A related bias is retrievability, which suggests that more attention is given to the most easily recalled information. Retrievability is consistent with the over-reaction hypothesis, one dimension of which is the over-emphasis on recent information and recent events when making investment decisions.

Ambiguity aversion suggests that investors prefer to invest in companies that they feel they understand. Over 90 per cent of the equity investments of investors in the US, UK and Japan is in companies in their own countries. This home bias exists despite the demonstrated benefits of international diversification. The preference for the familiar results in the holding of portfolios that are insufficiently diversified and consequently investors bear more risk than is necessary.

Some other biases have similarities with the concept of overconfidence. As a result of the confirmation bias investors pay more attention to evidence that supports their opinions than to evidence that contradicts them. This can cause investors to persist with inappropriate investment strategies. Another cognitive bias is the illusion of control. In some circumstances people behave as if they were able to exert control where this is impossible or unlikely. The illusion of control, together with the over-confidence hypothesis, may explain why so many investors choose actively managed funds when tracker funds outperform them and have lower charges.

A study by the Financial Services Authority has confirmed the findings of academic studies which established that the relative past performance of actively managed funds is no indicator of future relative performance. It may be that over-confidence in their own selection abilities, and the illusion of control provided by the facility of choosing between funds, cause investors (or their financial advisers) to select actively managed funds when tracker funds offer better potential value. Of course, financial advisers might be influenced by the fact that actively managed funds typically pay higher commissions.

Sandler addresses information but not psychology

The Sandler report into the long-term savings industry in the United Kingdom was published on 9 July 2002. It focused on a number of important issues but ignored the greatest deterrent to long-term saving. The deterrent that was ignored is stock market volatility.

The main points of the Sandler report included:

1 Individuals face a choice that is too large, too complex, and with too much obscure jargon.
2 Consumers do not understand savings products.
3 There should be simple low-cost stakeholder investments that could be sold without financial advisers.
4 Pensions taxation and rules should be simplified.
5 Consumers often pay heavily for poor performance.
6 There is no relationship between fund charges and performance.
7 Competition does not operate to keep charges down.
8 There is a wide disparity in charges.
9 Sales of tracker funds should rise relative to sales of actively managed funds
10 Financial advisers should be paid by means of fees rather than commission.
11 Life companies should not be able to take part of the profits of with-profit funds
12 Investors should receive information about the smoothing of with-profit funds.
13 Tax breaks on with-profits bonds should be ended

Information

One area of attention was the issue of actively managed versus tracker funds. Actively managed funds attempt to out-perform stock markets by stock selection and market timing. Tracker funds aim to move in line with stock markets. Sandler points out that, when allowance is made for charges, actively managed funds on average under-perform stock indices. Yet the vast majority of retail sales (93%) is of actively managed funds as opposed to funds that track a stock index. This is possibly because actively managed funds tend to pay financial advisers more commission. Index trackers are also less risky since they avoid the risk that an actively managed fund may perform particularly badly.

The average under-performance of actively managed funds is what would be expected on the basis of the Efficient Market Hypothesis. According to the Efficient Market Hypothesis, if the stock market is informationally efficient it is not possible for fund managers to consistently out-perform the market. This is consistent with the wealth of empirical research that indicates that there is little, if any, persistence in fund performance (e.g. Mark Rhodes, 'Past Imperfect? The performance of UK equity managed funds', Financial Services Authority Occasional Paper 9, August 2000). The evidence indicates that there is no reason to believe that funds that have performed well in the past will continue to do so in the future. In fact the winner–loser phenomenon, for which evidence exists, suggests that today's good performers will be tomorrow's bad performers, and vice versa.

Sandler does not suggest that there is no place for active fund management. However he says that most customers, and advisers, lack the expertise to choose between active fund managers in order to find the potentially successful ones.

Informational efficiency is conventionally divided into the weak, semi-strong, and strong forms. The weak form of the Efficient Market Hypothesis suggests that all historical market information (past

▶

prices, past trading volumes) is fully taken into account in current market prices.

An implication of the weak form hypothesis is that there is no scope for making profits from analysis of historical market prices and volumes. So technical analysis, including chartism, is expected to be of no value. Attempts to forecast stock prices using charts based on previous stock prices will fail since all the information available from past price data is already reflected in stock prices.

A semi-strong form efficient market is one in which security prices fully take account of all publicly available information. In addition to market information on past prices and trading volumes publicly available information includes macroeconomic data (such as interest rates and inflation rates), company data (such as profits and sales), and non-economic events (such as political events, technological developments, and discoveries of natural resources). The implication is that asset prices immediately move to reflect any new information so that no one can make profits by means of purchases or sales based on analysing the new information.

The fairly high level of informational efficiency in stock markets is to be contrasted with the low level in the market for retail investments. The retail investor is often very ignorant of institutional investments such as unit trusts and investment bonds. There is therefore asymmetric information between the client and the financial adviser, and between the fund manager and the individual investor. Individual investors have less information than the professionals with whom they deal. The asymmetric information can lead to adverse selection where advisers seek to sell the products that pay them the highest commission, rather than the products that offer the best value to their clients.

The report suggests that commission-based remuneration should be replaced by fees. This should remove commission bias where advisers recommend the investments that pay the highest commissions. It should also lead to competition based on charges that results in lower, and more uniform, charges.

Sandler points out that there is little consistency in charges with large variations in charges for essentially identical products. This is symptomatic of low informational efficiency and ineffective competition.

The report also points out that there is a lack of correlation between charges and performance.

George Akerlof, a Nobel prize-winning economist, wrote an article entitled 'The Market for "Lemons": Quality, Uncertainty and the Market Mechanism' in which he discussed asymmetric information and its implications. Asymmetric information is the term referring to the fact that the managers of a corporation know more about its operation than investors know. Investors cannot be sure about which corporations are good (the peaches) and which are bad (the lemons). However the managers do know whether their firm is a peach or a lemon. Likewise financial advisers may be peaches or lemons, but retail investors do not know which are the lemons. The same may be true of funds and their managers. Individual investors may be aware that some financial advisers do not offer good advice, and that many fund managers do not perform well. Since investors cannot easily distinguish between peaches and lemons, they are less willing to invest for fear of buying a lemon.

Another consequence of asymmetric information is moral hazard. Moral hazard is the temptation for the fund managers to take excessive risks, or engage in activities that are not in the interests of investors. A form of moral hazard is the principal–agent problem. Investors are the principals and managers are their agents. The agents may act in their own interests rather than in the interests of the principals. Likewise financial advisers may recommend investments that pay high commissions at the expense of the investors. This is a form of adverse selection and moral hazard. Many people believe that financial advisers provide free and unbiased advice. They do not realise that the adviser is paid according to the amount, and type, of sales.

Simple stakeholder products and more information about with-profits policies (both recommended by Sandler) would help to overcome problems of asymmetric information, adverse selection, and moral hazard. The Sandler report calls for the introduction of simple stakeholder investments that would have no initial charge, annual charges capped at 1%, and carefully designed investment policies. They could be sold without the need for a financial adviser.

With-profits policies were criticised for being opaque with respect to performance and charges.

▶

Sandler suggested that investors should be provided with more information about with-profits funds. Investors would have to be given information on smoothing the process by which managers hold money back in good years in order to top up policies in bad years. Customers should be given four figures each year: the redemption value of the policy, the proceeds available on death, projections of the pay-out at maturity, and the value of the unsmoothed assets.

Psychology

Recent falls in stock markets are probably more of a deterrent to long-term saving than any of the factors identified by Sandler. Behavioural finance applies the findings of psychological research on decision making to investment decisions. There is evidence from psychological studies that there are systematic biases in the way people think. One such bias is the tendency to give too much emphasis to the most recent information. Recent stock market falls, for example. Another bias, suggested by prospects theory, is the tendency for people to weigh prospective losses about twice as heavily as prospective gains. This is sometimes known as loss aversion. Loss averse savers take fright from declining stock markets.

Representativeness helps to explain why many investors seem to extrapolate price movements. Many investors appear to believe that if prices have been rising in the past then they will continue to rise, and conversely with falling prices. The concept of representativeness suggests that this is because those investors see an investment with recent price increases as representative of longer term successful investments, conversely with price falls. This helps to explain high levels of unit trust purchases as markets reach their peaks, and redemptions when share prices are near their bottom. This is consistent with market falls being a deterrent to investment by individuals.

A dimension of Narrow Framing is the focus on the short-term even when the investment horizon is long term. It is not rational for an investor accumulating assets for retirement 25 years hence to be concerned about the week by week performance of the portfolio. Yet long-term investors do focus on short-term volatility. Studies have shown that when, in experimental situations, people have been presented with monthly distributions of returns they are less likely to invest than when they are shown annual distributions (with the annualised volatility being the same in both cases). The implication is that focus on short-term volatility deters investment. It appears that people do not appreciate the effects of time diversification. By time diversification is meant the tendency for good periods to offset bad periods with the effect that the dispersion of investment returns does not increase proportionately with the period of the investment. Investors who focus too much on short-term fluctuations overestimate stock market risk and allocate too little of their money to investment in share-related investments. Again this is consistent with the deterrent effect of stock market volatility.

Other biases include retrievability which suggests that more attention is given to the most easily recalled information. Retrievablity is consistent with the over-reaction hypothesis, one dimension of which is the over-emphasis on recent information and recent events when making investment decisions. Stock market falls, and dramatic media headlines, remain in memories.

Another insight of behavioural finance is the existence of overconfidence. Overconfidence arises partly from self-attribution bias. This is a tendency on the part of investors to regard successes as arising from their expertise whilst failures are due to bad luck or the actions of others. This leads to excessive confidence in one's own powers of forecasting. Gains in a rising stock market are taken, by overconfident investors, to be evidence of their high investment skills. This encourages increased investment in rising stock markets. Conversely, falling markets remove the confidence with the result that investors sell and withdraw from the markets. Overconfidence is capable of explaining a number of types of apparently irrational behaviour. For example it can explain why some investors hold undiversified portfolios. If investors are highly confident about their stock selection abilities, they will not feel the need to reduce risk by means of diversification. It could also explain why some investors trade very frequently, to the point where transaction costs cause their investment behaviour to be loss making. Unbalanced portfolios and frequent trading (often referred to as churning) are characteristic of many active fund managers.

Source: Keith Redhead, *Company Accountant*, Issue 170, October 2002.

Discussion questions

1 Distinguish between unit trusts and investment trusts.

2 What are the relative merits of unit trusts, OEICs, investment trusts, investment bonds and endowment policies from the point of view of individual investors?

3 What might an investor consider when choosing between unit trusts, OEICs, investment trusts and investment bonds?

Chapter 4

Some types of institutional investment fund

After studying this chapter readers should be aware of three alternatives to actively managed unit trust funds, and be able to evaluate those alternatives, which are:

- *index (tracker) funds*
- *with profits funds*
- *annuities.*

Index (tracker) funds

An index fund, alternatively known as a tracker fund, aims to replicate the performance of a stock index. The emergence of index funds followed the observation that actively managed funds fail, on average, to outperform stock indices. This is related to the issue of market efficiency. Active fund management is predicated on the view that portfolio managers can forecast market movements and the performance of individual stocks relative to the market. If the efficient market hypothesis is correct, it is not possible to consistently forecast either overall market movements or the relative performance of individual stocks. If this is the case, investors should avoid the transaction and management costs associated with actively managed funds by investing in index funds whose aim is merely to move in line with the stock market.

One advantage of index funds to the individual investor in collective investments is that they avoid management risk. The performance of actively managed funds can, during any period of time, vary considerably. Some will outperform the index and others will underperform it. The difference between the best and the worst can be considerable. If the direction and size of the deviations from the index occur by chance, as empirical evidence seems to suggest, the individual investor faces a management risk. Individual investors run the risk that their chosen funds are relatively poor performers. By investing in index funds they avoid this management risk.

Another advantage of index funds, relative to actively managed funds, is that they ensure that the portfolio remains well diversified. Actively managed funds, in their attempts to outperform the market, may hold poorly diversified portfolios.

For example, they may tilt the portfolio towards particular industries. To the extent that actively managed funds hold inadequately diversified portfolios, they sacrifice part of the risk-reduction benefit of diversification.

Probably the greatest advantage of index funds is that they are much cheaper to run than actively managed funds. For example, many actively managed UK unit trusts and OEICs have a 6% initial charge, an annual 1.5% management charge and transaction costs around 1% per year. This compares with index tracker funds which typically have a zero initial charge, a 0.5% annual charge and minimal transaction costs.

A drawback of index funds is that they tend to omit the shares of very small firms. Even broad indices have a cut-off in terms of company size. For example, in the UK the FT All Share Index covers about 800 stocks. This eliminates more than 1,000 firms whose capitalisation is not sufficient. Actively managed funds are able to include any stocks, including those with very small capitalisations.

Tracking error

Portfolios constructed to replicate an index rarely succeed in precisely tracking the index. The tracking error is the difference between the total return on the replicating portfolio and the total return on the index. The total return consists of both dividends and capital gains (or losses).

The portfolio may hold all the stocks in the index, with weights corresponding to those of the index. This involves little tracking error but can involve significant transaction costs. Alternatively a subset of the index might be used. This approach reduces transaction costs but increases tracking error.

Even if the portfolio contains all the stocks in the index, appropriately weighted, there are sources of tracking error. The constituent stocks of an index are subject to change. Replacing stocks involves transaction costs. Furthermore the replacement is not instantaneous. Tracking is imperfect during the time taken to replace stocks.

Changes in the composition of an index can also affect stock prices. If index funds are widely used, stocks leaving the index will be sold in large numbers by index funds. As a result their prices fall and the funds receive unfavourable prices. Conversely stocks entering the index will be bought by index funds with the effect that their prices rise. The funds thus buy these stocks at raised prices. So the marginal stocks, those prone to move in and out of an index, are sold at low prices and bought at high prices. This weakens the performance of index portfolios.

● ● ● ● With-profits funds

Like unit trusts and investment trusts, with-profits funds offer the means of pooling the investments of thousands of small investors into a large fund that can hold a diversified portfolio of investments without incurring disproportionate transaction costs. Compared with unit and investment trusts with-profits funds provide a reduced-risk means of participating in stock market investment. Such a fund might be the basis of a pension plan or an endowment policy. If an investor puts a lump sum into a with-profits pension plan, for example, the value of that investment cannot fall irrespective of what happens in bond or stock markets. Furthermore the pension scheme provider (typically an insurance company) will add a sum of money to the planholder's personal fund each year. This sum is known as an annual or reversionary bonus and once added cannot be taken away. The money value of the investor's personal fund can only grow, it cannot fall. The scheme provider will normally add a further bonus, known as the terminal bonus, on the date that the investor's pension plan matures.

So a with-profits investment provides a high degree of security. It further reduces risk through the smoothing of investment returns over time. The insurance company (or other provider) will manage a fund that will typically consist of stocks, bonds, property and bank deposits (and other money market investments). Investments into a with-profits scheme will go into this fund and the returns on the fund will pay for the bonuses. The provider of the with-profits scheme will put some of these returns into a reserve in years in which the fund performs particularly well and will take money out of the reserve in order to pay bonuses in years that show relatively poor investment performance. Good and bad years are averaged out so that the private investor in the with-profits scheme is protected against the extremes of stock market fluctuations.

The operation of a with-profits scheme can be illustrated by means of Table 4.1, which shows the returns from £1,000 invested in 1989. The second column shows the percentage returns on the with-profits fund net of charges. The third column indicates the value of the individual's investment on the basis of having a proportionate share of the assets of the fund (proportionate to the initial investment) – this is sometimes referred to as the 'asset share'. The fourth column shows the percentage addition to the fund value allocated to the individual investor. This is often

Table 4.1 The returns from £1,000 invested in 1989

	Investment		Allocated		Guaranteed	
	% return	Cumulative total	% added	Cumulative total	% added	Cumulative total
1989	24.1	1,241	10.0	1,100	8.0	1,080
1990	−8.3	1,138	3.0	1,133	2.0	1,101
1991	13.5	1,292	9.0	1,235	6.0	1,167
1992	17.1	1,512	12.0	1,383	8.0	1,260
1993	28.8	1,948	21.0	1,673	14.0	1,436
1994	−4.2	1,866	4.0	1,740	3.0	1,479
1995	16.6	2,176	12.0	1,949	9.0	1,612
1996	10.7	2,409	10.0	2,144	8.0	1,741
1997	17.2	2,823	13.0	2,423	9.0	1,898
1998	13.3	3,198	12.0	2,714	9.0	2,069

referred to as the smoothed allocation since it reflects the principle of reallocating investment returns between time periods. For example, in 1993 only 21% of the 28.8% return was allocated to investors whereas in the following year the allocation was 8.2% higher than the returns on the fund.

The fifth column shows the cumulative total of allocations made to the individual investor, while the sixth contains the percentage allocations that are guaranteed and hence cannot be lost by the investor. These guaranteed returns correspond to the reversionary bonuses. The final column shows the cumulative guaranteed total which consists of the initial investment plus the sum of the annual reversionary bonuses. The values in this column constitute the lowest level that the investment could reach irrespective of what happens in stock markets.

At maturity of the pension or endowment plan (or at death if earlier) a terminal bonus is added to the guaranteed total. The terminal bonus is the difference between the total guaranteed and the total allocated. At maturity the investor receives the sum in the fifth column, made up of the guaranteed total (initial investment plus annual bonuses) and a terminal bonus. The difference between the sums in the third and fifth columns remains with the scheme provider as reserves. These reserves, sometimes known as orphan funds, are available for the payment of bonuses in future years in which returns are poor.

From the perspective of the scheme provider the value of the private individuals' investments constitutes a liability, whereas the underlying portfolio is an asset. The surplus (or excess) is the amount by which the value of the assets of the underlying fund exceeds the aggregate value of the liabilities (the total value of all the individual with-profits policies). Companies providing the schemes are required to maintain a minimum surplus as reserves. This minimum surplus is known as the solvency margin. The surplus remaining above the required minimum solvency margin will be divided between the current payment of bonuses to the scheme members, the reserves (available for bonus payments in future years) and dividends for shareholders (this is not applicable if the company is a mutual and hence owned by its with-profits policyholders – a mutual has no shareholders).

It is sometimes argued that the annual guaranteed bonuses reflect the current income on investments (dividends, interest, etc.) while the terminal bonuses arise from capital gains on the investments. This cannot be precisely true since in many years reversionary (guaranteed) bonus rates deviate substantially from the rates of income yield on investments. Nevertheless there may be a kernel of truth in the idea.

One question concerns the cost of the risk reduction provided by the guaranteed sums. Some argue that the risk reduction is more apparent than real. Instead of fluctuations in the current value of the policy, there is uncertainty as to the size of the terminal bonus. However, with-profits policies do provide a form of disaster insurance – in the event of an extreme collapse of share prices the policyholder is protected. It is likely that the provider covers its guarantees to policyholders by investing a sufficient proportion of the fund in low-risk securities such as government bonds, Treasury bills and high-grade bank deposits. A cost of the risk reduction is the reduction in investment returns arising from investment in low-risk (and hence low-return) assets.

Unitised with-profits policies were introduced in response to the emergence of unit-linked policies linked to unit trusts, making it easier to switch with other units within unit-linked policies. Investors can now sell units in one type of fund in order to buy units in another. The value of the with-profits units will never fall (so long as the policy is not terminated before the maturity date). The final return to the investor will be the value of the units plus any terminal bonus. Whether the policy is conventional or unitised, the maturity values should be similar. As with conventional with-profits policies, termination of a unitised with-profits policy before its maturity date could involve a reduction in value in the form of an exit penalty or market value adjustment.

The significance of financial strength

Financial strength refers to the amount of money that a life office has in its financial reserve. It is a measure of a life company's ability to meet its liabilities and provides an indication of how likely the company is to pay future bonuses. A company with large reserves has more investment freedom, allowing greater exposure to equities (more emphasis on shares). Large reserves also allow bonus rates to be maintained when markets fall.

Only those with sufficient financial strength can invest in the relatively volatile asset classes of equities and property and continue to deliver consistent returns. Weaker companies are forced to maintain a higher proportion of their investments in bonds and deposits, which tend to offer less growth potential than equities.

One way of determining a company's financial strength is to look at its 'free asset ratio'. This is a measure of the free assets that a company holds expressed as a percentage of total assets. Free assets are assets remaining after liabilities have been accounted for. However, the information provided by the free asset ratio is not unambiguous – free assets may be large because the company tends to be mean with its bonus payments.

Criticisms

One criticism made of with-profits policies is that the term 'with profits' is in reality a misnomer. Originally this term was used on the grounds that with-profits policyholders shared in the profits made from the company's other operations (non with-profits business). In reality, with-profits funds typically do not receive income from sources other than the with-profits fund itself.

Another criticism sometimes made is that most companies give policyholders little information – most give no feedback about investment returns, asset shares or the smoothing. It has been suggested that this lack of information allows companies to manipulate pay-outs so that transfer values (the sums transferred when switching to other providers) are reduced in order to boost maturity values (which are the values used in sales and marketing). It may also be possible that transfer values are trimmed for the purpose of replenishing reserves.

If a policyholder terminates a policy before maturity a transfer value is payable. This transfer value should equal the cumulative value of the allocated returns (inclusive of the initial investment). If this value exceeds the asset share (the accumulated assets resulting from the initial investment plus investment returns), the transfer value should equal the asset share. The use of the asset share rather than the cumulative smoothed allocation is referred to as a 'market value adjustment'.

Many observers suspect that, under the cover of incomplete information, some companies set transfer values below both the asset share and the smoothed allocation. The surplus might be used to enhance maturity values. Potential new clients may be made aware of maturity values but not experienced transfer values. It is possible for companies to boost their sales of new policies by boosting maturity values at the expense of transfer values.

● ● ● ● Annuities

Annuities are guaranteed incomes. They may be for specific periods, for example ten years. More frequently the income is guaranteed for the life of the holder. They are often used for pension purposes. Upon retirement a person would buy an annuity and thereby guarantee a retirement income payable until death. Once the annuity is taken out it cannot be changed. The buyer of the annuity also needs to be aware that the money used to buy the annuity is usually not refundable. If someone dies immediately after buying an annuity, the money used to buy the annuity is normally lost.

When an annuity is taken out, an annuity rate is stipulated. For example, an annuity rate of 7% p.a. means that a payment of £100,000 secures an annual income of £7,000 per year. Annuity rates vary with age, sex and sometimes also the health of the individual, and will improve as the age at which the annuity is undertaken increases. An older person will have a shorter life expectancy and so the income is expected to be paid over fewer years. The prospective shorter period allows for increased annual pay-outs. Since women have longer life expectancies than men, annuity rates tend to be lower for women than for men. Existing health problems that could shorten life might entail higher annuity rates. The same is true for lifestyle factors such as smoking.

Annuities as pensions

When used as a pension, an annuity is a regular payment made by an insurance company for the rest of the pensioner's life in return for a pension fund. The pension fund would have been built up over the working life of the pensioner. The annuity payments will depend upon the size of the pension fund available for the

rates depended on:
– size of fund
– bond yield

purchase of the annuity as well as on the rates of yield available from government bonds at the time that the annuity is purchased.

Annuities normally invest in government bonds (gilts). The annuity payments to the pensioner arise partly from the yield on the government bonds and partly from the repayment of the initial purchase price of the annuity. The purchase price of the annuity is returned to the pensioner over time at a rate that would return the entire sum by the (actuarially) expected date of death, which is determined by insurance company statisticians (actuaries).

To the extent that the annuity payments depend on the yields on government bonds, potential pensioners face a high degree of uncertainty. Yields on government bonds can vary considerably over time. In consequence annuity rates can change substantially from year to year. If a person retires in a year in which annuity rates are relatively low, that person suffers a low pension for the rest of his or her life. The system of obtaining a pension by buying an annuity at retirement involves a considerable amount of risk. The size of the pension depends upon when this occurs. Retirement at a time when government bond yields are low results in a low pension.

Alternative types of annuity

Alternatives available to the buyer of an annuity include the level annuity, escalating annuity, index-linked annuity, with-profits annuity and unit-linked annuity. A related possibility is an income drawdown scheme.

A level (or conventional) annuity pays a fixed amount each year for the rest of the person's life. An escalating annuity increases the payments by a predetermined percentage each year. The cost of these annual increases is a lower initial payment relative to a level annuity. Index-linked annuities guarantee that the payment rises each year to keep pace with inflation, again at the cost of a lower initial payment compared with a level annuity.

A with-profits annuity links the payments to the with-profits fund of an insurance company. When taking out the annuity, the holder specifies a growth rate for the with-profits fund (an anticipated bonus rate). A high specified growth rate implies a relatively large fund over time and hence a high level of income that can be drawn from the fund. However, if the fund fails to grow at the specified rate (the actual annual bonus falls short of the anticipated rate), those withdrawals will prove to be excessive. The consequence is a smaller fund and a lower income in subsequent years.

If the specified growth rate is less than the rate actually achieved, the fund size increases, as does the income that can be drawn in future years. A low specified rate implies an assumption that the fund will be relatively small in future. This entails a low initial income. If the actual growth rate turns out to be higher than the specified rate, the low initial income is less than could have been paid, with the result that the fund becomes larger. This means that future income payments will exceed the initial payment.

Unit-linked annuities operate in a similar way to with-profits annuities, but are linked to unit trusts. This entails an additional risk. Unit trust prices can go down as well as up (as opposed to an investment in a with-profits fund). A consequence is that the income payments can fall as a decline in unit trust prices pulls down the value of the fund (and hence the potential flow of income that it can support). Conversely there is a potential for increased income resulting from rising unit prices. As is normal for investments, the relatively high risk is associated with relatively high expected returns and hence income levels.

Income drawdown schemes

With-profits and unit-linked annuities may be attractive to pensioners who face low annuity rates at retirement due to low yields on government bonds. Another alternative for such pensioners is to use income drawdown. This enables people to defer buying an annuity while drawing an income from their pension fund.

The pensioner leaves the pension fund invested but takes part of the fund each year as an income. The amount taken is subject to upper and lower limits. The pensioner can choose to use the fund to buy an annuity when annuity rates are judged to be satisfactory. There is an upper age limit by which an annuity must be purchased (in the UK, at the time of writing, an annuity must be purchased by the age of 75).

One advantage of income drawdown is that it avoids the risk that the pension fund might be lost as a result of death shortly after retirement. In the event of death the remainder of the pension fund becomes part of the person's estate (subject to a tax deduction).

Calculating a level annuity

The calculation of an annuity rate can be illustrated by the following example. Someone has a pension fund of £100,000. The actuarial expectation is that the person will live for another ten years. If the ten-year interest rate (yield on government bonds) is 8.5% p.a., how much can be paid to the pensioner each year? The first payment is to take place one year from the present.

The annuity equation is:

$$p = M / [\{1 - (1 + r)^{-T}\} / r]$$

where p is the annual income, M is the size of the pension fund, r is the relevant rate of (redemption) yield on government bonds and T is the period for which the annuity is expected to be paid.

$$p = 100{,}000 / [\{1 - (1.085)^{-10}\} / 0.085]$$

$$p = £15{,}240.77$$

An annual income of £15,240.77 can be paid to the pensioner.

It can be noted that a mortgage is equivalent to a negative annuity. An annuity entails the initial payment of a lump sum and a subsequent series of cash receipts. A mortgage involves the initial receipt of a lump sum (which is typically used to buy a property) and a subsequent series of cash payments. This equivalence of annuities and mortgages implies that the annuity equation can be used for the purpose of calculating mortgage repayments.

There is a related equation for the calculation of the lump sum to be expected from a series of cash payments. The accumulation of a pension fund may entail periodic payments into an investment scheme. The equation for the expected value of the lump sum to be generated by those payments is:

$$M = p.[(1 + r)^T - 1]/r$$

where M is the expected final sum of money, p is the periodic payment into the fund, r is the average rate of return on the fund and T is the length of time for which the payments are made.

Exercise 4.1

(a) You are advising a client with savings of £100,000. The client wants to fund constant annual expenditure for ten years with a zero savings balance at the end. If the ten-year interest rate is 8.5% p.a., how much can be withdrawn each year? The first withdrawal is to take place one year from the present.

(b) A mortgage of £100,000 is to be paid off in equal monthly instalments over 25 years. What are the monthly mortgage payments at a constant interest rate of 6% p.a.?

(c) Someone is planning to retire in 40 years' time with a pension fund of £250,000. What is the required annual contribution to the pension fund if the rate of return on the fund is 5% p.a.?

Answers

(a) $p = M/ [\{1 - (1 + r)^{-T}\} / r]$
$p = 100,000 / [\{1 - (1.085)^{-10}\} / 0.085]$
$p = £15,240.77$

(b) $p = M/ [\{1 - (1 + r)^{-T}\} / r]$
$p = 100,000/ [\{1 - (1.005)^{-300}\} / 0.005]$
(Annual interest of 6% implies a monthly 6/12 = 0.5%)
$p = £644.30$

(c) $M = p. [(1 + r)^T - 1] / r$
$250,000 = p. [(1.05)^{40} - 1] / 0.05$
$250,000 = p \times 120.8$
$p = 250,000 / 120.8 = 2069.54$
The required annual contribution is £2,069.54

Exercise 4.2

A person has an annual income of £20,000, of which £2,500 each year is invested in a pension fund. The contributions to the fund are made over 40 years and the average rate of return on the fund is 5% p.a. The expected life expectancy at retirement is 20 years. The rate of return on government bonds at the time of retirement is 2.5% p.a. What annual pension should the person receive?

Answer

The first step is to calculate the expected value of the pension fund at the end of the 40 years during which contributions are made.

$M = p.[(1 + r)^T - 1]/r$
$M = £2,500 [(1.05)^{40} - 1] / 0.05$
$M = £302,000$

The next step is to calculate the annuity payments to be expected from that sum of money.

$p = M/ [\{1 - (1 + r)^{-T}\} / r]$
$p = £302,000/[\{1 - (1.025)^{-20}\}/0.025]$
$p = £19,372$

The annual pension is £19,372.

Discussion question

How would you explain the popularity of with-profits pension funds?

Chapter 5

Tax advantaged investment schemes

After studying this chapter readers should be able to evaluate:

● *tax advantaged investment schemes available in the United Kingdom, including pension plans, individual savings accounts, venture capital trusts and enterprise investment schemes*

● *the effects of taxation on investment returns.*

Tax advantaged investment schemes

Many governments allow investment schemes that provide tax advantages for people. What follows is a description of schemes allowed by the UK government. One purpose of such schemes is to encourage people to save and make their own provision for retirement. UK tax advantaged schemes motivated by this objective include personal pension plans, additional voluntary contributions, individual savings accounts and friendly society policies.

The main purpose of some schemes is to encourage investment in enterprises that might otherwise have difficulty raising finance. In the UK, venture capital trusts and enterprise investment schemes provide tax concessions for investments in companies that are too small to raise capital by means of issuing shares via a listing on the stock exchange.

Pension funds

One means of accumulating assets while enjoying tax breaks is to invest in a pension fund. In the UK, contributions to a pension fund are deductible against income tax. The investments in a pension fund accumulate free of capital gains tax. The income from bonds, cash and property within a pension fund is free of tax. Dividends from shares within the fund do not attract any tax liability beyond the basic rate, which is assumed to have been paid (a firm's payment of corporation tax is deemed to preclude shareholders from the requirement to pay tax at the basic rate).

There are limitations as to how much can be paid into a pension plan each financial year. In the case of personal pension plans the limit varies between 17.5% and 40% of earned income; the percentage rises with age. There is also an upper limit to the income that can be used as a basis for contributions into a personal pension fund (at the time of writing this upper limit is about 4.5 times average earnings).

In the case of employers' pension schemes, the maximum that an employee can pay into the fund is 15% of income (salary plus bonus). If the employee pays less than 15%, that employee is able to make payments into an AVC (additional voluntary contributions) fund so long as the total of the two payments does not exceed 15% of income. The AVC payments may be paid into the pension fund operated by the employer or into a fund operated by another provider (such as an insurance company). Employees whose pensions are not payable from the proceeds of investment funds (for example civil servants, teachers and armed forces personnel have their pensions paid from general taxation) can also pay into AVCs, so long as their superannuation contributions are less than 15% of income. AVC payments are tax deductible (they are subtracted from income when tax is assessed) and AVC funds attract the same tax advantages as other pension funds.

Individual savings accounts

ISAs were introduced in the 1999 Finance Act and were due to have a life of at least ten years. They provide tax advantaged investments. At the time of writing, an ISA investment can be in either a maxi ISA or in mini ISAs. If an investor chooses mini ISAs, he can hold up to three mini ISAs. Up to £3,000 per year can be invested in a cash mini ISA with a bank, building society or other deposit taker. The interest on the cash is tax free and the money can be withdrawn at any time without loss of the tax relief (although if the money is withdrawn subsequent to the financial year in which the investment was made, it cannot be reinvested in that year's ISA). In addition the capital (not interest) from a maturing TESSA (tax exempt special savings account) can be invested in a 'TESSA only ISA'; this could occur only once for an investor and would be subject to the TESSA investment limit of £9,000.

A further £3,000 per year can be invested in a stocks and shares mini ISA. The investment can be in the form of unit trusts, investment trusts, open ended investment companies (OEICs), shares or bonds. There are no geographical restrictions on the investments. The investments are free of capital gains tax, bond coupons are free of income tax, and share dividends benefit from a 10% tax credit for a few years. A further £1,000 can be invested in an insurance mini ISA, which takes the form of an insurance bond whose underlying fund has the same tax advantages as the cash and stocks and shares ISAs. The three mini ISAs can be with three different providers (the providers include banks, building societies, insurance companies and investment companies).

Alternatively an investor could invest up to £7,000 in a maxi ISA. Up to £7,000 can be in the form of shares and bonds, frequently in unit trusts, investment trusts or OEICs. However, the investor could choose to have up to £3,000 of the maxi ISA in cash and up to £1,000 in an insurance bond. There is no facility for switching between the three alternative components of a maxi ISA. Investments in a maxi ISA receive the same tax advantages as those in mini ISAs and can also be withdrawn at any time without loss of the tax advantages. The whole of a maxi ISA must be with one provider, although the investor may choose a different provider for ISAs in subsequent years. An investor cannot invest in both mini and maxi ISAs in a financial year. ISAs are illustrated by Figure 5.1.

Friendly society policies

Friendly society policies are a form of endowment policy. They are savings schemes with a small amount of life assurance attached. They differ from other endowment policies in that the fund is exempt from income and capital gains taxes. At the time of writing contributions are limited to £25 per month (£300 per year). The tax concessions are dependent upon a policy running for at least ten years.

The effects of taxation on investment returns

Taxation has a considerable effect on the returns to an investment. Table 5.1 illustrates the outcome of a lump sum investment of £1,000 over investment horizons of 10 years, 20 years and 30 years. It is assumed that the value of the investment grows at an average of 8% p.a.

The first row shows the outcome of an investment that is tax deductible and accumulates tax free. If the investment is tax deductible then the sum actually invested, as the result of an outlay of £1,000, is £1,000/0.6 = £1,667. The sums of money shown are the values of the investment at the end of the respective periods. The percentages in parentheses show the (average compound per annum) rates of return.

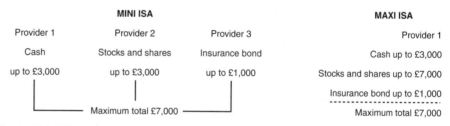

Figure 5.1 Mini and maxi ISAs

Table 5.1 A lump sum investment over 10 years, 20 years and 30 years

Period of investment	10 years	20 years	30 years
Tax deductible investment (at 40% Tax) plus tax-free accumulation	£3,598 (13.66%)	£7,768 (10.79%)	£16,771 (9.85%)
Tax-free accumulation	£2,159 (8%)	£4,661 (8%)	£10,063 (8%)
Deferred tax at 24%	£1,880 (6.52%)	£3,782 (6.88%)	£7,888 (7.13%)
Deferred tax at 40%	£1,695 (5.42%)	£3,197 (5.98%)	£6,438 (6.4%)
Annual taxation at 40%	£1,598 (4.8%)	£2,554 (4.8%)	£4,082 (4.8%)

The second row shows the outcome of an investment that is not tax deductible but which is allowed to accumulate free of tax. The third row shows the results of an investment that is free of tax during the life of the investment but which is subject to tax at 24% on investment returns when the investment is liquidated. The fourth row is similar to the third row except that the tax rate is 40%. The fifth row shows the outcomes when the investment returns are taxed each year.

It can be seen that the tax treatment makes a considerable difference. For example, the 30-year outcome with the most favourable tax treatment is more than four times the outcome with the least favourable treatment. In the UK, pension funds are highly favoured investments, in terms of tax treatment. Pension contributions are tax deductible, pension funds are free of capital gains tax, interest and bond coupon receipts are tax free, and dividends from shares receive favourable tax treatment (from the perspective of payers of the 40% tax rate).

Individual savings accounts and personal equity plans (PEPs), while not being tax deductible, do receive favourable tax treatment. Such investments are free of capital gains tax, interest and bond coupons are tax free, and dividends from shares receive favourable tax treatment (from the perspective of payers of the 40% tax rate).

In the UK, capital gains tax is payable only when investments are sold, in other words the tax is deferred. Furthermore the rate of capital gains tax is lower than the rate of income tax (24% as against 40% if the investment is held for ten years or more). So investments that provide returns in the form of capital gains are treated more favourably than investments whose returns are in the form of periodic payments such as interest, coupons or dividends. This means that shares are more favourably treated than bonds and bank (and building society) deposits.

These conclusions are applicable to payers of the standard rate of tax as well as to those who pay the higher (40%) rate. The relative advantage of shares is further reinforced by the fact that the first £7,500 (the figure at the time of writing) of capital gains in any financial year are free of tax.

Venture capital trusts (VCTs) and enterprise investment schemes (EISs)

VCTs and EISs are UK schemes that encourage investment in small companies through the provision of tax breaks. At the time of writing VCTs had been the more successful in attracting investors.

VCTs are similar to investment trusts. A VCT holds a portfolio of shares of unquoted companies. The VCT has a stock exchange listing and is professionally managed by a fund manager. Also, like investment trusts, the market value of the VCT usually differs from the sum of the values of the companies in which it invests. VCTs often trade at a discount to their net asset values.

Investments in a VCT attract tax relief at 20% up to the investment ceiling of £100,000 per year. Investments are also free of capital gains tax. Both of these tax breaks are subject to minimum holding periods (which can be as low as three years). A further tax concession relates to the facility of sheltering capital gains from other

Exercise 5.1

A unit trust fund has a prospective average annual return of 7.5% over the next 25 years. Estimate the value of a £1,000 investment after 25 years when the returns are (a) tax free, (b) subject to a deferred tax (i.e. taxed at the end of the 25 years) of 20%, and (c) subject to an annual tax of 20%.

Answer
(a) £1,000 $\times$ (1.075)^{25} = £6,098
(b) {(£6,098 − £1,000) $\times$ 0.8} + £1,000 = £5,078
    (The investor retains 80% of the accumulated return plus the initial investment of £1,000)
(c) £1,000 $\times$ (1.06)^{25} = £4,292
    (The annual tax of 20% turns a 7.5% p.a. return into a 6% p.a. return)

sources. Capital gains from other sources are sheltered from tax if they are invested in a VCT. The capital gains tax is not payable until the VCT investment is sold.

Enterprise investment schemes involve the investment being made in a single unquoted company rather than a portfolio of companies. Unlike VCTs, EIS investments do not have an upper limit to the annual investment. However, only the first £150,000 per year attracts the tax concessions of 20% relief plus freedom from capital gains tax. The whole of the investment can be used to shelter capital gains from other sources. Capital gains from other sources are not taxable until the EIS investment is sold. The EIS tax concessions may also be applicable to investments in AIM (Alternative Investment Market) quoted companies, where shares are being issued to raise capital for investment. EIS investments are likely to be less liquid than VCTs since EISs are not stock exchange listed and hence cannot be sold through the stock exchange.

Business as usual after boom and bust

During the internet boom, the venture capital model seemed omnipotent. Now, after scores of dotcoms backed by blue-chip venture capitalists have gone bust, it is time for a sober evaluation: in normal times, what are the advantages and limitations of the venture capital model?

Venture capitalists occupy an important niche as investors. Businesses backed by venture capital have profoundly influenced high-technology fields such as semiconductors and genetic engineering. Capital and advice provided by venture capitalists have helped propel companies such as Sun Microsystems and Compaq to global leadership. But

such cases are not typical. Contrary to popular belief, only exceptional entrepreneurs can secure start-up venture capital. Of nearly a million businesses formed each year in the US, venture capitalists fund a few hundred. Most companies, exemplified by Hewlett-Packard, Microsoft, Cisco and Dell, start with limited funds provided by founders or by their families and friends.

This article examines the attributes of companies in which venture capitalists tend to invest. As shown in Figure 1 entrepreneurs pursue opportunities with high subjective uncertainty and low resource requirements. When public companies mature they

▶

undertake projects that require substantial capital and managerial resources. Failure can lead to substantial losses but such projects do not involve much subjective uncertainty, because the risks and returns can be assessed.

Venture capitalists use criteria that demand investments with medium resource requirements and uncertainty. Only a few, unusual entrepreneurs meet these criteria. Some businesses, such as Cisco, that cannot raise venture capital at the outset can do so later, after uncertainty has declined and resource requirements have increased. The venture capital industry typically gives about two thirds of its funds to companies which are not start-ups. As these businesses prove themselves further, so uncertainty continues to decline and their resource requirements increase. Then they can access public capital markets. Thus venture capital is a source of medium-term, 'bridge' financing.

Evaluation

Investors in start-ups have an incentive to conduct more due diligence than investors in public companies. Investors in publicly traded shares are not rewarded for assuming company-specific risk. The risks are diversified by holding a portfolio. The 'market' or 'systematic' risk of the portfolio, rather than astuteness in choosing securities, determines an investor's long-term return. Efforts to analyse a company's prospects carry little reward because market prices already allow for all available information.

Funding start-ups is different. Discrimination among opportunities is crucial, because investors cannot depend on free research and due diligence reflected in market prices. Prudence demands some diversification but this is no substitute for choosing each investment carefully.

Buying 20 listed stocks at random eliminates most company-specific risk and provides a return that tracks the overall stock market. Historically, this return has been about 10 per cent a year. Providing venture capital to 20 random entrepreneurs will likely provide, given the dubious prospects of most new businesses, a return of close to zero. Moreover, backing randomly selected ventures makes investors vulnerable to opportunistic founders.

Investors in start-ups have to undertake considerable monitoring and oversight. In public markets, the diversified investor's ability to monitor and intervene is low. Companies cannot discuss strategy and performance with dispersed investors, so shareholders lack the confidential information to monitor managers and distinguish between their luck and skill. Also, the shareholder who incurs the costs of inducing a company to change must share the benefits with others who made no effort. Unhappy stockholders therefore sell shares rather than incur these costs. In small, private companies, however, investors can demand access to information they need on performance. And they cannot avoid intervention by selling their holdings in a liquid market.

Partnership terms

Professional venture capitalists, who invest others' funds rather than their own, face additional incentives to develop systems for evaluating and monitoring investments.

Wealthy individuals, pension funds and others who have the capital to invest in start-ups often lack the resources (or confidence) to evaluate and monitor such ventures. Instead, they invest in limited partnerships organised by venture capital companies. In such partnerships, venture capitalists have discretion over the funds under management. At or before the end of the life of the partnership, usually within 10 years, they sell the illiquid holdings of the partnership for cash or convert them into marketable securities and return the proceeds to clients. For this service, venture capitalists receive an annual fee (usually 1–2 per cent of assets managed) as well as a 'carried interest' or share (about 20 per cent) of profits generated.

The terms of their deals with clients encourage venture capitalists to formalise investment processes. Limited partnership structures allow venture capitalists to avoid delays and the leakage of information that might result from having to raise funds for individual investments. However, they also require clients to cede control over investment decisions for an extended period. The 'carried interest', which gives venture capitalists a share of the profits but not of the losses, creates an incentive to invest in excessively risky projects. Venture

▶

capitalists therefore have procedures to reassure clients that they will not make reckless investments.

Evidence suggests that venture capitalists devote considerable effort to due diligence, structuring deals and providing advice and oversight. Partners in venture capital companies, academic William Sahlman reports, usually have responsibility for just under nine investments and sit on five boards. They visit each company 19 times a year and spend 100 hours either on site or in contact by phone. They 'help recruit and compensate key individuals, work with suppliers and customers, help establish tactics and strategy, play a major role in raising capital, and help structure transactions such as mergers and acquisitions. They often assume more direct control by changing management and are sometimes willing to take over day-to-day operations'.

Typical criteria

The limited number of deals venture capitalists can manage sets a high threshold for the returns they require. Instead of dividing their time between many opportunities, they concentrate on a few ventures that have the potential – based on objective data – to make substantial returns. Significant failure rates and limited time horizons reinforce this preference. Even after extensive due diligence and monitoring, many venture capital investments yield disappointing returns.

One study of venture capital portfolios by Venture Economics reported that about 7 per cent of investments accounted for more than 60 per cent of profits, while a third resulted in a partial or total loss.

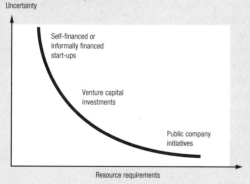

Figure 1: Three stages of investment

Uncertainty

Self-financed or informally financed start-ups

Venture capital investments

Public company initiatives

Resource requirements

Venture capitalists therefore avoid small opportunities where even substantial returns on a percentage basis will not cover the opportunity costs of their time or compensate for failures. Every venture must hold the promise of returns in millions of pounds, rather than in the tens or even hundreds of thousands.

The attractiveness of a company also depends on how long venture capitalists expect it will take them to sell their investment. Venture capitalists have to cash out before their partnership expires. In a 10-year fund, a venture that does not fold is taken public or sold to another company typically within five years. This consideration leads venture capitalists to favour investments with the potential for large payoffs: small companies cannot afford to go public and conform to regulatory and reporting requirements.

Unusual ventures

In trying to identify big winners, venture capitalists look for companies that serve large markets with a proprietary technology or process. A small company can be profitable as a result of its founders' drive, energy, relationships and so on, but a significant payoff, realised through the sale of the company or a public issue of its stock, generally requires something inherently proprietary in its products or processes. Venture capitalists also favour seasoned founding teams who can significantly increase a venture's chances of becoming large quickly.

Some entrepreneurs who start niche businesses without a proprietary model may discover large markets and build sustainable advantages. Similarly, inexperienced founders may learn how to manage rapidly growing companies. But it is difficult to predict which entrepreneurs will be able to do so. The absence of a specific plan or technology and verifiable credentials puts the subjective uncertainty of the venture above the venture capitalist's acceptable threshold.

My research suggests that most start-ups, including those in Inc. magazine's list of the 500 fastest-growing private companies in the US, do not meet the criteria used by venture capitalists. Most entrepreneurs do not have a proprietary product or service capable of generating significant revenues. They are often not the first or second entrants in their

▶

markets. Often, they copy from other companies or develop an idea independently but at the same time as others.

Usually the revenue potential of an initial concept is limited. Most entrepreneurs start in niches that cannot justify the million-dollar investment thresholds of venture capitalists. For example, Microsoft co-founders Bill Gates and Paul Allen launched the company in 1975 by writing a programming language for a computer sold to a tiny market of hobbyists. Even if such companies can find larger markets, their growth tends to fall short of the size necessary to meet venture capital standards of success. An investment in Microsoft in 1975 would probably not have produced an attractive return over the usual three- to five-year venture capital horizon. Five years after launch, Microsoft had sales of $5m. It took nine years to book the same revenues as the software company Lotus, which was backed by venture, did in its first year and 10 years to go public.

Most entrepreneurs don't have the experience that venture capitalists believe is necessary to build and manage large companies. The founders of Compaq had been senior managers at Texas Instruments. Michael Dell and Bill Gates were students when they started. In exceptional cases, an inexperienced founder may team up with a seasoned manager and venture capitalists can help entrepreneurs create such teams. This requires, however, a high-potential idea or technology. If, as is often the case, entrepreneurs start off with a me-too concept or a differentiated product for a small market, they cannot recruit partners or employees with the experience that venture capitalists consider necessary.

Later-stage finance
Many ventures whose prospects are small or uncertain at the outset qualify for venture capital later, as their business models and management capabilities are proven. And venture capitalists give more to these later-stage businesses than to start-ups. The National Venture Capital Association's annual report shows that in 1996, 77 per cent of companies receiving venture capital were three years or older and 80 per cent had more than 25 employees. Similarly, data collected for the US Federal Reserve by George Fenn, Nellie Liang and Stephen Prowse show only about a third of investments are 'early stage'.

Cisco illustrates how the fit with venture capital increases as subjective uncertainty declines. Sandy Lerner and Len Bosak started Cisco in 1984. They raised money by running up bills on their credit cards and persuaded friends and relatives to work for deferred pay. Although the business was consistently profitable it faced persistent cash shortages and at one point in 1986, Lerner took a job as a data processing manager to provide more cash. In 1987 Cisco received funding from Sequoia Capital – the 77th venture capital company the founders approached.

By then the products had proven themselves – Cisco had sales of about $300,000 a month, without a professional sales staff and marketing campaign. But not only did Cisco lack capital, it also lacked professional management. Sequoia partner Donald Valentine helped provide these by hiring an experienced manager, John Morgridge, to run Cisco in 1989. Morgridge paved the way for a public offering in 1990. After going public, Cisco became the leading supplier of routers that link computer networks. In 2000, it took revenues of nearly $19bn and profits of $874m.

Symbiotic relationship
Cisco exemplifies the relationship between venture capitalists and public markets. Markets provide exits for venture capitalists and venture capitalists create a 'product' for public investors. Public companies can then undertake projects whose resource requirements and time horizons lie outside the scope of venture capitalists. For example, the research and marketing costs of a drug compare with the total capital of many venture capital funds and the time taken just for regulatory approval typically exceeds their investment horizon.

Public companies have an obvious advantage in such projects with their extensive management structures. Investors are also more prepared to entrust funds for an indefinite time to organisations with well-developed management rather than to a few talented individuals. However, management systems make public companies more averse to subjective uncertainty than venture capital companies.

▶

Mania and its aftermath

The IPO mania that started in earnest with the 1996 flotation of Netscape distorted this natural order. Investing in any growth stock turns on the optimism that small profits will turn into large profits. With Netscape and subsequent offerings, investors were betting on a fundamental change in trajectory, believing that companies making significant losses would, one day, make substantial profits.

New economy optimism did wonders for venture capitalists. Before, they had to wait for ventures to establish a record of profits over several years. And they had to write off investments in businesses that, in spite of star-studded founding teams, could not develop profitable business models. As the IPO market became less discriminating, venture capitalists had fewer write-offs, holding periods shrank and exit values multiplied.

Contrast Sun Microsystems, incorporated in 1982, with Chemdex, incorporated in 1997. Both started with concepts that could lead to substantial long-term profits, had exceptionally capable founders and secured financing from Kleiner-Perkins. The difference? It took four years for Sun to go public and only two for Chemdex. In its pre-IPO fiscal year, Sun booked revenues of $115m on which it earned $8.5m in net income. Chemdex booked $29,000 in revenues and lost $8.5m. By design, Sun turned profitable in its first quarter and has remained so ever since. Chemdex (now renamed Ventro) has never made a profit. Its stock, which peaked at $243 last February, now trades for about $1. But as far as its venture capitalists are concerned, what might once have been a write-off counts as a winner.

By my calculations, returns from venture capital funds between 1981 and 1996 were indistinguishable from those of publicly traded stocks. Between 1996 and 1999 many funds sported triple-digit returns each year. These returns enabled venture capitalists to raise huge funds and attracted many new entrants and substitutes. The investment banks which underwrite IPOs moved up the value chain and put billions into their venture capital activities. All of the top consulting and accounting companies set up incubators. And as the money poured in, venture capital had neither the time nor the incentive to apply traditional criteria and due diligence procedures.

What happens next? The boom and bust in biotechnology companies provides a good preview. In the early 1990s markets seemed to think genetic engineering would help cure every disease. These companies could issue stock without any obvious route to profitability. Venture capitalists courted academics and medics with implausible business plans. Then the bottom fell out. According to Josh Lerner and Alexander Tsai, external financing raised by US biotechnology companies halved – from $5bn in 1992 to $2bn in 1994. Biotechnology stocks had a wilder ride. The Amex biotechnology index peaked at 250 and in the next two and a half years lost 80 per cent of its value. It would take almost a decade to regain that peak.

But research into drugs and therapies, and the formation of companies, did not end. It just reverted to more sensible patterns. And although biotechnology did not meet expectations, it will make significant contributions to medicine. So it will be with the new economy. Valuations and expectations will fall, but not forever. The party is over, but it isn't the end of the world. Once they have recovered from their hangovers, investors will resume their distinctive roles.

Source: Amar Bhidé, *Financial Times, Mastering Investment Supplement*, Part 9, July 9 2001, pp 2–4. Reprinted with permission.

Chapter 6

The rationale and conduct of regulation

After studying this chapter readers should appreciate:

- *the need for regulation of investment business and markets*

- *the drawbacks of regulation*

- *the system of regulation in the United Kingdom*

- *how systems of regulation differ between countries.*

Institutional investments can be mis-sold. There can be malpractice and misrepresentation. These could arise from inadequate training of advisers or from conflicts of interest. For example, if advisers are paid by commission they may be inclined to sell the products that pay the highest commission rather than the products most suitable for the needs of their clients. A major source of possible malpractice is asymmetric information – the supplier of an investment product knows much more about it than the consumer does and full and accurate information may be withheld from the consumer.

What follows does not attempt to describe a regulatory regime in a particular country at a particular time. It is concerned with general issues concerning regulation, especially its purposes.

The economic rationale for regulation can be described under three headings. The first is the need to correct market imperfections. The second relates to the existence of economies of scale in monitoring the suppliers of financial products. The third involves the establishment and maintenance of consumer confidence in the market by ensuring that the suppliers do not fall below a specified standard.

The correction of market imperfections

There are numerous potential imperfections in the market for retail financial products. A perfect market requires all participants to have full information. Consumers of financial services typically lack full information. It is difficult to ascertain the quality of financial products at the point of purchase. The technicalities of many products render them difficult to assess by consumers. Many financial products are long term in nature and the realisation that a poor product has been bought does not occur until it is too late. There is a temptation for consumers to take a 'free-rider' approach whereby each consumer assumes that other consumers have investigated the soundness of products and their providers. There may be a temptation for commission-seeking sales personnel to distort the information provided to consumers. Many financial products are not purchased frequently (for example pensions and endowment policies), with the result that consumers do not develop a knowledge of products and providers.

One purpose of regulation is thus the imposition of requirements upon providers in relation to the provision of information to consumers. This regulation should encompass not only the provision of adequate and accurate information to consumers but also the ability of sales personnel to communicate such information. Financial advisers should not only provide high-quality information but should be able to understand the information that they give. It is possible for poor advice to be given as a result of the adviser failing to fully understand the product being offered.

Economies of scale and delegated monitoring

In the absence of regulation and supervision by an agency, consumers would need to investigate and monitor the providers of financial services, requiring time, effort and money on the part of the consumers. This would entail considerable duplication as all consumers would be carrying out the same process. There would also be the loss of the economies of scale derived through a specialist regulator acquiring expertise by means of carrying out investigation and monitoring on a frequent basis.

In the absence of such a regulatory agency many consumers would find the investigation and monitoring of firms beyond their level of expertise or resources. Consumers might be tempted to take a free-rider approach wherein each would assume that other consumers were carrying out the investigations and monitoring (with the possible result that no one would perform these functions). Each individual consumer would be unable to derive the full benefits of their own supervision, since the benefits would accrue to all consumers (many of whom might not contribute to the process of supervision). Meanwhile the costs of investigation and monitoring would be likely to be disproportionately high for any individual consumer who chose to carry out a supervisory function.

Since there are high costs involved in investigating and monitoring the providers of financial services, it is rational for consumers to delegate some of the supervisory role to a regulatory agency. The rationality of this is reinforced by the economies of scale in regulation and by the desirability of spreading the costs of regulation among all those that benefit from it. This rationale is a variation on delegated monitoring theory.

Confidence in minimum standards

The theory relevant to this point is known as Akerlof's Lemons paradigm. In a situation in which consumers know that there are good and bad products on the market but do not have enough information to distinguish between them, they may decide not to buy in order to avoid the possibility of finding that they have bought a bad one. In this way the existence of substandard products can reduce the total level of demand in the market. When consumers know that there are low-quality products in the market, good products may become tarnished by the generalised reputation of poor products.

One role of regulation is to set minimum standards and thereby remove substandard products from the market. Suppliers also have an interest in regulation, which enhances consumer confidence by eliminating the possibility of low-quality products. It is doubtful whether such confidence can be created without formal regulation. There would always be the risk that unscrupulous firms would attempt to exploit the confidence created by reputable firms. The chance that some providers of financial services will fail to abide by an informal (explicit or tacit) agreement about minimum standards would disincline the honest providers from abiding by the agreement. Indeed, firms that abide by such an agreement, when other firms do not, may put themselves at a competitive disadvantage.

The hazards of regulation

Regulation has a number of potential hazards. Regulators may be subject to institutional capture, which means that those being regulated gain control of the regulatory process. Regulation involves costs, which are likely (at least in part) to be borne by the consumers that the regulation aims to protect. Regulation can reduce competition between firms supplying financial services. Regulators may pursue their own agenda with objectives other than the protection of consumers. Moral hazard can emerge, which means that consumers cease to take care in the mistaken belief that the regulator eliminates all risks.

Related to the point about institutional capture is the issue of whether self-regulation or statutory regulation is the most appropriate structure. More accurately the issue concerns the appropriate point on the spectrum between these two extremes. Self-regulation is regulation of the financial services industry by the financial services industry. Self-regulation, with no governmental dimension, is unlikely to command full public confidence. However, statutory regulation, that is regulation by central government, can be bureaucratic and inflexible.

Self-regulation can, in large part, be identified with practitioner input into the regulatory process. Practitioner input has advantages but also poses potential dangers. On the plus side it utilises the expertise of the firms being regulated. This helps to avoid the situation in which the regulated firms are able to hide or obscure deficiencies by exploiting the relative ignorance of non-practitioner regulators. Second, practitioners are likely to have a professional interest in ensuring that standards and public confidence are maintained. Third, those being regulated may be more prepared to co-operate if the regulators have experience within the industry. Fourth, practitioners would have an interest in ensuring that the potentially less scrupulous firms do not gain a free-rider advantage (exploiting an enhanced public image of the industry) arising from the responsible behaviour of the more scrupulous suppliers.

On the downside, self-regulation could be more susceptible to regulatory capture. This involves the financial services industry gaining control over the regulatory agency and using it for the industry's purposes. Related to this is the potential for using regulatory requirements as a means of hindering the entry of new firms to the industry. The imposition of such barriers to entry would reduce competition and thereby operate against the interests of consumers. Another drawback is that a regulatory agency without statutory powers may be unable to fully enforce its decisions. This would result in reduced credibility and low public confidence.

The costs of regulation

A regulatory authority supplies regulatory services to both consumers and providers of financial services. The costs of this regulation are likely to be borne partly by consumers and partly by the firms supplying financial services. The consumer pays through higher prices and the industry pays to the extent that it does not fully pass on its own costs to consumers. One problem is that there is not a market for regulation. So the beneficiaries of regulation are unable to express their preferences in terms of the amount of regulation and the price they are prepared to pay for it. Regulation, and its costs, are excessive if the regulator supplies more regulation than the beneficiaries would choose to pay for under a market mechanism. Since it is impossible for the recipients of regulation to express their preferences as to quantity and price through a market mechanism, it is impossible to know whether the extent of regulation exceeds or falls short of the level that the beneficiaries would demand.

Moral hazard

Investors may be unclear about the scope and level of protection that can be expected from a regulatory body. Consumers cannot expect to be protected against all possibility of losing money. It is possible that consumers perceive an implicit contract between themselves and a regulator. An implicit contract can create the impression that the consumer need not take care when buying financial services. Regulation cannot be expected to be watertight – there is always a risk that unscrupulous operators will slip through the regulatory net. Furthermore there are risks that regulation does not seek to reduce. For example, regulators do not seek to protect investors from the risk that the investments underlying the financial products may fall in value. The possibility that stock markets could fall and thereby reduce the value of a pension fund or endowment policy is not a risk that a regulator could try to reduce. A regulatory system cannot be expected to relieve the consumer of responsibility for exercising judgement and care.

● ● ● ● Regulation of investment business in the UK

Regulation of investment business in the UK is conducted by the Financial Services Authority (FSA). The FSA recognises that it is impossible to remove all risk and failure

Enron, WorldCom and lemons

George Akerlof, a Nobel prize-winning economist, wrote an article entitled 'The Market for "Lemons": Quality, Uncertainty and the Market Mechanism' in which he discussed asymmetric information and its implications. Asymmetric information is the term referring to the fact that the managers of a corporation know more about its operation than investors know. Investors cannot be sure about which corporations are good (the peaches) and which are bad (the lemons). However the managers do know whether their firm is a peach or a lemon.

Shares as lemons

The accounting scandals surrounding Enron and WorldCom have been used as explanations of stock market falls in the period subsequent to the revelations. This sequence of events can be interpreted as a problem of asymmetric information.

Since investors cannot easily distinguish between peaches and lemons, the price that they are willing to pay for shares will fall between the high value of a peach and the low value of a lemon. The price for the stock would be depressed by the knowledge that lemons are more likely, than peaches, to issue shares. Lemons are happy to sell shares since the price obtainable exceeds their value (the price being between the values for peaches and pears). Peaches are less prepared to sell their shares because they are priced too low. So lemons are more likely to sell shares with the result that investors are more likely to be offered shares in lemons than in peaches. This is known as adverse selection.

Another consequence of asymmetric information is moral hazard. Moral hazard is the temptation for the managers to take excessive risks, or engage in activities that are not in the interests of shareholders. A form of moral hazard is the principal–agent problem. Shareholders are the principals and managers are their agents. The agents may act in their own interests rather than in the interests of the principals.

Asymmetric information can interfere with the effective operation of stock markets. If good firms are unwilling to sell shares because the price is too low, and if investors are unwilling to buy shares since the corporations that sell them may be lemons, there will be an insufficient volume of trading in shares. It is thus desirable to increase the amount of information, about corporations, available to potential investors.

Information could be generated privately. Investors could engage in the search for information or employ others to do so. Unfortunately this encounters the free-rider problem. Some investors will stand back and allow others to bear all the effort and cost of information acquisition whilst sharing in the benefits. This discourages the active investors since they will not draw all the benefits arising from their information generating activities. The result is that the amount of information produced privately will fall below the most desirable level.

One way in which the free-rider problem may be reduced is by the use of collective investments (such as unit trusts, investment trusts, investment bonds and pension funds) to channel the wealth of individuals into stocks. The managers of such collective (institutional) investments might engage in information seeking activities on behalf of the individual investors. The fact that the cost of the information generation is spread amongst a large number of individuals moderates the free-rider problem. However there is a risk that the principal–agent problem might be present. The managers of the collective investments may reward themselves to such a degree that the benefits of the information acquired is used to enrich those managers rather than the individuals who provided the money for the collective investments.

An alternative would be for the government, or other regulatory authority, to intervene with a view to ensuring the provision of an adequate amount of information about firms. This normally entails a requirement, placed upon corporations, to produce accounts that meet prescribed standards and for those accounts to be verified by independent auditors. For this to be effective as a means of reassuring investors that they can distinguish between peaches and lemons, the audited accounts need to be regarded as reliable sources of information.

The revelations of accounting irregularities at Enron and WorldCom have undermined confidence in audited accounts. Investors found themselves unsure about which corporations were peaches, and which were lemons. Corporations that had appeared to be good could no longer be regarded as such with confidence. The perceived likelihood, of a firm turning out to be a lemon, had increased. To the extent that share prices reflect an average of the values of peaches and

▶

lemons, the increased probability that firms are lemons reduces that average and hence the share prices.

Bonds as lemons

It is useful to consider the implications of asymmetric information from the point of view of bondholders as well as from the perspective of shareholders. In relation to profit uncertainties, such as those arising from the revelation of accounting irregularities, bondholders suffer less than shareholders. Bondholders receive fixed coupon (interest) payments to which the corporation is legally committed. Bondholders will suffer only if the profit/loss position is so weak that the corporation is unable to meet its legal obligations to bondholders.

From a different perspective, bondholders are more vulnerable than shareholders. Borrowers may have an incentive to take on investment projects that are riskier than lenders (which include bondholders) would like. Risky investments may be very profitable, but entail the possibility that everything will be lost. In the event of high profits, bondholders do not share in the increased pay-outs. The gains accrue to shareholders, which may include the managers. The benefits to managers would be enhanced if they are incentivised by share option schemes. Bondholders receive the same coupon payments whatever the level of profit. If the investment fails bondholders, as well as shareholders, may lose everything. Shareholders have an incentive to take risks whilst bondholders would prefer a low risk approach.

This moral hazard increases as share prices fall. At low share prices, the shareholders have less to lose from taking risks. The incentive to take risks is therefore greater. Since falling share prices increase moral hazard, investors will become more reluctant to buy a firm's bonds when its share price falls.

The situation of shareholders can be analysed by using option theory. Shares can be seen as call options on the value of the corporation with a strike price of zero. The options increase in price if the expected value of the corporation becomes more volatile. In other words, increased risk increases share prices. This effect is magnified if the option loses intrinsic value, that is if the share price approaches the strike price of zero. A low share price increases the desirability of accepting risk.

Bondholders can be seen as having written (sold) put options. An increase in risk (expected volatility) worsens the position of option writers. An option is a liability to the writer and therefore an increase in risk, by increasing the value of that liability, works against option writers.

Bonds may be subject to legally binding restrictive covenants aimed at reducing moral hazard. Such restrictive covenants are of four types. Covenants to discourage undesirable behaviour, covenants to encourage desirable behaviour, covenants to keep collateral valuable, and covenants to provide information.

Restrictive covenants need to be monitored and enforced. Bondholders need to check on whether the covenants are being adhered to, and take legal action if they are not. The free-rider problem arises again. Not all bondholders will participate in policing restrictive covenants. Many will assume that others are doing it. Those that do participate may be discouraged from doing so by the fact that others are taking the benefits without incurring the costs. The free-rider problem is likely to cause the degree of monitoring and enforcement to fall below desirable levels.

Institutional investors, such as pension funds and insurance companies, may be more willing to monitor and enforce restrictive covenants since the benefits would accrue to a large number of individual investors in their funds. Such institutional investors may hold a significant quantity of the bonds. However the principal–agent problem remains. The institutional fund managers are agents operating on behalf of individual investors who are the principals. The agents may be more concerned with their own interests than with those of the principals.

The insurance of lemons

Adverse selection occurs when those most likely to benefit from a transaction are the ones who most actively seek out the transaction and are thus most likely to be selected. In the case of bonds, adverse selection implies that borrowers who are bad credit risks are the ones that most actively sell bonds (selling bonds is a form of borrowing). In the insurance market, the parties that are the most likely to suffer loss are those most likely to seek insurance. There is asymmetric information since such parties know more about their own situations than insurers do. An implication of adverse selection is that loss probability statistics for the whole population may not accurately indicate the loss potential for those who want to buy insurance policies.

Insurance companies tackle the adverse selection problem by seeking information about those to be

▶

insured. In addition to attempts to lessen the asymmetric information, insurance companies may exclude some risks from policies. The risks excluded may be those that are likely to have led to the adverse selection.

In addition to adverse selection, another problem faced by insurers is moral hazard. Once insured some people may become careless about looking after their property, knowing that losses would be covered by insurance. They may even increase their vulnerability to loss in the hope of receiving money from the insurer.

Insurance companies often tackle the moral hazard problem by requiring an excess. An excess is the amount of any loss that must be paid by the insured before the insurance company will pay anything. Moral hazard might also be tackled by placing, upon the insured, requirements that aim to ensure that the insured property is suitably protected by the party seeking insurance.

In addition there are general principles of insurance that have the objectives of preventing insurance being used as a means of gambling, of avoiding unnecessary risks for the insurer, and of making it possible to price insurance policies. These basic principles of insurance are:

1 There must be a relationship between the insured item and the potential beneficiary of insurance pay-outs. The beneficiary must be someone who stands to suffer potential harm.
2 The insured must provide full and accurate information to the insurance company (this reduces the problem of asymmetric information).
3 The insured is not to profit as a result of insurance coverage.
4 If a third party compensates the insured for the loss, the insurance company's obligation is reduced by the amount of the compensation.
5 The insurance company must have a large number of insureds so that the risk can be spread out among many different policies
6 The potential loss must be quantifiable.
7 The insurance company must be able to compute the probability of the loss occurring.

Source: Keith Redhead, 'Enron, WorldCom and lemons', *Company Accountant*, Issue 169, August 2002.

from the financial system. It therefore seeks to prioritise in seeking to achieve its four statutory objectives set out in the Financial Services and Markets Act (2000). These objectives are to (i) maintain market confidence, (ii) promote public understanding of the financial system, (iii) secure appropriate consumer protection and (iv) reduce financial crime.

The FSA has identified a set of generic risks to its objectives. For example, risks to the consumer protection objective could be classified under failure of companies; crime and market abuse; misconduct or mismanagement; market malfunction; and inadequate understanding of products or services.

After identifying risks to objectives, it is necessary to prioritise. The FSA assesses the likelihood of a risk being realised and evaluates the impact of such a realisation. The risks focused upon would be those with high likelihood of resulting in problems, and with substantial significance for the attainment of one of the four objectives.

Rather than carrying out routine compliance visits to all financial services companies, the FSA intends to focus on companies that pose the greatest risk. Each company is allocated to one of four categories, ranging from high risk to low risk. High-risk companies will receive close attention whereas low-risk firms will be monitored less closely. In addition the FSA will pursue themes that are common to large numbers of firms, for example the provision of comparative information about financial products to consumers so that consumers can make informed choices.

The coming of the single financial regulator

Economic slowdown may have hit the US, but the financial services industry in the UK remains buoyant. Most sectors have seen an expansion of business in the past year and in the number of authorised companies, in spite of continued consolidation. There are now 664 UK-authorised banks, a six per cent increase over last year, and more than 7,600 investment companies, a four per cent increase. London remains the leading international financial centre and continues to attract a growing volume of mobile international business. Most large US and Asian companies have their European headquarters in London.

One of the main reasons companies give for choosing to base their business in the UK is that the regulatory system is seen as strong, rigorous and cost-effective. But there has been general agreement that the sector-based approach needed updating and reform if the UK were to continue to keep its world-leading position in regulation.

The confusing mixture of self-regulating organisations and statutory bodies operating on different legal bases no longer reflected what was happening in the financial services industry. Distinctions between investment companies, banks and insurance companies were becoming blurred, with mergers and takeovers creating multi-purpose conglomerates.

Under the old regime, these groups had to apply to several regulators, comply with several sets of standards and grapple with differing regulatory styles. Further, no single regulator could take an overall view of a major financial group and the interactions between the risks it was taking.

So the government's decision to form a single regulator in the shape of the Financial Services Authority (FSA) – and a single statutory basis for regulation in the Financial Services and Markets Act 2000 – has been welcomed within the industry. That is particularly true in the investment sector, which had hitherto the most fragmented and complex regulatory structure.

Investors and their representatives were also enthusiastic, sensing an end to the alphabet-soup of

SIB, PIA, IMRO and SFA, and the confusion over ultimate responsibility that such fragmentation created (see Box).

In anticipation of the act coming into full force in November this year, the FSA has created a de facto single regulator, with staff of the former bodies working in a unified management structure in a single building. The FSA has also devoted much thinking to the question of what being a single regulator means in practice. How can it regulate in a more focused, efficient and effective way, to the benefit of companies and consumers?

Risk-based approach

The FSA has devised a risk-based approach to regulation, with a clear statement of the realistic aims and limits of regulation. It recognises both the proper responsibilities of consumers and of companies' own managers, and the impossibility and undesirability of removing all risk and failure from the financial system.

The prime aim of the strategy is to identify, prioritise and address risks to the four statutory objectives set out in the act – to maintain market confidence, promote public understanding of the financial

---

Box: The single regulator

Following the passage of the Financial Services and Markets Act, the Financial Services Authority in the UK will centralise the roles of the following institutions:
- IMRO (Investment Management Regulatory Organisation) is the regulator of companies in the field of investment management.
- SFA (Securities and Futures Authority) is the regulator of trading and dealing companies operating in organised

investment markets in the City of London.
- PIA (Personal Investment Authority) is the regulator of retail investment and financial advice companies.
- SIB (Securities and Investments Board) was the designated agency under the Financial Services Act 1986 for regulating investment businesses in the UK. In October 1997 it was renamed the Financial Services Authority.

▶

system, secure appropriate consumer protection and reduce financial crime. Risk in this specialised sense should not be confused with the commercial risks undertaken by finance companies and within financial markets as a core component of day-to-day business.

For regulators there are two basic questions. First, what developments, events or issues pose significant risk to the stated objectives? Second, how should they use resources to focus on the risks that matter most? In tackling these questions, the act requires the FSA to observe certain principles of good regulation, including economy and efficiency in the use of resources, the position of the UK as an international financial centre and the need to be proportionate in regulatory responses. The approach aims to ensure that the FSA uses its resources to deliver the most effective regulatory action within these parameters.

In developing the framework, the FSA first identified a set of high-level, generic risks to its objectives. For example, risks to the consumer protection objective can usually be classified under: failure of companies; crime and market abuse; misconduct or mismanagement by companies; market malfunction; and inadequate understanding of products or services preventing informed decision-making.

These stated risks provide a common language that enables us to assess possible sources or instances of risk in the same way. Traditionally, regulators have tended to focus on individual companies, but the framework recognises that risks to objectives can also arise from, for example, worldwide economic trends, new products, developments in social policy and changes in consumer behaviour.

After identifying and classifying risks to objectives, the next task is assessment and prioritisation. First, the FSA assesses how likely a risk to its objectives is to crystallise. But this is not the only relevant measure. Another question arises: 'How important is the risk?' It is this indicator of impact that helps us set priorities when allocating resources. Where we face different risks that are equally likely to occur, it makes sense that we should focus on those risks that are likely to have the most significance in terms of, for example, consumer loss.

New tools

Once risks have been assessed and prioritised, the question is how to deal with them. In the past, regulators have generally focused on the individual company. But past experience of financial regulators, the broad range of the FSA's statutory objectives and the powers given to it in the act suggest that this may not always be the most effective solution. In particular, it can often result in regulators only reacting to events in companies, when there are opportunities to be proactive and wide-ranging in managing risks. Hence the FSA must select from the full range of regulatory tools available to it, not just those that act on individual companies. The key point is to decide what is the most effective way of addressing risks.

A good example of such a tool is the provision of comparative information to consumers on a range of financial products. The FSA has asked all investment companies offering retail products to participate voluntarily by providing comparable information on their products, which will then be made available to investors on a website and in print. Market research shows that consumers want clear, up-to-date information, provided by an independent organisation to help them to make investment decisions. Comparative tables will be available from September.

The FSA is also introducing a more thematic approach to regulation – where it examines and responds to particular themes or issues that may affect its ability to meet objectives, such as those arising from particular markets, sectors, products or the external environment. Recent themes have been as diverse as the implications of a low-inflation environment, consumer protection beyond the point of sale and e-commerce.

Changing relations

How will this approach affect the way the FSA interacts with regulated companies? Investment companies should not imagine that because the FSA is looking at wider thematic issues it is going to abandon company-focused regulation. One of the most useful regulatory tools remains the power to set rules and requirements for the protection of consumers and to check that companies comply with them. (These are set out in the FSA Handbook of Rules and Guidance.) However, routine compliance visits will be

▶

a thing of the past. The FSA will instead focus on companies that pose the greatest risk and on areas of perceived highest risk to the authority's objectives.

The FSA has now assessed the 10,000 or so companies it regulates to identify the level of risk they pose to its objectives. That assessment will inform its relationship with each company. Where companies pose substantial risks, through a combination of their impact and the likelihood of problems arising, the regulator will have a strong incentive to anticipate problems by maintaining a close relationship. Where risk is lower, the relationship will be less intimate.

All companies, however, must comply with rigorous conduct standards and reporting requirements. Each will be allocated to one of four categories, imaginatively labelled A to D. At one end of the spectrum the FSA will maintain the closest relationships with category A companies (high-risk). At the other end of the risk scale, category D companies will be monitored remotely, supported by sampling of particular lines of business and thematic work.

Many of the 7,600 investment companies regulated at present by the PIA, IMRO and SFA will therefore see a substantial change in their relationship with the regulator. Companies that are part of large conglomerates will be regulated by a division covering major financial groups. Insurance companies monitored by the PIA for compliance with conduct-of-business rules will move to an insurance firm's division, which will have responsibility for all aspects of the regulatory relationship. However, most investment companies, ranging from global fund management operations and large UK brokers to solo financial advisers, will be regulated in the investment firm's division.

At present, this is organised in a way that reflects the old SRO responsibilities, with staff working in separate departments covering companies regulated by the PIA, IMRO or SFA. In future, however, issues will be handled as a portfolio of thematic projects, such as the Free Standing Additional Voluntary Contributions review or the development of a regulatory regime for energy market participants. These will be taken forward by a themes department, while the relationship management department will focus on the larger or higher-risk companies within the division. There are about 1,050 of these, engaged in a variety of investment businesses and operating in both wholesale and retail markets. The department will carry out risk assessments and design risk mitigation programmes.

Finally, the regulatory events department will mainly be responsible for the lower-impact category D companies, which number about 6,000. In practice, this means that an individual company supervised by the department will not have a relationship with a dedicated supervision team but material regulatory events will be dealt with case-by-case, using events teams assigned to particular industry sectors.

As the moment when the FSA takes on its full statutory powers draws near, it is not surprising that the financial community both in the UK and overseas is closely examining how it will operate. The FSA believes that its new approach will deliver better and more focused regulation of investment business, going with the grain of the market, rather than forcing companies to conform to a standard regulatory model.

Source: Howard Davies, *Financial Times*, *Mastering Investment Supplement*, Part 10, July 16 2001, pp. 8, 10. Reprinted with permission.

Comparative regulatory systems

An important issue arises as to how the regulation of asset managers can improve investor protection without limiting competition. Inadequate investor protection can cause investors to be reluctant to invest. Good companies can be tainted with the failure of bad companies. Conversely, excessive regulation may increase the costs of entry to the industry and hence reduce competition. For example, consumer protection may be improved by establishing high capital requirements, but if new entrants to the market need to have large amounts of capital, many potential financial services firms will be unable to enter the market, resulting in less competition and reduced innovation. More generally, excessive regulation can deter both companies and consumers by imposing substantial costs on them.

The organisation of the financial services industry can significantly affect investors' exposure to loss. Large groups have greater financial resources than small independent companies. Also large groups may wish to compensate investors for any losses in order to maintain their own reputations. Large groups thus have both the resources and the motive for protecting investors. Large groups dominate European markets with the exception of the UK and France, which have many smaller independent firms (the USA also has many independent investment companies). Arguably markets in which retail investment operations are predominantly within large financial conglomerates require less regulation by authorities.

Forms of regulation include (i) capital requirements, (ii) conduct of business rules, (iii) requirements concerning the separation of clients' assets, (iv) disclosure requirements, (v) auditing and (vi) investor compensation schemes. The respective importance of each of these reflects the organisational structure of the respective national markets. For example, countries in which investment services operations are part of large financial conglomerates tend to have less need of consumer compensation schemes than those in which there are many small independent investment companies.

European regulation tends to rely on monitoring by public agencies, such as the Financial Services Authority in the UK. The US system puts more emphasis on private contracting in which more responsibility falls on investors and investment firms. In the USA there is an emphasis on ensuring that investors have good information (through disclosure requirements) so that they can make informed decisions.

Chapter 7

Investing in bonds

After studying this chapter readers should:

- *understand the nature of bonds*
- *appreciate the role of bond rating agencies*
- *understand the various types of government bonds, as illustrated by UK gilts*
- *know what is meant by bond strips, bond yields and bond price volatility.*

Bonds are used for long-term borrowing by the issuer. Central governments are major issuers of bonds (in the UK government bonds are called gilt-edged securities, or gilts). Bonds are issued in a wide variety of forms. However, most government bonds conform to a conventional format. A conventional government bond pays a fixed sum of money, known as the coupon, at regular intervals such as every six months. It has a definite redemption date on which the government is obliged to pay the nominal, or par, value of the bond to its owner. Its market price is expressed in relation to its nominal or par value, for example, pounds per £100 nominal (so a market price of £96 means that £96 must be paid for every £100 to be repaid at redemption).

Governments are not the only issuers of bonds – firms in particular are major issuers. Corporate bonds vary considerably in terms of their riskiness. Some bonds are secured against property of the company that issued them, whereas other bonds are unsecured. The fact that unsecured bonds do not provide their holders with a claim on the property of the issuing firm in the event of default is normally compensated for by means of a higher rate of coupon payment. Sometimes there are bonds with differing priorities of payment in the event of the issuer becoming insolvent. Bonds with a high priority for repayment are often referred to as being senior debt, while those bonds that would be redeemed only after the senior debt (and only if sufficient funds remained) would be termed subordinated debt. The greater risk of non-redemption of subordinated debt is compensated for by a higher rate of coupon yield.

When new corporate bonds are issued, their yields are generally set with reference to government bonds. Corporate bonds offer a spread over the government bond yield in order to compensate for the greater risk of default. Companies, unlike the governments of developed countries, can find themselves in a position in which they cannot pay the money owing to the holders of their bonds.

Bond issues are typically credit rated. There are credit rating agencies (such as Moody's and Standard & Poor's) that give ratings to bond issues. A high credit rating indicates a low risk of default, whereas a low rating is suggestive of a high default risk. Low credit ratings are associated with high rates of yield. Bonds with very low credit ratings and hence subject to very high risk of default are often referred to as junk bonds.

Many corporate bonds have call features. This means that the issuer has the right to redeem the bonds before the maturity date. A bond is likely to be called if interest rates fall below the coupon rate, since the issuer could then redeem the bond with money borrowed at a lower coupon rate. This is to the disadvantage of investors since they can only reinvest the money at a lower rate of yield. This potential disadvantage would be compensated for by means of a higher coupon rate on callable bonds.

Some corporate bonds are putable. This means that the investor has the right to sell the bond to the issuer, at a predetermined price, before the maturity date. Investors might exercise this right when interest rates rise so that the proceeds can be reinvested at a higher rate of yield. Since this right provides potential advantages to investors, it would be offset by a lower coupon rate on the bond.

Eurobonds are bonds denominated in a currency which is not the currency of the country in which the bonds are issued. So a bond denominated in sterling but sold in Paris would be a eurosterling bond. Eurobonds are often issued in several financial centres at the same time, for example a US dollar eurobond might be issued simultaneously in London, Paris, Sydney, Hong Kong and Singapore (the prefix 'euro' has no geographical or currency significance). Eurobonds are often bearer bonds. This means that coupons and principal are payable to the holder (bearer) of a bond, and bonds are not registered in the names of investors, allowing investors to retain anonymity.

Eurobonds tap the large stateless pool of cash and are traded in a secondary market of screens and telephones. Eurobond markets are volatile and little regulated. They can become illiquid since there is no obligation on any body to make a market in eurobonds. In other words there is liquidity risk – in adverse market circumstances, holders of bonds may be unable to sell them because there is no one willing to buy.

Eurobonds are not the only form of international bond. Bonds may be issued in the country whose currency is being borrowed, by a borrower in another country. So a German company might borrow Canadian dollars by issuing Canadian dollar bonds in Canada. Such bonds sometimes have names that symbolise the country whose currency is being borrowed. For example, bonds issued in the US are called Yankees, bonds issued in Britain are known as Bulldogs, and those issued in Japan are called Samurais.

Bond rating agencies

A bond rating is an assessment of the default risk of a bond by an independent agency. The ratings reflect only default risk, which is the risk that the issuer of the bond will fail to meet coupon payments or the repayment of principal. The ratings do not reflect other types of risk such as interest rate risk (which includes the risk that interest rate changes will cause capital losses to holders of bonds). Ratings are specific to a bond issue rather than to the issuer.

There are a number of bond rating agencies worldwide, but the global market is dominated by two agencies. These are Standard and Poor's (S&P) and Moody's. The rating agencies assign debt issues to risk categories and label those categories with letters. Table 7.1 shows the letter grades used by S&P and Moody's.

Debt rated BBB (or Baa) and above is classed as investment grade. Bonds rated BB (or Ba) and below are classed as speculative grade. Speculative grade bonds are alternatively referred to as high yield or junk bonds. The first two categories (AAA/Aaa and AA/Aa) indicate a very strong capacity to pay coupons and repay principal. The next four categories (A to B) indicate that the issuer is currently able to meet payments but has some susceptibility to adverse changes in economic conditions. The issues in the next two categories (CCC/Caa and CC) are prone to default unless there is a favourable change in economic conditions. The next category (C/Ca) indicates that a bankruptcy petition has been filed but payments are still being made. The bottom category (D/C) indicates that the issuer has already failed to make coupon payments or principal repayments.

Alternative forms of coupon payment

The conventional pattern of coupon payments is often deviated from, particularly by corporate bonds and eurobonds. Some bonds have floating coupon payments

Table 7.1 The lever grades used by S&P and Moody's

Standard and Poor's	Moody's	
AAA	Aaa	
AA	Aa	
		Investment grade
A	A	
BBB	Baa	
BB	Ba	
B	B	
CCC	Caa	
		Speculative grade
CC		
C	Ca	
D	C	

wherein the coupon is changed periodically to reflect the general level of interest rates. Typically each coupon payment will be different, with the difference reflecting changes in interest rates. Floating rate bonds show less price variation than conventional bonds since changes in the coupon tend to match changes in the discount rate.

There are deferred coupon bonds which entail no coupon payments for a period of years, at the end of which coupon payments commence. Step up bonds pay a low coupon initially, but the coupon rises after a number of years. Zero coupon bonds pay no coupons – the return to the investor arises from the difference between the buying and selling prices.

Gilts

Gilts (gilt-edged stock) are bonds issued by the United Kingdom government as a means of borrowing money. Since they are backed by the government's ability to levy taxes, there is no risk of default (no risk that the issuer will fail to make payments to investors). This absence of default risk means that they are less risky than most other forms of long-term investment.

Issuing gilts

Gilts are issued through the Debt Management Office (DMO), which is a department of the Treasury. Up to 1997 they were issued by the Bank of England on behalf of the government. Gilts are issued by tender, by auction or as tap stock.

Sale by tender entails the DMO offering a quantity of gilts and stating a minimum acceptable price. The price at which the gilts are sold is the highest price at which all the gilts can be sold, or the minimum price. For example, £1 billion of gilts may be offered with a minimum price of £100. The total demanded by investors at prices at and above £102 may amount to the full £1 billion. In that case all investors pay £102. If the amount tendered for at £100 or above is less than £1 billion, the gilts will be sold at £100. The unsold gilts will be treated as tap stock. This means that the DMO will gradually sell them over time when investors become ready to buy them.

In the auction process, professional investors (largely institutional investors) state the quantities that they want and the prices that they are prepared to pay. If the auction is oversubscribed, only the highest bidders will receive the gilts. Successful bidders pay the price that they offered. Private investors, seeking small quantities of gilts, may apply for gilts on the basis of paying the average of the prices paid by the successful participants in the auction. Sale by auction involves no minimum price. The gilts are sold to the highest bidders. All the gilts are sold and none are left over as tap stock.

Tap sales involve the DMO selling newly issued gilts to market-makers. The market-makers subsequently sell them on to other investors. Market-makers undertake to be always ready to quote prices at which they are prepared to buy and sell. They hold gilts as principals which means that they invest in, and trade, gilts for their own profit.

The gilt-edged market is part of the London Stock Exchange and the market-makers, dealers and brokers are members of the stock exchange. The Central Gilts Office provides a computerised service for payments and settlements between buyers and sellers.

Gilt investments

This part aims to explain gilts as a form of investment for the private investor. It will comprise four sections: (i) the types of gilt available, (ii) the recent innovation of gilt strips, (iii) the nature of gilt yields and (iv) the causation and measurement of gilt price volatility.

Conventional gilts

Most gilts issued by the UK Treasury are conventional in nature. Conventional gilts have two standard characteristics. These are the payment of fixed coupons every six months and the repayment of the nominal value of the gilt on a specified maturity date. These two characteristics are detailed in the description of each gilt published in the financial media.

Most UK gilts are described as Treasury, Conversion or Exchequer. There is no significance for the investor in the name of the gilt. The name is followed by an interest rate and a year. These indicate the value of the coupon and the year in which the gilt is due to mature. The maturity date of a gilt is the date on which the final coupon and the nominal value are payable to the holder of the gilt.

If a gilt is described by the title Exchequer 8% 2015, this gilt pays £4 every six months (£8 a year) for each £100 of nominal value. The nominal value is the principal sum payable by the Treasury to the investor holding the gilt on the maturity date of the gilt. The year of maturity is shown in the title of the gilt. In this example maturity will occur in 2015.

Double-dated gilts

Double-dated gilts have two years in their title. This is because the Treasury can redeem them (pay the nominal value to bondholders) at any time between two dates. In effect the Treasury has a call option on the gilts (in the United States they are referred to as callable bonds). The Treasury has the right to buy back the gilts at the nominal value at any time between the two dates. If the current interest rate on other bonds is below the coupon rate of the gilt (the rate of interest on the nominal value), it is advantageous to the Treasury to redeem the gilts before the final maturity date. For example, if the current interest rate is 6% p.a. and a gilt pays a dividend of £8 a year (per £100 nominal), the Treasury could redeem it with money borrowed by selling gilts paying £6 a year.

The Treasury must pay for this call option. The Treasury has to pay for the right to redeem the gilts before the final maturity date. This payment is made by means of a coupon rate (percentage dividend) that is greater than the rate on gilts that lack the right to redeem before the final maturity date.

Undated gilts

Undated gilts have no maturity date – the Treasury is never obliged to redeem them, it may simply continue to pay coupons into perpetuity (hence these gilts are alternatively known as perpetuities). It has been several decades since such gilts were last issued, but a quantity of them remains in the market. They are unlikely to be redeemed by the Treasury so long as current interest rates are above the coupon rates of the undated gilts. The undated gilts in existence tend to have very low coupon rates.

Index-linked gilts

Index-linked gilts give investors automatic protection against inflation by continually raising the coupon payments and the principal sum to be paid to the investor at maturity in line with the Retail Price Index (RPI). Specifically the RPI figure used is the one current eight months before the date that the coupon, or principal, is to be paid. The eight-month time lag is used so that the money value of the next coupon is always known.

An index-linked gilt will have a nominal coupon and a nominal redemption value. The sum actually payable is adjusted to reflect inflation from a point in time eight months prior to the issue of the gilts. The sum payable is the nominal amount multiplied by the ratio of the new RPI to the initial RPI (the ratio of the RPI eight months before the present to the RPI eight months before the gilt was first issued). So, for example, a doubling of the level of retail prices causes a doubling of the money value of the coupons payable to the investor with the effect that the real value (purchasing power value) of the coupons remains unchanged. The real value of the principal payable to the investor at redemption (the redemption value) is also maintained by means of the inflation adjustment.

Rump stocks

A rump stock is a gilt of which little remains in the market. They are often the result of conversion offers. A conversion offer involves the Treasury making an offer to exchange holdings of an existing gilt issue for a new issue of gilts. Investors may then choose to replace existing gilts with new ones without incurring transaction costs such as dealing charges. Not all investors respond to conversion offers. As a result some of the original gilt issue remains in the market. If only a small amount remains in investors' hands, liquidity may become very poor. Poor liquidity means that it is difficult to buy or sell the gilts since there are few potential buyers and sellers.

Gilt strips

A gilt strip market began in the UK in December 1997. Strips is the acronym for Separately Traded and Registered Interest and Principal Securities. Stripping a gilt involves breaking it down into its individual cash flows which can be traded separately. Each individual coupon payment date becomes a maturity date for a strip and the coupon becomes the redemption value. These are alternatively known as zero coupon gilts since they provide the investor with just one cash flow, which is the redemption value of the strip payable at maturity. The nominal value of the original gilt can also be traded separately from the coupons – it becomes a strip with a redemption (maturity) date corresponding to the redemption date of the original gilt. For example, a gilt with five years to maturity can be broken down into 11 strips, one for each remaining coupon and one for the redemption value (principal sum). These strips would have maturities of six months, one year, eighteen months, two years, and so on.

Coupons from different strippable bonds that are paid on the same day are fungible (interchangeable) when traded as strips. The maturity value of a strip could contain coupons from a number of different conventional gilts. One purpose of conversion issues has been the replacement of gilts that lack fungibility with gilts that are fungible with others (share coupon payment dates).

Gilt yields

There are two frequently used measures of the yield of a gilt. One is known as coupon yield (alternatively known as interest, flat or running yield). This is calculated as the annual coupon divided by the current market price of the gilt. The deficiency of this measure is that it ignores potential capital gains or losses. The return from an investment comprises both periodic payments (coupons or dividends) and capital gains or losses arising from changes in the market value of the investment.

The other popular measure of yield, known as redemption yield or yield to maturity, takes both forms of investment return into account. It includes prospective capital gains or losses as well as coupons. It is the average annual rate of yield based upon the presumption that the investor will hold the gilt until its redemption (maturity) date. The redemption yield can be interpreted as the rate of discount that will equate the sum of the present values of the future cash flows to the current market value of the gilt. As such it is often treated as the rate of interest offered by the gilt (more accurately it approximates an average of interest rates relating to the various cash flows from the gilt).

When gilts are traded, the accumulated rights to the next coupon have to be paid for by the buyer. These rights are referred to as accrued interest. For example, if a bond that pays a £4 coupon every six months is sold three months after the last coupon payment date, there will be £2 accrued interest. This accrued interest is added to the market price when the buyer pays the seller. During the seven working days prior to the payment of the coupon, the reverse occurs. The coupon is payable to the investor who holds the gilt seven working days before the coupon payment date. If the gilt is sold during this seven-day period, the seller must compensate the buyer for the absence of coupon receipts during this period. The compensation is referred to as rebate interest. The gilt price exclusive of accrued or rebate interest is known as the clean price. The gilt price inclusive of such adjustments is the dirty price. Prices quoted in the financial media are clean prices.

Exercise 7.1

If a bond paid no coupon after six months but a coupon of £10 plus the redemption value of £100 after one year, what redemption yield is implied by a current price of £95? What is the interest yield?

Answer
The interest yield is £10/£95 = 0.1053 = 10.53% p.a.
The rate of capital gain is £5/£95 = 0.0526 = 5.26% p.a.
Interest yield plus rate of capital gain equals redemption yield, i.e. 10.53% + 5.26% = 15.79% p.a.

Alternatively:

Let r = redemption yield.
£95 = £110/(1 + r)
£95(1 + r) = £110
1 + r = £110/£95 = 1.1579
r = 1.1579 − 1 = 0.1579, i.e. 15.79 % p.a.

Exercise 7.2

(a) A bond pays an annual coupon of £5 and is priced at £96. It matures in 364 days. Calculate its interest yield and redemption yield. If it was due to mature in 1 year 364 days, would the redemption yield be higher or lower than in the first case?
(b) If a zero coupon bond is priced at £90 and matures in two years, what is its redemption yield?

Answer
(a) Interest yield = 5/96 = 0.0521 (5.21% pa)
Redemption yield = (5/96) + [(100−96)/96)] = 0.0521 + 0.0417 = 0.0938 (9.38% p.a.) If the bond was due to mature in two years rather than one, the annual rate of capital gain would be halved and the redemption yield would be lower.
(b) £90 = £100 / (1 + r)^2

$$£90 = £100 / (1 + r)^2$$
$$(1 + r)^2 = £100/£90 = 1.111$$
$$1 + r = \sqrt{1.111} = 1.0541$$
$$\therefore r = 0.0541 \ (5.41\% \ \text{p.a.})$$

Gilt price volatility

Gilt prices vary because interest rates vary. A relatively high sensitivity to interest rate movements is observed among undated gilts. Suppose that an undated gilt pays coupons amounting to £4 a year. If rates on other long-term investments (long-term interest rates) were 4% p.a., the undated gilt would be priced at about £100. A coupon of £4 on an investment of £100 provides an interest rate of 4% p.a. which matches rates of return elsewhere. If interest rates on other long-term investments rose to 8% p.a., rational investors would not pay £100 for a gilt paying £4 a year. Investors would be prepared to pay around £50 for the gilt since £4 on £50 produces a rate of return of 8% p.a. Conversely a fall in interest rates on other investments to 2% p.a. would imply a price of £200 for the gilt. The coupon of £4 a year provides 2% p.a. when the gilt price is £200. It can be seen that the gilt price is inversely proportional to the long-term interest rate available elsewhere in the market. A doubling of the interest rate causes a halving of the gilt price and vice versa. This degree of volatility is relatively extreme. There is always an inverse relationship between interest rates and gilt prices but rarely a proportionally inverse one. Usually the change in gilt price is less than proportionate to the interest rate change.

Gilt price volatility can be measured by modified duration. This is the percentage change in the gilt price divided by the change in interest rate. Modified duration provides an estimate of the percentage change in the price of a gilt to be expected from a change in the relevant interest rate. Three factors that affect the modified duration of a gilt are (i) the maturity of the gilt, (ii) the size of the coupon and (iii) the prevailing level of interest rates. These relationships can be understood by bearing in mind that gilt prices tend to equal the discounted value of future coupons and principal repayment.

Modified duration is higher when the maturity date is more distant (the present value of distant sums is more sensitive to changes in a discount rate). Modified duration is usually higher when coupons are low (low coupons give greater importance to the redemption value in the determination of the gilt price, and the redemption value is the most distant of the cash flows from the gilt). Modified duration is higher when interest rates are low (a 1% p.a. interest rate change is a quarter of 4% but a tenth of 10%. It is a larger proportion of the lower interest rate and hence has a larger proportionate effect on the gilt price).

Preference shares

Preference shares, despite their name, are more like bonds than ordinary shares since they pay a fixed dividend each year. Unlike bonds they confer part ownership of a company, but like bonds they normally entail no voting rights. They further differ from bonds in that the firm is not obliged to make the dividend payments on preference shares if profits are not sufficient. Preference shares come in various forms:

- irredeemable
- redeemable
- cumulative

- non-cumulative
- participating
- convertible.

Apart from the irredeemable/redeemable and cumulative/non-cumulative distinctions, these characteristics are not mutually exclusive. For example, a preference share could be irredeemable, cumulative, participating and convertible whereas another might be simply irredeemable and cumulative.

While most preference shares are irredeemable, some are redeemable (the sum received from the issue of the shares would be repaid by a specified date). In the case of cumulative preference shares, the firm is required to pay any missed dividends when profits become adequate. Back payments of missed dividends must be made before any dividends on ordinary shares (common stock) can be paid. In the case of a non-cumulative preference share, there is no obligation on the issuer to pay any previously missed dividends. So a missed dividend may be lost for ever.

Participating preference shares provide participation in unusually good profit levels. If the company's profits are exceptionally good, the payments to holders of participating preference shares will exceed the normal dividend level. Convertible preference shares are similar to convertible bonds in that the holder has rights to convert the preference shares into ordinary shares on predetermined terms.

Discussion question

How do bonds differ from shares? Why is there such a large variety of bonds?

Chapter 8

Stock exchanges

After studying this chapter readers should have a knowledge of:

- *the purpose and functions of stock exchanges*
- *the distinction between primary and secondary markets*
- *types of stock exchange*
- *stock market trading systems*
- *bid-offer spreads*
- *types of purchase and sale order*
- *processes by which shares are issued*
- *different types of share.*

The purpose of a stock exchange

The main purpose of a stock exchange is the transfer of money from investors to those wishing to obtain capital. The investors buy shares and bonds from issuers and thereby transfer money to them in exchange for potential future cash flows.

The direct transfer of money from investors to those wishing to obtain funds, without a financial intermediary such as a stock exchange, would be problematical for a number of reasons. First, there would be the difficulty of how investors and those seeking funds were to find each other. Second, companies and governments want to raise large amounts of capital whereas individual investors normally want to invest relatively small sums. Individual investors have limited sums to invest and they usually prefer to spread their investments among a number of companies so as to avoid the risk of suffering heavily from the poor performance of one firm. A stock exchange provides size transformation – relatively small sums from a large number of investors are aggregated so as to provide a large sum for the firm or organisation raising capital.

Third, stock exchanges provide maturity transformation. Companies need to obtain funds for the long term, whereas investors typically want immediate access to their money. A stock exchange provides a means of reconciling these two objectives. A firm may sell securities with distant maturities (or, in the case of ordinary shares, with no maturity date) while the buyers of such securities can obtain quick access to their money by selling the securities.

Another function of a stock exchange, which is performed as a byproduct of the financial intermediation, is to communicate information about the companies whose securities are being traded. The prices of stocks and bonds reflect the evaluation of investors and dealers (some of whom carry out very detailed analyses of the firms) of the performance of the firms. Share prices, and their changes, can communicate information of value to those inside as well as those outside the companies whose shares are being traded.

Primary and secondary markets

When stocks and bonds are issued initially they are said to be sold in the primary market. Subsequent to their initial sale they are traded in the secondary markets. Primary trading involves buying and selling newly created securities, whereas secondary trading involves shares and bonds that are already in existence. The fact that financial investments can be sold in a secondary market renders them more liquid and hence more attractive. This enhanced liquidity makes investors more willing to buy in the primary market and causes them to be less demanding in terms of required rates of return. An active secondary market improves the operation of the primary market and allows companies to raise money easily and on favourable terms. Secondary-market trading volume far exceeds the level of primary-market dealing.

The secondary market is the market in which previously issued securities are traded. It is the means by which stocks or bonds bought in the primary market can be converted into cash. The knowledge that assets purchased in the primary market can be resold easily and cheaply in the secondary market makes investors more prepared to provide borrowers with funds by buying in the primary market. A successful primary market depends upon an effective secondary market.

If transaction costs are high in the secondary market, the proceeds from the sale of securities will be reduced and the incentive to buy in the primary market will be lower. Also high transaction costs in the secondary market might tend to reduce the volume of trading and thereby reduce the ease with which secondary market sales can be executed. It follows that high transaction costs in the secondary market could reduce that market's effectiveness in rendering primary market assets liquid. In consequence there would be adverse effects on the level of activity in the primary market and hence on the total level of investment in the economy.

Price volatility in the secondary market might also be detrimental to the operation of the primary market. High volatility means that buyers in the primary market stand a considerable risk of losing money by having to sell at a lower price in the secondary market. This can reduce the motivation to buy in the primary market. Two factors that affect the price volatility of securities in the secondary market are the depth and breadth of that market.

The depth of the market is based on the likely appearance of new orders stimulated by any movement in price. If a rise in price brings forth numerous sell orders, the price rise will be small. A decline in price that stimulates buy orders will be small. A deep market would be characterised by the appearance of orders that tend to dampen the extent of any movement in price. Greater depth is thus associated with lower volatility.

The breadth of the market reflects the number and diversity of the traders in the market. If there are a large number of market participants with differing motivations and expectations, substantial price changes are less likely than would be expected when there is a small number of traders or when the traders have common views such that they buy or sell together. A broad market is a large heterogeneous market characterised by relative price stability.

Types of stock exchange

In many countries there are both national and regional stock exchanges. National exchanges tend to trade the stocks of large companies and impose demanding listing conditions. If shares in a company are to trade on a stock exchange, they must be listed. The exchange may prescribe criteria for listing in terms of history of the company, its profits, its capital, the integrity of its management and possibly other factors. Shares in a firm can be traded on a stock exchange only if the stock exchange authorities give approval: that is, list the stock. Examples of national stock exchanges include the New York Stock Exchange, American Stock Exchange, London Stock Exchange, Tokyo Stock Exchange, Paris Bourse and the Frankfurt Börse.

Regional exchanges tend to cater for the stocks of smaller companies. Their listing requirements are normally less stringent than those of the national exchanges. The financial costs involved in obtaining a listing also tend to be lower. So it is easier for a company to get its shares traded on a regional exchange, but probably at the cost of being traded on a less liquid market (i.e. on a market in which there is a lower frequency, and smaller volume, of trading). Regional stock exchanges also cater for small stockbroking firms by offering cheaper membership than the national exchanges. Examples of regional stock exchanges include the Pacific and Midwest exchanges in the United States, Osaka and Nagoya in Japan, Munich and Hamburg in Germany.

In addition to formal stock exchanges there are over-the-counter (OTC) markets. At one extreme these markets are unorganised with trading taking place between individuals on an unregulated basis, and typically there is no restriction on the ability of people to buy and sell outside of organised exchanges. At the other extreme over-the-counter markets may be highly organised and sophisticated. Examples of organised over-the-counter markets are the NASDAQ and upstairs markets in the United States.

The NASDAQ market specialises in the trading of high technology stocks. Trading takes place via telephone or computer contacts. Market-makers display the prices at which they are prepared to buy and sell on computer networks. Investors, normally via brokers, trade with the market-makers by means of telephone or computer links. The upstairs market is mainly used by institutional investors and handles large buy and sell orders (block trades). When an institution places an order with a broker, traders at the brokerage firm will contact other institutions in an attempt to find one willing to trade. In the absence of finding a trading counterparty, the dealers at the stockbroking firm will attempt to execute the order with market-makers.

Shares in a company may be listed on more than one stock exchange. This is referred to as multiple listing. Shares in a company may also be simultaneously traded on formal exchanges and over-the-counter markets. Stocks of very large multinational companies may be traded on more than one national stock exchange. For example, the London Stock Exchange lists more than 600 foreign stocks. Trading in such stocks can effectively be global and may operate on a 24-hour basis (as one exchange closes, trading may continue on others). This is one dimension of the globalisation of financial markets: that is the tendency for financial markets in different countries to become integrated into a single market. A major factor leading to globalisation has been the development of telecommunications. Other factors have been the tendencies towards international diversification of portfolios, and deregulation of national financial markets.

Stock market trading systems

Order-driven systems

Order-driven systems operate by matching buy and sell orders. Investors are proactive in terms of both price and quantity. Orders to buy and sell determine stock prices. Stock prices move towards the level at which orders to buy are matched by orders to sell. This can be illustrated by demand and supply curves, as shown in Figure 8.1.

In Figure 8.1 P_A is the ask (or offer) price which is the price at which investors buy. P_B is the bid price, at which investors sell. Investors offering P_A or more will buy at P_A. Sellers requiring P_B or less will sell at P_B. The quantity that buyers demand at P_A matches the quantity that sellers wish to supply at P_B. The excess of P_A over P_B (the bid-offer or bid-ask spread) constitutes a payment to the stock exchange, or other agent, for carrying out the matching process.

In an order-driven system stock prices are determined directly by demand and supply. The agent or body facilitating the trading process holds no position in shares and is entirely reactive to those seeking to buy or sell.

Order-driven systems involve investors stating the quantities that they wish to buy or sell. The quantities may be linked with maximum buying or minimum selling prices. Alternatively the order could simply state a quantity, with an acceptance of the market price. The operation is illustrated by Table 8.1, which shows a hypothetical situation at the beginning of a trading day.

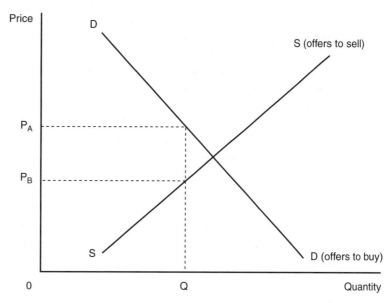

Figure 8.1 Demand and supply curves

The buy orders might consist of 1 million 'at best' orders (investors willing to accept whatever the market price may be), the remainder being limit orders (stipulating a maximum buying price). The quantities are cumulative (for example the orders at 103 comprise the 'at best' orders plus the 103 limit orders plus orders with higher limit prices).

The sell orders might consist of 1.5 million 'at best' orders, with the remainder being limit orders. Again the quantities are cumulative. However, as opposed to the buy orders, the cumulative number of sell orders increases with increasing price. The fall in the cumulative number of buy orders, and rise in the cumulative number of sell orders, as the share price rises is consistent with a downward sloping demand curve and upward sloping supply curve.

Table 8.1 A hypothetical situation at the beginning of a trading day

Stock price	Buy orders (millions of shares)	Sell orders (millions of shares)
95	6	1.5
96	5.5	1.5
97	5.2	2
98	5	3
99	3.5	3.2
100	3	3.75
101	2.75	4
102	2.5	4.25
103	2	5
104	1.75	6.5
105	1	8.5

At the beginning of the trading day the stock price will be set at the level that results in the highest number of shares traded. In Table 8.1 this price is 99 and the number of shares traded is 3.2 million.

After the trades at 99 are executed, the number of remaining orders at each price could be as shown in Table 8.2.

These orders remain on the book until they are withdrawn by the investors or until they can be executed as a result of new orders arriving. The arrival of buy orders at 100 or above will allow execution of some of the sell orders in Table 8.2. If sell orders at 99 or less are submitted, some of the buy orders in Table 8.2 can be executed. In this way order matching can be continuous throughout the trading day. Typically these order-driven matching systems are computerised.

If some but not all orders at a price can be executed, the oldest orders get priority. Normally buyers and sellers are not shown the whole of the limit order book, only the highest buy price and the lowest sell price are shown (99 and 100 in Table 8.2).

Quote-driven systems

In a quote-driven system, market-makers quote prices at which they are willing to sell (offer or ask prices) and prices at which they are willing to buy from investors (bid prices). Stockbrokers (on behalf of private investors), or institutional investors, transact with the market-makers on the basis of the quotes provided. Market-makers are proactive and investors reactive in terms of the prices. The firms that operate as market-makers are usually banks or stockbrokers.

Market-makers, or dealers as they are sometimes known, trade as principals. Trading as principals entails buying and selling for their own account and holding positions in the stocks for which they make a market. In terms of transactions, they are reactive rather than proactive. Their trading is in response to buy or sell orders from investors. If they wish to change their stock positions, they must move their price quotes.

Table 8.2 Remaining orders

Stock price	Buy orders (millions of shares)	Sell orders (millions of shares)
95	2.8	0
96	2.3	0
97	2	0
98	1.8	0
99	0.3	0
100	0	0.55
101	0	0.8
102	0	1.05
103	0	1.8
104	0	3.3
105	0	5.3

If investors are net buyers, market-makers find that their stockholdings decline. If they want to stop such a decline, they raise their quoted prices to deter buyers and encourage sellers. Conversely net sales by investors might raise the stock holdings of market-makers to undesirable levels. In response, market-makers would lower prices in order to encourage buyers and deter sellers. In these ways, market-makers' price quotes respond to the pressures of demand and supply.

The excess of the offer price over the bid price is known as the bid-offer spread. It provides a source of profit for the market-maker as well as compensating for the risks inherent in the process of market-making. The market bid-offer spread is the excess of the lowest offer price over the highest bid price and is normally smaller than the spreads of individual market-makers.

Bid-offer spreads

Bid-offer spreads (alternatively known as bid-ask spreads) are the spreads between the buying and selling prices of share dealers. A dealer, operating as a market-maker, quotes a price at which it is prepared to sell – the offer price – and a price at which it is willing to buy – the bid price. The offer price is always above the bid price. The difference between the offer and bid prices, the bid-offer spread, is the dealer's profit. The question arises as to what factors affect the bid-offer spread.

From the perspective of investors, dealers (in their role as market-makers) provide two important services. The first is immediacy. The dealer sells from, and adds to, its own holdings of a stock in order to accommodate the trades of investors. As a result investors can immediately execute a trade without having to wait for a counter-party to emerge. For example, a buyer need not wait for a seller to come forward since the dealer stands ready to sell. A second service is the maintenance of price stability. For example, buy orders, in the absence of corresponding sell orders, would tend to push up prices. Sell orders would push prices down. By being willing to trade from their own stock holdings, dealers reduce such price fluctuations.

The bid-offer spread of dealers can be seen as the price to be paid, by investors, for these services. The spread can also be seen, from the perspective of the dealer, as compensation for costs and risks. The costs would include the administrative costs of transferring shares. The risks arise from price fluctuations and information-based investors.

A dealer who operates as a market-maker holds shares. The dealer is at risk from a fall in share prices when shares are held (and from a price rise when the dealer has a short position). The bid-offer spread can be seen as a source of compensation for accepting such risks. For shares that are infrequently traded, such as shares in smaller companies, the risks are greater. This is because positions are held for longer between trades. If shares are held for a long time, the risk of losses from price falls is greater. As a result the bid-offer spreads for such shares tend to be relatively high.

Another form of risk arises from the possibility that some investors may possess information that the dealer does not. Such investors are able to make profits at the expense of the dealer. For example, if an investor has information that suggests a share price fall, that investor could sell the shares to the dealer at a price that turns out to be high. It is the dealer who suffers the loss from a fall in the share price. The bid-offer spread can be viewed as providing the dealer with compensation for bearing the risk that such information-based trading may occur.

The markets in which the trading systems operate

Order-driven systems are the most common. They predominate in Europe and the Far East. In the United States there is a much greater use of quote-driven systems. NASDAQ, which has become the main market in North America for high technology stocks, is quote-driven. Market-makers display their quotes on computer screens. Investors (or brokers on their behalf) will buy or sell at the quoted prices by means of computer or telephone links.

The New York Stock Exchange (NYSE) is probably the best known example of a hybrid system. On the NYSE there are firms acting as 'specialists'. Each stock is allocated to a specialist. Specialists will operate by matching orders when there is a sufficient volume of trading. When trading volumes are low, such that matching buy and sell orders is not possible, specialists will act as market-makers (providing a quote-driven system). In other words, to the extent to which specialists are unable to match buy and sell orders they will trade on their own account. They buy from unmatched sellers and sell to unmatched buyers. In this way they maintain the liquidity of the market.

It is to be noted that trades do not have to go through a specialist. There will be a 'crowd' of traders and brokers around each specialist. Members of this crowd are able to trade with each other. This is possibly an additional source of both order-driven and quote-driven trading.

On the New York Stock Exchange, specialists have the additional function of ensuring orderly markets. This function requires them to ensure that price changes between one deal and the next are small. To achieve this they must sell in rising markets and buy in falling markets. While most of the time the specialists succeed in moderating price movements, the system broke down during the stock market crash of October 1987. At the height of the crash, many specialists stopped trading, because they lacked the resources to cope with the huge volumes of sell orders with which they were presented.

The London Stock Exchange also uses a hybrid system. The major stocks (including the constituents of the FTSE 100 index) are traded by order-driven matching. Smaller stocks are traded on a quote-driven (market-maker) basis. Up to 1996 all stocks were traded by means of a quote-driven system. The change to a hybrid system reflected the belief that for major stocks order-driven systems generate lower bid-offer spreads, while for smaller stocks market-makers are required in order to ensure liquid markets. There is also a market-maker system for small deals, but the prices have to reflect the prices in the order-driven market.

The Amsterdam Stock Exchange is another example of a hybrid system. Large trades are order matched, while small trades are executed through intermediaries who may match orders or may operate as market-makers (buying and selling on their own account). Most other exchanges in the world are purely order-driven.

Types of order

An investor who wants to buy shares on a stock exchange has a number of different types of order available. The simplest, and most common, is the market order. A market order stipulates that the shares should be traded at the most favourable price available – the lowest available price for a purchase, the highest available price for a sale. The trade takes place at a price that is currently available in the market.

Other types of order specify particular prices. A buy limit order specifies that the purchase should take place only if the price is at or below a specified level. A sell limit order specifies a minimum selling price such that the trade should not take place unless that price, or more, can be obtained.

A market-if-touched order becomes a market order if the share price reaches a particular level. This differs from a limit order in that there is no upper limit to the buying price or lower limit to the selling price. As soon as there has been a trade in the market at the specified price, the order becomes a market order. The specified price is not necessarily obtained.

A stop order is also an order that becomes a market order once there has been a trade in the market at a particular price. However, it involves selling after the price has fallen to a specified level or buying after the price has risen to a level. Stop orders are concerned with protecting profits or limiting losses. They seek to ensure that a selling price is not too low or that a buying price is not too high.

Another dimension to an order is the length of time for which it remains in force. A fill-or-kill order is to be cancelled if it cannot be executed immediately. An open order, otherwise known as a good-till-cancelled order, remains in force until it is specifically cancelled by the investor. Alternatively the investor can specify the period of time for which the order should remain open, e.g. a day, a week, a month.

Selling shares in the primary market

The sale of shares in the primary market entails the sale of newly created shares. These may be the first issue of shares by a newly floated company. The other source of new shares is the issue of additional shares where an initial issue has already taken place.

The issue of shares by a company that has not previously sold shares could be through a number of routes. Three popular means of issue are public offers, tenders and placements. Public offers invite investors, including private investors, to subscribe for shares. Often there are application forms in newspapers. The share price is set by the issuing company. Investors choose the number of shares for which they apply and if the number applied for exceeds the number being issued, individual investors may receive fewer shares than the number for which they applied.

Tenders invite investors to quote prices. Those quoting the highest prices receive the shares for which they apply. Placements involve the investment bank that is handling the share issue selling the shares to institutional investors. Placements do not involve general invitations to apply for shares. Selected institutions are approached directly.

Introductions take place when there is already a number of shareholders and the company is simply seeking permission for the shares to trade on the stock exchange. Introductions do not entail raising capital. They may be part of the process of moving from AIM to the main market, or may allow a foreign company to have its shares traded in London as well as in its home country.

The issue of additional shares, when shares in the company are already in the market, is normally by means of rights issues. In many countries, any addition to the total number of shares must be offered first to existing shareholders. The offer would be in proportion to the number of shares already held. For example, a one for two rights issue entails one new share being offered for every two already held.

To encourage the take-up of the offer, the new shares are usually offered at a lower price than the existing shares. One effect of this discount is that the share price subsequent to the rights issue is lower than the share price before it. For example, if the shares are initially 100p and there is a one for two rights issue at 70p, the share price might be expected to fall to 90p [(100p + 100p + 70p)/3 = 90p]. As an alternative to buying additional shares, investors can sell their rights to new shares. In the current example, the buyer of such rights obtains the ability to pay 70p for shares that are expected to be worth 90p.

Share issues are often underwritten by banks. A bank underwriting a share issue agrees, for a fee, to buy any shares not taken up by investors. This guarantees that the issuing company receives the money that it expects. In the case of rights issues, firms sometimes avoid paying a fee to underwriters by using the deep discount route. In a rights issue, failure to sell the new shares would result from the share price (prior to the issue) falling below the sale price of the new shares. The deep discount method prices the new shares at such a low level that the market price is extremely unlikely to fall so far.

● ● ● ● Types of share

The most common type of share is known as the ordinary share (alternatively referred to as common stock). Ordinary shares represent part ownership of the issuing company. They pay dividends at regular intervals (typically every three or six months). The sizes of the dividends are at the discretion of the issuing company and are likely to be related to the level of profit made by the company. There is no legal obligation for the company to pay dividends. In the case of bankruptcy, holders of ordinary shares are the last to receive any proceeds from the winding up of the company, and typically will receive nothing. However, the holders of ordinary shares are not liable for any outstanding debts.

Another type of share is the preference (or preferred) share. In some ways preference shares are more similar to bonds than to ordinary shares. In particular, most pay a fixed dividend each year and typically do not confer voting rights on the holder. Unlike bonds, preference shares constitute part ownership of the issuing company and the company does not have a legal obligation to pay the dividends. The absence of the legal obligation to pay dividends is related to the fact that preference shares are seen as part of the equity of the company rather than the debt of the company (bonds are debts). However, no dividends can be paid to the holders of ordinary shares if preference shareholders have not received their full dividend payments. In the event of bankruptcy the holders of preference shares have a prior right, relative to the holders of ordinary shares, to the receipt of remaining assets. However, bondholders and other creditors have a prior right to the holders of preference shares.

There are many varieties of preference share. These include:

- cumulative preference shares;
- non-cumulative preference shares;
- redeemable preference shares;
- convertible preference shares;
- participating preference shares.

With the exception of the first two, these characteristics are not mutually exclusive. For example, it is possible to issue non-cumulative, redeemable, convertible preference shares.

Cumulative preference shares entail the obligation, on the part of the issuing company, to pay any missed past dividends before any dividends are paid to the holders of ordinary shares. Non-cumulative preference shares entail no such obligation, with the effect that missed dividends may be lost for ever. A redeemable preference share has a maturity date on which the original sum invested is repaid, whereas most preference shares have no maturity date (the issuer may pay the dividends for ever and never repay the principal sum). Convertible preference shares give the holder the right to convert preference shares into ordinary shares at a predetermined rate. Participating preference shares allow the issuing company to increase the dividends if profits are particularly high.

Discussion questions

1 What are the functions of stock markets? How do stock market trading systems differ?

2 What are the various types of share and bond? Why is there such a large variety?

Chapter 9

Financial anomalies

After studying this chapter readers should be able to:

- *critically evaluate the concept of short-termism*
- *identify factors involved in the creation of stock market bubbles*
- *apply concepts of behavioural finance to the understanding of stock market bubbles and crashes*
- *understand the role of borrowing in the development of bubbles and crashes*
- *appreciate how bubbles and crashes can occur in property markets*
- *understand how crashes can generate banking crises.*

Short-termism

The proponents of the short-termism view believe that stock markets systematically misprice shares. It is claimed that this results in a misallocation of investment funds such that long-term investment by companies falls below the level consistent with economic efficiency.

During the 1950s, 1960s and 1970s US and British rates of investment, and rates of economic growth, lagged behind those of Japan and West Germany. One theory put forward to explain this relates to the structure and behaviour of financial markets. In the United States and the United Kingdom stock markets have been important sources of corporate finance. In Japan and Germany banks have been the dominant source of funds for firms seeking to finance investment.

Adherents of the short-termist view say that stock market investors have been too concerned with immediate rather than long-term profits and dividends. They claim that stock prices are determined primarily by short-term profit and dividend prospects, with long-term profitability receiving too little attention. This has resulted in companies over-emphasising short-term profits. It is argued that companies have reduced investment in order to boost short-term profits. Firms that fail to focus on the short term, and which invest for the long term, find that the market undervalues their shares. The low share price renders these companies vulnerable to takeover by other firms. In order to protect themselves from takeover, firms avoid investment projects whose pay-offs are long term.

This short-termism theory is particularly popular among politicians and journalists and hence is widely publicised. Research undertaken by economists tends to refute the theory. Economists who have looked for evidence relating to short-termism have concluded that the facts do not support the view that US and British stock markets are short-termist.

If stock markets placed too much weight on current dividends, low-yielding stocks would be relatively undervalued. However, evidence from both the USA and the UK indicates that the opposite is the case – low-yielding stocks are overvalued relative to higher yielding stocks. Empirical evidence concerning the relationship between price-earnings ratios and relative mispricing is also inconsistent with the notion of short-termism. It is widely believed that the major factor underlying variations in price-earnings ratios relates to differences in growth prospects. A high ratio of stock price to profits per share is thought to reflect potential for future growth in profits. If participants in financial markets are short-termist, there is a tendency to shun such stocks which would thereby become undervalued. However, research evidence suggests that high price-earnings ratio stocks tend to be overvalued. Also the evidence from studies of the effects of announcements relating to investment projects indicates that announcements of investment spending result in stock price increases. This is opposite to what would be expected from short-termist financial markets.

Investment analysts often appear to focus strongly on current profits and dividends. However, this is not evidence of short-termism. Current profits and dividends convey information about the future. The proportion of profits that firms choose to pay out as dividends can provide clues about the knowledge and thinking of senior executives within the company with regard to its future prospects.

Fund managers are also often seen as being short-termist. This is believed to arise from the fund managers being subject to appraisal on a short-term, often quarterly, basis. Many would deny that the main appraisers take such a short-term view. Even if they did, the achievement of short-term performance depends upon taking a long-term view. A rise in the price of a stock, relative to the market, in the short-term is likely to be based on a re-evaluation of the firm's long-term prospects. By taking a long-term view of a company's prospects a fund manager can assess whether the stock is correctly valued. If the fund manager turns out to be right in deciding that a stock is mispriced and trades accordingly, the resulting profit could arise in the short term as other market participants subsequently revise their views of the firm's prospects (and trade accordingly). The stock price change that generates short-term profits occurs as a result of a re-evaluation of the company's long-term prospects. The fund manager makes a short-term profit by taking a long-term view.

It is sometimes claimed that institutional investors put pressure on companies to make large dividend payments. These large dividends are seen as reducing the funds available to finance investment. The problem with this line of argument is that it assumes that firms face a choice between dividend pay-outs and investment. There is no such choice since firms are able to finance investment by means other than undistributed profits. Investment can be financed by borrowing or by issuing shares.

The payment of dividends that investors may choose to use for the purchase of bonds or shares has advantages for the economy. Investors are likely to fund the companies with the most promising prospects. In this way the market works to ensure that money is directed towards its most productive uses. Profits retained by firms and used to finance internal investments might be used more profitably by other companies with better investment opportunities.

Another factor that concerns adherents of the short-termism theory is the effect of hostile takeover bids. The belief is that the threat of takeover encourages managers to maximise short-term profits and dividends in order to boost the stock price and deter predators. This is seen as involving the curtailment of long-term investment. However, as has been pointed out above, such a response would not be expected to result in an increase in the stock price. There is no evidence that companies that invest heavily are more likely to be taken over.

There may be other factors that lead to a sub-optimal level of investment. It is still the case that some firms use the payback period as the criterion for investments. A focus on the period of time required for a project to repay its costs tends to bias managements against long-term investment projects.

High inflation in the USA and the UK, relative to that in Japan and Germany, could also provide a rationale for the suggestion that firms have been short-termist in their approach to investment. High levels of inflation tend to bias the repayment of debt, in real terms, towards the early part of the repayment period. High inflation tends to be reflected in high interest rates. It also erodes the real value of debt. The effect of the high interest rates is immediate, whereas the process of eroding the real value of money (and hence of debt) takes time to have its cumulative effect. In consequence the real interest cost is biased towards the early years of the debt. This may incline management away from investment projects whose returns are not generated relatively quickly. It is interesting to note that the relatively poor performance of the US and UK economies during the 1960s and 1970s tended to coincide with the period during which their inflation rates were relatively high.

Stock market bubbles and crashes

Kindleberger, in *Manias, Panics and Crashes*, argued that most bubbles and crashes have common characteristics. Bubbles feature large and rapid price increases which result in share prices rising to unrealistically high levels. Bubbles typically begin with a justifiable rise in stock prices. The justification may be a technological advance or a general rise in prosperity. Examples of technological advance stimulating share price rises might include the development of the car and the radio in the 1920s and the emergence of the internet in the late 1990s. Examples of increasing prosperity leading to price rises could be the United States, Western Europe and Japan in the 1980s.

The rise in share prices, if substantial and prolonged, leads to members of the public believing that prices will continue to rise. People who do not normally invest begin to buy shares in the belief that prices will continue to rise. More and more people, typically those who have no knowledge of financial markets, buy shares. This pushes up prices even further. There is euphoria and manic buying. This causes further price rises. There is a self-fulfilling prophecy wherein the belief that prices will rise brings about the rise, since it leads to buying. People with no knowledge of investment often believe that if share prices have risen recently, those prices will continue to rise in the future. Some professional investors may also participate on the basis of the greater fool theory. The greater fool theory states that it does not matter if the price paid is higher than the fundamental value so long as someone (the greater fool) will be prepared to pay an even higher price.

Research on investor psychology has indicated certain features about the behaviour of uninformed investors, who are often referred to as noise traders in the academic literature. Tversky and Kahneman (1982) found that they have a tendency to over-react to news. De Bondt (1993) found that they extrapolate trends, in other words they tend to believe that the recent direction of movement of share prices will continue. Shleifer and Summers (1990) found evidence that they become overconfident in their forecasts. This latter point is consistent with the view that bubbles and crashes are characterised by some investors forgetting that financial markets are uncertain and coming to believe that the direction of movement of share prices can be forecast with certainty.

At the time of writing, the most recent bubble was in technology stocks. During 1999 and up to March 2000 such stocks rose dramatically in price. Novice investors piled in either through direct share purchases or via unit trusts specialising in technology stocks. Many people came to believe that they could make a living out of trading shares (as 'day traders'). It seemed that some people even believed that their profits were due to their investment skills (typically people with no prior knowledge of investment or financial markets).

The implications of behavioural finance for understanding bubbles and crashes

Behavioural finance applies the psychology of decision making to investment behaviour. Psychological research has indicated that there are a number of systematic distortions that cause investors to deviate from the model of rationality typically assumed by financial economists. Some of these biases help to explain how stock markets can experience bubbles and crashes.

Representativeness and narrow framing

Representativeness suggests that many investors extrapolate the past too readily. They see investments that have risen in value recently as representative of investments that will perform well in the longer term. Conversely, assets that have fared badly recently are seen as representative of long-term losers. As a result people tend to interpret recent share price movements as indicative of longer-term trends. Investments that have recently risen in price are then expected to continue to rise, and recent fallers are expected to continue to decline.

Narrow framing suggests that investors focus too much on the short term. In consequence the very recent behaviour of share prices is focused upon and the longer term past is ignored. This reinforces the tendency of representativeness to lead to unjustified long-term expectations on the basis of short-term price movements.

These ideas are consistent with the emergence of stock price bubbles and crashes. Recent price increases cause expectations of future increases and investors buy shares. This pushes prices up further, hence generates expectations of more increases and leads to yet more buying. There is an upward spiral often referred to as positive feedback trading or as 'chasing the market'. There is a corresponding, but opposite, pattern as the market falls.

Overconfidence

Psychological research has indicated that there is a self-attribution bias in decision making. When an investment is successful, the investor believes that it is due to his or her skill. An unsuccessful investment is seen as a result of bad luck or the actions of others. This self-attribution bias leads to overconfidence. Such overconfidence may be particularly characteristic of inexperienced investors who find that their initial investments are profitable. Their belief in their own skill leads them to invest more. So a bull market can generate overconfidence which causes more investing, thereby reinforcing the upward price movement. There is a Wall Street adage which says: 'Don't confuse brains with a bull market.' However, there are those who interpret their gains in a bull market as arising from their own skills. They see certainty where there is uncertainty. This can lead them to invest beyond a rational level, resulting in painful losses when the market falls.

Borrowing to buy

Another feature of bubbles is that share purchases are often financed with borrowed money. This is sometimes referred to as buying on margin, or leveraged buying. The shares are then used as collateral for further loans taken out for the purchase of yet more shares. This can bring about a circular process that entails rising share prices. This circular process is illustrated by Figure 9.1.

The bubble phase leads to share prices reaching unrealistic levels. These are share price levels far in excess of what can be justified by fundamental analyses using dividend discount models or price-earnings ratios. Indeed one feature of bubbles, identified by Kindleberger, is the emergence of 'new age' theories – ad hoc theories that seek to justify why prices should be far in excess of what conventional share valuation models suggest.

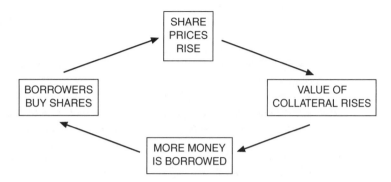

Figure 9.1 Circular process in share processing

The perils for investors of human nature

Your herds and flocks may increase, and you may amass much silver and gold – everything you own may increase. But your heart may then grow haughty, and you may ... say to yourself, 'It was my own strength and personal power that brought me all this prosperity'.

Deuteronomy 8: 13–14, 17

People constantly learn about their own abilities by observing the consequences of their actions. They assess their own abilities not so much through introspection as by observing successes and failures. Yet they tend to take too much credit for their own successes. This can lead to overconfidence. Investors, like others, may attribute too much of their success to personal skill and not enough to good fortune. They may become overconfident in their abilities and as a result make investment decisions that are not in their own best interests.

This process takes place in most walks of life: a newly graduated lawyer may be uncertain about her cross-examination skills, a teenager entering a new school may not fully appreciate his level of skill in a particular subject, or a footballer may not be able to ascertain precisely the level of success he can achieve as a professional. In these circumstances, people learn by doing, that is, they adjust their views about their ability to perform a given task through their performance of that task.

For investors, the learning process involves taking positions in financial securities and looking at the profits (or losses) that these positions then generate.

Psychologists have shown that there is a self-serving bias in how people learn about their own abilities. When successful, people tend to credit success to their own abilities. When they fail, they blame failure on bad luck or on others.

Self-serving bias can lead people to become overconfident in their abilities and knowledge. Such overconfidence has been observed in many fields. Clinical psychologists, physicians and nurses, investment bankers, engineers, entrepreneurs, lawyers, negotiators and managers have all been observed to exhibit overconfidence in their judgments. Investors, too, may be overconfident.

Effect on investors
Overconfidence is only potentially harmful to investors if it affects their behaviour. This is likely to be the case because overconfident investors believe their ability to profit from analysing and interpreting financial information is greater than it really is. Overconfidence will affect trading behaviour in a number of ways.

In a recent study, researchers Brad Barber and

▶

Terrance Odean found that investors at a large discount brokerage held an average of only four to five common stocks. While some gained further diversification through mutual funds, many did not. Overconfident investors may underdiversify portfolios because they are too sure their stock choices are the right ones. Investors who are sure they are right do not see the point of hedging. Such overconfident investors will invest too much in strategies that they perceive as profitable, underestimating or even ignoring the risks. As a result, the portfolios of overconfident investors will tend to be riskier than warranted by the available information and their ability to bear risk.

Overconfident investors tend to trade too much. While an investor who has no confidence in his ability to pick common stocks might buy and hold a broad-based mutual fund, the overconfident investor is likely to routinely buy stocks he feels are winners.

By trading too much, overconfident investors add to aggregate market trading volume. Increased trading activity is not necessarily damaging to financial markets (in fact, large trading volume may increase liquidity in these markets); however, unnecessary transaction costs can only be detrimental to investors.

Barber and Odean show that, in a sample of more than 60,000 households, the 20 per cent of investors who traded most actively underperformed the 20 per cent that traded least actively by more than five percentage points a year.

What happens to overconfident investors when the positions that they thought were justified by analysis do not pan out? For one thing, they start learning the errors of their ways and readjust their beliefs towards a more objective view of themselves.

In the long term, investors who systematically examine the outcomes of their decisions will gain a realistic appreciation of their abilities. The length of time a given investor takes to reach a more reasonable perspective depends on the frequency with which he gets feedback and the perspective and judgment he uses in examining such feedback.

This process is likely to be quicker for professional traders whose job is to analyse the market and whose absolute and relative performance is frequently examined. For a casual investor who makes only a few investment bets a year, the process may take longer.

Mature investors are therefore less likely to be overconfident than their younger counterparts or inexperienced investors who have not been trading for long. The relatively short trading history of young investors can make them more prone to errors in their self-assessment, especially if they have an early string of profits. While these profits could have resulted from innate ability, they could also be the product of simple luck. The problem is that it is difficult to distinguish ability from luck in the short term. As a result, investors who are young and lucky are likely to be overconfident.

Overconfidence and markets

The adverse effects of overconfidence on investors are clear, but does overconfidence also affect market prices? This is an unresolved controversy.

The extent to which investors affect market prices depends on their willingness and ability to trade. Wealthy investors who are willing to bear risk have more influence than those who are poor or averse to risk. Investors will not necessarily have greater influence on prices simply because they are not overconfident. Wealthy overconfident investors may influence markets as much as their less overconfident brethren.

Several investors – overconfident or not – may influence prices as much as one wealthy investor if they share the same opinions. If overconfident investors differ in their opinions, they will increase market trading volume but, because their actions are offsetting, have little influence on prices. If, however, a significant group of overconfident investors take aggressive positions in the same securities, they are likely to move prices.

'Don't confuse brains with a bull market,' warns an old Wall Street adage. Investors who fail to heed this advice are likely to become overconfident in a bull market. Those who profit from buying small speculative stocks may become convinced that this is the optimal investment for savvy investors such as themselves. They may pour more of their resources into such stocks, even borrowing on margin to do so, and drive prices still higher.

Even if other investors realise that their overconfident counterparts are misled, the risks associated with the short positions required to bring prices back to a justifiable level may be too high. Knowing that if

▶

prices rise further they may be forced to take losses on short positions may keep reasonable investors from acting. Thus self-attribution bias and overconfidence can contribute to and extend a price bubble.

Some argue that overconfident investors and others who do not behave optimally are of little importance because they will be driven out of markets as more strategic investors exploit their mistakes. If overconfident investors thereby decrease sufficiently in wealth and numbers, they may not affect prices.

If, however, success leads investors to become overconfident, many overconfident investors will be wealthy. They will be in no immediate danger of being driven from markets. These investors, who trade more aggressively due to their overconfidence and in greater quantities due to their wealth, are likely to affect prices, at least in the short to medium term.

What about the long run? At first, the destabilising effects of overconfidence seem possible only for short periods: after all, traders do eventually learn about their own abilities and overconfidence goes away. In a world where no new people decide to participate in financial markets, overconfidence may disappear.

However, every year, securities exchanges welcome new participants who have yet to learn about their abilities to assess the market. Furthermore, it is likely that investors who are fresh entrants to the trading bandwagon are, on average, overconfident at the outset. Overconfidence leads them to believe they can be successful traders. This process, in which new investors continue to stream into the market, leads to the propagation of overconfidence through people and time, with lasting effects on markets, even if the market is competitive.

Just as the overconfidence of an investor is likely to vary with personal experience, so too is the aggregate overconfidence of financial markets likely to vary. Most investors have long positions in financial assets. In a bull market, investors are successful and are likely to become overconfident, so aggregate overconfidence rises. This results in increased trading activity and, possibly, speculative bubbles. Conversely, bear markets tend to reduce aggregate overconfidence.

The extent to which overconfidence influences financial markets is, ultimately, an empirical question. Researchers face a significant challenge in separating the effects of overconfidence from those of other economic factors.

Conclusion

The human tendency to take too much credit for one's own successes while blaming one's failures on bad luck or others can lead successful investors to become overconfident. While successful investors may have more actual ability than others, they are likely not to have as much as they think they have.

Overconfident investors are likely to trade too actively and damage their own financial welfare. They may also buy portfolios that are inappropriately risky simply because they are too sure in their opinions and therefore underestimate their risks. Since successful investors will tend to become both overconfident and wealthy, overconfident investors may have a disproportionate influence on markets. This is particularly likely when such investors hold similar views. An individual investor's overconfidence will not flourish indefinitely; time and experience gradually rid him of it. However, in a market in which new investors are born every minute, overconfidence will flourish.

This article is based on 'Learning to be overconfident', published in the Review of Financial Studies *14, Spring 2001, 1–27.*

Source: Simon Gervais and Terrance Odean, *Financial Times, Mastering Investment Supplement*, Part 6, June 18 2001, pp. 6–7. Reprinted with permission.

There will then be an occurrence that causes prices to fall rapidly. One such occurrence might be the emergence of new companies. The new companies compete with existing ones and push down their profits. Also, when the new companies float on the stock market, the additional supply of shares will help to depress prices. Towards the end of the 1999–2000 technology stock bubble many new companies were issuing shares. This increased supply of shares overtook the growth in demand for shares. The result was that the prices of shares in the technology sector began to fall.

Rising interest rates could be another occurrence that leads to falling share prices. Bubbles often involve people borrowing money in order to buy shares. High interest rates could cause investors to sell shares in order to pay the interest. Such sales could set off a crash. In Japan in 1990 interest rates rose sharply. This was followed by collapses in the prices of both shares and property. At the time of writing (January 2002) the Japanese economy has still not recovered from the recession that followed the share and property price crashes.

Other factors that can precipitate share price collapses include share sales resulting from negative statements by people who are looked upon as experts. These may be genuine experts such as governors of central banks, or self-appointed experts such as newspaper gurus. Prospective investors may also stop buying because they deplete their sources of money. The flow of new investors on to the market will eventually stop. These factors can start a crash by increasing sales of shares and decreasing purchases.

To the extent that shares are bought with borrowed money (leveraged buying), stock market crashes can cause banking crises. If investors are unable to repay their debts, banks may become bankrupt. This could result in depositors losing their money. The 1929 stock market crash in the United States was worsened by the effects of leveraged buying. That crash was also followed by a banking crisis in which banks failed and depositors lost money. Figure 9.2 illustrates the vicious circle that can emerge when shares are used as collateral against borrowing.

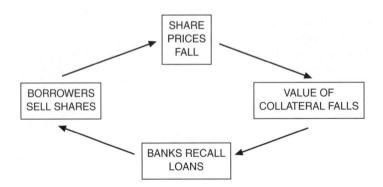

Figure 9.2 Vicious circle when shares are used as collateral against borrowing

● ● ● ● Price bubbles and banking crises

Crashes not only hurt investors, they can also damage banks. Slumps in stock prices can be detrimental to banks, particularly if banks have bought shares as well as lending to other buyers. The American stock market crash of 1929, and the Japanese stock market slump of the 1990s, involved stock price falls impacting on banks. However, stock market crashes do not always severely damage banks.

Property price slumps nearly always damage the banks. This is because property speculation is primarily financed with money borrowed from banks. Bubbles in property prices are typically based on borrowing from banks. Property developers and speculators finance their purchases by borrowing. The purchased property is used as collateral for the loans.

So long as property prices continue to rise, interest payments can be made and loans repaid. When prices stop rising, problems appear. If interest is paid out of the profits from price rises (or from increased borrowing based on the enhanced collateral), a pause in the rises means that interest cannot be paid. Banks may then require loans to be repaid.

The developers and speculators may then sell property in order to pay off the loans. The property sales cause prices to fall. The fall in property prices reduces the value of the collateral. As a result banks demand repayment of loans. More property is sold, prices fall further, collateral declines further and more repayment is demanded by the banks. There is a downward spiral leading to bankruptcy of property developers and speculators. The values of their properties fall below the values of their debts. Such bankruptcies mean that bank loans are not fully repaid. The banks lose money. The Japanese property market slump and banking crisis of the early 1990s involved banks being severely weakened by such a process.

Banks lend money to each other. If one bank became bankrupt, the banks from which it had borrowed would lose money. There could be a domino effect wherein the collapse of some banks causes others to fail. This systemic effect could lead to a collapse of the whole banking system.

The prospect of banks failing might cause depositors to panic and attempt to withdraw their money. If depositors rushed to withdraw their money, banks could run out of cash and hence be unable to pay out the money. This is especially so since bank loans normally are not repayable on demand and so banks cannot get their money back quickly. Such a run on the banks by depositors wanting to withdraw cash would hasten the collapse of the banks. Such behaviour by depositors was a feature of the American banking crisis that followed the Wall Street crash of 1929.

For such reasons central banks, such as the Bank of England, act as lenders of last resort. This means that they will lend to banks in an emergency so that banks can pay their customers. Governments also often guarantee that bank deposits will be repaid in order to avoid the panic that leads to runs on the banks.

Even if banks do not collapse (and normally they do not), the effect of losses on their capital can cause a credit crunch, a situation in which banks stop making new loans (or at least reduce the amount of new lending).

The curious case of Palm and 3Com

Former US Treasury secretary Lawrence Summers once described finance professors as practitioners of ketchup economics: 'They have shown that two quart bottles of ketchup invariably sell for twice as much as one quart bottle of ketchup except for deviations traceable to transaction costs … Indeed, most ketchup economists regard the efficiency of the ketchup market as the best established fact in empirical economics.' Summers was right. Arbitrage, defined as the simultaneous buying and selling of the same security for two different prices, is the central concept of modern finance. The absence of arbitrage is the basis of most modern financial theory, including option pricing and corporate capital structure.

In capital markets, the law of one price says that identical securities must have identical prices, otherwise investors could make unlimited profits by buying the cheap one and selling the expensive one. It does not require that investors be rational or sophisticated, only that they are able to recognise arbitrage opportunities. Because arbitrageurs can make profits by enforcing this law, it should be almost impossible to break in a well-functioning capital market. The law of one price is a basic, commonsense condition, so theorists have used it as a minimal condition, a starting point that leads to other implications.

Market disturbance

Unfortunately, something very disturbing happened in US capital markets during the recent technology stock mania. The law of one price was violated. A prominent example is the price of Palm relative to 3Com. On March 2 2000, 3Com sold part of its stake in handheld computer maker Palm. In this transaction, called an equity carve-out, 3Com sold about 4 per cent of its stake in Palm in an initial public offering and about 1 per cent to a consortium of companies. It kept 95 per cent of the shares. Palm shares were issued at $38. On the first day of trading, Palm immediately went to $150 and later rose to $165, before ending the day at $95.06.

Based on the relative number of shares of Palm and 3Com, a holder of one share of 3Com stock indirectly owned 1.5 shares of Palm stock. Based on 3Com's ownership of Palm alone, at the end of the first day of trading, 3Com shares were worth at least $142.59. 3Com, in addition to owning Palm, held cash and securities worth more than $10 a share, and ran a substantial and profitable network business. Thus one might expect 3Com to trade substantially above $142.59.

In fact, 3Com's value was $81.81 (3Com's stock price actually fell 21 per cent during the day). The 'stub value', or implied value of 3Com's non-Palm assets and businesses, is the difference between the lower bound of $142.59 and observed price $81.81, or −$60.78. The equity market gave a negative implied value to 3Com's other assets, which is puzzling since stock prices cannot be negative.

Most puzzling of all, 3Com had announced its intention to spin off its remaining shares of Palm, pending a decision from the US Internal Revenue Service on the tax status of the spin-off. The spin-off was expected to take place by the end of the year and a favourable ruling was highly likely. To profit from the mispricing, an arbitrageur would need to buy one share of 3Com, short 1.5 shares of Palm and wait less than a year. In essence, the arbitrageur would be buying a security worth at least zero for −$60.78, and would not need to wait long to realise the profits. As shown in Figure 1, this strategy (if one had been able to implement it with no transaction costs) would have been very profitable. The stub value of 3Com gradually rose until the distribution took place.

This mispricing was not in an obscure corner of capital markets, but in an IPO that attracted frenzied attention. On the day after the issue, the mispricing was discussed in several newspaper articles.

The 3Com example is not unique. In 1923, for instance, the young Benjamin Graham, later to co-author a classic book on security analysis, became the manager of what would now be called a mutual fund. Graham noticed that Du Pont's market capitalisation was about the same as the value of a stake it owned in GM. Du Pont had a stub value of about zero, despite the fact that it was a major company with many valuable assets. Graham bought Du Pont, short-sold GM, and profited when Du Pont later rose in value.

Something is terribly wrong here. This negative implied 'stub value' should not be happening. Economists have known about other apparent violations of the law of one price for many years. But these cases have special features that might explain the discrepancy between price and value. While one might be able to dismiss such cases as freakish anomalies, large capitalisation stocks trading in Nasdaq should not be mispriced.

Correcting prices

In understanding any violation of the law of one price, there are two questions. First, why don't arbitrageurs correct the mispricing by selling the overpriced security and buying the underpriced security? Second, even if something prevents the arbitrageurs from correcting the mispricing, why would anyone ever buy the overpriced security when they can buy the underpriced security?

The answer to the first question lies in transaction costs. To implement the arbitrage trade, one needs to sell short shares of Palm. Transaction costs arise in two ways: finding shares to short and the cost of holding the short position over time. To be able to sell short a stock, one must borrow it; for institutional reasons borrowing shares can be difficult or impossible for many equities, especially on the day of the IPO. Even weeks after the IPO, shorting can be difficult.

To borrow shares, an investor needs to find a willing lender. Much of this borrowing is typically done through financial institutions, such as mutual funds, trusts or asset managers, who lend their securities. In the case of Palm, retail investors rather than institutions held most of the shares, making Palm hard to borrow. For short sellers who could find shares to borrow, lenders demanded a high payment. This comes in the form of a daily cost to those shorting the stock. In the case of Palm, there were reports of very high holding costs, in the order of 40 per cent a year.

Thus the arbitrage opportunity is more apparent than real, since it is difficult and expensive to sell Palm short. Although not an easily exploitable arbitrage opportunity, this is a case of blatant mispricing. And it's worth noting that some investors did make substantial profits.

While these investors did not make infinite arbitrage profits, they were making very high returns on near-arbitrage opportunities.

For example, a young finance professor who took advantage of negative stub situations used the proceeds to buy a new car. Finance professors are not generally known for their market savvy or stock-picking success. Compared with institutional investors, they certainly have higher information-gathering and trading costs. So the apparent ability of professors to earn excess returns is troubling for the efficient markets hypothesis.

Evidence from the level of short-selling is consistent with the idea that Palm was overpriced. The level reached an amazing 148 per cent of floating shares, meaning that more than all the available shares had been sold short. This is possible if shares are borrowed, then sold short to an investor who permits the shares to be borrowed again. But it takes time to build this supply of shares, because this shorting market works sluggishly.

Initially, demand for shares was too large for the market to supply via short sales, creating a price that was too high. The upward trend in the stub value of Palm is matched by the upward trend in short sales, so that the graph traces out the demand curve for Palm. As supply of shares grows, we move down the demand curve of Palm investors and the Palm price falls relative to 3Com.

Option prices

The options market offers further evidence on mispricing. Exchange-traded options were introduced two weeks after the IPO. A basic relation that should hold in well-functioning options markets (and another manifestation of the law of one price) is put-call parity. Put-call parity almost always holds (taking into account transactions costs) for most stocks. Without going into detail, put-call parity says that the price of Palm should be the same as the price of a synthetic security, constructed using puts and calls (types of

▶

options) on Palm. This synthetic security has the same pay-off as Palm stock, so it should have the same price. Options prices for Palm massively violated put-call parity: puts were very expensive, calls were very cheap. These option prices are consistent with Palm being overpriced but costly to sell short.

We have three ways of inferring Palm's true value: the embedded value reflected in 3Com's share price, the value reflected in options prices and the actual price. The market for options and shareholders in 3Com seemed to agree: Palm was worth far less than its market price. The direction of the deviation from the law of one price is consistent with the difficulty of shorting Palm. To profit from the difference between the synthetic security and the underlying security, one would need to short Palm and buy the synthetic long. If shorting is costly, then the deviation from the law of one price can be interpreted as the cost of borrowing Palm shares.

By comparing option prices with the actual price for Palm, one can calculate the implied cost of shorting. During 2000, this cost of shorting fell as the stub value rose. The pattern shows that options prices adjust to virtually eliminate profitable trading opportunities. Put differently, the implied cost of shorting falls as the desirability of shorting falls.

Although it is difficult to profit from the mispricing, one can always turn around the question and ask why anyone buys Palm. Options give investors a third way to buy Palm: they can buy Palm directly, buy it indirectly by buying 3Com, or buy it indirectly by buying calls (and selling puts). The second two methods are much cheaper than the first, so it is puzzling why anyone would buy Palm directly.

Figure 1: 3Com/Palm stub (2000)

Why buy Palm?

Putting aside the failure of arbitrage, the second question is why anyone would buy a share of Palm for $95.06 when they could buy a share of 3Com (embedding 1.5 shares of Palm) for $81.81. One superficially appealing explanation for the mispricing is that the price of Palm is high because demand for shares outstrips supply. While undoubtedly true, this does not explain much. Why were Palm shareholders content to pay so much more when cheaper choices where available (such as 3Com stock or Palm options)? At one point when the stub value of 3Com was negative, investors worth more than $2.5bn thought that Palm was a better buy than 3Com.

While it is impossible to say what, if anything, was going through these investors' minds, there are clues. Numerous press reports mentioned that without Palm, 3Com's future growth was expected to be lower. For example, in the week after the IPO, a headline from The Wall Street Journal read '3Com faces bleaker future without Palm'. Investors may have simply pursued the idea that Palm was good and 3Com was bad, without pausing to do the calculations.

More generally, early 2000 was a time of great optimism about technology stocks. Between February 1999 and February 2000, the tech-heavy Nasdaq Composite Index more than doubled. One dramatic illustration of this optimism occurred in Hong Kong. In February 2000, chaos erupted when crowds gathered at 10 banks and police were called. Some branches closed and others extended their hours to accommodate the mob. A bank run? Sort of. But instead of fighting to get their money out, people were fighting to get their money in. They were applying to subscribe to the IPO of tom.com, an internet company. According to some sources, 300,000 people queued to apply and more than 453,000 applications were submitted, so that almost 7 per cent of the population subscribed to the IPO.

Market implications

There are two important implications of the efficient market hypothesis. The first is that it is not easy to earn excess returns. The second is that prices are 'correct' in the sense that they reflect fundamental value. This latter implication is, in many ways, more

▶

important than the first. Do asset markets offer rational signals to the economy about where to invest real resources? If some companies have stock prices that are far from intrinsic value, they will attract too much or too little capital.

While important, this aspect of the efficient market hypothesis is difficult to test because intrinsic values are unobservable. That is why the example of 3Com and Palm is important. It demonstrates that market prices can be wrong when transaction costs prevent arbitrageurs from correcting market mistakes. The example casts doubt on the claim that market prices reflect only rational valuations because it is a case that should be particularly easy for the market to get right. If markets are failing this easy test, what else are they getting wrong?

Stock market prices affect the real world. When prices are wrong, the world suffers. The technology stock mania that peaked in 2000 had real consequences. Money, time and talent were poured into ventures that gave little return.

Financial economists have regarded 'frictions', such as transaction costs, as minor concerns. Using an analogy from physics, the trajectory of a ball thrown in the air can be predicted using a simple formula that ignores complications such as wind resistance; one can pretend the ball has been thrown into an airless vacuum. While all agree that transaction costs, like wind resistance, exist, the traditional view is that these minor deviations are safe to ignore.

This is a misleading analogy. The case of 3Com and Palm shows that frictions are not minor details, but are central to understanding how market prices are determined. It is as if the ball, rather than being thrown into a vacuum, were hurled into a tornado. Although one is sure that the ball will eventually return to earth, ignoring complications is not a good idea.

Source: Owen Lamont, *Financial Times*, *Mastering Investment Supplement*, Part 6, June 18 2001, pp. 8, 10. Reprinted with permission.

Discussion question

Can behavioural finance help to explain stock market bubbles and crashes?

Chapter 10

Stock options

After studying this chapter readers should be able to:

- *understand the profit and loss potential of call and put options*
- *appreciate the factors that affect option prices*
- *evaluate the risks and potential pay-offs from selling (writing) options*
- *understand the gearing effects of call options.*

Introduction

A stock option is the right to buy or sell a specified number of shares at a pre-arranged price on or before a particular date. A right to buy is referred to as a call option, and the right to sell a put option. There are two other important distinctions; first, between European-style and American-style options. European-style options can be exercised (the right to buy or sell can be used) only on the maturity date of the option, which is known as the expiry date. An American-style option can be exercised at any time up to and including the expiry date. It is to be noted that the distinction has nothing to do with geography. Both types of option are traded throughout the world.

The other distinction is between over-the-counter (OTC) options and exchange-traded options. OTC options are the result of private negotiations between two parties (typically a bank and a client). They may relate to any amount of any stock at any agreed price and have any expiry date. In other words, they can be tailor-made to the specific requirements of the client buying the option. Exchange-traded options are bought and sold on an organised exchange. They are standardised as to the amount and price of the stock and the available expiry dates. There is also a limitation as to which stocks are available. Contracts would provide a limited range of exercise prices and expiry dates. Most exchange-traded options are American-style.

Call options

A call option gives the buyer of that option the right, but not the obligation, to buy shares at a particular price. That price is known as the exercise or strike price. At the time of buying the option there will be at least two exercise prices available to choose from. For example, when the price of BP Amoco shares was 568p on 30 March 2001, the option exercise prices available were 550p and 600p. If the holder of a call option decides to exercise it, he or she will buy a specific number of shares at the strike price chosen when buying the option. The number of shares covered by one option contract varies from country to country; examples are USA 100, UK 1,000, Germany 50.

It could be profitable to exercise a call option if the market price of the stock turns out to be higher than the strike price. In the event of the market price being lower than the strike price, the option holder is not obliged to exercise, and presumably will not, since exercising would realise a loss. The buyer of an option thus has potential for profit without the risk of a loss. For this favourable situation, the buyer of an option pays a premium. Continuing the previous example, the premiums for BP Amoco call options, at the close of trading on 30 March 2001, were as shown in Table 10.1. January, April and July were expiry months. The expiry month of an option is the month in which it ceases to be exercisable. Option premiums (i.e. prices) are expressed in the same currency units as the shares, e.g. pence in the UK, dollars in the USA. Premiums are payable at the time the option is bought.

Example 10.1

An investor buys a 550p call option on BP Amoco shares at a premium of 27p per share when the share price is 568p. Since each option contract on LIFFE relates to 1,000 shares, the cash outflow is £270. (LIFFE is the acronym for the London International Financial Futures and Options Exchange – LIFFE is pronounced 'life'.) Subsequently, the share price rises to 650p. The investor can then exercise the right to buy at 550p. There is a 100p pay off (£1,000 per option contract). This 100p pay off is the intrinsic value of the option. The net profit must take account of the 27p premium paid for the option. The net profit is thus 100p − 27p = 73p (£730 per option contract). The investor has guaranteed that the effective price to be paid for the shares will not exceed 577p, this consisting of the strike price plus the premium paid for the option.

The profit/loss profile at expiry

Since an option buyer is not obliged to exercise an option, he or she has the right simply to disregard it. In such an event the premium paid is lost, but there will be

Table 10.1 Premiums for BP Amoco call options at close of trading on 30 March 2001

Strike price	Calls			Puts		
	April	July	October	April	July	October
550p	27p	49p	64p	7p	27.5p	36p
600p	5p	26.5p	41p	35p	55p	63p

The BP Amoco share price was 568p.

no further loss. The premium paid is the maximum loss that can be incurred. On the other hand, the profit potential is subject to no limits. In principle, there is no upper limit to the stock price and hence no upper limit to the potential profit from the option. Figure 10.1 shows the profit/loss profile of a call option at expiry.

The option used for the illustration is the April 550p BP Amoco call whose premium is 27p. If the buyer holds the option to the expiry date and the share price turns out to be 550p or less, there will be no point in exercising the option. There is no benefit from exercising an option to buy shares at 550p when those shares can be bought at the same, or a lower, price in the market. In such a situation, the option buyer makes a net loss because of the payment of the 27p premium, which is non-returnable. This is shown in Figure 10.1, which depicts a loss of 27p at all stock prices up to 550p.

If the price of the share turns out to be greater than 550p, it could be worthwhile to exercise the option. The option holder could choose to exercise the right to buy at 550p and then immediately sell the shares at the higher price, thereby realising a profit. At a share price of 577p, this gross profit would exactly offset the premium paid. Hence, 577p is the breakeven price at which net profit is zero. At prices above 577p, the gross profit exceeds the premium so that there is a net profit. (These figures would need some adjustment if bid-ask spreads and commission costs were to be taken into account.)

The gross profit referred to is alternatively known as the intrinsic value of the option. Intrinsic value can be defined as the pay-off to be obtained by immediately

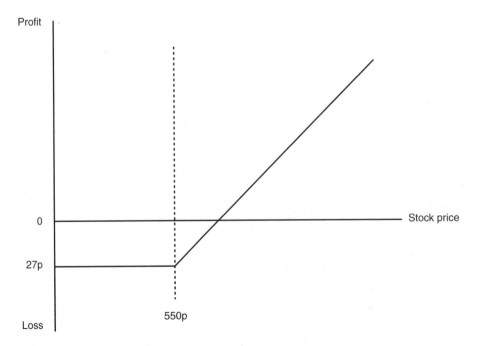

Figure 10.1 Profit/loss profile of a call option at expiry

exercising the option (disregarding the premium) and is equal to the difference between the exercise price and the market price of the stock when the option is in-the-money.

An in-the-money call option is one whose exercise price is less than the market price of the stock and which therefore offers an immediate gross profit. An at-the-money option is one whose exercise price is equal to the market price. An out-of-the-money call option is one whose exercise price is greater than the market price. Only in-the-money options have intrinsic value.

The profit/loss profile prior to expiry

At the time that a traded option expires, its price (premium) will be equal to its intrinsic value. Prior to expiry the premium would normally exceed the intrinsic value. This excess of the price of the option over the intrinsic value is known as the time value. When an option is exercised, only the intrinsic value is realised. The seller of an option would obtain a price that incorporates time value as well as the intrinsic value – see Figure 10.2.

Time value is at its highest when the option is at-the-money. Time value declines as the option moves either into or out of the money and will approach zero as the market price of the stock diverges substantially from the exercise (strike) price.

When account is taken of the time value, the profit/loss profile of an option differs from the at-expiry profile depicted in Figure 10.1. A prior-to-expiry profile is shown by the broken curve in Figure 10.3.

The broken curve indicates the market price of the option minus the initial premium paid (27p in this case). The net profit shown by this prior-to-expiry profile is the price that the trader could sell the option for, minus the price (premium) that was paid for it. At stock prices below the option exercise price, the option premium consists of time value only. Above the exercise price, the option premium consists of both time and intrinsic value.

Determinants of the option price (premium)

The explanation of an option premium subdivides into ascertaining intrinsic value and assessing the influences on time value. The intrinsic value of a call option is

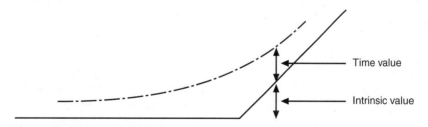

Figure 10.2 Time value and Intrinsic value

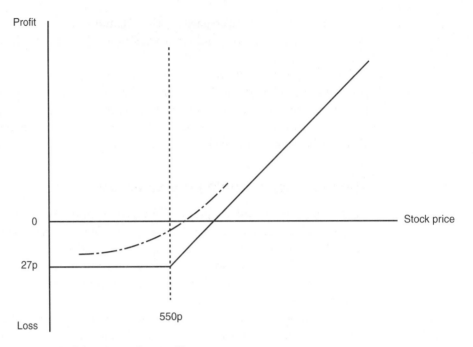

Figure 10.3 Prior-to-expiry profile

equal to the stock price minus the exercise price of the option, with zero being the minimum intrinsic value. In principle, the option premium cannot fall below the intrinsic value. If the option premium were below the intrinsic value, there would be a guaranteed profit from buying the option and immediately exercising it (and selling the shares acquired). It would be irrational for anyone to sell an option for a price that is less than its intrinsic value, since more could be obtained from exercising it.

The determination of time value is more complex. Major influences on time value are the expected volatility of the stock price, the length of the period remaining to the expiry date, and the extent to which the option is in or out of the money.

The higher the expected volatility, the greater will be the premium. An option on a volatile stock has a strong chance of acquiring intrinsic value at some stage prior to expiry. Similarly, the probability of an option acquiring intrinsic value prior to expiry rises with the length of time remaining to its expiry date. It can be seen from Table 10.1 that the options with the more distant expiry dates have the higher premiums.

Time value is at its peak when the option is at-the-money and declines as the option moves either into or out of the money. Out-of-the-money options have less time value than at-the-money options because the stock price has further to move before intrinsic value is acquired. In-the-money options have less time value than at-the-money options since their prices contain intrinsic value which is vulnerable to a fall in the stock price, whereas at-the-money option premiums contain no intrinsic value. The risk that existing intrinsic value might be lost reduces the attractiveness of the option and lowers its price.

● ● ● ● Put options

A put option gives its holder the right, but not the obligation, to sell shares at a specified price prior to, or on, the expiry date of the option. The holder of an option can exercise it, sell it or allow it to expire. It is worthwhile exercising an option – that is, exercising the right to sell shares at the strike (exercise) price – only if the market price of the stock turns out to be lower than the strike price. If the strike price is greater than the stock price, the option is said to have intrinsic value. The intrinsic value would be equal to the excess of the strike price over the stock price. An option without intrinsic value might simply be allowed to expire since its holder is not obliged to exercise it and presumably would not if the strike price were below the market price of the stock (it would be better to sell the stock in the market).

Table 10.1 shows the premiums of BP Amoco put options at the close of trading on 30 March 2001. The price of BP Amoco shares was 568p. The months referred to are expiry months. At any one time the buyer of a BP Amoco put option would have three expiry dates from which to choose. When the April expiry date is reached, options with a January expiry date will be introduced. Substantial movements of the stock price would invoke the introduction of additional strike prices so that there are strike prices either side of the stock price. As a result the number of available strike prices would exceed two.

Example 10.2

An investor buys a 550p put option on BP Amoco shares at a premium of 7p per share when the share price is 568p. Since each option contract relates to 1,000 shares, the cash outflow is £70. Subsequently, the share price falls to 400p. The investor can exercise the right to sell at 550p. There is a gross profit from the option of 150p (£1,500 per option contract). This gross profit of 150p is the intrinsic value of the option. The net profit from the option must take account of the 7p premium paid for the option. The net profit is thus 150p − 7p = 143p (£1,430 per option contract). The investor has guaranteed that the effective selling price of the shares cannot fall below 543p, this sum being the sale receipts of 550p minus the 7p premium paid for the option.

The profit/loss profile at expiry

In the case of traded stock options, the premium is usually payable in full on the day following the purchase of the option. However, since the buyer is not obliged to exercise the option and presumably will not do so if it involves selling at less than the market price of the share, the premium paid is the maximum loss the buyer of the option can incur. So, for example, a buyer of BP Amoco April 550p puts faces a maximum loss of 7p per share, which amounts to £70 per contract, since each put option contract is for the sale of 1,000 shares.

The maximum profit is limited only by the fact that stock prices cannot fall below zero. Since a stock price can fall to zero, the net gain from a put option can be as much as the strike price minus the premium paid. The buyer of April 550p BP Amoco puts stands to gain as much as 550p − 7p per share. This amounts to £5,430 per option contract.

Figure 10.4 shows the profit/loss profile of BP Amoco April 550p puts at expiry (i.e. on the day in April upon which the option ceases to be capable of being exercised). If the stock price is 550p or higher when the option expires, the holder of the option records a net loss of 7p per share (£70 per option contract). If the stock price turns out to be less than 550p there is a gross profit to be made by exercising the option. Exercising the option will allow the option holder to sell shares at 550p while buying them at a lower price. This gross profit from exercising the option minus the premium paid is the net profit. If the stock price lies between 543p and 550p there is a net loss, whereas below the breakeven stock price of 543p there is a net profit.

The profit/loss profile prior to expiry

Intrinsic value is the gross profit to be made from exercising the option. At expiry an option would have only intrinsic value, which could be equal to zero. Prior to expiry the option would have time value as well as intrinsic value. The profit/loss profile of Figure 10.4 is based on intrinsic value only. Since intrinsic value is the

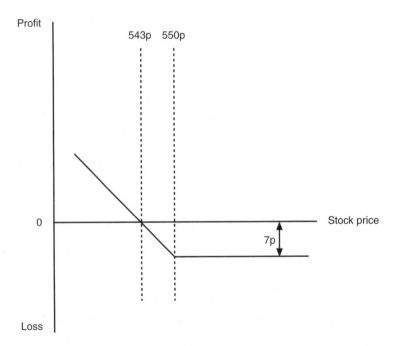

Figure 10.4 Profit/loss profile of BP Amoco April 550p puts at expiry

gross profit to be made from exercising the option it will be zero at stock prices at or above the strike price of 550p, whereas below 550p it will be equal to the difference between the stock price and the strike price. The net profit or loss at expiry is equal to the intrinsic value minus the premium paid.

Prior to expiry the price of an option will exceed its intrinsic value. The difference is the time value and is shown by the vertical distance between the prior-to-expiry profile and the at-expiry profile in Figure 10.5.

The prior-to-expiry profile indicates the current market price of the option minus the price that the present holder paid for it. As time passes, the prior-to-expiry profile will tend to converge on to the at-expiry profile, with the convergence becoming complete as expiry is reached.

This convergence reflects the tendency for the time value of an option to decline with the passage of time. This erosion of time value can be explained in terms of the likelihood of a substantial increase in intrinsic value falling as the time available for the requisite stock price movement declines. A second factor affecting time value is the expected volatility of the stock price. With high volatility there is a relatively high chance of substantial gains in intrinsic value at some stage prior to expiry. So, the greater the expected volatility of a stock price, the greater will be the time value of an option on that stock.

A third factor affecting time value is the relationship between the stock price and the strike price of the option. Time value is at its highest when the stock price is equal to the strike price. When the stock price is equal to the strike price, the option

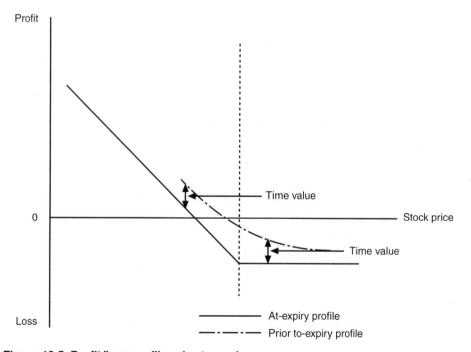

Figure 10.5 Profit/loss profile prior to expiry

is said to be at-the-money. As the stock price and strike price diverge, in either direction, time value declines.

When the stock price exceeds the strike price, the put option is said to be out-of-the-money. A better price can be obtained by selling the shares in the market than by exercising the option. Time value declines as the option moves further out of the money (in other words, as the stock price rises), reflecting the decreasing likelihood of the stock price declining sufficiently to cause exercise of the option to become profitable.

When the stock price is lower than the strike price, the put option is said to be in-the-money. A better price can be obtained by exercising the option than by selling the shares in the market. The option has intrinsic value since there would be a pay-off from immediate exercise of the option.

Time value declines as the option becomes deeper in the money (i.e. as the stock price falls). This can be understood in terms of there being an increasing amount of intrinsic value that is at risk of being lost. The price of an in-the-money option contains the intrinsic value of that option. The buyer of an in-the-money option bears this risk, whereas the buyer of an at-the-money option does not. The risk borne rises as the option becomes deeper in the money. This risk is reflected in the time value. The buyer of an at-the-money option pays a higher price for time value than the buyer of an in-the-money option, with the price paid for time value declining as the option becomes deeper in the money.

Writing options

For every buyer of an option there must be a seller. The seller of an option is often referred to as the writer. The buyer of an option is said to have a long option position, whereas the writer of the option is said to have a short position. The profit/loss profile of a short (written) option is the mirror image of that of the long (bought) option. Profits of the buyer must equal losses of the seller, and vice versa. Figures 10.6 and 10.7 compare long and short positions for call and put options respectively.

The premium paid by the buyer obviously equals the premium received by the writer. The profit (loss) of the buyer will always equal the loss (profit) of the writer. It should be noted that the buyer of a call option has loss potential limited to the premium paid, but unlimited profit potential. Conversely, the writer of a call has a maximum profit equal to the premium received, but unlimited loss potential. In the case of put options, the buyer has a maximum loss equal to the premium, which constitutes the maximum profit of the writer. With put options the maximum profit of the buyer (maximum loss of the writer) occurs at a stock price of zero.

In the case of traded options, a long option position can be closed out by selling an identical option, leaving no option position remaining. Likewise, a written option can be closed out by buying an identical option.

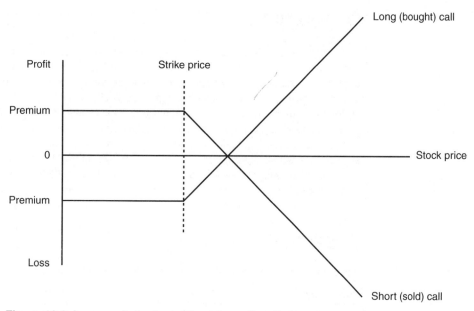

Figure 10.6 Long and short positions for call options

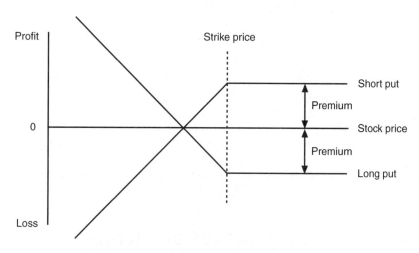

Figure 10.7 Long and short positions for put options

Example 10.3

An investor writes a 550p call option on BP Amoco shares at a premium of 27p per share when the share price is 568p. Since each option contract on LIFFE relates to 1,000 shares, the premium receipts amount to £270. Subsequently, the share price rises to 650p. An option buyer might then exercise the right to buy shares at 550p. If the option writer is assigned to the option buyer (assignment of writers to meet the requirements of buyers who exercise is usually carried out on a random basis), the writer must sell shares for 550p to the option buyer. The option writer may need to buy shares at 650p in order to sell them at 550p. This entails a gross loss of 100p (the intrinsic value of the option). Taking account of the option premium received indicates a net loss of 73p (£730 per option contract). The loss of the option writer is equal to the profit of the option buyer.

Exercise 10.1

It is 6 January. The Lonrho share price is 662p. Lonrho March expiry option prices are:

Strike price	Calls	Puts
650	55	43

(a) Calculate the intrinsic and time value for both of the options.
(b) Suggest two alternative option strategies for profiting from a price rise. In each case what would be the profit, or loss, in the event of the share price reaching (i) 700p, and (ii) 800p, by the expiry date of the option?

Answers
(a) Calls: intrinsic value 662 − 650 = 12p , time value 55 − 12 = 43p.
    Puts: intrinsic value 0, time value 43p.
(b) Buy a call: at 700p there would be a net cash flow of 700p − 650p − 55p = −5p,
        i.e. a loss of 5p.
        at 800p there would be a net cash flow of 800p − 650p − 55p = 95p,
        i.e. a profit of 95p.
    Write a put: at 700p there would be a net cash flow of 43p, i.e. a profit of 43p.
        at 800p there would be a net cash flow of 43p, i.e. a profit of 43p.

Market practices and terms

All the call options on a particular underlying stock together constitute a class of options. Similarly, all the puts on the same underlying stock together comprise another class. Within each class there will be a number of series. An option series is specific to a particular exercise price and a particular expiry month, as well as to a particular stock and call/put categorisation. So, for example, $50 December calls and $60 January calls on the stock of ABC are two different series within the same class (the class being ABC call options).

An opening purchase is a transaction whereby the buyer of an option becomes its holder; a closing purchase is a transaction in which a writer of an option buys an option identical to the one previously written, whereupon the two positions are deemed to cancel each other out. An opening sale is a transaction in which the seller of an option becomes its writer; a closing sale involves the cancellation of a previously purchased option.

Premiums in respect of traded options are normally payable via the broker to the clearing house on the morning following the day of the trade. Payment to the writer of the option would come from the clearing house, which usually acts as a registrar for all open contracts. If the holder of an option exercises it, the clearing house, using a random selection process, chooses a writer who is then assigned to sell shares (in the case of calls) or buy shares (in the case of puts) to or from the holder of the option at the exercise price.

There are often position limits to the number of options in any one class that can be held or written by any one individual or organisation.

The effects of gearing

Options can be looked upon as either low-risk or high-risk instruments. In both cases the interpretation of risk is based upon the gearing effect offered by options. An option can be bought for a fraction of the price of the stock to which the option relates. The maximum loss from buying stock is the price of that stock, whereas the maximum loss from buying a call option on that stock is the option premium. So buying a call option on 1,000 shares of stock can be seen as less risky than buying 1,000 shares of stock.

However, if the choice is between investing £1,000 in stock and spending £1,000 on stock options, the options are the more risky. Again, this arises from the gearing offered by the options. Since the price of the option is a fraction of the price of the stock, percentage changes in the option price are prone to be much greater than percentage changes in the stock price. Suppose that XYZ stock is priced at 100 and a call option to buy at 100 is priced at 5. A rise in the stock price to 110 might plausibly cause a rise in the option price to 13. The stock price rises by 10%, whereas the option price rises by 160%. This arises from the gearing offered by the option. However, the possibility of high percentage profits is accompanied by potential large percentage losses. A fall in the stock price to 90 might cause a fall in the option price to 3. The 10% fall in the stock price is accompanied by a 40% drop in the option premium (and hence a 40% loss on the option). It may be that a more substantial fall in the stock price, say to 75, virtually eliminates the value of the option so that a 25% fall in the stock price brings about a 100% fall in the option price. So if the choice is between £1,000 invested in stock and £1,000 in options, the latter is the more risky.

The foregoing example involved an at-the-money option gaining just 8 in value as a result of the stock price rising by 10. One might think that the right to buy at 100 should rise in price by 10 as a result of a rise in the stock price from 100 to 110. However, although there is an additional 10 in intrinsic value, the other component of the option premium, time value, falls as the stock price moves away from the option strike price (the initial option price of 5 was entirely time value; at the stock price of 110, the time value of the option is 3). The change in the option price as a proportion of the change in the stock price is known as the delta of the option (in the present example the delta is $(13 - 5)/10 = 0.8$).

Chapter 11

Option related investments

After studying this chapter readers should be able to:

- *Appreciate the return potential and risks of warrants*
- *understand the nature and investment potential of convertible bonds*
- *construct options funds*
- *analyse split-capital investment trusts.*

Warrants

Warrants are long-term options. They may have expiry dates that lie as much as five years or more in the future (in contrast to stock options which often have a maximum life of nine months). Most warrants are issued by the company upon whose shares they are based. If they are exercised, the company will issue new shares. So, unlike options, warrants are usually used as a means of raising corporate finance. The issuing company receives the money from the sale of the warrants and subsequently receives the money paid upon exercise. In contrast to options, warrants entail the expansion of the number of shares in issue.

Warrants are often attached to company debt, such as loan stock, when they are issued. The presence of such warrants renders the debt more attractive to the investor, and hence the issuing company can raise money on more advantageous terms in that it needs to pay a lower rate of interest than would otherwise be the case. In most instances, the warrant is detachable from the host debt instrument and can be traded in its own right. Some warrants are issued naked, i.e. without the presence of corporate debt instruments. Since warrants pay no dividend or coupon, they provide an issuing company with a source of finance that involves no servicing costs.

Some warrants are not connected with the raising of corporate finance. Third party warrants (sometimes named 'covered' warrants) might be written by a bank without any involvement of the company on whose stock the warrants are based. One type of third party warrant is, however, used for the raising of corporate finance. This involves the company that is raising the finance issuing warrants on the stock of another company. Third party warrants do not entail the issue of new shares upon exercise of the warrants.

● ● ● ● Convertible bonds

A convertible might be looked upon as a corporate bond with an attached warrant (which cannot be detached from the bond). Convertibles are often referred to as convertible loan stock (or convertible unsecured loan stock, since most are unsecured) and involve the right to convert the loan stock into shares at specified rates and points in time. Convertible preference shares are preference shares with the right to convert to ordinary shares. Some convertibles provide the right to convert to other loan stock rather than shares.

The number of shares for which the bond can be exchanged is referred to as the conversion rate. So, for example, the convertible may allow the conversion of £100 par value of loan stock into 20 shares. Multiplication of the conversion rate by the share price provides the conversion value. A share price of £6 would imply a conversion value of £120. Convertible loan stock would also exhibit an investment, or straight bond, value. This is the value of the bond in the absence of the right to convert. The investment value is the price of a corresponding straight bond.

The market value of a convertible would normally be higher than the greater of the conversion and investment values. The excess of the market value over the greater of the conversion or investment value is often referred to as the premium. Figure 11.1 illustrates the relationship between the conversion, investment and market values of a convertible. It is assumed that the conversion rate is 20 and that the investment value is £90 per £100 par value. The market value (price) of the convertible is shown by the broken line.

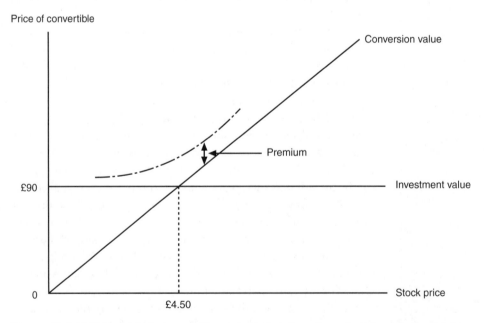

Figure 11.1 Relationship between the conversion, investment and market values of a convertible

It must be realised that the investment value, and hence the strike price of the implicit option, is not immutable. A rise in interest rates would lower the investment value and strike price. Similar effects would arise from a decline in the credit standing of the company. Such a decline in credit standing requires a higher rate of return which, given a constant coupon, implies a fall in the price of the loan stock.

Convertibles are hybrids in that they constitute a compromise between bonds and shares. They provide more upside exposure to share price movements than bonds, but less than ordinary shares. They provide less downside protection than bonds, but more than shares. The percentage rate of dividend or coupon yield would be less than that of a straight bond (because the market value exceeds the investment value), but probably more than that of the ordinary share (a rate of dividend yield on the share that exceeds the rate of coupon yield on the convertible would probably induce conversion of the convertible into the share).

The fact that a convertible involves a lower rate of coupon yield than a straight bond renders it attractive to the issuer. The attached warrant causes the investor to require a lower coupon yield. Convertibles thus provide a cheaper source of finance than loan stock or preference shares. Their advantage over ordinary shares, from the point of view of the issuer, is that they constitute a form of deferred equity. In particular, voting rights do not accrue to the holder until conversion takes place.

Holders of a convertible have the right to convert during a conversion period. If conversion does not take place during that period, the convertible might simply become a loan stock or preference share. So, for example, a convertible might offer the right to convert on 1 June of the sixth, seventh, eighth, ninth or tenth year of its life and, if conversion does not take place on any of those dates, it then becomes unsecured loan stock maturing at the end of a life of a further ten years, at which point it would be redeemed at par. The conversion rate would normally imply a high purchase price of the share (if acquired through conversion) on the issue date of the convertible so that a significant share price advance would be necessary for conversion to become worthwhile. The conversion price is the market value of the convertible divided by the number of shares obtained upon conversion. At the time that the convertible is issued, the conversion price will be greater than the share price.

The question arises as to why the holder of a convertible would exercise the right to convert, since it might be expected that the market value would exceed the conversion value so that the sale of the convertible appears to be preferable to conversion. The circumstances in which conversion would take place are (1) call by the issuing corporation, (2) the existence of a final conversion date, or (3) the dividend yield of the share rising above the coupon yield of the convertible.

Sometimes the issuer of the convertible has the right to call it. This means that the holder must either accept redemption of the convertible (probably at the par value of the loan stock) or convert it into shares. If the latter provides the greater value, conversion will take place. When the final conversion date passes, the implicit option disappears, leaving only the investment value of the convertible. If the conversion value exceeds the investment value on the final conversion date, it would be rational to exercise the right to convert.

The excess of the conversion price over the share price, when expressed as a percentage of the share price, is known as the conversion premium:

Conversion price = Market value of convertible / Number of shares on conversion

Conversion premium (%) = {(Conversion price − Share price) / Share price} × 100

In most circumstances the conversion premium would be positive. However, a time may come when the dividend on the share exceeds the coupon on the convertible (the coupon is fixed, whereas the dividend is likely to rise over time). If conversion dates are at distant intervals (such as a year apart), the prospect of a lower rate of yield on the convertible than on the share could render it less valuable than the shares into which it might be converted. So a share dividend above the coupon of the convertible, together with a long time before the next conversion date, could entail a negative conversion premium. The prospect of a negative conversion premium subsequent to a conversion date could lead to conversion on that date.

Exercise 11.1

A convertible bond has a maturity of ten years and a conversion rate of 100. The current share price is £1.10p. Conversion can take place on 1 June of the fifth, sixth, seventh and eighth years.

(a) Calculate the conversion value.
(b) What would be the significance for the market value of the convertible if conversion could take place in year five only, rather than in any of the four years?

Answers
(a) Conversion value = 100 × £1.10 = £110
(b) The ability to convert in year five only would reduce the time to expiry of the implicit option and hence reduce its time value. So the convertible should have a lower market value.

Options funds (guaranteed investment funds)

Options funds, or guaranteed investment funds, are a means of providing some of the potential profits from stock market investment whilst guaranteeing the return of the investors' capital. Such funds are marketed under a variety of different names such as guaranteed investment bonds, guaranteed equity bonds, guaranteed investment accounts and guaranteed capital bonds. They are investments for fixed terms, often five years. These funds typically guarantee the return of at least the initial investment plus a proportion, such as 70%, of any increase in a stock market index.

The risks are of opportunity costs. The opportunity cost, when compared with a bank deposit, is the interest foregone. The opportunity cost, when compared with buying shares, is the proportion of the stock market profit that fails to accrue to the investors (typically some of the capital gain and all of the dividends).

Investors should be aware that generally the guarantees apply only if the investments are held for the full fixed term. Another potential problem concerns taxation. Many of the funds are subject to income tax rather than capital gains tax. This is a disadvantage for many investors, since it is often the case that an individual is above the threshold for paying income tax but below the threshold for paying capital gains tax.

An options fund is characterised by upside exposure to a stock index together with a lower limit to the value of the fund. This profile of returns can be achieved in two main ways. One is the fiduciary call, which involves investment in risk-free assets (such as bank deposits) and call options. The risk-free assets provide the guaranteed minimum value, while the call options provide the exposure to the stock market.

The fiduciary call approach involves calculating the present value of the guaranteed sum and investing it in bank deposits (or other risk-free assets such as Treasury bills). This generates the minimum value upon maturity of the fund. The remainder is used to buy call options. The cost of the downside protection is reduced profit on the upside. Potential returns from a rising stock market are less than would be obtained if the entire fund were to be invested in shares.

Whether guaranteed investment funds turn out to perform better than the alternatives, of a bank deposit or investment in shares, depends upon the performance of the stock market. This is illustrated by Exercise 11.2.

Exercise 11.2

(a) A fund manager has £1,000,000 and invests £952,381 in a bank deposit for one year at 5% p.a. The remaining £47,619 is used to buy a FTSE 100 at-the-money call option on £900,000 of stock when the FTSE 100 stands at 5,000. The option expires in one year. What is the value of the fund at the end of one year if the FTSE 100 is (i) 4,000, (ii) 5,000, (iii) 6,000 and (iv) 7,000.

(b) How does the investment strategy in (a) compare with (1) investing the £1,000,000 in a bank deposit and (2) investing the £1,000,000 in a balanced portfolio of FTSE 100 shares?

Answers

(a) (i) £1,000,000, (ii) £1,000,000, (iii) £1,180,000, (iv) £1,360,000.

(b)

(1) In cases (i) and (ii) the investment strategy in (a) is inferior to the deposit by £50,000 (5% interest on £1,000,000). In cases (iii) and (iv) the strategy in (a) is superior to the deposit by £130,000 and £310,000 respectively (since the deposit of £1,000,000 would grow to £1,050,000).

(2) In case (i) the strategy in (a) is superior to the investment in shares (which would have provided £800,000 plus dividends). In case (ii) the strategy in (a) is inferior to the investment in shares by the amount of the dividend yield on the shares. In case (iii) the investment in shares would have provided £1,200,000 plus dividends, and in case (iv) the share investment would have produced £1,400,000 plus dividends. So in cases (iii) and (iv) the investment in shares would have out-performed the strategy in (a).

The other main approach is that of the protective put. This consists of a holding of stock together with put options that guarantee a minimum value of that shareholding. Protective put strategies (sometimes referred to as portfolio insurance) also tend to involve some investment in risk-free assets in order to fully guarantee the minimum value. The minimum value is ensured by a combination of an investment in assets such as bank deposits, and a lowest possible value of the shareholding based on the strike price of the put options.

In the case of options funds created using the protective put approach, since the guaranteed minimum value is provided from two sources – the investment in risk-free assets and a shareholding combined with put options – it is necessary to use simultaneous equations to calculate the amounts of the constituent components. If M is the guaranteed minimum value, X is the amount to be invested in risk-free assets, K is the option strike price, r is the interest rate on risk-free assets, T is the maturity of the fund and N is the number of put options (which matches the amount of stock purchased), then:

$$M = X(1 + r)^T + NK$$

i.e. the guaranteed minimum fund value equals the maturity value of the investment in risk-free assets plus the minimum value of the shareholding guaranteed by the put options.

The value of N can be calculated as:

$$N = (V - X)/(S + P)$$

where V is the value of the fund, S is the value of stock covered by one option and P is the price of a put option. N is thus the number of combinations of stock and put option that can be purchased after X has been allocated to investment in risk-free assets.

The two equations can be simultaneously solved for X and N. In this way, the amount to be invested in risk-free assets can be ascertained together with the number of matched combinations of stock and put option.

High yield funds

Another use of options, in the construction of funds, is their use in enhancing income. In some high-yield funds, options are written and the premiums received are used to enhance the income paid to investors. This is likely to be at the cost of the capital value of the funds. Such a fund is illustrated by Exercise 11.3.

Exercise 11.3

A high yield fund has £10,000,000 in a balanced portfolio of FTSE 100 shares. The dividend yield of 3% p.a. is added to by way of the premium receipts from writing options. The FTSE 100 stands at 5000 and the investment horizon is one year. The fund manager writes European style options that expire in one year. FTSE 100 option prices are:

Strike price	Calls	Puts
4900	315	205
5000	250	240
5100	215	305

What would the income yield be if the equity exposure were matched by written:

(a) out-of the-money call options?
(b) at-the-money call and put options?
(c) out-of-the-money call and put options?
(d) What are the risks to investors in these three cases?

Answers

(a) 215/5000 = 4.3. The total income yield becomes 3% + 4.3% = 7.3%. (Dividends plus option premium receipts)
(b) (250+240)/5000 = 9.8. The total income yield becomes 3% + 9.8% = 12.8%.
(c) (215+205)/5000 = 8.4. The total income yield becomes 3% + 8.4% = 11.4%.
(d) In the case of (a) the investor risks losing part of any increase in share prices so that long-term capital growth is reduced. In the case of (b) any movement, up or down, of the index would reduce the value of the fund. In the case of (c), upward movements are restricted and downward movements may be exaggerated. In all three cases, the increased income yield could be at the expense of the capital value of the fund.

● ● ● ● Split-capital investment trusts

Closed-end funds, such as investment trusts, have become the source of various financially engineered investments. One approach has been to divide funds into income shares and capital shares. Buyers of income shares receive all of the dividends from the fund but are entitled to only a pre-set amount of capital, which could be the initial share price, when the fund is wound up. Such funds have a pre-determined date on which the assets of the fund are sold and the proceeds returned to investors in the fund.

The holders of the capital shares of a split-capital investment trust receive all or most of the capital growth from the fund. In effect they hold call options on the fund, with the capital returnable to holders of income shares constituting the strike price of the call options.

The holders of the income shares of a split-capital trust are effectively the sellers (writers) of put options, since there is a maximum return of capital but no minimum other than zero. If the fund becomes bankrupt, there will be no capital to be returned to investors.

The combined position of the holders of the income and capital shares is illustrated by Figure 11.2. Adding the values of the income and capital shares produces the value of an ordinary share (an ordinary share constitutes an income share plus a capital share). Figure 11.2 illustrates the case in which the capital returnable to holders of income shares equals the initial (issue) price of the ordinary shares.

Another way in which a closed-end fund (investment trust) might take a split-capital form is through division into geared ordinary shares and zero dividend preference shares (sometimes referred to simply as zeros). Money raised from the issue of zero dividend preference shares is used to fund additional investment by the investment trust. The fund is thus geared (i.e. partly financed by borrowing) and in consequence the ordinary shares of the fund can be regarded as being geared. A geared ordinary share might be looked upon as an ordinary share partly financed through borrowing by means of the issue of zero dividend preference shares. Geared ordinary shares receive all of the dividends and some of the capital growth.

The zero dividend preference shares would have redemption values above their initial issue price. The difference between the redemption value and the issue price of the zero dividend preference shares provides the investment return to their holders. If capital growth is more than that required to meet the redemption value, the surplus capital growth accrues to the holders of the geared ordinary shares.

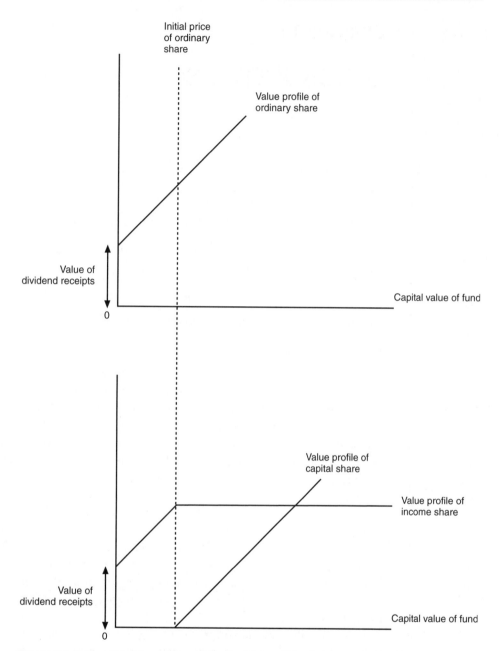

Figure 11.2 Combined position of the holders of the income and capital shares

Chapter 12

Stock indices

After studying this chapter the reader should be able to:

- *indicate how stock indices differ in respect to the method of calculation*
- *use unweighted, price weighted and value weighted approaches to the calculation of stock indices*
- *use arithmetic and geometric means in the calculation of stock indices*
- *adjust for changes in the constituent stocks of an index*
- *evaluate alternative stock indices.*

Stock indices are measures of the price performance of stock portfolios which may be seen as representative of a stock market as a whole, or a segment of the market. The better known indices include the Dow Jones Industrial Average, the Standard & Poor's 500, and the NASDAQ in the United States; the FTSE 100 in the United Kingdom; the Nikkei 225 in Japan; the DAX in Germany; the CAC 40 in France; and the Hang Seng in Hong Kong. All countries with stock markets have at least one index, and some countries (in particular the United States) have numerous indices.

Indices are not only calculated for national stock markets. There are also regional and global market indices. For example the FTSE Eurotop 300 measures the performance of the shares of the 300 largest companies in Europe. The index represents about 70% of the region's total market capitalisation. The index is broken down into three regional sub-indices: one for Eurotop 300 companies located in the euro-zone, one for those outside the euro-zone, and one excluding companies located in the UK.

Indices are also calculated for bonds. There are indices of bond yields as well as indices of bond prices. Each bond index relates to a particular type of issuer (e.g. government, AAA rated corporate, etc.) and to a specific maturity band.

This chapter is primarily concerned with the mechanics of the calculation of indices. This is of importance since it determines the comparability of the movements of different indices, and the interpretation that can be put upon a change in a particular index. Indices can be categorised in a number of ways: (i) the number of stocks included; (ii) the method of weighting the stock prices; and (iii) the nature of the averaging.

The number of stocks can vary from a small number of large company stocks (for example, the Dow Jones Industrial Average is based on just 30 stocks) to inclusion of every stock traded on a particular market (for example the New York Stock Exchange Composite Index). The indices based on a small number of stocks have the advantage of easy calculation, but the disadvantage of being imperfectly representative of the market as a whole.

The contribution of individual stock prices to an index may be unweighted (as in the case of the Financial Times Ordinary Share Index), value weighted (for example the Financial Times Stock Exchange [FTSE]100) or price weighted (such as the Dow Jones Industrial Average).

In the case of unweighted indices an average of daily rates of price change is calculated each day. The product of such changes (that is multiplying them together) since a base date provides the index. Such a calculation gives all stocks equal influence irrespective of the sizes of the companies. To illustrate the calculation of an unweighted index, suppose that it is to be based on just three stocks whose prices and numbers issued are as shown in Table 12.1. It is further supposed (a) that stock A rises in price by 15% while the other two prices remain unchanged, and (b) that stock C undergoes a 15% price rise while the other two prices remain constant. Before the price rise, the index equals 100.

In the event of a 15% rise in the price of A, the new index will be (using arithmetic means):

$$\frac{\text{New value}}{\text{Old value}} \times 100 = \frac{(1.15 + 1 + 1)}{(1 + 1 + 1)} \times 100 = 1.05 \times 100 = 105$$

If the price of C rises by 15%, the new index will be:

$$\frac{\text{New value}}{\text{Old value}} \times 100 = \frac{(1 + 1 + 1.15)}{(1 + 1 + 1)} \times 100 = 1.05 \times 100 = 105$$

It can be seen that a 15% rise in either stock price has the same effect on the index despite the fact that C has a higher stock price and is issued by a larger company.

Price weighted indices weight percentage price increases by the initial stock prices. The index at time T can be calculated as follows:

$$\frac{\text{Sum of stock prices at time T}}{\text{Sum of stock prices on the base date}} \times \text{Base value}$$

The calculations, using the data in Table 12.1 and 15% price rises for stocks A and C respectively but based on a price weighted approach, produce the following indices:

Table 12.1 Prices and numbers of three stocks

Stock	Price	Number of shares
A	50p	10 million
B	100p	10 million
C	200p	5 million

(a) $\dfrac{\text{New value}}{\text{Old value}} \times 100 = \dfrac{(57.5\text{p} + 100\text{p} + 200\text{p})}{(50\text{p} + 100\text{p} + 200\text{p})} \times 100$

$\qquad = 1.0215 \times 100 = 102.15$

(b) $\dfrac{\text{New value}}{\text{Old value}} \times 100 = \dfrac{(50\text{p} + 100\text{p} + 230\text{p})}{(50\text{p} + 100\text{p} + 200\text{p})} \times 100 = 1.086 \times 100 = 108.6$

It can be seen that the impact on the index is four times as great when the price rise is in stock C rather than stock A. This reflects the fact that stock price C is initially four times stock price A. So high priced stocks have the greatest influence on the index.

Using the same example but calculating a value weighted index (weighting percentage increases by the market capitalisations of the companies: that is, stock price times number of shares issued) may be based on the formula:

$$\text{Index at time T} = \dfrac{\text{Sum of the market capitalisations at time T}}{\text{Sum of the market capitalisations on the base date}}$$
$$\times \text{ Base value}$$

Using the figures from the previous example, a 15% increase in the price of stock A raises the index from 100 to:

$\dfrac{\text{New value}}{\text{Old value}} \times 100 = \dfrac{(£5.75\text{m} + £10\text{m} + £10\text{m})}{(£5\text{m} + £10\text{m} + £10\text{m})} \times 100 = 1.03 \times 100 = 103$

whereas a 15% increase in the price of stock C raises the index to:

$\dfrac{\text{New value}}{\text{Old value}} \times 100 = \dfrac{(£5\text{m} + £10\text{m} + £11.5\text{m})}{(£5\text{m} + £10\text{m} + £10\text{m})} \times 100 = 1.06 \times 100 = 106$

The impact of the rise in stock price C is double that of the rise in stock price A. This reflects the fact that the initial market capitalisation of C (200p × 5 million) is twice that of A (50p × 10 million). When indices are value weighted, large companies have the greatest influence. Rather than using the full market capitalisation, some indices use the value of shares available to investors in the free float. This alternative excludes shares held by the issuer and not available for purchase by investors.

All the calculations thus far have used arithmetic means. It is interesting to repeat the calculations using geometric means. The computations and resulting indices are as follows:

Unweighted

(a) $\dfrac{\text{New value}}{\text{Old value}} \times 100 = \dfrac{\sqrt[3]{(1.15 \times 1 \times 1)}}{\sqrt[3]{(1 \times 1 \times 1)}} \times 100 = \sqrt[3]{1.15} \times 100 = 104.8$

(b) $\dfrac{\text{New value}}{\text{Old value}} \times 100 = \dfrac{\sqrt[3]{(1 \times 1 \times 1.15)}}{\sqrt[3]{(1 \times 1 \times 1)}} \times 100 = \sqrt[3]{1.15} \times 100 = 104.8$

Price weighted

(a) $\dfrac{\text{New value}}{\text{Old value}} \times 100 = \dfrac{\sqrt[3]{(57.5 \times 100 \times 200)}}{\sqrt[3]{(50 \times 100 \times 200)}} \times 100 = 104.8$

(b) $\dfrac{\text{New value}}{\text{Old value}} \times 100 = \dfrac{\sqrt[3]{(50 \times 100 \times 230)}}{\sqrt[3]{(50 \times 100 \times 200)}} \times 100 = 104.8$

Value weighted

(a) $\dfrac{\text{New value}}{\text{Old value}} \times 100 = \dfrac{\sqrt[3]{(5.75 \times 10 \times 10)}}{\sqrt[3]{(5 \times 10 \times 10)}} \times 100 = 104.8$

(b) $\dfrac{\text{New value}}{\text{Old value}} \times 100 = \dfrac{\sqrt[3]{(5 \times 10 \times 11.5)}}{\sqrt[3]{(5 \times 10 \times 10)}} \times 100 = 104.8$

As a consequence of the fact that calculating geometric means involves multiplying values together, the unweighted, price weighted and value weighted computations produce identical results. It also entails the result being the same irrespective of whether the 15% increase is in the price of stock A or the price of stock C.

If the value weighted arithmetic mean is regarded as the most accurate method of ascertaining the index, it can be seen that the geometric mean overestimates the effects of rises in the prices of smaller company stocks and underestimates the effects of changes in the stock prices of larger companies. Since large corporations are large because of rapid growth in the past, it follows that the use of geometric means gives too little weight to the stock prices of rapidly growing companies and too much weight to the stock prices of slow growth companies. So the use of geometric means under-weights stocks whose prices rise rapidly and over-weights stocks whose prices increase slowly. In consequence, over time, indices based on geometric means tend to understate the true rate of increase in stock prices. The same argument and conclusion applies to indices based on unweighted arithmetic means.

Adjusting for changes in the constituent stocks of an index

In most cases the constituent stocks in an index are changed as some firms grow and others experience relative decline. For example every three months some companies are removed from the FTSE 100 index and replaced by others in order to ensure that the index covers the largest 100 firms by market capitalisation. Such changes in the composition of the index portfolio should not affect the value of the index, since they do not result from overall market movements. This requires adjustments to the formula used for calculating the index.

Suppose that a value weighted index stands at 1120 and is based on the three stocks in Table 12.2.

Exercise 12.1

A stock index portfolio consists of stocks A, B and C.

Stock	Price	Number of shares issued
A	100p	10 million
B	400p	5 million
C	500p	1 million

Assess the effects of a 10% increase in the price of share A on stock indices that are (a) unweighted, (b) price weighted and (c) value weighted.

Consider the effects for stock indices that are based on arithmetic means and for indices based on geometric means.

Answer
Suppose that the indices initially stand at 100.

ARITHMETIC

Unweighted

$$\frac{1.1 + 1 + 1}{1 + 1 + 1} = \frac{3.1}{3} = 1.033$$

$$1.033 \times 100 = 103.3$$

Price weighted

$$\frac{110 + 400 + 500}{100 + 400 + 500} = \frac{1010}{1000} = 1.01$$

$$1.01 \times 100 = 101$$

Value weighted

$$\frac{11 + 20 + 5}{10 + 20 + 5} = \frac{36}{35} = 1.029$$

$$1.029 \times 100 = 102.9$$

GEOMETRIC

$$\frac{\sqrt[3]{(1.1 \times 1 \times 1)}}{\sqrt[3]{(1 \times 1 \times 1)}} = 1.032$$

$$1.032 \times 100 = 103.2$$

Table 12.2 Market capitalisations of three stocks

Stock	Market capitalisation
Shoddigoods plc	£100 million
Nore Turn Airlines plc	£50 million
Cowboy Construction plc	£40 million

When the periodic review date is reached, it is found that the constituents of the index portfolio are no longer the three largest companies. The index is still at 1120 and the market capitalisations are still as shown in Table 12.2. However, the market capitalisation of a fourth company, Gonoff Foods plc, has grown to £45 million. As a result Gonoff Foods replace Cowboy Construction in the calculation of the index (so that the index continues to be based on the three largest firms).

The index had been calculated as:

$$\frac{\text{Sum of market capitalisations on the current date}}{\text{Sum of market capitalisations on the base date}} \times 1000$$

i.e. $$\frac{£100m + £50m + £40m}{\text{Sum of market capitalisations on the base date}} \times 1000 = 1120$$

Consequent upon the change in the constituent stocks, an adjustment needs to be made to the formula to ensure that the change in the composition of the index portfolio does not change the index. A change in the stocks used to calculate the index should not, in itself, cause a change in the index. The adjustment factor is shown as AF in the following equation.

$$\frac{£100m + £50m + £45m}{\text{Sum of market capitalisations on the base date}} \times 1000 \times AF = 1120$$

AF will take the value of $(100 + 50 + 40) / (100 + 50 + 45) = 190/195 = 0.974$.

Evaluating alternative stock indices

When evaluating a stock index, it is necessary to consider it in relation to the functions that it is expected to perform. If an index fulfils its intended purposes, it will be evaluated positively.

Indices have a number of uses. First, they are used to measure and monitor market movements. Second, they should provide a means of ascertaining changes in aggregate wealth over time. Third, they have a role as barometers of the wider economy; in particular stock market movements tend to be leading indicators which means that they provide indications of likely future changes in the level of activity in the economy as a whole. Fourth, they provide a means of evaluating the performance of fund managers by providing benchmarks against which portfolio managers can be compared. Fifth, they provide the basis for derivative instruments such as futures and options. Sixth, they provide the framework for the creation of tracker funds whose aim is to closely reflect the performance of a stock market. Seventh, they are required by capital market models, in particular the capital asset pricing model (CAPM), for a number of purposes: ascertaining discount rates for capital projects, estimating required rates of returns on shares, and deriving fair rates of return for utilities.

Unweighted, price weighted, and geometrically averaged indices are much less satisfactory than indices that are value weighted and arithmetically averaged. For

Exercise 12.2

A value weighted index is based on three stocks: A, B and C. The current value of the index is 1000. The share prices and numbers of shares are:

Stock	Share price	Number of shares
A	100p	1,000,000
B	200p	1,000,000
C	40p	2,000,000

(a) If stock C were to be replaced by stock D, which is priced at 20p with 5,000,000 shares issued, calculate the adjustment factor required to ensure that the replacement does not affect the index.

(b) Subsequent to the replacement, the price of stock D rises to 25p. What will the new index be?

Answers

(a) The total market capitalisation before the replacement is:

(£1 × 1,000,000) + (£2 × 1,000,000) + (£0.4 × 2,000,000) = £1,000,000 + £2,000,000 + £800,000 = £3,800,000

The total market capitalisation after the replacement is:

(£1 × 1,000,000) + (£2 × 1,000,000) + (£0.2 × 5,000,000) = £1,000,000 + £2,000,000 + £1,000,000 = £4,000,000

The adjustment factor required is:

£3,800,000/£4,000,000 = 0.95

Use of this adjustment factor produces an index of:

$$\frac{£4,000,000}{£3,800,000} \times 1000 \times 0.95 = 1000$$

(b) If the price of stock D rises to 25p, the new market capitalisation will be:

(£1 × 1,000,000) + (£2 × 1,000,000) + (£0.25 × 5,000,000) = £1,000,000 + £2,000,000 + £1,250,000 = £4,250,000

So the new index should be:

$$\frac{£4,250,000}{£3,800,000} \times 1000 \times 0.95 = 1062.5$$

Alternatively

$$\frac{£4,250,000}{£4,000,000} \times 1000 = 1062.5$$

the purpose of measuring stock market values, it is necessary to have an index that accurately reflects the total market capitalisation of the market. An arithmetically averaged value weighted index does accurately measure the aggregate value of the stocks covered by the index, whereas other indices do not. A reliable measure of the total value of the market is also required for ascertaining changes in aggregate wealth over time and as a basis for derivative instruments.

An index will also perform its functions most effectively if it covers a large number of stocks. Indices that provide a very broad coverage, and hence reliably reflect the whole market, include the Wilshire 5000 in the US (which covers about 7,000 stocks) and the FT All Share Index in the UK (which covers about 800 stocks). It is ironic that the world's most closely followed index, the Dow Jones Industrial Average, covers only 30 stocks and is price weighted.

Unfortunately most stock indices consider only stock prices and fail to incorporate dividends. An index that incorporates dividends would be most appropriate if the aim is to have a benchmark against which to evaluate fund managers, a structure that tracker funds can try to replicate, and a measure of market return that can be used in models such as the capital asset pricing model.

In recent years there has been a change in the way that value weighted indices are constructed. The move has been towards a free float basis and away from a total capitalisation basis. Free float includes only those shares that are seen as available for purchase, rather than all shares. The free float basis excludes shares held by governments, founding families and non-financial companies. The stock index weighting is thus based on the total value of a company's shares available for purchase, and not on the full market capitalisation of the company. One reason for this change has been the growth of funds that seek to track stock indices. Such a fund may aim to buy shares in proportion to their weights in an index. If the weights are based on total capitalisation but only a small proportion of the shares are available in the market, the purchases by index tracking funds could distort the market by causing unjustified increases in the prices of such stocks.

Institutional investors, such as unit trusts, use stock indices as benchmarks for performance measurement. Tracker funds aim to replicate the performance of an index. European Union legislation prevents unit trusts (and OEICs) holding more than 10% of their portfolio in a single stock. Vodafone's takeover of Mannesmann in 2000 raised its market capitalisation to more than 10% of the FTSE 100. To enable institutional investors to benchmark against a relevant index, FTSE International (a major indexing organisation) has introduced capped versions of its FTSE 100 and All-Share indices. These capped indices limit the maximum weighting of a stock in the index to 10%.

Discussion questions

1 What is a stock index? What are the different approaches to the calculation of a stock index? Are the various approaches equally useful with respect to satisfying the purposes of stock indices?

2 Is it possible that two different stock indices, both measuring movements of the same stock market, can move in opposite directions?

Chapter 13

Stock index futures

After studying this chapter readers should be able to:

- *prepare to commence trading in financial futures*
- *distinguish between hedging, speculative and arbitrage trades*
- *understand the margin system and closing out*
- *construct futures funds*
- *evaluate the relative merits of using futures and stocks for achieving investment objectives.*

Financial futures

A financial future is a notional commitment to buy or sell, on a specified future date, a standard quantity of a financial instrument at a price determined in the present (the futures price). It is rare for a futures contract to be used for the exchange of financial instruments. Indeed many contracts, including stock index futures, have no facility for the exchange of the financial instrument. Instead, financial futures markets are independent of the underlying cash market, albeit operating parallel to that market.

The main economic function of futures is to provide a means of hedging. A hedger seeks to reduce an already existing risk. This risk reduction could be achieved by taking a futures position that would tend to show a profit in the event of a loss on the underlying position (and a loss in the case of a profit on the underlying position).

Positions in futures markets can be taken much more quickly and much more cheaply (in terms of transaction costs) than positions in the underlying spot markets. For example, a position in stock index futures can be established within a few minutes (from the time of the decision) at little cost in terms of commissions and bid-ask spreads. The construction of a balanced portfolio of stocks would take much longer and be more costly in terms of commissions and spreads. For these reasons, futures markets tend to be more efficient than the underlying spot markets; futures prices respond to new information more quickly. So futures have a second economic function, which might be termed price discovery. Futures prices may be indicative of what prices should be in the markets for the underlying instruments. This price discovery function is particularly important where the underlying spot market is poorly developed or illiquid, as in countries with poorly developed financial systems or for instruments that are not frequently traded.

Hedging with futures

The FTSE 100 Index stands at 6000 on 14 February and a fund manager expects to receive £900,000 on 15 March. The intention is to invest that money immediately in a balanced portfolio of shares. The fund manager fears that share prices will rise by 15 March, meaning that fewer shares can be bought with the £900,000. Since the risk is that share prices will rise, the requisite futures position is one that would profit from a rise in share prices. Stock index futures are bought. A FTSE 100 futures contract relates to a value of stock equal to the futures index multiplied by £10. So, if the futures index were 6000, each futures contract would relate to 6000 × £10 = £60,000 worth of shares. Hedging a purchase of £900,000 of stock (at 14 February prices) requires the purchase of 15 FTSE 100 futures contracts.

Suppose that the index rises by 600 points by 15 March. The quantity of stock that could have been bought for £900,000 on 14 February now costs £990,000. This could be regarded as a loss of £90,000. However, if the futures FTSE 100 Index also rises by 600 points, there will be a futures profit of £90,000.

600 index points × £10 per point × 15 contracts = £90,000

The futures profit, when added to the £900,000, provides the £990,000 required to buy the quantity of stock that £900,000 would have bought on 14 February.

● ● ● ● Types of trader

Hedgers are not the only traders active on futures exchanges. Speculators buy and sell futures simply to make profit, not to reduce risk. They buy when they believe futures to be under-priced, and sell when they view them as over-priced. Frequently, speculative trades heavily outnumber hedging trades.

Speculators are vital to futures markets. They facilitate hedging, provide liquidity, tend to ensure accurate pricing and can help to maintain price stability. It is unlikely that hedgers wishing to buy futures will precisely match hedgers selling futures in terms of numbers of contracts. If hedgers are net sellers, there will be a tendency for futures prices to fall and that may generate profit opportunities for speculators. Speculators will buy the under-priced futures. The purchases by speculators will allow the net sales on the part of the hedgers. In effect, speculators fill the gap between sales and purchases by hedgers. In so doing, they tend to maintain price stability since they will buy into a falling market, and sell into a rising one (in the event of hedgers being net buyers).

A liquid market is one in which there is considerable buying and selling on a continuous basis. In a liquid market, hedgers can make their transactions with ease. Speculative transactions add to market liquidity. In the absence of speculators, hedgers may have difficulty in finding counterparties with whom to trade.

Speculators also help to make a market informationally efficient. A market is informationally efficient when prices fully reflect all available relevant information. Speculators are likely to consider all relevant information when deciding upon the appropriate price of a futures contract. If actual prices differ from those judged appropriate, they will be brought into line with the estimated prices by speculative trades; under-priced futures will be bought (and so their prices will tend to rise), while over-priced futures will be sold until their prices have fallen to the level considered correct.

In addition to hedgers and speculators, there is a third category of trader known as arbitragers. Arbitragers also help to make markets liquid, ensure accurate pricing and enhance price stability. Arbitrage involves making profits from relative mispricing. Futures prices should bear a consistent relationship to stock prices. If this relationship is violated, an arbitrage opportunity may arise. If the futures price is too high relative to the stock price, a profit can be made by buying stocks and simultaneously selling futures. Such trades will tend to restore the appropriate relationship between stock prices and futures prices (by raising stock prices and reducing futures prices).

● ● ● ● The margin system

The margin system is central to futures markets. There are three types of margin: initial margin, maintenance margin and variation margin. The initial margin is a sum of money to be provided by both the buyer and the seller of a futures contract when they make their transaction, it is a deposit that is returned when the contract expires or is closed out. This margin is a small percentage of the face value of the contract (perhaps 5%). The initial margin is subject to variation (by a clearing house) and will depend on the volatility of the stock market. One function of initial margin is the provision of market discipline. The payment of initial margin may deter poorly capitalised speculators from entering the market.

Whereas initial margin is the sum to be initially deposited (with a clearing house), the maintenance margin is the sum that must remain deposited while the futures position is held. Initial and maintenance margins are frequently identical in value. Initial and maintenance margins could be in the form of money (which may earn interest) or other securities (which continue to provide a yield to the holder of the futures position). The margin will be drawn upon (by the clearing house) in the event of the holder of a futures position failing to make a variation margin payment.

Variation margin is payable and receivable on a daily basis. It reflects the profit or loss made from a futures contract during the course of a day. If the futures price moves to the holder's advantage, the holder will receive variation margin; if the futures price moves adversely, a payment must be made. This process of realising profits and losses on a daily basis is known as marking to market. If a contract holder fails to make a variation margin payment, the contract will be automatically closed out and the outstanding sum deducted from the maintenance margin (which is set at a level that is expected to exceed any likely variation margin call).

When a futures deal is agreed between a buyer and a seller, a clearing house takes over the role of counterparty to both buyer and seller. So, although buyer A bought from seller B, once the deal is registered the clearing house becomes the seller to buyer A and the buyer from seller B. An implication of this is that there is no need to investigate the creditworthiness of the person or entity with whom a deal is made (the need for such investigation could slow up futures dealing and undermine market efficiency). All default risk is taken by the clearing house. The clearing house protects itself from counter-party default risk by means of the variation and maintenance margins. Marking to market prevents the accumulation of counter-party debt and the maintenance margin is a source from which one day's outstanding variation margin payment can be drawn. Another implication of the margin system is that futures are highly geared investments. For example, an initial margin of 5% of the underlying stock means that the exposure acquired is 20 times the initial money outlay.

Closing out

The majority of futures contracts are closed out before they mature. Since there are typically only four maturity dates each year, it is unlikely that the needs of futures users will coincide with one of those four dates (for most futures contracts there are maturity dates in March, June, September and December). Closing out involves taking a futures position opposite to the original position. If the position was opened by buying a contract with a March maturity date, it would be closed out by selling a March futures contract; likewise, a short position (futures sold) would be closed out by buying futures with the same maturity date. When futures contracts are closed out, the transactor is left with no futures position; the purchases and sales are deemed to cancel each other.

The closing transaction will typically not be with the same counter-party as the opening transaction, but nonetheless, the transactions will cancel out, leaving the trader with no remaining futures position. This is because of the counter-party role of the clearing house. As soon as a futures trade is agreed, the clearing house becomes the counter-party to both buyer and seller. It is as if the buyer has bought from the clearing house and the seller sold to the clearing house. So when a closing out transaction occurs, the transactor is left with identical long (bought) and short (sold) positions with the clearing house and the clearing house deems these to cancel each other out.

Futures funds

Futures funds are collective investments that operate by means of keeping most of their assets in a liquid form such as short-term bank deposits, while the remainder are used to finance the margin requirements of futures trading. The gearing offered by futures provides an opportunity for such funds themselves to be highly geared. The market exposure of a futures fund might be several times the value of the fund. Obviously, such highly geared funds are very risky.

Futures funds often contain a wide variety of futures contracts. Multi-sector funds would contain not only a range of financial futures, but also commodity futures. Furthermore, the contracts are likely to derive from exchanges in a number of different countries. Such diversification helps to reduce the risk inherent in the futures funds. Commodity futures may be particularly attractive to fund managers since they are likely to exhibit little or no correlation with the assets (such as stocks and bonds) that constitute the major part of investment portfolios. An asset that has low correlation with the other elements of a portfolio will tend to reduce the risk of the portfolio.

Trading on market movements can normally be achieved more quickly and cheaply by using futures than by means of the spot instruments. Futures bid-offer spreads and commissions are often much lower than in the spot markets and time need not be spent on deciding between specific securities. It follows that a fund that is likely to shift frequently between asset classes (e.g. between shares and bonds) would benefit from the use of futures rather than spot market instruments.

Futures allow quick and cheap movement not only between types of asset, such as equities and gilts, but also between national markets. The time and expense of researching foreign stocks can be avoided by using stock index futures relating to the foreign stock markets. Furthermore, only margin payments are subject to currency exposure (exchange rate risk); the bulk of the fund can remain in the home currency.

Futures funds commonly guarantee that the initial investment is safe (in the sense that this is the minimum repayment at the end of the investment term, which may be several years). In such cases the loss is limited to the interest forgone, and even this loss can be ameliorated by a guaranteed rate of interest. A futures fund might, for example, hold 60% of the original fund on deposit while making the remaining 40% available for futures trading. A quarter (for example) of the money available for futures trading might be deposited as (initial or maintenance) margin at any one time.

A futures fund would involve most of the fund being invested in short-term money market assets such as bank deposits or Treasury bills and the remainder being used for the margin requirements arising from futures positions. The futures may relate to a sum of securities equal to the value of the fund, but not necessarily. Futures provide the flexibility to gain exposure to a quantity of assets in excess of the value of the fund, or to take a short position in the underlying investment.

Exercise 13.1

The manager of a futures fund has £1,000,000. The fund manager buys FTSE 100 futures relating to £1,000,000 of shares when the FTSE 100 stands at 5,000. The futures mature in one year.

(a) How many futures contracts are bought?
(b) Does any of the £1,000,000 need to be used in the purchase of the futures?
(c) What is the approximate capital gain on the fund over a year if the FTSE 100 rises by 10%?
(d) What must be added to the capital gain in order to find the total return on the fund?

Answers
(a) £1,000,000/(5000 × £10) = 20 contracts.
(b) Initial margin must be provided.
(c) 10% minus the net cost of carry.
(d) Interest on the money on deposit (i.e. interest on approximately £1,000,000).

Chapter 14

Stock index futures prices

After studying this chapter readers should be able to:

- *ascertain whether stock index futures are fairly priced*
- *design an arbitrage strategy to make profits from any observed mispricing*
- *use basis trading to enhance profits*
- *appreciate the roles of hedgers and speculators in the determination of futures prices.*

The pricing of stock index futures can be looked upon as being based on cash-and-carry arbitrage. The futures price should be such that there is no arbitrage profit from buying stock (with borrowed money) and simultaneously selling futures. Likewise there should be no profit opportunity from selling stock and simultaneously buying futures.

The excess of the financing cost of holding the stock over the dividend receipts constitutes the net cost of carry. The selling price guaranteed by the futures should match the initial cost of the stock plus the net cost of carry. In other words, the futures price should provide a guaranteed capital gain that exactly compensates for the excess of the interest payments over the (expected) dividend receipts. Such a futures price is referred to as the fair futures price.

The fair value premium is the excess of the fair futures price over the spot (i.e. actual) stock index. The formula for the fair value premium is:

$$FP = I \times [\{(r-y)/100\} \times \{d/365\}]$$

FP is the fair value premium, I is the spot FTSE 100 Index, r is the interest rate over d days, y is the expected percentage yield on the index portfolio, and d is the number of days to maturity of the futures contract.

For example, let $I = 6000$, $r = 7\%$ p.a., $y = 2\%$ p.a. and $d = 91$ days. Then:

$$FP = 6000 \times [\{(7-2)/100\} \times \{91/365\}] = 75 \text{ index points}$$

(So the fair futures price is $6000 + 75 = 6075$.)

Short cash and carry involves selling stock and buying futures. In this case the excess of interest over dividends is a net inflow and this gain should be matched by having a guaranteed future purchase price that exceeds the spot sale price by the amount of this net inflow. The money from the stock sale is put on deposit, but dividends are foregone. The excess of interest over foregone dividends is a net inflow that should be matched by a capital loss guaranteed by the futures price.

Exercise 14.1

If the rate of interest on risk free bank deposits were 7.5% p.a., and if money could be borrowed at the same rate of interest, estimate the price of a FTSE 100 futures contract which matures in four months on the basis of a spot index of 4,000 and a zero expected rate of dividend yield on the FTSE 100 portfolio. How would the answer change if the expected rate of dividend yield were 4.5% p.a. (while the other values were as before)?

Answer
Using the formula

$$FP = I \times \frac{(r - y)}{100} \times \frac{d}{365}$$

and treating four months as exactly one-third of a year gives (with zero expected dividend yield):

$$FP = 4,000 \times \frac{(7.5 - 0)}{100} \times \frac{1}{3}$$

$$FP = 4,000 \times 0.025 = 100$$

If the fair value premium is 100, the fair futures price is $4,000 + 100 = 4,100$.
With an expected rate of dividend yield of 4.5% p.a. the calculation becomes:

$$FP = 4,000 \times \frac{(7.5 - 4.5)}{100} \times \frac{1}{3}$$

$$FP = 4,000 \times 0.01 = 40$$

If the fair value premium is 40, the fair futures price is $4,000 + 40 = 4,040$.

Cash-and-carry arbitrage, in the absence of transaction costs, determines the fair futures price. However, the actual futures price may differ from the fair futures price. This is due to transaction costs such as commissions and bid-offer spreads. An arbitrager must make a gain that covers transaction costs before showing a net profit. The actual futures price can deviate from the fair futures price by as much as the transaction costs without arbitrage taking place.

In the absence of transaction costs, cash-and-carry arbitrage would tend to keep the actual futures price equal to the fair price because under-valued futures would be bought by arbitragers (pushing up the futures price) and over-valued futures would be sold (pushing the futures price down towards its fair value). In the presence of transaction costs, the cash-and-carry arbitrage merely keeps the futures price within a range of values known as the no-arbitrage band. When the futures price is within the no-arbitrage band, there will be no further buying or selling by arbitragers to move the futures price towards the fair futures price (i.e. towards the

Exercise 14.2

A fund manager has £1 million for a futures fund. The fund has an investment horizon of one year. The FTSE 100 stands at 5,000. The one-year interest rate is 5% and the expected rate of dividend yield on the FTSE 100 over the coming year is 3%. The fund manager puts £1 million in a bank deposit and obtains market exposure by buying futures.

(a) How many futures contracts, with a one-year maturity, are required for a fund that has a £1 million exposure to the FTSE 100?

(b) What is the fair futures price?

(c) What is the rate of capital gain on the fund if the FTSE 100 rises by 20% over the year, and the futures price is initially at its fair level?

(d) What is the total return on the fund if the FTSE 100 rises by 20% over the year?

(e) How would the answers to (a), (c), and (d) change if the futures contracts were to provide a market exposure of £2 million (while the sum of money on deposit remains at £1 million)?

(f) Is it the case that the whole of the £1 million can be kept in a bank deposit?

Answers

(a) £1,000,000/(5000 × £10) = 20 contracts.

(b) The fair futures price is 5000 + 5000(0.05 − 0.03) = 5,100.

(c) (6000−5100)/5000 = 18%. (The futures price rises from 5,100 to 6,000.)

(d) 18% + 5% = 23%. (Capital gain on futures plus interest on deposit. Note that this is equal to the capital gain on the shares plus the dividends on the shares.)

(e) The number of contracts required would be 40. The futures profit would double to 1800, so the rate of capital gain doubles to 36%. The total rate of return is then 36% + 5% = 41%.

middle of the no-arbitrage band). Within the no-arbitrage band, the gains from arbitrage are not sufficient to offset transaction costs. Figure 14.1 illustrates a no-arbitrage band.

If the futures price falls below the bottom of the no-arbitrage band, arbitragers would buy futures until the futures price reaches the bottom of the band, at which point arbitrage would stop. A futures price above the top of the no-arbitrage band would induce long cash-and-carry arbitrage, which involves selling futures. The sale of futures would move the futures price to the top of the no-arbitrage band, but no further. Once the futures price is within the band, arbitrage opportunities cease.

So the arbitrage pressure that tends to prevent deviations of actual futures prices from fair futures prices merely serves to keep the actual futures prices within a range (the no-arbitrage band) rather than ensuring equality with the fair futures price. Arbitrage occurs only when the actual futures price moves outside the no-arbitrage band (i.e. away from the fair futures price by the sum of the transaction costs). This is illustrated by Exercises 14.3 and 14.4.

Since cash-and-carry arbitrage merely determines a band of possible futures prices around the fair futures price, there may be opportunities for enhancing

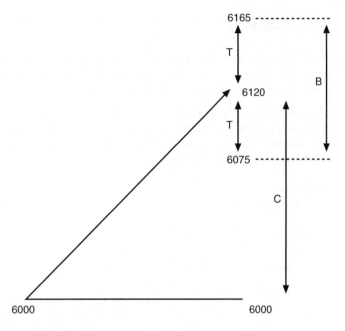

SPOT INDEX = 6000
NET COST OF CARRY (C) = 120
FAIR FUTURES PRICE = 6000 + 120 = 6120
TRANSACTION COSTS (T) = 45
THE NO ARBITRAGE BAND (B) IS 6075 TO 6165 i.e. (6120 – 45) TO (6120 + 45)
NB ALL VALUES (SPOT AND FUTURES) RELATE TO THE SAME POINT IN TIME

Figure 14.1 The no-arbitrage band

profits by buying futures when the futures price is towards the bottom of the range of possible values (i.e. below the fair futures price). A rise in the actual futures price relative to the fair futures price would add to the profits arising from movements in the fair futures price. Buying when the actual futures price is below the fair futures price enhances the probability of a rise of the actual futures price relative to the no-arbitrage band of possible values. This is known as basis trading and can be used to enhance the profits of hedgers and investors.

If the futures contracts are held to maturity, such an addition to profit is assured since the actual futures price converges on to the fair futures price at maturity (at that point in time the spot price, the fair futures price and the actual futures price are the same).

The role of hedgers and speculators

Arbitrage determines that the futures price will fall within a range of values. However, it does not determine where, within that range, the futures price will lie.

Exercise 14.3

The FTSE 100 is 6000. The three-month interest rate is 8% p.a. and the expected rate of dividend yield over the next three months is 4% p.a. What is the fair futures price for a futures contract maturing in three months' time?

How might an arbitrage profit be made if the actual futures price were (a) 6100 and (b) 6000 and there were no transaction costs. If the total transaction costs (commission, bid-offer spreads, stamp duty) amounted to £500 per £60,000 of stock would there still be arbitrage profits available?

Answers
The fair futures premium is:

$$6000 \times \frac{(8-4)}{100} \times \frac{1}{4} = 60$$

So the fair futures price is: 6000 + 60 = 6060.

(a) If the actual futures price were 6100, the futures would be over-valued. In the absence of transaction costs a profit is available from a long cash-and-carry arbitrage which entails buying stock and selling futures. There is a guaranteed profit from the stock and futures of 100 index points (amounting to 100 × £10 = £1000 per £60,000 of stock and 1 futures contract). The corresponding net cost of carry is 60 index points (£600). So there is a net profit of 40 index points (£400).

(b) If the actual futures price were 6000, the futures would be under-valued. So stock should be sold and futures bought (short cash-and-carry). There is neither profit nor loss from the stock and futures position. The net cost of carry accrues as profit and is 60 index points (60 × £10 = £600).

If the total of transaction costs were £500, there would be no net profit remaining in case (a) and only £600 − £500 = £100 in case (b). The futures price has to deviate by 50 index points from its fair value before any arbitrage profits become available.

In this case there is a no-arbitrage band of 50 index points either side of the fair futures price (6010 − 6110). Futures prices within this band do not induce arbitrage since they offer no net arbitrage profit.

In the absence of transaction costs, cash-and-carry arbitrage would tend to keep the actual futures price equal to the fair futures price because under-valued futures would be bought by arbitragers (pushing up the futures price) and over-valued futures would be sold (pushing the futures price down towards its fair value). In the presence of transaction costs, the cash and carry arbitrage merely keeps the futures price within the no-arbitrage band. When the futures price is within the no-arbitrage band, there will be no further buying or selling by arbitragers to move the futures price towards the fair futures price (that is towards the middle of the no-arbitrage band).

If the futures price falls below the bottom of the no-arbitrage band, arbitragers would buy futures until the futures price reaches the bottom on the band, at which point arbitrage would stop. A futures price above the top of the no-arbitrage band would induce long cash-and-carry arbitrage, which involves selling futures. The sale of futures would move the futures price to the top of the no-arbitrage band, but no further. Once the futures price is within the band, arbitrage opportunities cease.

Exercise 14.4

The FTSE 100 is currently 5000, the three-month interest rate is 7% p.a., and the expected dividend yield on the FTSE 100 portfolio is 3% p.a.
(a) What is the fair price of a FTSE 100 futures contract due to mature in three months?
(b) If each stock transaction incurs costs of 0.6% of the value of the stock, within what range of values should the actual futures price lie? (Ignore transaction costs on futures contracts.)
(c) If the actual futures price were 5200, how could an arbitrager make a profit? What might be the effects of arbitragers pursuing such a profit?

Answers
(a) The futures premium over spot, FP, is given by:
FP = I × [(r − y)/100] × [d/365]
Treating d/365 as 0.25 (a quarter of the year) gives:
FP = 5000 × [(7 − 3)/100] × 0.25 = 50
So the fair futures price is 5000 + 50 = 5050

(b) Both long and short cash-and-carry arbitrages involve the purchase and sale of stock. So each arbitrage incurs transaction costs amounting to 1.2% of the value of the stock. Based on an index of 5000 this amounts to 60 index points. So the no-arbitrage band would be 5050 +/− 60, i.e. 4990 to 5110.

(c) A futures price of 5200 would be above the no-arbitrage band. Arbitragers could sell the over-priced futures and simultaneously buy stock (long cash-and-carry arbitrage). These transactions would tend to reduce the futures price and to raise the spot index (and hence the fair futures price and the no-arbitrage band). The futures price would fall, and the no-arbitrage band rise, until the futures price equalled the top of the no-arbitrage band. At that point arbitrage would cease, since it would no longer be profitable.

This provides a role for hedgers and speculators to influence futures prices. Net buying by hedgers and speculators would move the futures price towards the top of the no-arbitrage band, while selling would induce a price movement towards the bottom of the band. Since net purchases would result from bullish views and net sales from bearish views, it follows that market expectations will play a part in determining the position of the futures price within the band.

Not only might such expectations affect the position of the futures price within the no-arbitrage band, but they also have the potential of moving stock prices and hence the position of the band. To understand the processes involved, consider the situation in which hedgers and/or speculators buy futures to the extent that the futures price rises above the top of the no-arbitrage band. When the futures price rises above the top of the band, the opportunity for long cash-and-carry arbitrage arises. Arbitragers buy stock and sell the (over-priced) futures. This tends to put upward pressure on stock prices (and hence the no-arbitrage band).

Exercise 14.5

The FTSE 100 is 6000, the three-month interest rate is 6% p.a. and the expected rate of dividend yield on the FTSE 100 over the next three months is 3% p.a.
(a) What is the fair price of a futures contract due to mature in three months?
(b) If financial institutions face transaction costs of 0.3% on both purchases and sales of stock, plus 0.5% tax on purchases, what is the no-arbitrage band of futures prices?
(c) If speculators adopt the view that the FTSE 100 will be 6200 in three months from the present, what would you expect to happen in the futures and spot markets?

Answers
(a) The fair futures premium is:

$$6000 \times \frac{(6 - 3)}{100} \times \frac{1}{4} = 45$$

The fair futures price is:
6000 + 45 = 6045

(b) The no-arbitrage band will be 1.1% each side of the fair futures price. The 1.1% is based on buying costs of 0.3% plus 0.5% tax, and selling costs of 0.3%. These costs are incurred in the case of both long and short cash-and-carry arbitrage.

Based on the initial index of 6000, the 1.1% is equivalent to 66 index points. So the no-arbitrage band should be:

6045 + 66 = 6111
to 6045 − 66 = 5979

(c) If speculators believe that the FTSE 100 will be 6200, they will buy futures at any price below 6200 with a view to selling when the price rises to 6200 (on the futures maturity date spot and futures prices are equal). These purchases would tend to pull the futures price out of the no-arbitrage band. As the futures price rises above the no-arbitrage band, arbitrage opportunities emerge. Arbitragers would sell the relatively over-priced futures and buy the relatively under-priced stock. This would put downward pressure on the futures price and upward pressure on the FTSE 100 (and hence the no-arbitrage band). If both speculators and arbitragers have adequate funds, the no-arbitrage band should rise until the value of 6200 falls within the band. Speculation will cease when the FTSE 100 futures price reaches 6200 and arbitrage will stop when the no-arbitrage band encompasses the value of 6200.

The role of risk

The arbitrage process is not entirely risk-free. Stock prices might move against the arbitrager during the time taken to assemble the portfolio. Furthermore, future dividends cannot be known with certainty. In consequence, some risk remains and arbitragers may require compensation for such risk. Any compensation for risk tends to widen the no-arbitrage band, but by amounts that vary between arbitragers and over time. So the boundaries of the no-arbitrage band should be seen not as definite values but as imprecise borders.

Chapter 15

Portfolio diversification

After studying this chapter readers should be able to:

- *use the Markowitz equations to calculate the expected return and risk of a portfolio*

- *appreciate how an efficiency frontier can be derived*

- *evaluate the merits of international diversification*

- *demonstrate the advantages of adding a risk-free asset to the investment alternatives.*

The idea that investment portfolios should be diversified is well established. The saying 'Don't put all your eggs in one basket' expresses a basic principle of diversification. Spreading one's assets among a large number of investments lessens the risk of losing everything as a result of adverse developments. Share portfolios are often in the form of 20 or more different stocks since poor performances on some of the investments tend to be offset by strong performances on others. The observation that industries vary in their performances over time leads to the shareholdings being spread across a number of industries. So a portfolio may have shares in firms involved in engineering, chemicals, banking, electricals, transport, brewing, insurance, food processing, retailing, oil, computing, water and pharmaceuticals. Spreading investments across industries, as well as across individual firms, allows for poor performances in some industrial sectors to be offset by strong performances elsewhere. A more complete diversification would involve a spread of investments across asset classes. The main asset classes are equities (shares), bonds, deposits and property (real estate).

Spreading one's wealth among asset classes, and within those classes among different sectors, will tend to provide most of the benefits of diversification. This approach is sometimes referred to as naive diversification. A more sophisticated approach has been suggested by Harry Markowitz. This involves basing the choice of investments upon their correlations (or upon their covariances) in order to maximise the expected degree of offset between them. What follows will focus on this latter form of diversification, often known as Markowitz diversification. The exposition will initially be concerned with diversification between asset classes, particularly equities, bonds and deposits. A more complete approach would extend to the choice of individual securities, for example the specific shares to be bought and the relative size of individual shareholdings within the overall portfolio.

The Markowitz equations

There is an equation for the expected return on a portfolio (in the sense of statistical expectation) and an equation for the expected variance (risk) of the portfolio. The equations used here will be based on the choices between the three asset classes of equities, bonds and deposits.

The equation for the expected rate of return can be written as:

$$E(R_p) = (W_e)E(R_e) + (W_b)E(R_b) + (W_d)E(R_d) \tag{1}$$

where $E(R_p)$ is the expected return on the portfolio; (W_e), (W_b), and (W_d) are the portfolio weightings in equities, bonds and deposits respectively (which add to 1); $E(R_e)$, $E(R_b)$, and $E(R_d)$ are the expected returns on equities, bonds and deposits respectively.

The equation for the expected portfolio variance can be written as:

$$V_p = (W_e)^2 \sigma_e^2 + (W_b)^2 \sigma_b^2 + (W_d)^2 \sigma_d^2 + 2(W_e)(W_b)\sigma_e\sigma_b \rho_{eb} + 2(W_e)(W_d)\sigma_e\sigma_d \rho_{ed} + 2(W_b)(W_d)\sigma_b\sigma_d \rho_{bd} \tag{2}$$

where V_p is the variance of the portfolio; σ_e, σ_b and σ_d are the expected standard deviations of returns on equities, bonds and deposits respectively; ρ_{eb} is the expected correlation between the returns on equities and bonds, ρ_{ed} and ρ_{bd} have corresponding interpretations. The portfolio standard deviation is the square root of the portfolio variance, i.e. $\sigma_p = \sqrt{V_p}$.

By using equations (1) and (2) it is possible to find the highest expected return for any level of expected risk, and the lowest risk for each level of return. This optimisation procedure is based on the use of the coefficients of correlation and standard deviations of returns. This use of correlation coefficients and standard deviations distinguishes Markowitz diversification from naive diversification. Markowitz diversification achieves the best (optimal) level of diversification possible, whereas naive diversification cannot aspire to such optimality.

The role of correlation in the determination of portfolio risk can be seen from the following example in which the combination of risky assets produces a risk-free portfolio.

There are two securities in this example, A and B. There are three possible eventualities (circumstances). Table 15.1 shows the returns from the securities in each of the three different circumstances. Table 15.2 shows the returns from a portfolio

Table 15.1 Returns from securities A and B

Eventuality	Return on A	Return on B
1	7.5%	20%
2	10%	10%
3	12.5%	0%

Table 15.2 Returns from a portfolio comprising 0.8A and 0.2B

Eventuality	Portfolio return (0.8A + 0.2B)
1	6 + 4 = 10%
2	8 + 2 = 10%
3	10 + 0 = 10%

comprising 0.8A and 0.2B. In eventuality 1 the contribution to total return from holding 0.8A is $0.8 \times 7.5 = 6\%$, the contribution from the 0.2B is $0.2 \times 20 = 4\%$, giving a total return of $6 + 4 = 10\%$. In the second circumstance A provides $0.8 \times 10 = 8\%$, B contributes $0.2 \times 10 = 2\%$, so that the total portfolio return is $8\% + 2\% = 10\%$. In eventuality 3 security A contributes $0.8 \times 12.5 = 10\%$, B contributes $0.2 \times 0 = 0\%$, with the result that the total portfolio return is 10%.

The portfolio of 0.8A plus 0.2B is a risk-free portfolio. Under all three of the possible eventualities the return is 10%. Since there is no uncertainty about the return, there is no risk. The expected return is 10% and the standard deviation of returns is 0%. So by combining two risky investments in an optimal ratio, risk has been eliminated. The optimal proportions of 0.8 and 0.2 (4 to 1) arise from the ratio of standard deviations, B has a standard deviation four times that of A. The other factor involved in ascertaining the optimal proportions in a portfolio is the correlation of returns, although this factor was not relevant to ascertaining the proportions in the example above since only one correlation was involved (between A and B).

The Markowitz approach seeks to incorporate securities with low correlations of returns. By minimising correlations the chance of poor performances by some investments being offset, by strong returns on others, is increased. In the example above the coefficient of correlation was −1, with the result that it was possible to completely eliminate risk. Although negative correlations rarely exist, there is still scope for reducing risk by using the criterion of low correlation. It can be seen from equation (2) that lower correlations will tend to result in lower variances. An important insight of the Markowitz approach is the observation that the risk reduction effects of diversification can be maximised by choosing investments with relatively low correlations with each other.

Another conclusion of the Markowitz analysis is that it is possible to construct a set of points, in risk-return space, that cannot be improved upon. Such a set of points is depicted in Figure 15.1.

The curve in Figure 15.1 is known as the efficiency frontier. Portfolios that produce points on the efficiency frontier provide the highest expected returns for each level of risk, and the lowest level of risk for each expected rate of return. Once on the efficiency frontier it is not possible to increase expected returns without increasing risk, nor is it possible to reduce risk without reducing expected returns. Points on the efficiency frontier are said to dominate points in the shaded area below it. Any point below the efficiency frontier can be improved on, in terms of increasing expected returns and/or reducing risk, by changing to a portfolio on the efficiency frontier. Rational investors would be expected to hold portfolios on the efficiency frontier.

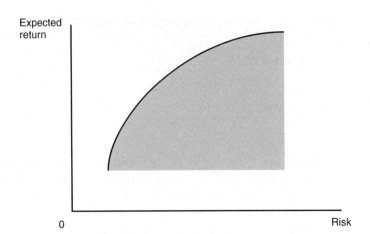

Figure 15.1 Risk-return points

Combining assets in a portfolio achieves an expected return that is a weighted average of the expected returns of the individual assets. However, the risk is less than the average of the individual risks, unless the coefficients of correlation all equal +1. Consider equations 3 and 4, which are generalised versions of equations 1 and 2 (generalised to allow for any number of assets in a portfolio).

$$E(R_p) = \sum_{j=1}^{n} W_j \, E(R_j) \tag{3}$$

$$V_p = \sum_{j=1}^{n} W_j^2 \, \sigma_j^2 + \sum_{j=1}^{n} \sum_{k=1}^{n} W_j \, W_k \, \sigma_j \, \sigma_k \, \rho_{jk} \; (j \neq k) \tag{4}$$

The expected return, $E(R_p)$, is the weighted average of the expected returns from the individual securities. The weighting of security j (the proportion of the portfolio in security j) is represented by W_j and the expected return on security j is shown as $E(R_j)$.

In equation 4, V_p is the variance of the portfolio returns (therefore $\sqrt{V_p}$ is the standard deviation of returns). The standard deviations of securities j and k are represented by σ_j and σ_k respectively. The coefficient of correlation between the returns of j and k is shown as ρ_{jk}.

If all the coefficients of correlation equal 1, the portfolio standard deviation will be a weighted average of the standard deviations of the individual securities. This averaging of the standard deviations is illustrated by Example 15.1.

If the coefficient of correlation is less than +1, the portfolio risk will be less than the average of the risks of the individual securities. This is illustrated by Example 15.2.

It can be seen that as the correlation falls below +1, the risk of the portfolio falls below the average of the risks of the individual securities that comprise the portfolio. As the correlation falls, the risk of the portfolio declines. Portfolio risk is at its lowest when the correlation is −1. When the correlation is −1 it is possible to find a proportion, for the two securities, that reduces risk to zero.

Figure 15.2 illustrates some possibilities.

Example 15.1

Suppose that a portfolio comprises equal values of two securities with standard deviations of return of 0.2 (20% p.a.) and 0.4 (40% p.a.). If the correlation between returns is 1 then:

$$V_p = (0.5)^2(0.2)^2 + (0.5)^2(0.4)^2 + 2(0.5)(0.5)(0.2)(0.4)$$
$$= (0.25)(0.04) + (0.25)(0.16) + 0.04$$
$$= 0.01 + 0.04 + 0.04 = 0.09$$
$$\sigma_p = \sqrt{0.09} = 0.3$$

The standard deviation (risk) of the portfolio, shown as σ_p, is 0.3 (i.e. 30%). This is the average of the risks on the individual securities (20% and 40%).

Example 15.2

If the correlation is 0.4 but other values are the same as in Example 15.1, the portfolio risk would be calculated as follows:

$$V_p = (0.5)^2(0.2)^2 + (0.5)^2(0.4)^2 + 2(0.5)(0.5)(0.2)(0.4)(0.4)$$
$$= (0.25)(0.04) + (0.25)(0.16) + (0.04)(0.4)$$
$$= 0.01 + 0.04 + 0.016 = 0.066$$
$$\sigma_p = \sqrt{0.066} = 0.257$$

The standard deviation (risk) of the portfolio is less than the average of the standard deviations (risks) of the two securities.

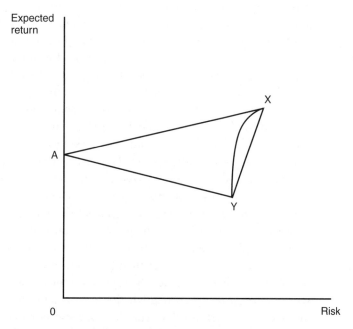

Figure 15.2 Expected return/risk combinations for securities X and Y

Figure 15.2 shows the expected return/risk combinations for securities X and Y. If the correlation of returns between X and Y were −1, it would be possible to find a portfolio of X and Y that reduces risk to zero. It would be possible to achieve a point such as A. If the correlation were +1, a portfolio of X and Y would be on the straight line XY. The risk of the portfolio would be an average of the risks of the two securities.

Between these extremes lie the more realistic correlations. Correlations would usually be between 0 and +1. In such cases portfolio risk would be greater than zero but lower than an average of the risks of the two securities. The possible combinations of expected return and risk would lie on a curve such as XY. The curve XY is an efficiency frontier for portfolios comprising X and Y. Along this curve the expected return is an average of the expected returns of X and Y, but the portfolio risk (standard deviation) is less than an average of the two risks.

Security risk is often subdivided into systematic and non-systematic risk. Systematic risk is the risk arising from movements in the market as a whole. Systematic risk cannot be removed by diversifying a portfolio (hence it is also known as non-diversifiable risk). Non-systematic risk is the risk that is specific to a particular firm or industry sector. Non-systematic risk can be removed by diversifying a portfolio (and is therefore alternatively known as diversifiable risk).

The importance of correlations in the estimation of portfolio risk is illustrated by Exercises 15.1, 15.2 and 15.3.

●●●● Foreign investments and portfolio risk

Investing in the securities of foreign countries has two opposing effects on the risk of a portfolio. Risk is reduced since the foreign investments increase the degree of diversification of the portfolio. On the other hand there is an additional source of risk to the extent that foreign investments are priced in foreign currencies. The consensus view is that the risk reducing effects are greater than the risk enhancement effects.

Both of these effects can be interpreted in terms of the Markowitz equation for the measurement of portfolio risk. The risk reduction effect of increased diversification is enhanced by choosing investments in those countries whose stock markets show the lowest correlations with the domestic market (and with one another). The effects of international diversification on portfolio risk can be illustrated by means of Figure 15.3.

Figure 15.3 shows how the risk of a portfolio tends to decline as the number of different stocks in the portfolio increases. The decline is most rapid when the correlation of returns between the stocks is low. The correlation is likely to be lower between a domestic and a foreign stock than between two domestic stocks. As a result the risk of the international portfolio (comprising both domestic and foreign stocks) tends to decline faster than the risk of the portfolio containing only domestic stocks. Furthermore since the returns on the domestic and foreign stock markets will not be perfectly correlated, the lowest achievable risk will be lower for the international portfolio than for the domestic portfolio. Systematic (non-diversifiable) risk for internationally diversified portfolios is lower than systematic risk for domestic portfolios.

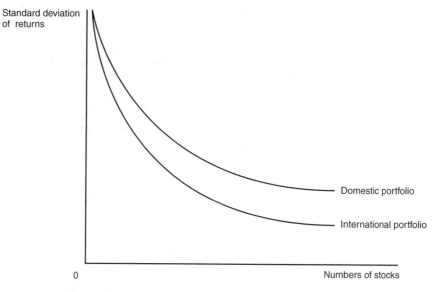

Figure 15.3 Portfolio risk

Exercise 15.1

A portfolio consists of stocks A, B and C in equal proportions. Each has an expected return of 10% p.a. and an annual standard deviation of returns of 8%. The coefficient of correlation between the returns of A and B is 0.9, while the correlations between A and C and between B and C are both 0.

(a) Calculate the expected return and risk of the portfolio. (b) Show how risk can be reduced by changing the proportions of A, B and C. Why has the risk reduction occurred?

Answers

(a) Let $E(R_p)$ = expected return on the portfolio.
$E(R_p) = (1/3)10\% + (1/3)10\% + (1/3)10\% = 10\%$ p.a.
Let V = variance of the portfolio.
$V = (1/3)^2 8^2 + (1/3)^2 8^2 + (1/3)^2 8^2 + 2(1/3)^2 8^2 (0.9) + 2(1/3)^2 8^2 (0) + 2(1/3)^2 8^2 (0)$
$V = (0.11)64 + (0.11)64 + (0.11)64 + 2(0.11)64(0.9)$
$V = 7.11 + 7.11 + 7.11 + 2(7.11)(0.9)$
$V = 21.33 + 12.8 = 34.13$
Standard deviation $= \sqrt{V} = \sqrt{34.13} = 5.84$

(b) Increase the proportion held in C to 40% and reduce the proportions held in A and B to 30% each.
$V = (0.3)^2 8^2 + (0.3)^2 8^2 + (0.4)^2 8^2 + 2(0.3)^2 8^2 (0.9)$
$V = 5.76 + 5.76 + 10.24 + 10.37 = 32.13$
Standard deviation $= \sqrt{V} = \sqrt{32.13} = 5.67$
Portfolio risk has been reduced because there is now a higher proportion in the stock, whose correlation with both of the other stocks is low.

Exercise 15.2

An investor has a portfolio of three stocks. Their expected returns are A 7%, B 8% and C 9% p.a. The expected standard deviations of returns are A 12%, B 14% and C 16% p.a. The correlations between returns are AB 0.3, AC 0.8 and BC 0.2.

(a) Calculate the portfolio expected return and risk if each of the stocks constitutes one third of the portfolio.

(b) Suggest weightings for A, B and C that would produce a portfolio with lower risk. Explain why risk is reduced.

Answers

(a) Expected return is: $(0.33 \times 7) + (0.33 \times 8) + (0.33 \times 9) = 8\%$ p.a.
Portfolio variance, V_p, is:
$V_p = (1/3)^2(0.12)^2 + (1/3)^2(0.14)^2 + (1/3)^2(0.16)^2 + 2(1/3)(1/3)(0.12)(0.14)(0.3) +$
$\qquad 2(1/3)(1/3)(0.12)(0.16)(0.8) + 2(1/3)(1/3)(0.14)(0.16)(0.2)$
$V_p = 0.0016 + 0.00218 + 0.00284 + 0.00112 + 0.00341 + 0.001$
$V_p = 0.01215$
Standard deviation $= \sqrt{0.01215} = 0.1102$ i.e. 11.02% p.a.

(b) Risk might be reduced by increasing the weighting of the relatively low risk share, A, and increasing the weighting of the share with low correlations, B. For example 40% A, 40% B and 20% C.
$V_p = (0.4)^2(0.12)^2 + (0.4)^2(0.14)^2 + (0.2)^2(0.16)^2 + 2(0.4)(0.4)(0.12)(0.14)(0.3) +$
$\qquad 2(0.4)(0.2)(0.12)(0.16)(0.8) + 2(0.4)(0.2)(0.14)(0.16)(0.2)$
$V_p = 0.0023 + 0.00314 + 0.00102 + 0.00161 + 0.00246 + 0.00072$
$V_p = 0.01125$
Standard deviation $= \sqrt{0.01125} = 0.1061$ i.e. 10.61% p.a.

Whereas the increased diversification provided by foreign investments reduces risk, the acquisition of currency exposure increases it. For the most part foreign stocks are priced in foreign currencies. If a foreign currency loses value relative to the domestic currency, the domestic currency value of the foreign investment will fall. A security may provide high returns in terms of its own currency, but a relative fall in that currency would offset those returns for foreign investors. Exchange rate movements can turn strong profits into heavy losses (or vice versa). A US dollar investment might produce a 10% return in dollar terms, but if the dollar falls 20% against the euro the result for a European investor is a 10% loss.

This can be expressed in terms of the Markowitz formula. The risk of a foreign security, held as an investor's only asset, is represented by σ_F in equation 5.

$$\sigma_F^2 = \sigma_D^2 + \sigma_C^2 + 2\,\rho_{DC}\,\sigma_D\,\sigma_C \qquad (5)$$

In equation 5, σ_D represents the risk (standard deviation of returns) of the security from the point of view of a domestic investor. The currency risk faced by a foreign investor is shown as σ_C. The correlation between the domestic returns on the security and the exchange rate movements is represented by ρ_{DC}. It might be noted that

Exercise 15.3

Stocks A, B and C have expected rates of return of 6% p.a. and standard deviations of returns of 10% p.a. The coefficients of correlation between the returns are:

A and B 0.9
A and C 0.2
B and C 0.2

(a) Calculate the risk of a portfolio of 40% A, 40% B and 20% C.
(b) Suggest a portfolio with lower risk.
(c) What practical difficulties would an investment manager face when calculating the risk of a portfolio of stocks?

Answers

(a) $V = (0.4)^2(0.1)^2 + (0.4)^2(0.1)^2 + (0.2)^2(0.1)^2$
$\qquad + 2.(0.4)^2(0.1)^2(0.9) + 2(0.4)(0.2)(0.1)^2(0.2)$
$\qquad + 2.(0.4)(0.2)(0.1)^2(0.2)$
$\quad = 0.0016 + 0.0016 + 0.0004 + 0.00288 + 0.00032 + 0.00032$
$\quad = 0.00712$

Standard deviation of portfolio returns = 8.44% p.a.

(b) Since C has a low correlation with both A and B, a higher proportion of C might reduce risk. One possibility could be 30% A, 30% B and 40% C. In this case the risk would be calculated as
$V = (0.3)^2(0.1)^2 + (0.3)^2(0.1)^2 + (0.4)^2(0.1)^2$
$\qquad + 2(0.3)^2(0.1)^2(0.9) + 2(0.3)(0.4)(0.1)^2(0.2)$
$\qquad + 2(0.3)(0.4)(0.1)^2(0.2)$
$V = 0.00598$

Standard deviation of portfolio returns = 7.73% p.a.

(c) The calculations in (a) and (b) have involved just three stocks. In reality there are thousands of stocks that might be incorporated into a portfolio and calculating correlation coefficients between each possible pair of stocks would be problematic. Even a portfolio of 50 different shares (not an unusual number) would involve 1,225 correlation coefficients. Correlating each stock with a stock index would be a little less accurate but would reduce the number of correlations required to 50.

Another practical difficulty is that past statistical data may not be a reliable guide to future values. Returns, risks and correlations can change over time so that the past is not always a reliable guide to the future.

the weighting for both the security risk and the currency risk is 1; this is because they both relate to the full value of the investment.

A numerical example can illustrate some of the implications of equation 5. Suppose that the risk (standard deviation of returns) for a domestic investor is 20% p.a. and that a foreign investor faces a 15% p.a. exchange rate risk. If this relates to a British investor buying a US security, the risk for a US investor is 20% whereas the British investor faces that risk plus a 15% p.a. currency risk. Suppose further that there is zero correlation between the domestic returns on the security and the currency movements. Introducing these values into equation 5 gives:

$$20^2 + 15^2 = 400 + 225 = 625$$

$$\sigma_F^2 = 625$$

$$\therefore \sigma_F = 25$$

The combination of a domestic security risk of 20% p.a. and a currency risk of 15% p.a. is a foreign security risk of 25% p.a.

Finally, it could be argued that not all of the currency risk should be included in the calculation of total risk. For example, the investor's annual expenditure might be spent partly on imported goods. This may give a currency risk which is opposite to that on foreign investments. A rise in the US dollar against the euro will make imports from the US more expensive for Europeans, but that currency movement enhances investment returns on US securities held by Europeans. One currency exposure off-sets the other. To the extent that this happens, the exchange rate exposure of foreign investments can be seen as reducing risk rather than increasing it.

The significance of including a risk-free asset among the investment alternatives

If a risk-free asset (Treasury bill or bank deposit) is available to them, investors may hold combinations of the risk-free asset and a portfolio of risky assets. Rational investors would choose a portfolio of risky assets on the efficiency frontier. More specifically they would choose the portfolio depicted by A in Figure 15.4. This is known as the market portfolio.

The rate of return on the risk-free asset is shown as R_f. Rational investors would hold combinations of the risk-free asset and the portfolio at A. Point A indicates the expected return/risk combination of the portfolio that produces the highest capital market line. The capital market line is the set of points that represent combinations of the risk-free asset and the market portfolio.

To the left of point A investors are combining positive amounts of the risk-free asset with the portfolio at A. To the right of A investors combine negative amounts of the risk-free asset with the portfolio. In other words, to the right of A investors borrow money in order to hold an amount of the market portfolio that exceeds their wealth.

Asset allocation lines

Farrar (1962) found that US mutual funds (unit trusts) were, typically, not on the efficiency frontier. This finding has been supported by subsequent studies by other researchers. Individual investors can nevertheless create investment opportunities

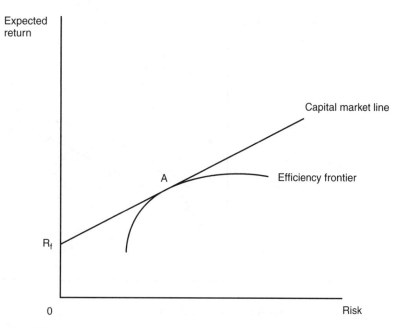

Figure 15.4 Market portfolio

that correspond to the capital market line by combining holdings of risk free assets (e.g. bank or building society deposits) with holdings of a unit trust. The resulting opportunities will be on what is termed an asset allocation line. Such an asset allocation line is illustrated in Figure 15.5.

The point marked by X describes the risk-return characteristics of a unit trust. An investor can attain a point along the asset allocation line by combining a holding of the unit trust with a bank deposit (or debt if the chosen position is to the right of point X).

The investor could get closer to the capital market line by holding a portfolio of unit trusts (which will further reduce non-systematic risk and move point X towards the efficiency frontier). Alternatively the investor might choose a unit trust that invests in a broad index of the market, for example, the FT All Share index. In this way an investor can get close to the capital market line (however, even index tracker funds based on broad indices do not fully correspond to the market portfolio at A in Figure 15.4, since the market portfolio contains all possible investments – domestic stocks, foreign stocks, bonds, property, etc.).

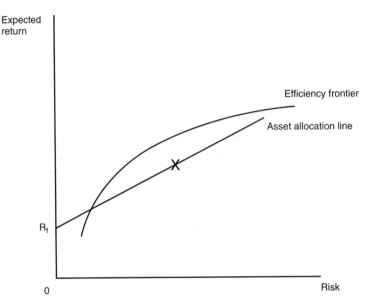

Figure 15.5 Asset allocation line

Exercise 15.4

A fund manager intends to construct a portfolio of shares, bonds and deposits. The expected returns on these asset classes are 10% p.a., 5% p.a. and 3% p.a. respectively. The expected standard deviations of returns are 20% p.a., 15% p.a. and 0% p.a. respectively. The coefficients of correlation between returns are:

shares/bonds 0.5
shares/deposits 0
bonds/deposits 0

(a) Calculate the expected return and standard deviation of a portfolio comprising 60% shares, 30% bonds and 10% deposits.
(b) How could the fund manager construct a portfolio with half the risk of the portfolio of part (a)?

Answers
(a) The expected return would be:
$(10 \times 0.6) + (5 \times 0.3) + (3 \times 0.1) = 7.8\%$ p.a.
The expected variance would be:
$$V = (0.2)^2(0.6)^2 + (0.15)^2(0.3)^2 + (0)^2(0.1)^2 + 2(0.2)(0.15)(0.6)(0.3)(0.5) +$$
$$2(0.2)(0)(0.6)(0.1)(0) + 2(0.15)(0)(0.3)(0.1)(0)$$
$V = 0.0144 + 0.002025 + 0 + 0.0054 + 0 + 0 = 0.021825$
The expected standard deviation is:
$\sqrt{V} = \sqrt{0.021825} = 0.1477$ i.e. 14.77% p.a. (to 2 decimal places)

(b) One approach would be to halve the weightings of the risky assets so that the portfolio becomes:
30% shares, 15% bonds, 55% deposits
The expected variance would now be:

$V = (0.2)^2(0.3)^2 + (0.15)^2(0.15)^2 + (0)^2(0.55)^2 + 2(0.2)(0.15)(0.3)(0.15)(0.5) +$
$\quad 2(0.2)(0)(0.3)(0.55)(0) + 2(0.15)(0)(0.15)(0.55)(0)$
$V = 0.0036 + 0.00050625 + 0 + 0.00135 + 0 + 0 = 0.0054562$
The expected standard deviation is:
$\sqrt{V} = \sqrt{0.0054562} = 0.073866$ i.e. 7.39% p.a. (to two decimal places)

Exercise 15.5

There are two risky assets available, a share and a bond. The share has an expected return of 8% p.a. and an expected standard deviation of returns of 16% p.a. The bond has an expected return of 4% p.a. and an expected standard deviation of returns of 10% p.a. There is also a risk-free asset available, a bank deposit paying 2% p.a. The coefficient of correlation between the expected returns on the share and the bond is 0.3. The coefficient of correlation between the bank deposit and the share is 0, as is the correlation between the bank deposit and the bond.

(a) Calculate the expected return, and the standard deviation of returns, of a portfolio comprising 50% of the share and 50% of the bond.
(b) Calculate the expected return, and the standard deviation of returns, of a portfolio comprising 25% of the share, 25% of the bond and 50% of the deposit.
(c) How could an investor raise the expected return to 10% p.a.? What level of risk might be involved?

Answers
(a) $E(R_p) = (0.5)8 + (0.5)4 = 6\%$ p.a.
$\quad V_p = (0.5)^2(0.16)^2 + (0.5)^2(0.1)^2 + 2(0.5)(0.5)(0.16)(0.1)(0.3)$
$\qquad = 0.0064 + 0.0025 + 0.0024 = 0.0113$
$\quad \sigma_p = \sqrt{V_p} = \sqrt{0.0113} = 0.1063$ i.e. 10.63% p.a.

(b) $E(R_p) = (0.25)8 + (0.25)4 + (0.5)2 = 4\%$ p.a.
$\quad V_p = (0.25)^2(0.16)^2 + (0.25)^2(0.1)^2 + (0.5)^2(0)^2 + 2(0.25)(0.25)(0.16)(0.1)(0.3)$
$\qquad + 2(0.25)(0.5)(0.16)(0)(0) + 2(0.25)(0.5)(0.1)(0)(0)$
$\quad V_p = 0.0016 + 0.000625 + 0 + 0.0006 + 0 + 0 = 0.002825$
$\quad \sigma_p = \sqrt{V_p} = \sqrt{0.002825} = 0.05315$ i.e. 5.315% p.a.

Note that this is exactly half the risk as that provided by the portfolio in part (a). This is to be expected since the portfolio of part (b) comprises 50% of the portfolio of part (a) and 50% the risk-free asset.

(c) The investor could borrow a sum equal to his or her wealth. The whole of the investor's wealth, plus the sum borrowed, would be invested in the portfolio of part (a). The expected return would be 10% p.a.
$\quad E(R_p) = (1.0)8 + (1.0)4 - (1.0)2$
$\quad 10 = 8 + 4 - 2$
The expected standard deviation of returns would be:
$\quad 2 \times 10.63 = 21.26\%$ p.a.
The expected return could be found from the equation of the capital market line:
$\quad E(R_p) = 2 + (4/10.63)\sigma_p$
$\quad 10 = 2 + [(4/10.63) \times 21.26]$

The logic that lies behind overseas diversification

How internationally diversified should a portfolio be? Advice varies widely. In February, the New York Times reported that Merrill Lynch advises a limit on foreign stocks of five per cent, down from 35 per cent. The article noted that Goldman Sachs advises 15–20 per cent and Morgan Stanley 25–35 per cent. Stefano Cavaglia, a global equity strategist at UBS Brinson, advises US investors to hold half of their portfolio in foreign equity. Who's right?

The case for diversification begins with the fact that investors must make decisions under uncertainty. Because future returns cannot be known, smart investors will assess the uncertainty of returns by specifying probability distributions (see Box).

These distributions, which reflect the subjective views of an investor, describe the expected values and variances of the returns, as well as correlations between returns. Investors are rational when their subjective views coincide with what is objectively true. Unfortunately, objective probability distributions are not published anywhere, so differences about diversification can be traced to differences of opinion about the probability distributions of future returns. One way to generate these distributions is to estimate them using historical data, assuming the future will look like the past. Let's suppose this is true.

Table 1 gives statistics for dollar-denominated excess returns on 12 country portfolios. The raw data are the Morgan Stanley Capital International total monthly returns for each country in excess of the return on a eurodollar deposit, which is a reasonable proxy for the risk-free return.

Mean monthly excess returns are annualised and standard deviations are calculated to correspond to

Table 1: Statistics from annualised excess returns by country
US dollars; 1970-2000

Country	US	JP	GB	FR	DE	IT	NL	BE	CH	SE	AT	SG	
Mean	5.7	8.8	7.8	7.6	6.7	3.3	8.4	8.9	7.3	11.2	3.5	10.9	
Standard deviation	15.3	22.9	23.9	23.0	20.4	26.4	18.8	17.8	19.0	22.3	25.1	30.9	
Correlation	1.00	0.27	0.50	0.45	0.38	0.25	0.42	0.57	0.49	0.43	0.47	0.47	**US**
		1.00	0.36	0.39	0.36	0.35	0.40	0.42	0.42	0.38	0.29	0.34	**JP**
			1.00	0.54	0.43	0.34	0.51	0.64	0.56	0.42	0.47	0.48	**GB**
				1.00	0.61	0.44	0.66	0.61	0.61	0.40	0.37	0.28	**FR**
					1.00	0.39	0.64	0.69	0.68	0.47	0.30	0.28	**DE**
						1.00	0.41	0.37	0.37	0.36	0.23	0.19	**IT**
							1.00	0.66	0.63	0.42	0.30	0.31	**NL**
								1.00	0.71	0.47	0.41	0.41	**BE**
									1.00	0.50	0.39	0.37	**CH**
										1.00	0.40	0.36	**SE**
											1.00	0.42	**AT**
												1.00	**SG**

US = United States
JP = Japan
GB = Great Britain
FR = France
DE = Germany
IT = Italy
NL = Netherlands
BE = Belgium
CH = Switzerland
SE = Sweden
AT = Australia
SG = Singapore

Note: The means and standard deviations are measured in per cent per annum. The raw data are MSCI monthly country returns in excess of the eurodollar rate (which averaged 7 per cent). Figures are annualised by multiplying the mean monthly returns by 12 and the standard deviation of monthly returns by the square root of 12.

an annualised holding period. The highest average is Sweden's 11.2 per cent and the lowest is Italy's 3.3 per cent. The US average is 5.7 per cent. Standard deviations range from a low of 15.3 per cent a year for the US to 30.9 per cent for Singapore. Because returns are in dollars, the return for any country other than the US contains both the local currency equity return and the change in the value of the US dollar relative to the local currency, which provides an additional source of volatility.

After assessing the probability distributions, the rational investor must consider preferences for risk and return. It is uncontroversial to assume that an investor likes high expected returns on a portfolio and dislikes variance in future returns. What trade-offs between risk and return do financial markets offer?

For a US investor with a US portfolio, there is a trade-off in terms of how much the expected return rises with an increase in the portfolio's standard devi-

Equation 1

Expected portfolio excess return = (% invested in US × expected US excess return) + (% invested in GB × expected GB excess return)

Equation 2

Variance of portfolio return = [(% invested in US)² × (variance of US excess return)] + [(% invested in GB)² × (variance of GB excess return)] + [2 × (% invested in US) × (% invested in GB) × (covariance of US excess return and GB excess return)]

Equation 3

Risk-return trade-off improves if:

$$\frac{\text{expected GB excess return}}{\text{covariance of US excess return and GB excess return}} > \frac{\text{expected US excess return}}{\text{variance of US return}}$$

▶

ation as the investor moves from risk-free assets to equities. This trade-off can be calculated using the mean return and standard deviation statistics in Table 1. In the case of the US portfolio, the trade-off is 5.7/15.3 = 0.37. So for each percentage point increase in the standard deviation of a US portfolio, the investor is compensated with a 0.37 per cent increase in expected return. Depending on their tolerance for risk, investors will choose a portfolio, for example, two-thirds in US equities and a third in risk-free securities. However, this analysis ignores a key issue, which is the potential improvement in the trade-off between risk and return that comes from diversifying internationally.

Now, suppose our US investor is willing to add British equity to the portfolio if doing so improves the trade-off between risk and return. Some investors might look at the ratio of British expected excess return to British standard deviation, which, from Table 1, is 7.8/23.9 = 0.33 and conclude they should not diversify because the British trade-off of 0.33 is worse than the US figure of 0.37. This conclusion is wrong.

Underlying logic

To see why, one should recognise that the expected excess return on a portfolio of US and British equity would be the weighted sum of the expected excess returns on the two country returns, where the weights are the shares of wealth invested in each of the two countries (see Equation 1).

The variance of the portfolio is the squared weight on the US return times the variance of the US return, plus the squared weight on the British return times the variance of the British return, plus two times the product of the two investment weights times the covariance between the two country returns (see Equation 2).

From differential calculus we know that the effect of adding British equity to the expected portfolio excess return is simply the British expected return, while the effect on the variance of the portfolio is given by the covariance of the British return with the US return.

Thus, the ratio of expected portfolio return to the variance of the portfolio return goes up if the ratio of the expected return on British equity to its covariance with the US is larger than the ratio of the expected return on the US to the variance of the return on the US (see Equation 3).

We can rephrase the argument in terms of expected returns and standard deviations by recognising that the covariance is the correlation coefficient times the product of the two standard deviations. So,

US investors should add British equity if the ratio of British expected return to standard deviation divided by the correlation between the US and British returns is greater than the ratio of US expected return to its standard deviation. The British statistics produce a result of: 7.8/(23.9 × 0.50) = 0.65.

This easily exceeds the US figure of (5.7/15.3) = 0.37. A similar result comes out for the other countries, except Australia comes out lower, at 0.30.

The average correlation between the US return and returns on the other countries is 0.43. It is this low correlation between country returns that generates a significant improvement in the risk-return trade-off. Let's see how our US investor can use this to generate a portfolio that has an optimal risk-return trade-off.

An optimal portfolio

Figure 1 has expected return on the vertical axis (equal to the excess return from Table 1 plus the eurodollar rate, which averages out at 7 per cent) and standard deviation of return on the horizontal axis. Points corresponding to expected returns and standard deviations from Table 1 are labelled with the country codes. The upper half of the solid curved line represents the efficient frontier, that is the minimum standard deviation of a portfolio of the 12 country returns that can be achieved for a given level of expected return on the portfolio. The dashed line represents the efficient frontier for a US investor who only invests in G5 countries (US, Japan, Great Britain, France and Germany).

The point labelled MVE, the mean-variance efficient point, corresponds to the point of tangency between a straight line starting from the risk-free return on the vertical axis and the efficient frontier. The MVE point

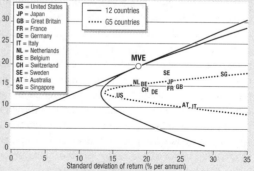

Figure 1: Mean-standard deviation frontiers 1970-2000

A statistical refresher

- A probability distribution lists the values returns may take and the probabilities associated with different possible returns.
- The expected value of a future return is also called the mean of the probability distribution and is calculated as the probability-weighted average of the possible future values of that return. This is the sum of the probabilities of the events times the values of the return if those events occur.
- The variance of the distribution of a future return is the probability-weighted average of the squared deviations from the mean return.
- A related concept is standard deviation, which is measured in the same units

as returns because it is the square root of variance.
- The covariance of two returns describes how the possible realisations of these returns move together. It is measured by the probability-weighted average of the deviations from the mean for one return times the deviations from the mean of another return.
- A related concept is the correlation coefficient – the covariance of two returns divided by the product of the two respective standard deviations. Correlations range between −1 and +1. If two returns are perfectly correlated, the correlation is +1; if they are not at all correlated, the correlation is 0; and if they are perfectly negatively correlated, the correlation is −1.

corresponds to a specific portfolio investment in the 12 countries that I'll call the global portfolio.

An investor with no equities gets the risk-free return, which averaged 7 per cent during this sample period. Increasing investment in the global portfolio moves the investor to the top-right along the straight line, increasing expected return and risk. Because the expected excess return of the global portfolio is 12.6 per cent and the standard deviation of the global portfolio is 18.6 per cent, the trade-off between the expected excess return and standard deviation for the global portfolio is 12.6/18.6 = 0.68.

Notice that for the same standard deviation as the US equity portfolio – 15.3 per cent – the global investor can have an increase of almost five per cent in expected return, from 12.7 per cent to 17.6 per cent. Alternatively, the investor can accept the same expected return as the US portfolio while reducing the standard deviation of the portfolio to below 10 per cent. Investing only in G5 countries also offers an improvement in the risk-return trade-off for a US investor, but the improvement is not as great as from the global portfolio.

This analysis uses historical data from 1970 to 2000 to estimate true expected returns, variances and covariances. Why might it misrepresent the case for diversification?

First, estimating expected returns is difficult, so average excess returns are measured with substantial error. In choosing a sample period, it is important to include several good and bad periods to avoid bias. For example, calculating average returns from 1980 to 2000 would substantially overstate the true expected excess returns because this period does not contain sufficiently problematic experiences, such as recessions and major wars, that are associated with poor equity performance. Omitting the 1970s, the average excess returns on equities exceed the average returns in Table 1 by anywhere between 1.5 per cent and 5 per cent, depending on the country.

One can also use theory to help determine an appropriate expected return. When academic Jacob Thomas and analyst James Claus combine analysts' earnings forecasts for major countries with a financial valuation model, they find expected excess returns of just 3 per cent.

Second, some past returns are probably poorer representations of what to expect than others. Japan's average excess return of 8.8 per cent represents very good performance in the 1980s, yet is poor for the 1990s. What should we expect going forward? Is Japan mired in recession, or is a return to growth around the corner?

Third, the analysis does not constrain all the portfolio positions in the different countries to be positive, and the MVE portfolio takes short positions in five of the 12 countries. Many investors avoid short positions in portfolios. Allowing only long positions reduces, but does not eliminate, gains from international diversification. For example, the risk-return trade-off for a global portfolio whose weights correspond to the average market capitalisations of the 12 countries during the sample period is 6.9/14.0 = 0.49.

Fourth, there is evidence that correlations of country returns are increasing, especially in down markets. As technology progresses and markets become more integrated, we should expect correlations to increase. The average correlation between returns for the US and the other countries calculated for the last five years of the sample is 0.58, substantially above the 0.43 for the full sample period. Could future correlations be even higher?

The New York Times article cited earlier indicates that correlations calculated over three-year rolling intervals between the US market and developed foreign markets were as low as 0.15 in early 1987 and now stand slightly below 0.8. Further, academics François Longin and Bruno Solnik have demonstrated that correlations across countries are especially large when the US market experiences a large drop. Thus, exactly when US investors have the greatest need for the benefits of diversification, they do not materialise. Does this evidence indicate that international diversification is unwarranted?

Academics Andrew Ang and Geert Bekaert have found that correlations across countries do increase in highly volatile markets, confirming the findings of Longin and Solnik. Yet Ang and Bekaert still find substantial value from international diversification because correlations fall when equity markets are doing well and volatility is lower. It seems unlikely that the world economy is so integrated that future correlations are going to remain as high as they may now seem. There is simply too much diversity in government policies and business cycles to think otherwise.

It is also possible to diversify internationally by choosing the equities of a country based on some measurable criterion and not just by their geographic location. Investment managers often use the ratio of a company's book value to its equity market value (the B/M ratio) to classify companies as 'value' stocks (ones with high B/M) and 'growth' stocks (ones with low B/M).

Academics Eugene Fama and Kenneth French found that value stocks in the US and major countries in MSCI's EAFE index have substantially higher average returns than growth stocks between 1975 and 1995.

Fama and French rank companies in the MSCI index of a country by B/M. This ranking produces a high book-to-market portfolio (HB/M) of companies in the top 30 per cent of B/M, and a low book-to-market portfolio (LB/M) of companies in the lowest 30 per cent. Differences between country portfolios are substantial, from Japan's 9.9% to Italy's −7.0%; with the US at 6.8% and the UK at 4.2%.

There is also benefit from diversification because the correlations of returns across countries on portfolios that long the HB/M companies and short the LB/M companies of a country are low. For example, the average correlation of returns on the high and low portfolios for these countries with the equivalent US portfolio is 0.10.

These arguments suggest there is ample opportunity for a US investor to form a globally diversified portfolio that improves upon the risk-return trade-off from investing only in the US. However, knowing the right percentage of foreign equity is difficult.

A world market portfolio would require US investors to put half of their investments in foreign equity because US equity represents about half of the world economy. This is the UBS Brinson advice. Will US investors diversify that much? Probably not, because the US did very well in the past decade and correlations of returns across countries are high. Even so, this author is uncomfortable with Merrill Lynch's five per cent level. The US has not always produced the best returns. I also expect future correlations to be low enough to give a substantial benefit from international diversification.

Source: Robert Hodrick, *Financial Times*, *Mastering Investment Supplement*, Part 3, May 28 2001, pp. 6–7. Reprinted with permission.

Chapter 16

Capital market theory: the capital asset pricing model

After studying this chapter readers should be able to:

- *interpret beta values*

- *use the security market line to estimate the expected return of a stock or a portfolio*

- *use the security market line to identify mispriced stocks*

- *appreciate the role of demand and supply in the determination of share prices.*

The meaning of beta

The beta of the capital asset pricing model can be interpreted in several ways. One is as the relationship between expected percentage changes in the stock price and percentage changes in a stock index. A beta of 1 indicates that a 1% rise in a stock index would be expected to be associated with a 1% rise in the stock price. Likewise a stock with a beta of 2 would be expected to experience a 2% price rise. A stock with a beta of 0.5 has an expected price rise (fall) of 0.5% when the stock index rises (falls) by 1%. This view of beta sees it as a measure of market risk (systematic risk). High beta stocks tend to show high price volatility.

A second interpretation of beta views it in terms of the characteristic line. The characteristic line relates the excess return of the individual stock (the excess of the stock return over the risk free rate) to the excess return of the stock index portfolio. A graph is drawn based on a set of points that have excess return on the stock on the vertical axis, and the excess return on the market index on the horizontal axis. These points are based on a series of observations from past time periods (a time series). Figure 16.1 shows a hypothetical example of a characteristic line.

The points marked by an X are observed combinations of the excess return on the individual stock ($r_i - r_f$) and the excess return on the stock index portfolio ($r_m - r_f$), where the stock index portfolio is used as a proxy for the market portfolio. The characteristic line is the straight line that provides the best fit to the set of observed points. The beta of the stock is the gradient of the characteristic line (a/b). The intercept of the characteristic line with the vertical axis is the alpha (α) of the

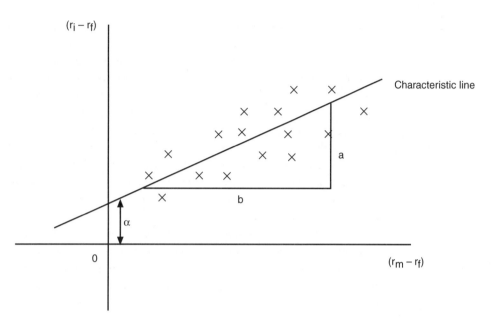

Figure 16.1 A characteristic line

stock. The vertical distances between the characteristic line and the observed points reflect non-systematic risk.

The alpha of a stock is its risk adjusted excess return, in other words the amount by which the excess return is above the level justified by beta. In equilibrium alpha will be zero. Arbitrage will tend to move alpha towards zero (through purchases of positive alpha stocks and sales of negative alpha stocks).

A third interpretation of beta is in terms of covariances and variances or, equivalently, in terms of correlations and variances.

$$\text{Beta} = \sigma_{im}/\sigma_m^2 \qquad \text{alternatively beta} = \rho.\sigma_i/\sigma_m$$

σ_{im} is the covariance between the returns on the individual stock and those on the stock index portfolio, σ_m^2 is the variance of the stock index portfolio, ρ is the coefficient of correlation between the returns on the individual stock and the returns on the index portfolio, σ_i is the standard deviation of returns on the individual stock, and σ_m is the standard deviation of returns on the stock index portfolio.

These three interpretations of beta are different ways of looking at the same thing. They are alternative perspectives on the same measure of systematic (market) risk.

It is to be emphasised that stock index portfolios are used as proxies for the market portfolio, which cannot be measured. It is therefore to be expected that the resulting measure of beta is imperfect. Some researchers have noted that other sources of risk premiums are positively correlated, and hence might be incorporated into a measure of beta. These sources include firm size, price-earnings ratio, and the price/book-value ratio. A beta that takes account of the fundamental characteristics of the firm, as well as its covariance with the market portfolio, is known as a fundamental beta. Evidence suggests that fundamental beta produces a better estimate of future beta than does historical beta alone (Rosenberg and Guy, 1976). Another refinement used in forecasting beta is to adjust historical beta to reflect the observation that portfolio betas tend to regress towards 1 over time (Blume, 1971).

It has been widely observed that betas for individual stocks are unstable over time whereas portfolio betas exhibit much greater stability. This is consistent with the view that beta encompasses a number of different sources of systematic risk (such as interest rates, exchange rates, and commodity prices). An individual stock beta may be unstable as a result of the stock returns reacting to changes in some of the sources of systematic risk underlying beta but not to others. The market as a whole reacts to all sources of systematic risk but an individual stock responds to only some of them. So the individual stock will appear to have a high beta at some times and a low one at others, dependent upon which source of systematic risk is changing at the time. Portfolios are likely to contain stocks which, taken together, react to a wide variety of sources of systematic risk.

The single index model

The estimation of portfolio risk using the Markowitz equation requires a huge input of data. The standard deviation of returns is required for every security. In addition the coefficient of correlation of returns between each pair of securities is required. Since the available securities are numbered in thousands, the number of correlations to be estimated is massive. Although the development of computer technology has rendered the task feasible, there is an alternative approach that requires less information. This alternative is the single index model, which has proven to be effective in portfolio analysis.

The single index model requires just the beta of each stock and the standard deviation of the market portfolio. The systematic risk of each stock equals its beta multiplied by the standard deviation of the market portfolio. The standard deviation of returns of the market portfolio is usually proxied by the standard deviation of a market index portfolio, such as the portfolio on which the FTSE 100 or the S&P 500 is based.

The beta of a portfolio is the weighted average of the betas of the individual shares in that portfolio. The systematic risk of the portfolio is the portfolio beta multiplied by the standard deviation of returns of the market portfolio. For a well-diversified portfolio, systematic risk approximates total risk.

The security market line

Risk on the capital market line is total risk. Total risk is the sum of systematic (non-diversfiable) risk and non-systematic (diversifiable) risk. However, all rational investors would be expected to hold the market portfolio. The market portfolio would contain all marketable assets. It follows that the market portfolio is perfectly diversified and has only systematic (non-diversifiable) risk. If the market portfolio has only systematic risk, the variable on the horizontal axis could be beta.

Investments along the capital market line are available to all investors. The risk of any investment along that line (any combination of the risk-free asset and the market portfolio) will be limited to systematic risk. Therefore when considering investments on the capital market line, beta can be the measure of risk on the horizontal axis.

The derived relationship between required rates of return and betas is known as the security market line. For any security, or portfolio of securities, there is a required (expected) rate of return related to the beta of the investment. Increases in beta (systematic risk) are associated with increases in the expected rate of return. Systematic risk is compensated for by enhanced expected return. The acceptance of non-systematic risk does not result in higher expected returns. Since non-systematic risk can be eliminated by diversification, and since rational investors are assumed to eliminate it in this way, the acceptance of non-systematic risk is not rewarded by increased expected returns.

The security market line (often referred to as the capital asset pricing model) can be described by means of equation 1. In equation 1, $E(R_i)$ represents the expected (required) rate of return on security i. R_f is the return on the risk free asset, β is the beta of the security, and $E(R_m)$ is the expected return on the market portfolio.

$$E(R_i) = R_f + \beta[E(R_m) - R_f] \qquad (1)$$

The expected (required) rate of return on security i consists of two components. The first component is the risk free rate of return, R_f. The second component is the risk premium, shown as $\beta[E(R_m) - R_f]$. The risk premium is the reward for accepting systematic risk, which is measured by beta.

The market portfolio is treated as having a beta of 1. So the risk premium of the market portfolio is $[E(R_m) - R_f]$ and the expected return is:

$$R_f + E(R_m) - R_f = E(R_m).$$

It might also be noted that if beta is zero, indicating an absence of systematic risk, the expected return is the risk-free rate R_f.

The application of the security market line is illustrated by Exercise 16.1.

Trading rules based on the security market line (Capital Asset Pricing Model)

The security market line provides a required rate of return. In equilibrium the required rate of return would equal the anticipated rate of return. However, the market for a particular security may not be in equilibrium. If the market is out of

Exercise 16.1

The rate of return on Treasury bills is 5% p.a. over the next three months. The expected rate of return on the FT All Share index portfolio over the same period is 8% p.a. An investment trust portfolio has a beta of 1.2 and an expected rate of dividend yield of 4% p.a. What might be the expected rate of capital growth of the investment trust portfolio?

Answer

The security market line of the capital asset pricing model states that:

$E(R_p) = r_f + \beta(E[R_m] - r_f)$
i.e. $E(R_p) = 0.05 + 1.2\,(0.08 - 0.05) = 0.086$
i.e. 8.6% p.a.

So the expected rate of return on the investment trust portfolio is 8.6% p.a. of which 4% p.a. is in the form of dividend yield. So the expected rate of capital gain on the investment trust portfolio is 8.6% − 4% = 4.6% p.a. (which is 1.15% over the three-month period).

equilibrium, trading opportunities will be available. A trading opportunity is the ability to achieve an anticipated return in excess of the required rate of return (or to avoid an anticipated rate of return lower than the required rate). Such opportunities are illustrated by Figure 16.2.

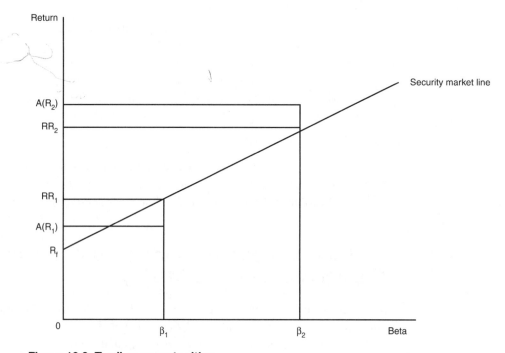

Figure 16.2 Trading opportunities

In Figure 16.2: β_1 =   beta of share 1
              RR_1 =   required (expected) rate of return on share 1
              $A(R_1)$ =   anticipated (forecast) rate of return on share 1
              $A(R_1) - RR_1$ =   alpha of share 1

              β_2 =   beta of share 2
              RR_2 =   required rate of return on share 2
              $A(R_2)$ =   anticipated rate of return on share 2
              $A(R_2) - RR_2$ =   alpha of share 2

Share 1 has a negative excess rate of return and should be avoided (or sold if already held). Share 2 has a positive excess rate of return and should be considered as a possible purchase.

Exercise 16.2

The rate of return on Treasury bills is 4% p.a. The expected return on the FT All Share index portfolio is 9% p.a. Stocks A and B both have anticipated returns of 10% p.a. and a price of 100p. Stock A has a beta of 0.8 and stock B has a beta of 1.7.
   Are these shares mispriced? If so, should they be bought or sold?

Answer
The required rate of return for A should be, according to the security market line:

$$4 + 0.8(9 - 4) = 8\% \text{ p.a.}$$

The anticipated return of 10% p.a. indicates that A should be bought (i.e. A is under-priced).
   For stock B:

$$4 + 1.7(9 - 4) = 12.5\% \text{ p.a.}$$

The anticipated return of 10% indicates that B should be sold (i.e. B is over-priced).

If the anticipated rate of return on a share differs from that derived from the security market line (the required rate), the market is out of equilibrium. Since each investor has their own anticipations, investors are likely to differ in their opinions as to whether the market for a security is in equilibrium. Investors would also tend to differ in their views as to whether alpha is positive or negative.

This is consistent with a downward sloping demand curve for the asset. Investors who believe that there is an anticipated return in excess of the required rate would see the market price as being too low, and could be prepared to buy at a higher price than the current market price. Investors with the opposite view regard the share as overpriced and would require a lower price before they considered buying. As the stock price falls an increasing number of investors will see it as under-priced (offering an anticipated return in excess of the required return). So as the stock price falls, the number of investors willing to buy increases. The demand, supply and equilibrium price for the share are shown by Figure 16.3.

The line DD shows the number of shares demanded (by investors in aggregate) at each price. The vertical line S indicates the number of shares issued. P_e is the equilibrium share price. The price that each investor is prepared to pay could be based on that investor's use of a dividend discount model (with the required rate of return obtained from the security market line) and/or the price-earnings ratio.

Discussion question

What is a security market line? How useful is a security market line as a guide to choosing which shares to buy or sell?

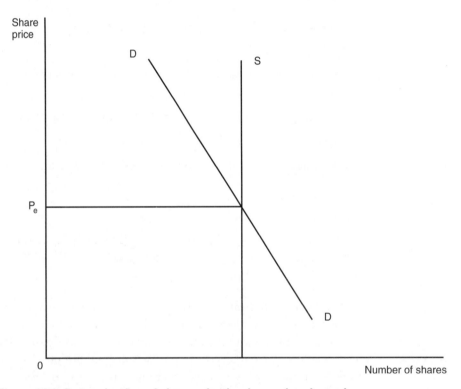

Figure 16.3 Determination of share price by demand and supply

Chapter 17

Capital market theory: alternatives and criticisms

After studying this chapter readers should be able to:

● *assess the arbitrage pricing model*

● *apply the factor approach to bonds*

● *critically evaluate capital market theory.*

The arbitrage pricing model

Arbitrage pricing theory (APT) has been proposed as an alternative to the capital asset pricing model. A central idea of the CAPM is that there is only one risk that affects the long-term average return on an investment. That risk is market risk, which is the tendency of a stock to move in response to movements in the stock market as a whole. Market risk is measured by beta. Beta is often approximated as the expected percentage change in a share price divided by the percentage change in a stock index. High beta stocks embody greater market risk, their price volatilities tend to be high relative to that of the market as a whole.

The capital asset pricing model is reflected in the security market line (SML). The equation for the security market line is shown by equation 1.

$$E(R_i) = R_f + \beta(E\{R_m\} - R_f) \tag{1}$$

where $E(R_i)$ is the expected (or required) rate of return on security i, R_f is the risk-free rate of return (e.g. the return on Treasury bills), β is the beta of the share and $E(R_m)$ is the expected return on the market portfolio (where the market portfolio is often approximated by a stock index portfolio). The term $\beta(E\{R_m\} - R_f)$ is referred to as the risk premium.

A core idea of arbitrage pricing theory is that several systematic influences (rather than just one) affect the long-term average returns of securities. As in the CAPM, risks other than the systematic influences are regarded as diversifiable and hence are not compensated for by way of increased expected returns. The several sources of systematic risk are dealt with by means of using several betas. Each beta captures the sensitivity of the stock to the corresponding systematic factor. Examples of systematic factors could include the market risk used in the CAPM but might also include influences such as unexpected interest rate changes, unexpected exchange rate movements, unexpected changes in the rate of inflation, and unexpected changes in the level of industrial production.

Arbitrage pricing theory suggests that the security market line should be replaced by the following equation (which uses the example of three systematic influences):

$$E(R_i) = R_f + \beta_1(RPF1) + \beta_2(RPF2) + \beta_3(RPF3) \tag{2}$$

where $E(R_i)$ is the expected (or required) rate of return on the security and R_f is the return on a risk free asset. The three beta values applicable to the three risk factors are shown as β_1, β_2 and β_3. The three risk premiums are shown as RPF1 (risk premium of factor 1), RPF2 and RPF3. The theory stipulates neither the number nor the nature of the risk factors. This information has to be obtained by empirical investigation.

The role of arbitrage

In the case of the capital asset pricing model, equilibrium exists when all stocks lie on the security market line. If stocks exhibit risk/return combinations that deviate from the security market line, arbitrage opportunities will arise. Those stocks that exhibit returns below the line can be sold (sold short if necessary) and the proceeds used to buy stocks with expected returns above the line. Such an arbitrage procedure increases expected returns without committing more capital (in the case of short selling no capital is used). This arbitrage will involve selling overpriced securities and buying under-priced securities. This will tend to move securities on to the security market line and hence restore market equilibrium.

There is a corresponding equilibrium relationship in the arbitrage pricing model. Instead of the one dimensional relationship of the CAPM (i.e. the security market line which uses only beta as a risk factor) APT has an n-dimensional relationship (n being the number of risk factors). In the case of the CAPM, equilibrium required all stocks to be on the security market line. This equilibrium condition could alternatively be expressed as an absence of arbitrage opportunities. The equilibrium relationship of arbitrage pricing theory can also be expressed as an absence of arbitrage opportunities. However the arbitrage of APT needs to take account of all n risk factors.

If the arbitrage entails short selling (borrowing shares and selling them), the short positions provide negative betas. The arbitrage transactions would be in a proportion that involves the positive betas of purchased stocks exactly cancelling the negative betas of the short positions in stocks. There would be net zero betas. The difference between the market values of the short and long positions would be matched by investing, or borrowing, at the risk-free rate.

The stocks sold would tend to fall in price and hence their expected rates of return would rise towards the equilibrium rates. The stocks purchased would rise in price with the effect that the expected rates of return fall towards the equilibrium rates. The pursuit of arbitrage profits thus tends to move stocks towards equilibrium.

According to the arbitrage pricing model, all investments with identical risk characteristics should exhibit the same expected rate of return. If this is not the case, it is possible to short sell stocks (or portfolios) with low expected returns and buy those with high expected returns. The purchases and sales should be such as to render all the net betas equal to zero. In other words, the resulting portfolio is risk-free. The difference in the costs of the two portfolios (short sold and bought) is matched by investing or borrowing at the risk-free rate. The result is an arbitrage that produces a rate of return without risk. Pursuit of such arbitrage profits will tend to move stock prices towards their equilibrium values. Equilibrium exists when all securities and portfolios with identical risk characteristics provide the same expected rate of return.

Returns on bonds

The factor approach to ascertaining the required rate of return on bonds parallels the approaches of the capital asset pricing model and arbitrage pricing theory. Whereas the CAPM uses just one factor (the excess return on the market portfolio) and APT uses a number of factors which can vary according to the user, the factors employed when analysing bond returns tend to be related to the yield curve. The yield curve is the relationship between bond yields on a per annum basis (vertical axis) and bond maturity in years (horizontal axis). The two most important factors relate to the level and slope of the yield curve. In particular an intermediate rate of interest (e.g. the redemption yield on bonds with ten years to maturity) may be used to proxy the level of the yield curve and the spread between short and long term interest rates (i.e. the difference between them) may be used to proxy the slope of the yield curve. The equation for the required rate of return can be presented as shown by equation 3.

$$R_b = R_f + (b_1 \times F_1) + (b_2 \times F_2) \tag{3}$$

R_b = required rate of return on bond
R_f = risk free rate of return
b_1 = exposure to intermediate rate
F_1 = risk premium per unit exposure to intermediate rate
b_2 = exposure to spread
F_2 = risk premium per unit exposure to spread

Criticisms of capital market theory

There are three main criticisms of the capital asset pricing model. There is the argument that it is impossible to identify, and measure, the market portfolio. There is the point that it is not possible for individual investors to borrow at the risk free rate of interest. Third, there is the observation that not all empirical studies have established a direct link between beta and average annual returns.

The argument that it is not possible to identify the market portfolio is often referred to as the Roll critique. Since every investor is assumed to hold the same portfolio, that portfolio must contain all available investments. All available investments include not only stocks, bonds and deposits but also a wide range of other investments. These other investments include property, land, works of art, human capital and other tangible and intangible assets. Furthermore, these assets would be drawn from throughout the world. To approximate the market portfolio with a national stock index would involve limiting the measure to one type of asset (equities) in one country. Even an international stock index would exclude a wide variety of financial and non-financial wealth. The Roll critique suggests that the capital asset pricing model can be neither tested nor used since it rests on a wealth aggregate that cannot be measured, or even fully identified.

The arbitrage pricing model avoids this critique because it does not require the use of the market portfolio. The risk factors to be used are not predetermined by theoretical considerations, they are to be established by empirical research.

The point about risk-free borrowing is that it is as troublesome to arbitrage pricing theory as it is to the capital asset pricing model. Individual investors are able to acquire risk free assets, for example Treasury bills issued by national governments. However, individuals are not free of default risk, consequently they cannot expect to be able to borrow at a risk-free rate. The lenders would require a risk premium to compensate for the risk of default by individual investors. One consequence of this is that the capital market line takes the shape shown in Figure 17.1.

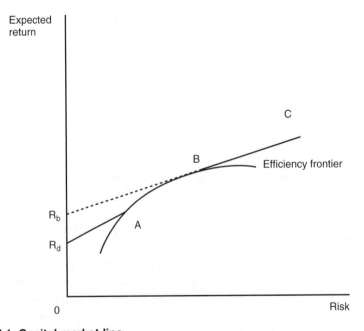

Figure 17.1 Capital market line

In Figure 17.1, R_d is the rate of interest at which money can be deposited or invested. The rate of interest at which money can be borrowed is shown as R_b. The range of investment alternatives is no longer shown as a straight line tangent to the efficiency frontier. The range is shown as R_d–A–B–C. Significantly this new range includes part of the efficiency frontier, A–B. An implication of this is that investors will not all hold exactly the same portfolio of risky assets. Any portfolio between A and B could be held by rational investors.

Another implication of an inability to borrow and lend at the same rate concerns the choice of techniques for acquiring high beta portfolios. If an investor wants a high beta portfolio, there are two alternatives. The investor could buy a portfolio of high beta stocks, or the investor could borrow in order to hold a larger portfolio of lower beta stocks. If borrowing rates are relatively high investors are more likely to choose the first method. The demand for high beta stocks would be higher than the CAPM predicts. In consequence high beta stocks would be relatively overpriced and their returns lower than would be predicted on the basis of their betas. High beta stocks would not provide full compensation, by higher expected returns, for their relatively high systematic risks.

The third source of criticism of the CAPM arises from the empirical evidence on the relationship between beta and average annual returns. Not only is the evidence mixed, it is bedevilled by the difficulty of separating tests of the capital asset pricing model from tests of the efficient market hypothesis. A failure to find a relationship between beta and returns could be due to an inadequacy of either, or both, of the theories. There have been fewer tests of the APT than of the CAPM and hence it remains to be seen whether the APT is a better predictor of investment returns than the CAPM.

A model weighting game in estimating expected returns

Overstating the importance of expected returns in investments is difficult. For money managers, expected returns on assets are important inputs to portfolio decisions. For corporate managers, the expected return on their company's stock is central to the company's cost of capital and thereby affects which projects the company decides to undertake.

Expected return estimates also affect consumers. Charges set by utility companies are set to ensure the utility earns a 'fair rate of return', defined by regulators as the utility's cost of capital. Our energy bills partly depend on how regulators estimate expected returns on utility stocks.

Unfortunately, expected returns are elusive as well as important. Finance professionals differ on how they should be estimated. This article compares the relative merits of common approaches to this challenging task and argues that the best estimates are produced by combining theory with historical returns data and judgment.

Looking to history

'I know of no way of judging the future but by the past,' said American revolutionary Patrick Henry. One simple estimator of an asset's expected return is a sample average of its historical returns. Unless we

▶

suspect that expected return changes in a non-trivial way over time, the sample average return is an unbiased estimator of expected future return – that is, it is not systematically higher or lower than the true expected value. The unbiased nature of this method is its main advantage.

However, getting things right on average is not the only objective. You might have overheard a joke about three econometricians who went hunting and came across a deer. The first one fired a shot and missed by 10 metres to the left. The second one missed by 10 metres to the right. Instead of firing, the third one shouted in triumph: 'We got it!'

The main disadvantage of the sample average is its imprecision. Suppose we want to estimate expected return on the stock of General Motors, traded on the New York Stock Exchange. Using monthly returns from January 1991 to December 2000, the sample average return on GM is 14 per cent a year. The standard error, the usual statistical measure of imprecision, is huge: 10 per cent a year. With 95 per cent confidence, the true expected return is within two standard errors of the sample average, or between – 6 per cent and 34 per cent a year. We want to be more confident than that!

Would the precision increase if we used weekly instead of monthly data? No. Although higher-frequency data helps in estimating variances and covariances of returns, it does not help in estimating expected returns. Intuitively, what matters for expected return is the beginning and ending prices over a given period, not what happens in between.

The only way to get a more precise average is to collect more data. For example, if we use GM returns back to December 1925, the historical average is 15.5 per cent and the 95 per cent confidence interval narrows to between 8.7 per cent and 22.3 per cent. However, the gap is still too wide.

Moreover, GM today is very different from 70 years ago, so the estimate could be contaminated by old data. In general, as we add older data, we gain precision at the expense of introducing potential bias. Striking a balance is difficult and needs sound judgment.

Despite its drawbacks, the long-run average return is a popular estimator for expected returns on aggregate market indices. Unfortunately, we have no theory for what the expected market return should be.

Luckily, for individual stocks and most portfolios, we can rely on estimates produced by theoretical asset pricing models. Those estimates tend to be substantially more precise than sample averages.

Theory is good

Finance theory says riskier assets must offer higher expected returns and asset pricing models quantify this. The Capital Asset Pricing Model (CAPM), says a stock is riskier the more closely its price moves with prices in the market as a whole.

The appropriate measure of risk is therefore the degree of a stock's co-movement with the market, which is summarised by a measure called beta (β). Expected return, $E(r)$, on a given stock is linearly related to the stock's beta. Specifically, the expected stock return in excess of the risk-free rate r_f ('expected excess return') can be expressed using:

$$E(r) - r_f = \beta \times E(r_m - r_f)$$

The constant of proportionality, $E(r_m - r_f)$, is the expected excess return on the market as a whole. It is often called the equity premium.

The value we choose for the risk-free rate r_f depends on our objectives. To forecast expected stock returns over the next month, the appropriate risk-free rate is the yield to maturity on a Treasury bill that matures in one month. If we want to estimate a company's cost of capital to value the company's future cash flows, the risk-free rate should be derived from a longer-term Treasury bond. The bond's duration should be close to the duration of the company's cash flows. Very long-term bonds should be avoided, because their yields might also reflect premiums for risks such as inflation.

Does the above equation solve all our problems? Not quite. The elements on the right side, beta and the equity premium, need to be estimated. Beta is typically estimated by regressing monthly stock returns on market returns over the most recent five to 10 years. For example, the estimate of GM's beta using its monthly data from January 1996 to December 2000 is 1.11.

How much data should we use to estimate beta? The trade-off is similar to that involved for sample averages: the further we go back in time, the higher the statistical precision of the estimate, but the bigger the possibility of introducing bias from old data.

▶

Unlike sample averages, however, here it often pays to use more frequent data. For example, whereas the 95 per cent confidence interval for GM's beta based on the monthly data is 0.65 to 1.57, this interval based on weekly data is tighter, 0.69 to 1.08. GM's beta estimated using weekly data is 0.88.

However, going from monthly to weekly data is recommended only for the most liquid and volatile stocks. For other stocks, some week-to-week price changes are simply movements between the bid and ask prices around the true price, which introduces additional error. Also, it may take time for market-wide news to affect the prices of illiquid stocks, which biases the usual beta estimates downward. Conveniently, betas of illiquid stocks can be estimated using an alternative approach developed by economists Myron Scholes and Joseph Williams.

It is clear from the GM example that estimates of beta contain a fair amount of noise. A useful way of reducing that noise is to 'shrink' the usual estimates to a reasonable value, such as 1. This is reasonable because the average beta across all stocks is 1, by construction.

The 'shrinkage' estimate of beta is the weighted average of the usual sample estimate and of the shrinkage target. For example, the 'adjusted' betas reported by Merrill Lynch put a 2/3 weight on the sample estimate and a 1/3 weight on the value of 1. The adjusted beta for GM is therefore:

$(2/3) \times 0.88 + (1/3) \times 1 = 0.92$

Shrinkage betas can be justified as 'Bayesian' estimators, named after the 18th century English mathematician Thomas Bayes. They reflect not only data but also prior knowledge or judgment. Bayesian estimators have solid axiomatic foundations in statistics and decision theory, unlike many other estimators used by statisticians.

Before seeing data on GM, we know it is a stock, so a good prior guess for GM's beta is 1. Also, we know more about the company; for example, we know which industry it operates in. Since the average beta among carmakers is about 1.2, a reasonable prior guess for GM's beta is 1.2.

How much weight we put on the guess and how much on the estimate depends on the precision of the sample estimate and on the strength of our prior beliefs. Those beliefs can be based for example on the dispersion of betas among carmakers: the stronger the concentration around 1.2, the more weight we put on the prior guess. With equal weights on the prior guess and the weekly sample estimate, GM's industry-adjusted beta is:

$(1/2) \times 0.88 + (1/2) \times 1.2 = 1.04$

Unfortunately, the CAPM says nothing about expected market return and estimating the equity premium is more difficult than estimating betas. More frequent data does not help and there is no obvious prior guess. The most common approach is to average a long series of excess market returns, which leads to equity premium estimates of 5–9 per cent a year, depending on the sample period.

A recent equity premium study by Robert Stambaugh and the author puts the current premium in the US at 4.8 per cent a year. This estimate comes from a model in which the premium changes over the past 165 years. Combining this estimate with GM's industry-adjusted beta and a 6 per cent risk-free rate, the CAPM estimates GM's annual expected return (its cost of equity capital) at 6 per cent plus (1.04 × 4.8 per cent), which comes out at 11 per cent.

Imperfect models

The CAPM is just a model, not a perfect description of reality. Indeed, many academic studies reject its validity because some stock return patterns seem inconsistent with the model. Does this mean we should throw the model away and rely only on model-free estimators, such as the sample average return?

No! Every model is 'wrong', almost by definition, because it makes simplifying assumptions about our complex world. But even a model that is not exact can be useful.

It is again helpful to adopt a Bayesian perspective and combine what the data tell us with our best prior guess. While the data speak to us about expected return through the sample average return (14 per cent a year for GM), our prior guess can be based on finance theory such as the CAPM (11 per cent a year for GM). The resulting estimate is a weighted average of the two numbers. The weights depend on how strongly we believe in the model and on how well the model compares with the data.

This Bayesian approach is developed in another study by Robert Stambaugh and the author. The

▶

study finds that even if we have only modest confidence in a pricing model such as the CAPM, our cost of capital estimates should be heavily weighted towards the model. Average stock returns are noisy, so they should receive small weights. In other words, theory is more powerful than data when estimating expected stock returns.

To make the water muddier, the CAPM is not the only theoretical model of expected returns. Competition comes from multifactor models, in which expected return depends on the stock's betas with respect to more factors than just the market. The factors can be either macroeconomic variables (for example, a five-factor model developed by Naifu Chen, Richard Roll and Stephen Ross), or portfolios formed based on companies' characteristics (for example, a three-factor model of Eugene Fama and Ken French), or even return series constructed using statistical techniques such as factor analysis.

Opinions vary on which model is best and the jury is still out. Meanwhile, what are we to do? A sensible solution is to construct a weighted average of expected return estimates from all models that we are willing to consider, including the 'no-theory' model that produces the sample average estimate. Each estimate should be weighted by the probability that its parent model is correct.

Where do we get these probabilities? It helps to be aware of the relevant research, but in the end this is a matter of judgment. The author believes that, despite its weaknesses, the CAPM has the strongest theoretical foundation and should receive the largest weight. Other models should be weighted according to their theoretical support and empirical success.

Uncertainty

Although pricing models generally produce expected return estimates that are significantly more precise than sample averages, uncertainty remains. Research by Fama and French shows standard errors of more than 3 per cent a year are typical for estimates of industry costs of equity based on common pricing models.

Where does the uncertainty come from? Is it more important that we do not know the true beta, the exact value of the equity premium, or that we do not know the right model?

Interestingly, not knowing which model is right turns out to be less important on average than not knowing the parameters within each model. That is one conclusion from the author's cost of capital study mentioned earlier. We should therefore spend less time searching for the right model and more time trying to improve estimates within each model.

In addition, uncertainty about the premium is bigger than uncertainty about betas, which makes the intangible equity premium the biggest source of uncertainty in the companies' cost of capital estimates.

As popular as they are, asset pricing models are not the only option for estimating the cost of capital. Another approach that is often used for regulated utilities in the US is based on the Gordon growth model, described by M.J. Gordon in 1962. This gives the cost of equity as equal to the sum of the current dividend yield and the long-term dividend growth rate.

This approach is generally favoured less by academics, for several reasons. It makes the strong assumption that dividends will grow forever at the same rate. Besides, there is no theory to help us estimate the dividend growth rate, which is unfortunate because the cost of equity estimate is very sensitive to that rate. This approach therefore strongly reflects opinions about a company's prospects.

A moving target

There is an emerging consensus in academia that expected returns vary over time. For example, expected stock returns seem to be related to the business cycle – they tend to be higher in recessions and lower in expansions.

Among the variables that have been found useful in explaining the time-variation in expected stock market returns are the aggregate dividend-price ratio (D/P) and earnings-price ratio (E/P). Low values of these ratios have historically predicted low returns. In other words, when prices are high relative to the fundamentals, future returns are on average low, especially at longer horizons such as 10 years ahead.

The predictive power of the D/P and E/P ratios was reinforced last year, when the Standard & Poor's 500 index lost 10 per cent of its value while the ratios were at their historical lows. However, these predictors worked poorly in the 1990s, when low D/P and E/P peacefully coexisted with high stock market returns.

▶

'If you torture the data long enough, Nature will confess,' said the Nobel Prize winning economist Ronald Coase. If you search enough variables, you will find a variable that appears to predict returns. However, this apparent predictability exists by chance and such 'data-mined' variables will not work in the future.

An interesting example of data mining was provided in an article by Peter Coy, who quoted David Leinweber, managing director of First Quadrant, a money-management company. Leinweber 'sifted through a United Nations CD-Rom and discovered that historically, the best predictor of the S&P 500 was butter production in Bangladesh'. Good luck if you try to make money on this – you'll need it.

Fortunately, economists have come up with reasons for D/P and E/P having predictive power. Difficult questions remain, though. Is the predictive relation linear? What is the best way to estimate the unknown parameters of this relation? What other predictors should we include?

If it is hard to estimate expected returns when they are constant, it is even harder when they change with time. There is no simple recipe for estimating expected returns. Since data are noisy and no theory is flawless, judgment enters the process at several points. There is nothing wrong with that. After all, economic theories themselves ultimately reflect our judgment about how the world behaves.

Given the importance of expected returns and the huge uncertainty associated with them, the finance profession clearly needs to invest more in their estimation. Such an investment will undoubtedly provide a high expected return. But please don't ask me for an exact number.

Source: Ľuboš Pástor, *Financial Times, Mastering Investment Supplement*, Part 2, May 21 2001, pp. 6–7. Reprinted with permission.

Chapter 18

Evaluating the performance of fund managers

After studying this chapter readers should be able to:

- *measure money weighted and time weighted rates of return*

- *assess portfolio performance using reward per unit of risk*

- *evaluate portfolio performance using differential return*

- *appreciate the inadequacies of the alternative measures of portfolio performance*

- *attribute the performance of a fund manager between asset allocation and stock selection.*

The evaluation of portfolio performance is often made on the basis of returns alone. Since maximising the rate of return is seldom the sole objective of a fund manager, the evaluation of performance should address itself to a number of criteria of success. Furthermore, merely measuring realised performance is insufficient – attention should also be paid to the sources of over or under-performance.

Portfolio return is the most obvious criterion of success, but it is not obvious how return is to be measured. In addition to the question of the start and end dates to be used (a decision that can make a huge difference to apparent performance) there is the choice between money and time weighted measures. These alternatives will be detailed in the first section.

Risk is the second most frequently cited measure of performance. The second section will look at alternative measures of risk. This will be followed by a consideration of risk-return relationships and the various measures that aim to provide a single number which simultaneously evaluates return and risk. Related to this is the matter of the benchmarks against which these measures and others are to be judged.

Although return and risk will be the criteria to receive most attention in what follows, it is important to bear in mind that they are not the only criteria. Other criteria will relate to specific fund objectives. For example, a high-income fund might be judged to have failed if its income yield is less than that on the average general fund, or an ethical fund could be viewed negatively if it is found to be holding shares in a tobacco company. Management, administration and trading costs may be another criterion for evaluation. Although it may be argued that if returns are measured net of costs then the figure for returns takes costs into account, some people might contend that relative returns are partly due to luck and hence cannot be relied on to be repeated in the future whereas costs are less prone to variation.

● ● ● ● Money and time weighted measures of return

The distinction between money and time weighted measures of return arises when there are cash inflows to, or outflows from, the portfolio during the period of assessment. The money weighted measure uses the rate of discount that equates the present values of the inflows and outflows. Suppose that a share is bought for £1 and one year later another is purchased at the new price of £1.06. The price at the end of the second year is also £1.06. A dividend of £0.04 per share is received at the end of each year. The money weighted rate of return is given by r in the following expression:

$$£1 + £1.06/(1+r) = £0.04/(1+r) + £0.08/(1+r)^2 + £2.12/(1+r)^2$$

This gives a rate of return of about 5.8% p.a.

The time weighted approach calculates a rate for each period separately and finds the average. Thus:

Period 1 (£0.04 + £0.06)/£1 = 0.1 i.e. 10%

Period 2 £0.08/£2.12 = 0.0377 i.e. 3.77%

This implies a compound average rate of:

$$\sqrt{(1.1)(1.0377)} - 1 = 0.0684 = 6.84\% \text{ p.a.}$$

The time periods used will depend on the frequency of cash flows. The time weighted measure of return should be based on periods during which no cash flows take place.

Although it is not the case that one measure is always more appropriate than the other, the time weighted approach seems to be more favoured than the money weighted method when evaluating the performance of fund managers. This preference arises because portfolio managers typically do not control the cash inflows and outflows to which their funds are subjected. Additions to, and withdrawals from, a fund will affect the money weighted rate of return. Two fund managers may choose identical portfolios but differ in their money weighted rates of return because of different patterns of additions and withdrawals on the part of clients. Money weighted rates of return should not be compared with rates on a benchmark portfolio since the two portfolios are unlikely to have the same pattern of cash inflows and outflows, and the pattern of such cash flows will affect the money weighted rate of return.

A third approach is to take the arithmetic mean of a succession of periodic returns. For most purposes this is unsatisfactory. To illustrate its unsatisfactory nature, consider an outcome in which an investment doubles in value during one period and halves the next period. Obviously the investment has the same value after the two periods as it had at the beginning. The two-period return is zero. Using an arithmetic average, the two-period return is calculated as:

$$(100\% - 50\%)/2 = 25\%$$

which is clearly incorrect. In this case the time weighted approach provides the correct answer, since it uses a geometric rather than an arithmetic average.

$$2 \times 0.5 = 1$$

$$\sqrt{1} - 1 = 0$$

There is one possible use of the arithmetic average. It could be seen as indicating the typical periodic return. Consider the following series of returns:

$$10\% \quad 15\% \quad 20\% \quad 10\% \quad 15\% \quad 20\%$$

Arguably the typical rate of return is 15%. This figure is provided by the arithmetic average, but not by the geometric average. If the investor asks the question 'What rate of return can I expect this period?', the answer is provided by the arithmetic average. The arithmetic average has its worth when the focus is on the return of a single period. It is not satisfactory when the concern is with the average rate of return over a number of periods.

The evaluation of risk

Much of the academic work on portfolio performance evaluation has been concerned with whether the returns are more than, or below, what would be expected on the basis of the level of risk incurred. Substantial attention will be paid to such risk adjusted measures of portfolio return in what follows. Prior to that, two general points relating to risk should be mentioned.

If the fund objectives include maintenance of a particular risk profile, then deviation from the corresponding risk level would be regarded negatively. A fund with the objective of below average risk should not exhibit risk levels above those of otherwise similar funds.

There is a widespread acceptance that some risk cannot be diversified away, whereas other forms of risk can. It is reasonable to expect that a fund manager will diversify the portfolio to the extent required to remove unnecessary risk. Although some funds, for example high technology funds, may have objectives that render full diversification impossible, portfolio managers should still be expected to avoid risk that can be removed by means of the level of diversification permitted by the fund policy. While some risk will always remain, fund managers should be judged negatively if they fail to employ diversification to the full extent consistent with fund objectives.

Reward per unit of risk

Risk adjusted measures of return fall into two types. One type is concerned with the returns relative to the risk undertaken and involves a division of returns by the level of risk incurred in order to obtain those returns. This is often referred to as 'reward per unit of risk'. This section will elaborate that approach. The following section will be concerned with the alternative approach which ascertains the difference between the returns on the managed portfolio and those on a benchmark portfolio, often referred to as the 'differential return' measure.

Two portfolio performance measures that use reward per unit of risk are the 'Sharpe' and 'Treynor' measures. Both use excess return in the sense of the excess of the portfolio return over the return on a risk-free investment such as a Treasury bill or a short-term bank deposit. This excess return is then divided by a measure of risk so as to ascertain the amount of excess return for each unit of risk undertaken. The Sharpe measure uses the standard deviation of returns of the portfolio to measure risk whereas the Treynor measure uses the portfolio beta as the numerical indicator of risk.

Algebraically these can be described as:

Sharpe measure $(R_p - R_f)/S_p$

Treynor measure $(R_p - R_f)/\beta_p$

R_p is the rate of return on the portfolio, R_f is the rate of return on a risk-free investment, S_p is the standard deviation of returns on the portfolio and β_p is the portfolio beta.

The Treynor measure tends to be favoured when the portfolio being assessed is one of a number of portfolios being held such that any non-systematic (firm-specific) risk can be expected to be removed by diversification. In such a case only the non-diversifiable (systematic) risk is relevant. Beta is a measure of non-diversifiable risk.

The Sharpe measure is appropriate when the portfolio stands alone rather than being part of a portfolio of portfolios. In that case all risk should be included. So the portfolio standard deviation, which encompasses both diversifiable and non-diversifiable risk, should be used.

Differential return

The differential return method of evaluating fund performance involves comparing the return on the fund with the return on a benchmark portfolio. The benchmark could be a stock index portfolio, such as the FTSE 100, or could be an average of funds with similar objectives to the fund being assessed. Using a stock index fails to take account of differences in risk between the stock index portfolio and the fund being evaluated. Comparison with the average performance of similar funds comes closer to comparing like with like, in particular it involves a benchmark with broadly equivalent risk. However, the risk adjustment is crude, and it could be the case that funds on average underperform some absolute benchmark (one advantage of using a stock index portfolio is that it can be interpreted as an absolute benchmark).

An alternative benchmark could be the returns on a hypothetical portfolio whose risk matches that of the fund being evaluated. This provides a relatively precise risk adjustment together with provision of an absolute benchmark (but begs the question as to whether it represents an attainable portfolio – only portfolio characteristics that can be attained with an actual portfolio can reasonably be used to assess the performance of real portfolios).

One technique that utilises hypothetical fund characteristics is the 'Jensen' measure. This derives a benchmark rate of return using the securities market line from the capital asset pricing model. The securities market line provides a theoretical rate of return composed of two components. The first component is a risk-free rate of return (such as the return on Treasury bills or deposits in blue chip banks), the second component is a reward for accepting risk.

The component of expected return that is seen as the reward for accepting risk is the product of the portfolio beta (the beta of the portfolio being evaluated) and the market excess return. The market excess return is the difference between the return on a balanced portfolio consisting of a mix of all available investments (often approximated by a stock index portfolio), and the return on risk free assets. Algebraically:

$$R_b = R_f + \beta_p(R_m - R_f) \tag{1}$$

where R_b is the expected or theoretical rate of return on the assessed portfolio, R_m is the return on the market portfolio, R_f is the risk free rate of return, and β_p is the beta of the portfolio being assessed. By using the beta of the fund under assessment, the comparison of the observed and expected returns provides a risk-adjusted evaluation.

The differential return is expressed as $R_p - R_b$. If this is positive the realised return on the fund being evaluated exceeds the benchmark rate of return and the fund is viewed as over performing. Conversely, a negative value indicates underperformance. $R_p - R_b$ is often referred to as Jensen's alpha. It is estimated simultaneously with beta by regressing portfolio excess returns (portfolio returns minus the risk-free rate of interest) against market excess returns. Both positive and negative alphas often fail to be (statistically) significantly different from zero.

The use of beta as the measure of portfolio risk is appropriate when diversifiable risk can be ignored. Such would be the case if the portfolio being evaluated was extremely well diversified or was part of a larger portfolio such that the final portfolio contained no diversifiable (firm-specific) risk. If neither of these conditions holds then the standard deviation of returns becomes the relevant measure of risk.

Parallel to the use of beta and the securities market line by the Jensen measure it is possible to produce a benchmark rate of return using the portfolio standard deviation within the capital market line of the capital asset pricing model. The algebraic formulation would be:

$$R_b = R_f + (R_m - R_f)S_p/S_m \qquad (2)$$

which differs from the Jensen measure in using the ratio of the standard deviation of the evaluated portfolio (measuring the total risk, diversifiable as well as non-diversifiable) to the standard deviation of the market portfolio. This ratio is used in the place of beta, which measures non-diversifiable risk only.

Problems with portfolio performance evaluation

In relation to the performance measures that use beta a problem arises because of the unreliability of estimates of beta. Betas are calculated from historical price data. The values of beta derived from the statistical analysis will vary according to the time intervals used (i.e. upon whether weekly, monthly or quarterly data is employed). They will also vary with differences in the time spans from which the data is taken (i.e. upon whether prices are taken from the last six months, last year or last two years). Betas can also vary when different stock indices are used as proxies for the market portfolio (which in principle contains all assets). The rankings of portfolios, relative to one another, will thus be dependent upon the database used for the estimation of beta.

Measures of performance using standard deviations of return face problems of interpretation when a fund manager deliberately changes the beta of the portfolio during the period of assessment. Such variations in beta are likely to reflect market views taken by the portfolio manager; a bullish view leads to an increased beta, vice versa for a bearish view. Changes in beta are associated with changes in expected portfolio returns. In effect the fund manager is engineering variations in portfolio returns. These controlled fluctuations in returns should not be regarded as resulting from uncertainty and should not be deemed to be due to portfolio risk. Unfortunately the standard deviation of returns incorporates such variations and hence treats them as reflecting risk.

In addition, over or underperformance may be the result of luck rather than the relative skills of the fund managers. Over or underperformance needs to be shown to persist for a number of years before conclusions can be drawn about fund managers' investment skills.

Attribution

The performance of a fund manager depends partly on the allocation of the portfolio between asset classes (for example, between equities, bonds and deposits) and partly upon selection within classes (which stocks to buy). If a portfolio contains foreign currency investments there is a currency dimension to the returns, profits or

Exercise 18.1

The interest rate on a risk-free bank deposit is 5% p.a. The return on the FT All Share Index portfolio has been 10% p.a. with an annual standard deviation of 8%. Portfolio A has had a beta of 0.5, an annual standard deviation of 5%, and has provided a return of 8% p.a. Portfolio B has had a beta of 1.5, an annual standard deviation of returns of 15%, and has provided a return of 12% p.a.

Evaluate the performances of portfolios A and B relative to each other and relative to the FT All Share index.

Answer

(a) Sharpe measure

Portfolio A $(8 - 5)/5 = 0.6$

Portfolio B $(12 - 5)/15 = 0.47$

Market (FT All Share index) portfolio $(10 - 5)/8 = 0.625$

Portfolio A is superior to portfolio B but inferior to the All Share index (market) portfolio.

Portfolio B is inferior to portfolio A and to the All Share index (market) portfolio.

(b) Treynor measure

Portfolio A $(8 - 5)/0.5 = 6$

Portfolio B $(12 - 5)/1.5 = 4.67$

Market portfolio $(10 - 5)/1 = 5$

(The beta of a market index is normally treated as being equal to 1.)

Portfolio A is superior to portfolio B and to the All Share index (market) portfolio.

Portfolio B is inferior to portfolio A and to the All Share index (market) portfolio.

(c) Capital market line measure

Portfolio A

$R_b = 5 + (10 - 5)5/8 = 8.125\%$ p.a.

$8\% - 8.125\% = -0.125\%$ p.a.

Portfolio B

$R_b = 5 + (10 - 5)15/8 = 14.375\%$ p.a.

$12\% - 14.375\% = -2.375\%$ p.a.

(Note that the index has an R_b equal to the actual return: $R_b = 5 + (10 - 5)8/8 = 10$. So $R - R_b = 0$.)

A is superior to B but inferior to the All Share index (market) portfolio.

B is inferior to A and inferior to the All Share index (market) portfolio.

(d) Jensen measure

Portfolio A

$R_b = 5 + 0.5(10 - 5) = 7.5\%$ p.a.

$8\% - 7.5\% = 0.5\%$ p.a.

Portfolio B

$R_b = 5 + 1.5(10 - 5) = 12.5\%$ p.a.

$12\% - 12.5\% = -0.5\%$ p.a.

(The index will have an R_b equal to the actual return. $R_b = 5 + 1(10 - 5) = 10$. So $10 - R_b = 0$.)

A is superior to B and to the All Share index (market) portfolio.

B is inferior to A and to the All Share index (market) portfolio.

losses arising from exchange rate movements. It is possible to measure the contribution of each of these different decisions (asset allocation, stock selection and currency choice) to the overall performance of the portfolio.

To separate the effects of asset allocation from those of stock selection, it is necessary to compute an average return for all investments (weighted by the total market value of each asset class) for the investment period being considered, e.g. the past year. Then an average rate of return of each asset class is calculated. The results may (hypothetically) be those illustrated by Table 18.1. It can be seen that equities over-perform by 1.8% p.a., bonds underperform by 2.2% p.a. and deposits underperform by 4.2% p.a. relative to the average rate of return for the aggregate of all investments.

The next step is to compare the portfolio that is being evaluated with the average portfolio. The average portfolio reflects the total values of the different asset classes available to be held. Table 18.2 compares hypothetical figures for a portfolio being evaluated and an average portfolio.

It can be seen that the portfolio being evaluated is 15% overweight in equities, 10% underweight in bonds and 5% underweight in deposits. The portfolio return arising from the asset allocation decision is based on the extent to which it is overweight in the over-performing asset class and underweight in the underperforming asset classes. The asset allocation contribution to portfolio performance is thus calculated as shown in Table 18.3.

Table 18.1 Average rate of return of each asset class

Asset class	Rate of return (% p.a.)
Equities	10
Bonds	6
Deposits	4
All investments	8.2

Table 18.2 Hypothetical figures for a portfolio being evaluated and an average portfolio

Asset class	Weightings of average portfolio (%)	Weightings of evaluated portfolio (%)
Equities	60	75
Bonds	30	20
Deposits	10	5

Table 18.3

Asset class	Over-weighting (1)	Overperformance (2)	Contribution to performance: (1) × (2)
Equities	0.15	1.8%	0.27%
Bonds	−0.10	−2.2%	0.22%
Deposits	−0.05	−4.2%	0.21%

It can be seen that the total contribution of the asset allocation decision to fund performance is :

0.27 % + 0.22 % + 0.21 % = 0.7 % p.a.

The portfolio being evaluated has a rate of return of 9% p.a., whereas the average portfolio has a rate of return of 8.2% p.a. Thus there is an additional return of 0.8% p.a. of which 0.7% is due to asset allocation. It follows that the return arising from stock selection is 0.1% p.a.

In order to determine the currency contribution to portfolio return when foreign investments are included it is necessary to compare a fully hedged version of the fund with a version that is completely unhedged against currency movements. The profit or loss on the forward or futures position that is needed to hedge the portfolio equals the loss or profit on the currency exposure. The currency contribution to portfolio return is the negative of the profit or loss on the forward or futures position that would be needed to hedge the fund against currency movements.

Assessing market timing skills

Market timing entails forecasting market movements with a view to adjusting a portfolio to take advantage of the expected movements. If a fund manager is capable of timing the market, that manager would succeed in raising the portfolio beta before the market rises and lowering it before it falls. The characteristic line for a successful market timer would be concave to the vertical axis as illustrated in Figure 18.1. The concave characteristic line shows that excess returns, on the portfolio being managed, rise more than proportionately to those on the market portfolio; and fall less than proportionately. In Figure 18.1, R_p represents the return on the portfolio being managed and R_m represents the return on the market portfolio.

Treynor and Mazuy have tested US mutual funds (unit trusts) to find whether the fund managers exhibit market timing ability. The research involved testing whether an equation of the form shown by equation (3) had a positive β_2.

$$R_p = \alpha + \beta_1 R_m + \beta_2 R_m^2 \tag{3}$$

A positive β_2 would show that the portfolio excess return rises more than in proportion to (and falls less than proportionately to) the excess return of the market portfolio. They found that β_2 was not significantly different from zero and therefore concluded that their sample of mutual fund managers did not exhibit market timing ability.

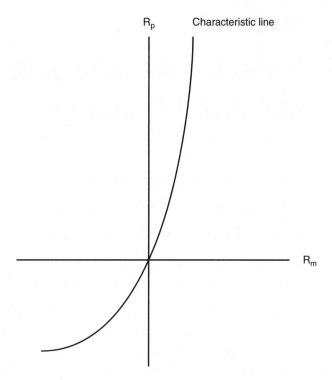

Figure 18.1 Characteristic line for a successful market timer

Chapter 19

Investment analysis: discount models

After studying this chapter readers should be able to:

- *discount future cash flows to obtain a present value*
- *use dividend discount models to obtain the fair prices of shares*
- *use variations on the dividend discount model, such as the Gordon growth model, stochastic dividend discount models and multi-period models*
- *appreciate the effects of investment opportunities on share prices.*

Investment analysts need to produce estimates of what stock prices should be. Stock selection requires views as to which shares are under-priced or over-priced in the market. There are two major approaches. One involves discounting prospective future dividends in order to arrive at their present value, which is regarded as the fair price of the share. The other proceeds by obtaining estimates of the price-earnings ratio and of prospective earnings. These estimates are then used to ascertain the appropriate, or fair, price of the stock.

Discounting cash flows

A sum of money received (or paid) in the present is worth more than the same sum in the future. One explanation for this runs in terms of the fact that money can earn interest. A unit of money received now is worth more than the same unit received one year from now because it can earn interest over the year. If the interest rate is 10% p.a., receipts in the present are worth 10% more than identical receipts one year hence.

To render a future cash flow comparable with a current one, the future sum is discounted. This involves dividing the future sum by one plus the decimalised rate of interest. In the case of a receipt of S one year hence, when the interest rate is 10% p.a., the present value (PV) is given by:

PV = S/(1.1)

More generally:

PV = S/(1 + r)

where r is the decimalised rate of interest.

If the cash flow is to occur two years from now, then (assuming a rate of interest of 10% p.a.) because of compound interest an identical sum in the present is worth 21% more. The present value of the future sum would be:

$$PV = S/(1.1)^2 = S/(1.21)$$

More generally:

$$PV = S/(1 + r)^2$$

Correspondingly the present value of a sum three years hence is $S/(1 + r)^3$, four years hence $S/(1 + r)^4$, and so on. It follows that the present value of a future stream of cash flows is:

$$PV = S/(1 + r) + S/(1 + r)^2 + S/(1 + r)^3 + \ldots + S/(1 + r)^n$$

where the final receipt (or payment) occurs n years from the present. This can be more formally expressed as:

$$PV = \sum_{k=1}^{n} S/(1 + r)^k$$

which states that the present value equals the sum of the discounted cash flows (the cash flow being S at the end of each year) relating to the next n years.

Example 19.1

The present value of £100, to be received at the end of each of the next three years, with a discount rate (i.e. interest rate) of 10% p.a. would be:

$$PV = \sum_{k=1}^{3} 100/(1.1)^k$$

i.e. $PV = £100/1.1 + £100/(1.1)^2 + £100/(1.1)^3$
$= £100/1.1 + £100/1.21 + £100/1.331$
$= £90.91 + £82.64 + £75.13$
$= £248.68$

The time period is not necessarily a year. If it is not, an adjustment needs to be made to the interest rate. For example, for six-monthly cash flows an interest rate of 10% p.a. would be expressed as a rate of 5% per six-month period. (Interest rates are always expressed on a per annum basis; a six month rate of 10% p.a. means 5% over six months. Likewise a three-month rate of 10% p.a. means 2.5% over three months.)

The cash flow may not be the same at the end of each time period, in which case the equation becomes:

$$PV = S_1/(1 + r) + S_2/(1 + r)^2 + S_3/(1 + r)^3 + \ldots + S_n/(1 + r)^n$$

or

$$PV = \sum_{k=1}^{n} S_k/(1 + r)^k$$

where S_1, S_2, S_3, ..., S_n are the cash flows at the ends of periods 1, 2, 3, ..., n respectively. There may also be a different interest rate (discount rate) for each time period.

Discounting future dividends

This approach to share price valuation uses variations on the discounted cash flow model. The simplest variant is based on an unchanging annual dividend payment on the shares.

$$P = D/(1 + r) + D/(1 + r)^2 + D/(1 + r)^3 + \ldots + D/(1 + r)^n \tag{1}$$

P is the fair price of the share, D is the annual dividend on the share, r is the discount rate and n is the number of years for which the firm is expected to exist. The rate of discount, r, is also known as the required rate of return. The required rate of return is the rate required by investors in the light of what is available on other investments. The required rate of return can be looked upon as composed of the rate of yield on long term government bonds plus a risk premium to reflect the fact that shares are riskier than government bonds. The required rate of return is often calculated by means of the security market line, which is derived from the capital asset pricing model.

If the firm is assumed to last for ever, that is n is treated as infinite, equation (1) can be simplified to equation (2).

$$P = D/r \tag{2}$$

The Gordon growth model

The assumption of an unchanging annual dividend is unrealistic for most stocks. The Gordon growth model takes a step towards greater realism by allowing for a growth in annual dividends. Dividends are assumed to grow at a constant annual rate. This growth rate of dividends is shown as g in equation (3).

$$P = D(1 + g)/(1 + r) + D(1 + g)^2/(1 + r)^2 + D(1 + g)^3/(1 + r)^3 + \ldots + D(1 + g)^n/(1 + r)^n \tag{3}$$

D is the most recent dividend, so that $D(1 + g)$ is the next dividend. Equation (3) assumes that the next dividend is payable one year from the present. If the company is expected to continue for ever (n approaches infinity), equation (3) can be simplified to equation (4).

$$P = D(1 + g)/(r - g) \tag{4}$$

Estimating the growth rate of dividends

An investment analyst using the Gordon growth model would need to forecast the rate of dividend growth. This can be done by using equation (5).

$$g = ROE \times (1-d) \qquad (5)$$

In equation 5, g is the growth rate of profits, ROE (return on equity) is the rate of return that the company can obtain from reinvested profits and d is the dividend pay-out rate (the proportion of profits paid as dividends to shareholders). With a constant dividend pay-out rate, the growth rate of dividends will equal the growth rate of profits.

For example, if the firm pays out 60% of profits as dividends (while reinvesting 40%) and the new investment yields 20% p.a. then:

$$g = 0.2 \times (1 - 0.6) = 0.08.$$

Dividends (and profits) are expected to grow at 8% p.a. Out of each pound of profit, 40p is reinvested to yield $40p \times 0.2 = 8p$ more profit per year. For every £1 profit this year, there will be £1.08 profit next year.

Stochastic dividend discount models

Stochastic dividend discount models allow for the possibility that dividends do not increase every year. A stochastic form of the Gordon growth model is shown by equation (6).

$$P = D(1 + pg)/(r - pg) \qquad (6)$$

In equation (6), p is the probability that the dividend will increase in a period (e.g. a year). For example, if p is 0.5, there is a 50% chance of a dividend increase in a particular year.

Stochastic dividend discount models provide a distribution of possible future stock prices rather than a single price. The equation indicates the average (mean) of a distribution of possible prices but actual prices could differ from that average. Stochastic models can be refined to allow for the possibility of dividend reductions.

●●●● Multi-period models

A further step towards greater realism is provided by multi-period dividend-discount models. The simplest of these is the two-period model. The two-period model assumes dividend growth at an untypical rate for a number of years after which growth proceeds at a normal rate. The first step when using a two-period model is to estimate the share price that will prevail at the future point in time at which the growth rate will change. If the untypical growth rate is G, the normal growth rate g, and the untypical growth is expected to continue for N years, the estimate of what the share price will be N years from now (using the Gordon growth model) is given by equation (7).

$$p = D(1 + G)^N(1 + g) / (r - g) \tag{7}$$

The term $D(1 + G)^N(1 + g)$ represents the dividend expected at the end of period $N + 1$. Application of the Gordon growth model then estimates the share price N years from the present. This expected future share price is represented by p. The current fair price of the stock is given by discounting the expected future price and the dividends expected during the period of untypical dividend growth. The current fair price is given by equation (8), which assumes that the untypical dividend growth continues for three years.

$$P = D(1 + G)/(1 + r) + D(1 + G)^2/(1 + r)^2 + D(1 + G)^3/(1 + r)^3 + p/(1 + r)^3 \tag{8}$$

Some investment analysts use three-period models in which the period of untypical growth is followed by a period during which growth changes from the untypical to the typical rate. At the end of the transition period the third period, during which growth proceeds at a normal rate, begins. The Gordon growth model, used in multi-period dividend-discount models, could be either stochastic or non-stochastic.

Effects of investment opportunities on the share price

The Gordon growth model has implications for the relationship between the dividend policy of a firm and its share price. This can be illustrated by the case of a firm that has to choose between (a) distributing all of its profits and (b) distributing half its profits. In these two cases the rate of reinvestment would be zero and 50% respectively. Suppose that expected next period profits are 20p per share and that the required rate of return is 10% p.a. In the first case the expected rate of growth is zero (ignoring the possibility of growth unrelated to investment). So in case (a) the fair price of the share, using the Gordon growth model, is given by:

$$P = 20p / (0.1 - 0) = 200p.$$

In the second case 50% of profits are reinvested. Suppose that profits can be reinvested to earn 16% p.a. The growth rate of profits (and dividends) would be:

$$0.16 \times 0.5 = 0.08 \text{ (i.e. 8\% p.a.)}.$$

With profits of 20p, this entails reinvestment of 10p at 16% yielding 1.6p. Hence profits grow at the rate of $1.6/20 = 0.08$. A constant dividend pay-out rate implies a growth rate of dividends of 0.08.

Using the Gordon growth model (noting that the next period dividend is expected to be $20p \times 0.5 = 10p$):

Exercise 19.1

(a) The most recent dividend paid on shares in WMB plc was 10p per share. WMB dividends are expected to grow at 5% p.a. The required rate of return is 8% p.a. What is the fair price of the shares?

(b) What would be the fair price of the shares if dividend growth were expected to fall to 4% p.a. after three years?

(c) If the rate of dividend growth were to remain at 5% p.a. but with a 20% chance that there would be no dividend growth in a year, what would be the fair price of the share?

Answers

(a) Using the Gordon growth model:

$P = D(1+g)/(r - g) = (10 \times 1.05)/(0.08 - 0.05) = 10.5/(0.03) = 350p$

(b) The first step is to estimate what the share price will be in three years' time. This can be done by means of the Gordon growth model. The dividend expected in four years is:

$10p \times (1.05)^3 \times 1.04 = 12.04p$

Using the Gordon growth model, the expected future share price (for three years from the present) is:

$P_3 = 12.04/(0.08 - 0.04) = 12.04/0.04 = 301p$

This expected share price is discounted to the present together with the next three dividends in order to estimate the current fair price of the share.

$P_0 = 10(1.05)/1.08 + 10(1.05)^2/(1.08)^2 + 10(1.05)^3/(1.08)^3 + 301/(1.08)^3$
$P_0 = 9.72 + 9.45 + 9.19 + 238.94$
$P_0 = 267p$ (to nearest whole number)

(c) The equation for the stochastic version of the Gordon growth model is:

$P = D(1 + pg)/(r - pg)$

So $P = 10(1 + 0.8[0.05])/(0.08 - 0.8[0.05])$
$P = 10(1.04)/(0.08 - 0.04) = 10.4/0.04 = 260p$

$P = 10p / (0.1 - 0.08) = 10p / (0.02) = 500p.$

It can be seen that the decision to reinvest half the profits raises the fair price of the share from 200p to 500p.

The conclusion that lowering the dividend pay-out rate increases the share price rests on the fact that the profits can be reinvested to earn a rate of return that exceeds the required rate of return. It can be shown that if the best investment opportunity available to the firm offers a rate of return lower than the required rate, reinvestment of profits will tend to reduce the share price. For example, if reinvested profits were expected to earn 4% p.a., the expected growth rate of dividends would be:

$0.04 \times 0.5 = 0.02$ (i.e. 2% p.a.)

Exercise 19.2

AB plc has a new product and is enjoying rapid growth. The company has just paid an annual dividend of £2 and expects dividends to grow at an annual rate of 20% over the next three years. The growth rate of dividends is expected to be 10% p.a. after three years. Calculate the fair price of the share if the required rate of return is 12% p.a.

Answer
The first step is to calculate the share price expected for a point in time three years from the present. The dividend expected to be paid four years from now is $£2(1.2)^3((1.1) = £3.80$. The expected share price, for the point in time three years hence, is:

$P_3 = D_4/[r - g] = £3.80/[0.12 - 0.1] = £3.80/[0.02] = £190$

The present fair value of the share is:

$P_0 = D_1/[1+r] + D_2/[1+r]^2 + D_3/[1+r]^3 + P_3/[1+r]^3$
$P_0 = £2[1.2]/[1.12] + £2[1.2]^2/[1.12]^2 + £2[1.2]^3/[1.12]^3 + £190/[1.12]^3$
$P_0 = £2.14 + £2.30 + £2.46 + £135.24 = £142.14$

Exercise 19.3

A high technology stock is expected to pay no dividends during the first five years. It is expected to pay a dividend of 50p at the end of year 6. Dividends are expected to grow at 14% p.a. after year 6. The required rate of return is 16% p.a. Estimate the fair price of the shares.

Answer
The first step is to forecast what the share price will be at the end of year 6. The Gordon growth model can be used for this purpose.

$P_6 = 50(1.14)/(0.16 - 0.14)$
$P_6 = 57/0.02$
$P_6 = 2850$

This predicted price, and the year 6 dividend, are then discounted to the present.

$P_0 = 50/(1.16)^6 + 2850/(1.16)^6$
$P_0 = 1190p$

So the fair price of the shares is 1190p, i.e. £11.90.

The fair price of the share would be:

$$P = 10p / (0.1 - 0.02) = 10p / 0.08 = 125p.$$

In this case the reduction of the dividend pay-out rate (and increase in the reinvestment rate) reduces the fair price of the share from 200p to 125p. When the firm lacks strong investment opportunities, reinvestment of profits will tend to reduce the value of the firm.

Markets and the business cycle

The stock market has predicted nine out of the last five recessions! Paul Samuelson, *Newsweek*, 1966

Markets and the economy often are not synchronised, so it comes as no surprise that many investors dismiss economic forecasts when planning their market strategies. The substance of Paul Samuelson's quote from *Newsweek* remains true more than 30 years later.

Yet investors should not dismiss the business cycle too quickly when choosing a portfolio. The stock market still responds powerfully to changes in economic activity. Although there are many 'false alarms', akin to 1987, when the market collapse was not followed by a recession, stocks almost always fall before a recession and rally rigorously at or even before signs of an impending recovery. If you can predict the business cycle, you can beat a simple buy-and-hold strategy for equity investments.

But this is not easy. To make money by predicting the business cycle, you must be able to identify peaks and troughs of economic activity before they occur, a skill very few if any economists possess. Business-cycle forecasting is popular not because it is successful – most of the time it is not – but because the potential gains from successfully calling business booms and busts are so large. But before we do this, it is important to look at who calls the business cycle.

Marking the cycle

In the US, business cycles are dated by the National Bureau of Economic Research, a private organisation founded in 1920. In its early years, the bureau's staff compiled comprehensive chronological records of changes in economic conditions in many industrialised countries. In other countries, recession may not be declared in such a formal manner. In the UK, for example, investors might look to the Bank of England, the UK Treasury or the Confederation of British Industry for indications of a recession.

It is commonly assumed that a recession occurs when real gross domestic product, the most inclusive measure of economic output, declines for two consecutive quarters. But this is not necessarily so. Although this is a reasonable rule of thumb, it is not used by the

NBER. For example, the 1981 recession occurred when there was only a single disastrous quarterly decline in GDP followed by a flat quarter. The bureau looks at many other indicators, including real personal income and sales, employment and industrial production to date peaks and troughs of the business cycle.

Between 1802 and 1997, there were 41 US recessions, averaging nearly 18 months, while expansions averaged almost 38 months. This means that, over 195 years, a third of the time has been spent in recession. However, since the Second World War there have been nine recessions, averaging 10 months, while the expansions have averaged 50 months. So in the post-war period, the economy has been in a recession only a sixth of the time.

Turning points

Almost without exception, the stock market turns down before recessions and rises before recoveries. In fact, of the 41 US recessions, 38, or 93 per cent, have been preceded (or accompanied) by declines of 8 per cent or more in the total stock returns index. The three that were not were the 1829–30 recession, the recession that followed economic adjustment immediately after the Second World War and the 1953 recession, where stock declines fell just shy of the 8 per cent criterion.

Table 1 summarises return behaviour for the nine US recessions since the Second World War. You can see that the stock return index peaked anywhere from zero to 13 months before the beginning of a recession. The recessions that began in January 1980 and July 1990 are among the few where the stock market gave no advance warning of the downturn.

During the post-war period, if you wait until the stock returns index has declined by 8 per cent before signalling a business-cycle peak, then the stock market leads the business cycle by an average of only 1.3 months. This signal ranges from a lead of 10 months in the 1970 recession to a lag of three months in the 1990–91 recession. In all but two of the post-war recessions, an 8 per cent decline in the returns index led the business-cycle peak by less than one month, giving little advance warning of an impending recession.

▶

Table 1: Recessions and stock returns

Recession	Peak of stock index 1	Trough of business cycle 2	Lead time between peaks 3	% decline in stock index from (1) to (2) 4	Months between 8% stock index decline and (2) 5	Maximum 12-month % decline in stock index 6
1948–49	May 1948	Nov 1948	6	−8.74	0	−8.19
1953–54	Dec 1952	Jul 1953	7	−3.91	no decline	−7.18
1957–58	Jul 1957	Aug 1957	1	−5.05	−1	−13.90
1960–61	Dec 1959	Apr 1960	4	−8.28	0	−8.20
1970	Nov 1968	Dec 1969	13	−12.19	10	−25.50
1973–75	Dec 1972	Nov 1973	11	−16.20	7	−40.10
1980	Jan 1980	Jan 1980	0	−0.00	−2	−8.90
1981–82	Nov 1980	Jul 1981	8	−4.08	−1	−14.20
1990–91	Jul 1990	Jul 1990	0	0.00	−3	−13.92
		Average	**5.6**	**−6.49**	**1.3**	**−15.56**
		Std. dev.	4.4	5.10	4.4	10.17

As the Samuelson quote indicates, the stock market is prone to false alarms and these have increased since the war. Excluding the war years, there have been 12 episodes since 1802 when the cumulative returns index for stocks fell by 8 per cent, but the drop was not then followed by a recession within the next 12 months. In the 19th century this happened five times and in the 20th century seven times. Every occasion in the past century occurred after the Second World War.

The 1987 decline of 29 per cent, from August to November, is the largest decline in the nearly two-century history of US stock returns data after which the economy did not fall into a recession. Table 2 compares the trough in the stock return index and the trough in the NBER business cycle. The average lead time between a market upturn and an economic recovery has been 5.1 months and the range has been narrow. This compares to an average 5.6-month lead time between the peak in the market and the peak in the business cycle, with a much greater variability in these figures. As we shall see, stock returns rise more in a recession in anticipation of a recovery than they fall before an economic downturn.

Timing the cycle

Table 3 displays the excess returns to investors who can time their investment strategy in relation to the

Table 2: Expansions and stock returns

Recession	Trough of stock index 1	Trough of business cycle 2	Lead time between troughs 3	% rise in stock index from (1) to (2) 4	Months between 8% stock index rise and (2) 5
1948–49	May 1949	Oct 1948	5	15.59	3
1953–54	Aug 1953	May 1954	9	29.13	5
1957–58	Dec 1957	Apr 1958	4	10.27	1
1960–61	Oct 1960	Feb 1961	4	21.25	2
1970	Jun 1970	Nov 1970	5	21.86	3
1973–75	Sep 1974	Mar 1975	6	35.60	5
1980	Mar 1980	Jul 1980	4	22.60	2
1981–82	Jul 1982	Nov 1982	4	33.13	3
1990–91	Oct 1990	Mar 1991	5	25.28	3
		Average	**5.1**	**23.86**	**3**
		Std. dev.	1.73	8.59	1.41
2000–01	Apr 2001	Sep 2001?	?	14.78	?

▶

Table 3: Percentage excess returns around business cycle turning points

		Lead				Peak	Lag			
		4 month	3 month	2 month	1 month		1 month	2 month	3 month	4 month
Lead	4 month	**4.8**	4.0	4.2	4.1	3.3	2.7	2.1	2.2	1.9
	3 month	4.0	**3.3**	3.5	3.3	2.6	1.9	1.4	1.5	1.3
	2 month	3.3	2.6	**2.8**	2.6	1.9	1.2	0.7	0.8	0.7
	1 month	2.5	1.8	2.0	**1.8**	1.1	0.5	0.0	0.1	0.0
	Trough	1.9	1.2	1.4	1.2	**0.5**	−0.2	−0.7	−0.6	−0.7
Lag	1 month	1.5	0.8	1.0	0.8	0.1	**−0.6**	−1.1	−1.0	−1.1
	2 month	0.9	0.2	0.4	0.2	−0.5	−1.1	**−1.7**	−1.6	−1.7
	3 month	0.5	−0.2	0.0	−0.2	−0.9	−1.5	−2.1	**−2.0**	−2.1
	4 month	0.3	−0.4	−0.2	−0.3	−1.1	−1.7	−2.2	−2.1	**−2.2**

peaks and troughs in economic activity. Since stocks fall before a recession, investors want to switch out of stocks and into Treasury bills, returning to stocks when prospects for recovery look good. Excess returns are calculated by assuming that investors who lead the business cycle switch out of stocks and into bills before the peak of business expansions and switch back before the trough of recessions.

In contrast, investors who lag the business cycle switch out of stocks and into bills after the cycle peak and back into stocks after the cycle trough. The excess returns are measured relative to a buy-and-hold stock strategy of the same risk as the timing strategies employed previously.

In the post-war period, the excess return is minimal over a buy-and-hold strategy if investors switch into bills at the peak and into stocks at the trough of the business cycle. In fact, investors switching into bills just one month after the business cycle peak and back into stocks just one month after the business cycle trough would have lost 0.6 per cent a year compared with the buy-and-hold strategy.

Interestingly, it is more important to forecast troughs than peaks. An investor who buys stocks before the trough of the cycle gains more than an investor who sells stocks an equal number of months before the business-cycle peak.

The maximum excess return of 4.8 per cent per year is obtained by investing in bills four months before the business-cycle peak and in stocks four months before the business-cycle troughs. The strategy of switching between bills and stocks gains almost 30 basis points (30/100 of a percentage point) in average annual return for each week during the four-month period in which investors can predict the business-cycle turning point.

Extra returns from forecasting the cycle are impressive. An increase of 1.8 per cent a year in returns, achieved by predicting the business-cycle peak and trough only one month before it occurs, will increase your wealth by 60 per cent more than any buy-and-hold strategy over 30 years. If you can predict the market four months in advance, the annual increase of 4.8 per cent in returns will more than triple your wealth over the same time compared with a buy-and-hold strategy.

Can the cycle be predicted?

Billions of dollars are spent trying to forecast the business cycle. The previous section showed it is not surprising that Wall Street employs so many economists desperately trying to predict the next recession or upturn since doing so dramatically increases returns. But the record of predicting exact cycle turning points is poor.

For more than 15 years, Robert J. Eggert has been summarising the forecasts of a noted panel of economic and business experts. These forecasts are compiled each month in Blue Chip Economic Indicators. In July 1979, the publication indicated that a strong majority of forecasters believed a recession had started – forecasting negative GNP growth in the second, third and fourth quarters of 1979. However, the NBER declared that the peak of the business cycle did not occur until January 1980 and that the economy expanded throughout 1979.

By the middle of the next year, the forecasters were convinced a recession had begun. But as late as June 1980 they believed the recession had started in February or March and would last a year, a month longer than the average recession. This prediction was reaffirmed in August, when forecasters indicated

▶

the US economy was halfway through the recession. In fact, the recession had ended the month before, in July, and the 1980 recession turned out to be the shortest since the war.

Forecasters' ability to predict the 1981–82 recession, when unemployment reached a post-war high of 10.8 per cent, was no better. The headline of the July 1981 Blue Chip Economic Indicators read: 'Economic exuberance envisioned for 1982'. Instead, 1982 was a disaster. By November 1981 forecasters realised the economy had faltered and optimism turned to pessimism. Most thought the economy had entered a recession (which it had done four months earlier), nearly 70 per cent thought it would end by the first quarter of 1982 (which it did not, instead tying the record for the longest post-war recession, ending in November) and 90 per cent thought it would be mild, like the 1971 recession. Wrong again.

In April 1985, with expansion well underway, forecasters were asked how long the economy would be in an expansion. The average response was 49 months, which would put the peak at December 1986, more than 3 years before the cycle actually ended. Even the most optimistic forecasters picked spring 1988 as the latest date for the next recession to begin.

Following the stock crash of October 1987, forecasters reduced their GNP growth estimates of 1988 over 1987 from 2.8 per cent to 1.9 per cent, the largest drop in the 11-year history of the survey. Instead, economic growth in 1988 was nearly 4 per cent, as the economy failed to respond to the stock market collapse.

Conclusion

Going into 2001, the US is enjoying its longest economic expansion in history. Yet signs of a slowdown are unmistakable and there are strong indications that the economy is in, or soon will be in, a recession. The bull market topped out at the end of March 2000 and by April 2001 the S&P 500 index had fallen almost 27 per cent, exceeding the average twelve-month declines before post-war recessions.

Since the April low, the index has rallied significantly as investors predict that the economic slowdown will end soon. Using the historical average, the market says the bottom of the economic slowdown will be five months after the low, in September. Only time will tell if the market again can predict the end of recession.

Stock values are based on corporate earnings, and the business cycle is a prime determinant of these earnings. The gains of being able to predict turning points in the economic cycle are enormous. Yet doing so with any precision has eluded economists. And in spite of the growing body of economic statistics, predictions are not getting much better.

The worst course an investor can take is to follow the prevailing sentiment about economic activity. This will lead to buying at high prices when times are good and everyone is optimistic, and selling at the low when recession nears its trough and pessimism prevails.

Lessons to investors are clear. Beating the stock market by analysing real economic activity requires a degree of prescience that forecasters do not yet have. Turning points are rarely identified until several months after the peak or trough has been reached. By then, it is too late to act.

This article is adapted from the article 'Does it pay stock investors to forecast the business cycle?' in Journal of Portfolio Management, *Fall 1991, 18, 27–34 and chapter 12 of* Stocks for the Long Run, *2nd edition, McGraw-Hill, 1998. The material benefited significantly from discussions with Professor Paul Samuelson.*

Source: Jeremy Siegel, *Financial Times, Mastering Investment Supplement*, Part 2, May 21 2001, pp. 8, 10. Reprinted with permission.

Discussion questions

1 How can the constant dividend discount model be rendered more realistic as a method for estimating the fair prices of shares?

2 How reliable are dividend discount models as means of estimating the fair prices of shares? How can two-period dividend discount models be used for ascertaining fair prices of shares?

Chapter 20

Investment analysis: ratios

After studying this chapter readers should be able to:

- *ascertain a price-earnings ratio and earnings per share*
- *use price-earnings ratios and earnings per share to estimate the fair prices of shares*
- *calculate, and interpret, financial adequacy ratios.*

Price-earnings ratios

Price-earnings ratios provide a means of ascertaining the appropriate price of a stock. The price-earnings ratio is the ratio of the share price to the earnings (profits) per share. This can be expressed by equation 1.

$$PE = P / eps \qquad (1)$$

PE is the price-earnings ratio, P is the current share price and eps is the earnings (i.e. profits) per share.

The price-earnings ratio can be either backward looking or forward looking. In the backward looking version, eps is interpreted as the most recent earnings per share. In the forward looking version, eps is an estimate of earnings per share during the next period. Published price-earnings ratios (in the financial press or company reports) are normally backward looking. For the purposes of investment analysis, it is necessary to have a forward looking ratio.

Estimation of a forward looking price-earnings ratio, and the simultaneous forecast of earnings for the corresponding future period (normally the next period), allows for the estimation of a fair price for the share. This is shown by equation 2.

$$FP = PE \times eps \qquad (2)$$

Multiplication of the price-earnings ratio by the earnings per share provides an estimate of the fair price (FP) of the share. The fair price of the share is the price that the analyst believes that it should be. If the fair price differs from the actual price, there may be a perceived profit opportunity from trading in the share.

The use of equation (2) requires that PE is estimated separately from eps. The estimation of PE can be carried out in at least four distinct ways. First an average of past price-earnings ratios for the company (whose share price is being analysed) can be used. Second, an average of price-earnings ratios for similar firms can be used. The similarity may be based upon sector, for example the appropriate price-earnings ratio for a firm in the airline sector could be estimated from other companies in the same sector.

A third approach is based on the Gordon growth model. The Gordon growth model can be written as shown in equation 3.

$$P = D / (r - g) \tag{3}$$

P represents the fair price of the share, D the expected next dividend, r the required rate of return (comprising an interest rate plus risk premium), and g is the expected growth rate of dividends. Dividing both sides of equation 3 by eps gives equation 4.

$$P / eps = (D/eps) / (r - g) \tag{4}$$

P/eps is the price-earnings ratio (PE). The term D/eps is the dividend pay-out rate; that is, the proportion of earnings (profits) paid as dividends to shareholders.

From equation 4, it can be seen that the price-earnings ratio rises with increases in the dividend pay-out rate and the expected growth rate of dividends. However, it should be noted that these two variables are not independent – a higher dividend pay-out rate involves lower reinvestment of profits and hence tends to reduce the growth rate. Equation 4 also shows that the price-earnings ratio is inversely related to the required rate of return. This implies that a rise in interest rates or an increase in the perceived riskiness of the share (which raises the risk premium) would cause a fall in the price-earnings ratio. High price-earnings ratios would tend to be associated with relatively low risk shares with above average expected dividend growth rates.

Suppose that the dividend pay-out rate is 0.5, the required rate of return is 12% p.a. and the expected growth rate of dividends is 2% p.a., then putting these figures into equation 4 gives:

$$PE = 0.5 / (0.12 - 0.02) = 5.$$

If the expected next period earnings per share are £3, use of equation 2 gives:

$$FP = 5 \times £3 = £15.$$

The fair price of the share is £15. If the market price is below £15, this stock should be considered for purchase.

Regression analysis constitutes a fourth means of estimating the price-earnings ratio. Regression analysis is a technique for ascertaining the statistical relationship between one variable and one or more other variables. Equation 5 illustrates a hypothetical example of the result of a regression analysis.

$$PE = 3 + 2g + 0.5 \, (D/eps) \tag{5}$$

This hypothetical regression equation estimates the price-earnings ratio to be equal to three plus twice the growth rate of company earnings plus half the dividend pay-out rate. Putting forecasts of the growth rate of earnings, and of the dividend pay-out rate, into equation 5 yields a number which is the estimated price-earnings ratio.

Exercise 20.1

A company has a dividend pay-out rate of 0.4, the required rate of return on its shares is 12% p.a., there is a 2% p.a. expected growth rate of dividends, and earnings per share are forecast to be 50p during the next year. Estimate a fair price for the share.

Answer
Using the formula for the price-earnings ratio that states:

$$\frac{P}{eps} = \frac{D/eps}{r - g}$$

P/eps = 0.4/(0.12 − 0.02) = 0.4/0.1 = 4

With a price-earnings ratio of 4, and earnings per share forecast at 50p, the fair price of the share is estimated to be:

P = (P/eps) × eps = 4 × 50p = 200p

Exercise 20.2

Shares in LM plc are currently £40. LM's latest 12-month earnings were £4 per share, of which £2 was paid as dividends.
(a) What is the current price-earnings ratio?
(b) If earnings are expected to grow at 8% p.a. and the required rate of return is 12% p.a., what is the justified price-earnings ratio?
(c) Would you buy this share?

Answers
(a) The current price-earnings ratio is £40/£4 = 10.
(b) The justified P/E = [D/E]/[r − g] = [£2/£4]/[0.12 − 0.08] = 0.5/0.04 = 12.5.
(c) On the basis of a price-earnings ratio of 12.5, the fair price of the share is [P/E] × E = 12.5 × £4.32 = £54 [£4.32 is used in preference to £4 for earnings on the view that it is the future earnings per share that determines the current share price: £4.32 = £4 × 1.08]. At £40 the share appears to be under-priced and hence should be regarded as a potential purchase.

●●●● Earnings per share

The earnings per share ratio can be broken down into two other ratios. These are return on equity and book value per share. Thus:

Earnings per Share = Distributable Earnings/ Number of Shares

= (Distributable Earnings/ Stockholder's Equity) × (Stockholder's Equity/ Number of Shares)

The ratio 'Distributable Earnings/Stockholder's Equity' is the return on equity (ROE). Distributable earnings are the earnings (profits) available for distribution to shareholders. The second ratio, 'Stockholder's Equity/Number of Shares', is the book value per share.

The return on equity ratio can be broken down into two other ratios. These are the return on assets (ROA) and the asset/equity ratio. The return on assets ratio is:

Distributable Earnings/Total Assets

The asset/equity ratio is:

Total Assets/Stockholder's Equity.

The Return on Equity is thus calculated as:

ROE = ROA × (Asset/Equity).

The ROA can be seen as the product of two further ratios, these being the profit margin and the turnover of assets.

ROA = Profit Margin × Turnover of Assets

where

Profit Margin = Distributable Earnings/Sales

and

Turnover of Assets = Sales/Total Assets.

Other ratios

Ratios that can be used in addition to the price-earnings ratio are the price/cash flow ratio and the EV/ebitda ratio. To calculate the former ratio it is necessary to ascertain free cash flow.

To obtain a figure for free cash flow, depreciation and amortisation charges (and any other charges that are book entries rather than cash expenses) are added to profits after interest and tax paid. From this figure, maintenance capital spending (spending needed to maintain capital) should be subtracted. The figure needs to be adjusted to recognise that profits that result from changes in unpaid invoices or stock levels do not provide cash flow. Division of free cash flow by the number of shares issued gives free cash flow per share. Division of the share price by the free cash flow per share produces the price/cash flow ratio.

EV is an abbreviation for enterprise value, which is market capitalisation (share price times number of shares) plus debt minus cash. Ebitda stands for earnings before interest, tax, depreciation and amortisation. It is calculated by adding back interest, depreciation and amortisation to pre-tax profit.

Financial adequacy ratios

Three sets of ratios are used as indicators of the ability of a firm to meet its financial obligations. First, short-term solvency ratios indicate the ability of the firm to repay debts becoming due over the coming year. Second, financial leverage ratios show the extent to which the firm is financed by debt. Third, coverage ratios assess the ability of the firm to meet the obligations arising from its debts.

Short-term solvency ratios

Before buying a stock the investor must feel sure that liquidity problems are not likely to appear. Four ratios may be calculated in order to assess the adequacy of a firm's working capital. These are the current ratio, the acid-test ratio, the inventory-turnover ratio and the accounts-receivable-turnover ratio.

The current ratio is shown as:

Current Ratio = Current Assets/ Current Liabilities

Current assets are assets either in the form of cash or due to be converted into cash during the coming year (i.e. liquid assets). Current liabilities are either payable already or due to be payable in the coming year. The current ratio thus provides an assessment of the company's ability to meet its immediate liabilities.

Current assets include inventories, and in some circumstances there may be difficulty in converting inventories into cash. The acid-test ratio recognises this by removing inventories from current assets.

Acid-Test Ratio = (Current Assets − Inventories)/ Current Liabilities

The inventory-turnover ratio indicates the speed with which inventories can be converted into cash. The accounts-receivable-turnover ratio shows how quickly the firm's customers pay their bills. These factors also affect the ability of the firm to meet its commitments.

Financial leverage ratios

Debt provides risk for a company since servicing of the debt must be undertaken whatever the operational profitability of that company. There is a possibility that operational profits are insufficient to meet debt interest and repayments with the result that the firm becomes bankrupt. This risk rises with increased importance of debt in the financing of the firm, that is with increased leverage. (Debt arises from bank loans and the sale of bonds. The sale of shares does not constitute debt, the firm has no legally binding commitment to make payments to shareholders.)

There are many forms of financial leverage ratio. Two possibilities are as follows:

Long-Term Debt to Equity = Long-Term Debt/Shareholder's Equity

and

Total Debt to Equity = (Long-Term Debt + Current Liabilities)/Shareholder's Equity

Long-term debt is debt that is repayable more than a year into the future, current liabilities constitute debt that matures in a year or less. Long-term debt includes bonds issued by the firm. For the purposes of the ratios, bonds are valued at book value. Book value is the price at which the bonds were originally sold. Shareholder's equity is the total value of all the shares held by stockholders. Often each ratio is calculated twice, once using the original issue price of the shares and once using the current market price of the shares. High ratios indicate high leverage and hence risk.

Coverage ratios

Coverage ratios are concerned with the assessment of the ability of a firm to meet interest and other inescapable payments. They relate the resources available for the payments to the level of payments due. The interest coverage ratio is:

(Earnings + Interest Charges Paid)/Interest Charges Paid

Since earnings are quoted net of interest payments, it is necessary to add the interest payments back in order to ascertain the total sum available for the payment of interest.

A more comprehensive coverage ratio that takes lease payments into account is the fixed-charge coverage ratio which is:

$$\frac{\text{Earnings + Interest Charges Paid + Lease Payments}}{\text{Interest Charges Paid + Lease Payments}}$$

Problems with ratio analysis

Care needs to be taken when using ratio analysis for investment analysis. One source of difficulty is that companies use differing accounting methods in the measurement of earnings and other values. Reported values would be affected by accounting practices. Variations in ratios between companies may reflect differences in accounting methods rather than more fundamental differences.

This effect is particularly extreme where creative accounting is used. Creative accounting involves the deliberate abuse of the subjectivity inherent in accounting to select accounting policies or make assumptions which tend to bias the figures in the direction chosen by management. At a less extreme level figures could be distorted by window dressing, for example advancing or delaying transactions so that they are included in, or excluded from, the end of year accounts.

Looked at from the viewpoint of some financial ratios a firm may be seen as healthy while other ratios may indicate that it is less healthy. There is no established means of weighting the relative importance of different ratios. There will therefore be ambiguity with regard to the evaluation of the company.

There is a risk that the focus on ratios distracts the analyst from the multitude of other factors that are pertinent to the potential success of a company. Also some analysts believe that it is the direction of change in the ratios, rather than the ratios themselves, that reveals most about a company.

It should also be borne in mind that the past is not necessarily a reliable guide to the future. A company may be successful because it responds to poor financial ratios by reorganising its structure and procedures.

Chapter 21

Investment analysis: technical methods

After studying this chapter readers should be able to:

- *recognise, and critically appraise, some popular techniques of technical analysis.*

Technical analysts believe that stock markets have a dynamic of their own, independent of outside economic forces. Technical analysis is the study of internal stock market information. Any relevant outside information is seen as being embodied in stock market data so that there is no need to look for information outside the market. Technical analysts study the market itself, not the external factors that might be reflected in the market prices and volumes. The information produced by the stock market, particularly in relation to prices, is all that technical analysis is concerned with.

Technical analysts usually attempt to forecast short-term price movements. The methodology rests on the belief that stock market history tends to repeat itself. If a certain pattern of prices and volumes has previously been followed by particular price movements, it is suggested that a repetition of that pattern will be followed by similar price movements. Technical analysts assert that the study of past patterns of variables such as prices and trading volumes allows investors to identify times when particular stocks (or sectors, or the overall market) are likely to fall or rise in price. The focus tends to be on the timing of purchases and sales. Most technical analysts use charts of stock prices (and possibly also volumes of buying and selling). The following exposition aims to describe some of the more frequently used charts.

Figure 21.1 shows a bar chart. For each day, or other chosen time interval, there is a vertical line. The top of the vertical line indicates the highest price reached during the day, the bottom shows the lowest price. There is a short horizontal line on each vertical line – this horizontal line indicates the closing price on the day.

Figure 21.2 illustrates a line chart. It involves daily closing prices joined by straight lines to make a graph.

Figure 21.3 illustrates a point and figure chart. A price interval is decided upon, for example 10p. For every successive one interval increase in price, an X in entered in the same column (going upwards). If the stock price falls by 10p from a previous high, a O is entered in the next column. Each successive 10p price decline is then indicated by a O (going downwards) in the same column. When the price rises by 10p above the lowest price, an X is entered in the next column.

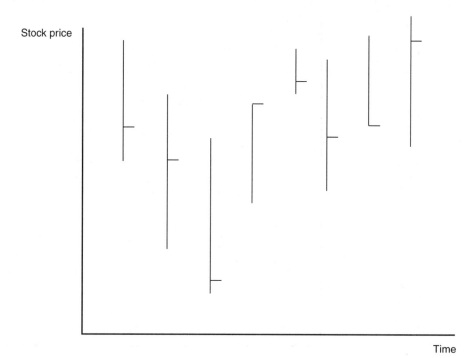

Figure 21.1 Bar chart

Figure 21.2 Line chart

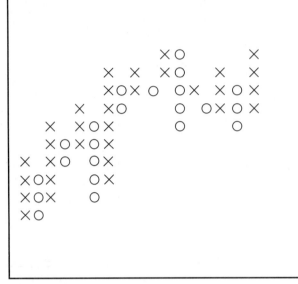

Figure 21.3 Point and figure chart

Chart patterns

There are a vast number of chart patterns employed by technical analysts. What follows is merely indicative of some of the patterns. Line charts will be used for the examples. Figure 21.4 illustrates a rising trend channel.

The stock price remains within the channel shown by the upward sloping parallel lines until point A. At point A, it breaks out of the channel in a downward direction. The chartist may interpret this as a signal to sell the stock since it is seen as forecasting a fall in the stock price. Trend channels could also be horizontal or downward sloping. In these cases a break-out in the upward direction could be seen as indicative of a price rise, and would therefore be a buy signal.

The lines constituting the bounds of a trading range are not necessarily parallel. Figure 21.5 illustrates a triangle. In this case converging lines bound the series of stock prices. The upward break-out at point A might be interpreted as an indication of subsequent price rises.

A particularly popular chart pattern is the head and shoulders. This is illustrated by Figure 21.6. The peak at C is the head, and the peaks at A and E are the shoulders. When the stock price falls from E to a level below D, further price falls are forecast. In other words, such an eventuality constitutes a sell signal.

Support and resistance patterns may be based on the premise that people remember past stock prices and may regret lost opportunities. These patterns may be

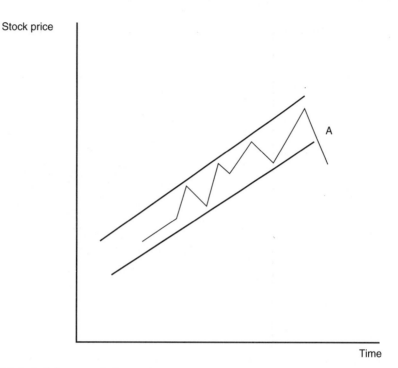

Figure 21.4 A rising trend channel

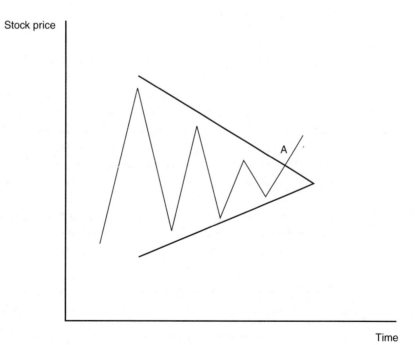

Figure 21.5 A triangle

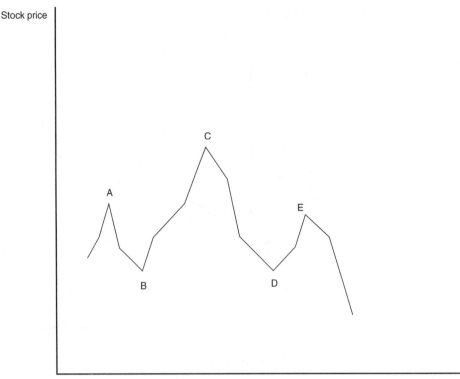

Figure 21.6 Head and shoulders

based on horizontal price channels, or trading ranges. Figure 21.7 illustrates such a channel.

Users of this approach suggest that for a period of time stock prices trade within the range bounded by the support and resistance levels. If the share price breaks out of the range in an upwards direction people who had not previously bought regret not having done so. As a result they will buy if the price re-enters the trading range. There would be buying at the top of the trading range, the support level. This buying will tend to prevent the share price falling below the support level.

If the stock price falls below the bottom of the trading range, the investor regrets not having sold. Investors decide to sell if they can do so within the trading range. If the stock price returns to the trading range, many investors will sell. The bottom

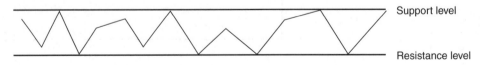

Figure 21.7 Horizontal price channel

of the trading range becomes an upper limit to the share price. This is the resistance level. If the share price rises above the resistance level, many investors will sell with the result that prices fall.

Chartists frequently believe that when the direction of a stock price changes, characteristic chart patterns may develop as the turn occurs. The head and shoulders configuration illustrated by Figure 21.6 is one of these reversal patterns. Figures 21.8 to 21.11 illustrate some other reversal patterns looked for by chartists. In each case the broken line indicates the general pattern that the actual charts (unbroken lines) are interpreted as revealing.

Technical analysts use not only prices relating to individual dates but also moving averages. A moving average is an average of a series of previous prices, for example the average of the last 200 daily prices. (Each day the oldest price is removed from the calculation of the average and the most recent price introduced.) Chart patterns can be based on moving averages as well as daily prices.

One popular technique is to use moving averages and daily prices on the same chart. If the current price is a predetermined percentage above or below the moving average, a buy or sell signal may be indicated. Points, at which a chart of daily prices crosses a chart of moving averages, are seen as significant. For example, a daily price chart that crosses a moving average chart from below might be seen as providing a buy signal. The signal may be dependent upon whether the moving average is rising or falling at the time. Each investor will have his or her individual trading rules.

One of the oldest technical tools is the Dow theory. Its main purpose is to forecast the future direction of the overall stock market. The Dow theory is based on

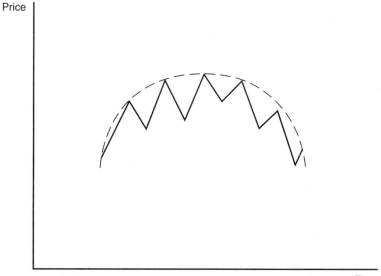

Figure 21.8 Rounding top reversal

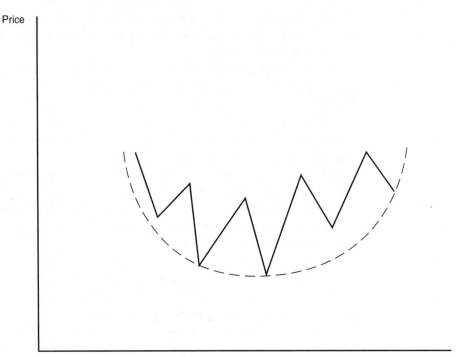

Figure 21.9 Rounding bottom reversal

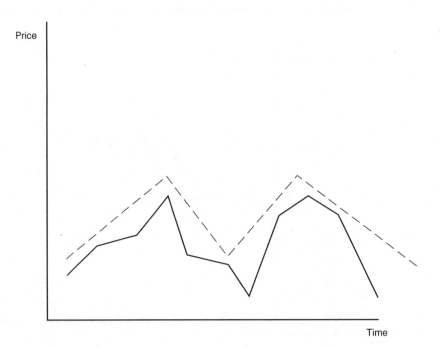

Figure 21.10 Double top reversal

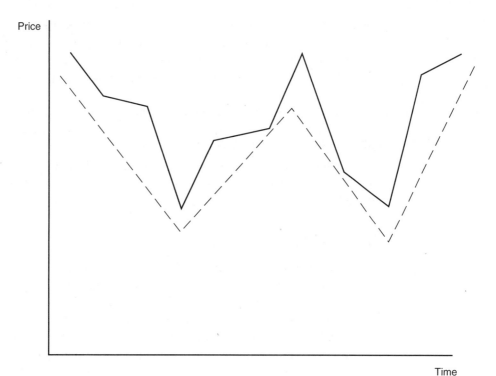

Figure 21.11 Double bottom reversal

the belief that market movements are analogous to movements of the sea. It sees three simultaneous movements in the market. Hourly or daily fluctuations correspond to ripples. Secondary movements (which last a few weeks) are the waves. Primary trends of up to a year or more are analogous to tides. It is the primary trend that is referred to as either a bull or a bear market. The hourly or daily movements are seen as having little or no predictive value. However, secondary movements in stock indices are used to forecast changes in the direction of the primary trend.

Other technical indicators

The forecasting techniques of technical analysts are not limited to charts. Technical analysts also use filter rules, relative strength and short interest ratios, among many other indicators. A filter rule states that an investor should buy when a stock price (or market index) has risen by a predetermined percentage above a previous low point. Conversely, the investor should sell when the price or index falls by a particular percentage below a previous high. The percentages are at the discretion of the investor, but should be established prior to the market movements.

Relative strength is measured by the ratio of a stock price to a market index. Changes in the ratio are taken to indicate buying or selling opportunities. A momentum trader would take a rise in the ratio as a signal to buy the stock (and a fall as a signal to sell). A contrarian would interpret a rise in the ratio as a sell signal (and a fall as a buy).

The short interest ratio is the ratio of short sales to total trading. A rise in the ratio has two opposing interpretations. Some technical analysts see a rise in the ratio as indicative of bearish sentiment and hence as constituting a sell signal. Others interpret a rise as a buy signal on the grounds that the short positions will have to be covered by stock purchases. These stock purchases would tend to push up stock prices.

Some caveats

The foregoing should be seen as merely indicative of the wide range of technical analysis techniques employed. However, what might appear as mechanical trading rules are in reality subject to a high degree of subjective interpretation. Technical analysts differ as to which charts, or other indicators, they use. They also differ as to the interpretation and significance to be assigned to a particular chart pattern or indicator. They even differ as to whether a particular chart pattern is present at all.

A point to note about technical trading rules is that speed is of the essence. Even if it is accepted that there are objective trading rules that provide clear and unambiguous price forecasts, those forecasts will not allow profits to be made if others act on them more quickly. Any rewards for accurate forecasting go to those who are first to trade on the basis of the forecasts. A buy signal (if correct) will provide profits only to the investors who are the earliest to react. Their purchases will pull up the stock price with the effect that the under-pricing is eliminated and the opportunity to profit from the price rise disappears.

Games people play

If one takes the view that the fundamentals that should determine share prices are factors such as the level of savings available for stock market investment, the profitability of businesses, and the rates of return available on other investments (e.g. interest rates), then technical analysis may be seen as focusing on irrelevant factors. Technical analysts could be seen as playing games with each other, probably with professionals tending to out-play amateurs. Much of technical analysis is concerned with forecasting the behaviour of other technical analysts. Those who are the first to identify (and act upon) the trend or indicator that everyone else is looking for will be able to profit when the others act upon it. Double guessing the behaviour of other investors is more important to a technical analyst than assessing the true values of shares based on factors such as the expected profitability of companies.

Such points were identified by J. M. Keynes (1936) in *The General Theory of Employment, Interest and Money*. A few quotations from the book may be of interest.

'The actual, private object of the most skilled investment to-day is "to beat the gun", as the Americans so well express it, to outwit the crowd, and to pass the bad, or depreciating, half-crown to the other fellow.' (p. 155)

'For it is, so to speak, a game of Snap, of Old Maid, of Musical Chairs – a pastime in which he is victor who says *Snap* neither too soon nor too late, who passes the old maid to his neighbour before the game is over, who secures a chair for himself when the music stops.' (pp. 155–6)

'We have reached the third degree where we devote our intelligences to anticipating what average opinion expects the average opinion to be.' (p. 156)

Chapter 22

Market efficiency: concepts and weak form evidence

After studying this chapter readers should be able to evaluate prospects for investment analysis in the light of:

- *the concepts of weak, semi-strong and strong form informational efficiency*

- *empirical evidence on the weak form of the efficient market hypothesis*

- *evidence on overshooting and mean reversion*

- *evidence on momentum and contrarian strategies.*

Market efficiency can be subdivided into three types: allocative efficiency, operational efficiency and informational efficiency. Allocative efficiency is concerned with whether funds are directed to their most productive uses. This is mainly a primary market issue, the primary market being the market in which borrowers issue securities and receive payment from the initial investors. Allocative efficiency is concerned with the issue of which borrowers receive the finance. An allocatively efficient market is one in which the available funds go to the borrowers who will make the most productive use of them. Allocative efficiency is not the main concern here. However, it is important to be aware that allocative efficiency is dependent on operational and informational efficiency.

Operational efficiency relates to the costs and risks involved in the process of carrying out transactions in financial markets. One dimension relates to transaction costs such as bid-offer spreads and brokers' commissions. High transaction costs in the primary market would raise the cost of funds for borrowers and lower returns for investors. The result would be a reduction in the total level of investment in the economy. High transaction costs in the secondary market would also adversely impact on the primary market and hence on the total volume of investment.

The secondary market is the market in which previously issued securities are traded. It is the means by which stocks or bonds bought in the primary market can be converted into cash. The knowledge that assets purchased in the primary market can easily and cheaply be resold in the secondary market makes investors more prepared to provide borrowers with funds by buying in the primary market. A successful primary market depends upon an effective secondary market.

If transaction costs are high in the secondary market, the proceeds from the sale of securities will be reduced and the incentive to buy in the primary market will be lower. Also high transaction costs in the secondary market would tend to reduce the volume of trading and thereby reduce the ease with which secondary market sales can be executed. It follows that high transaction costs in the secondary market would reduce that market's effectiveness in rendering primary market assets liquid. In consequence there would be adverse effects on the level of activity in the primary market and hence on the total level of investment in the economy.

Price volatility in the secondary market can also be detrimental to the operation of the primary market. High volatility in the secondary market means that buyers in the primary market stand a considerable risk of losing money by having to sell at a lower price in the secondary market. This can reduce the motivation to buy in the primary market. Two factors that affect the price volatility of securities in the secondary market are the depth and breadth of that market.

The depth of the market is based on the likely appearance of new orders stimulated by any movement in price. If a rise in price brings forth numerous sell orders, the price rise will be small. A decline in price that stimulates buy orders will be a small decline. A deep market would be characterised by the appearance of orders that tend to dampen the extent of any movement in price. Greater depth is thus associated with lower volatility.

The breadth of the market reflects the number and diversity of the traders in the market. If there are a large number of market participants with differing motivations and expectations, there are less likely to be substantial price changes than would be expected when there are a small number of traders, or when the traders have common views such that they buy or sell together. A broad market is a large heterogeneous market characterised by relative price stability.

Operational efficiency is important for informational efficiency. An informationally efficient market is one in which security prices reflect all relevant information. By buying underpriced securities and selling overpriced securities traders will tend to move prices to the levels that correspond with the available information. High transaction costs will reduce (or even eliminate) the potential profits from buying low or selling high (with a view to reversing the transaction when the pricing error has been corrected). Since such transactions are required for the purpose of moving prices to the levels consistent with the available information, transaction costs that deter them will lessen the informational efficiency of the market.

Informational efficiency of the secondary market is important for the operation of the primary market. This is because issuers of stocks or bonds in the primary market are likely to look at prices in the secondary market when determining the prices of new issues. If the secondary market is informationally inefficient, the guidance provided will be poor. The primary market, and its allocative efficiency, is thus dependent upon the operational and informational efficiency of the secondary market.

The meaning of informational efficiency

Informational efficiency is conventionally divided into the weak, semi-strong and strong forms (a classification originally suggested by Fama). The weak form of the efficient market hypothesis suggests that all historical market information (past prices, past trading volumes) is fully taken into account in the current market price.

An implication of the weak form hypothesis is that there is no scope for making profits from analysis of historical market prices and volumes. So technical analysis, including chartism, is expected to be of no value. Attempts to forecast stock prices using charts based on previous stock prices will fail since all the information available from past price data is already reflected in the stock price.

The weak form hypothesis is closely related to the idea of random walks. A random walk involves each day's price movement being independent of every previous day's price movement. Upward and downward movements are regarded as having equal likelihood on a day, irrespective of the previous direction of movement. Price movements reflect news coming into the market, and news is random both in timing and in nature (good and bad news have equal likelihood). However, the weak form hypothesis deviates from a pure random walk since it allows for upward price movements to dominate downward movements so that over the long term share prices tend to move upwards (there are random fluctuations around a rising trend).

A semi-strong form efficient market is one in which security prices fully take account of all publicly available information. In addition to market information on past prices and trading volumes, publicly available information includes macroeconomic data (such as interest rates and inflation rates), company data (such as profits and sales) and non-economic events (such as political events, technological developments, and discoveries of natural resources). The implication is that asset prices immediately move to reflect any new information so that no one can make profits by means of purchases or sales based on analysing the new information.

Both types of market efficiency require prices to fully reflect any new information without any time lag. Incomplete or slow price movements will allow traders successfully to forecast price movements, and to make profits from those movements. Although allowance is made for the possibility that a security price will not attain its true level until time has been taken to carry out the relevant analyses, it is proposed that any initial deviation from the true level is equally likely to constitute an over or under-valuation. There remains the paradox of how asset prices move to their new levels if no one is able to profit from trading in the assets following the emergence of new information. One might expect that those traders who respond most quickly to new information will be able to make profits from the use of that information. A further paradox is that the market efficiency that results from their trading depends upon those traders believing that markets are not efficient.

Strong form efficiency allows no information to be used profitably, not even insider information. It suggests that security prices reflect all available information even if some of that information is held by only one person. The puzzle of how the information becomes reflected in the asset prices without trading by the possessor of the information is even greater in this case.

● ● ● ● Assumptions of the efficient market hypothesis

The efficient market hypothesis makes five important assumptions. One is that investors are rational. This does not require all investors to be rational, but it does require that the rational investors outweigh the irrational ones. However, there are times when irrational investors are dominant. A possible cause of market over-reaction is the tendency of some investors (often small investors) to follow the market. Such investors believe that recent stock price movements are indicators of future price movements. In other words they extrapolate price movements. They buy when prices have been rising and thereby tend to push prices to unrealistically high levels. They sell when prices have been falling and thereby drive prices to excessively low levels. There are times when such naïve investors outweigh those that invest on the basis of fundamental analysis of the intrinsic value of the shares. Such irrational investors help to generate bubbles and crashes in stock markets.

A second assumption is that rational investors have adequate funds. If rational investors are going to dominate the markets, they must have the funds necessary to take advantage of all investment opportunities. It is only by being able to trade shares, which requires resources, that they are able to incorporate information into share prices. A related point is that rational investors should be able to sell shares short. Selling short means borrowing shares and selling those borrowed shares. The ability to sell is as important as the ability to buy in relation to ensuring that share prices reflect all relevant information.

A third assumption is that information is available instantaneously to many investors and that rational investors immediately use the information to make good assessments of share prices. If some investors were able to make good assessments more quickly than others, they would be able to make profits from the information received. Although this assumption will not hold in its absolute form, a high degree of market efficiency would be achieved if a substantial number of rational investors analyse the information, and trade on it, within one day of the information being available.

A fourth assumption is that rational investors do not believe that markets are semi-strong form efficient. This is a paradox. The existence of market efficiency depends upon rational investors not realising that it exists. If rational investors believed that markets are semi-strong efficient, they would not carry out investment analysis and trade on the basis of that analysis. Investment analysis is based on the belief that shares may be mispriced so that profit can be made by estimating the correct price and buying or selling accordingly. It is only through fundamental analysis and trades based on that analysis that share prices come to reflect new information.

A fifth assumption is that transaction costs, market impact effects and required compensation for risk are not large enough to deter trading at prices close to fundamental value. Transaction costs include brokers' commissions, bid-offer spreads and taxes such as stamp duty. Market impact effects are the effects of an investor's own purchases and sales on the share price. An investor may require some additional expected profit to compensate for the possibility that their own analysis may provide an inaccurate forecast. These factors could lead to investors not trading unless their estimate of fundamental value is substantially different from the actual share price. Investors would react only to very important pieces of new information. In consequence smaller deviations of share prices from their fundamental values are not corrected. Less important news would not be acted upon. Share prices would remain at levels that do not reflect all relevant information. Shares would not be efficiently priced.

Empirical evidence on the weak form of the efficient market hypothesis

Kendall (1953) attempted to identify cycles in stock indices. He could not find any. One day's level appeared to be equal to the previous day's plus or minus a random amount. Roberts (1959) showed that a series of cumulative random numbers looked like a series of share prices such that observers believed that they could identify price patterns. Osborne (1959) found that share price movements conformed to the Brownian motion of physics in that successive movements appeared to be random and the standard deviation of cumulative changes was proportional to the square root of time. Moore (1964) looked for correlations between share price changes and previous price changes (serial correlation). The average coefficient of correlation was not significantly different from zero (statistically). He concluded that past price changes cannot be used to forecast future price changes. Fama (1965) confirmed the absence of serial correlation. He also employed runs tests, which sought to ascertain whether runs of successive upward or downward price movements were longer or shorter than would be expected on the basis of random price movements. He concluded that lengths of runs were consistent with a random series of price movements. So there was no observable tendency for prices to trend upwards or downwards. However, Niederhoffer and Osborne (1966) found slight evidence of serial correlation and runs using intra-day rather than weekly or daily data. Intra-day serial correlation appeared to be slightly negative.

The vast majority of studies, testing for correlation between current and previous returns, have shown that there is not a significant coefficient of correlation. The small relationships that have been seen do not provide the possibility of excess returns net of transaction costs. Transaction costs exceed any potential gains. Efficient markets should be characterised by transaction costs setting upper limits to correlation coefficients, with higher transaction costs allowing greater serial correlation. Jennergren and Korsvold (1975) observed higher correlation coefficients in markets with higher transaction costs when examining Norwegian stocks.

Another approach to testing for weak form efficiency is to ascertain whether trading rules, such as those used by chartists, have any predictive value. One trading rule that has been investigated is the filter rule. A typical filter rule might involve buying when a stock price rises 5% above its previous low point and selling when the stock price falls 5% from its previous high. Alexander (1964) and Fama and Blume (1966) concluded that it was not possible to make profits by using filter rules to forecast price movements. However, Sweeney (1988, 1990) suggested that filter rules can produce statistically significant risk-adjusted excess returns after adjusting for the types of transaction costs faced by professional traders.

Chartists argue that tests of simple and mechanical trading rules cannot be used to draw conclusions about the complex and subtle techniques actually employed. There is also the point that it is impossible to test the whole infinite variety of trading rules and hence it is always possible that effective trading rules exist among those that have not been tested. Furthermore technical analysts would not publicise effective techniques for fear that widespread knowledge of the techniques would reduce the profits available to themselves. Perhaps it is only the ineffective trading rules that become widely known and hence subject to testing.

There are counterviews and debates about the evidence. Shiller (1984, 1988) has suggested that there may be fads and fashions in investment. If such fashions spread slowly, share price trends could emerge as a result. Fashion is not the only possible driving force. Since the late 1990s some people have argued that demographic trends are having a similar effect. In North America and Europe the post-war bulge generation (people born in the baby boom of the late 1940s to the early 1960s) is moving into the last decade or so before retirement. They are reaching the stage at which family responsibilities are lessening as their grown-up children leave home, their mortgages are being paid off, and the necessity of saving for retirement is becoming increasingly apparent. They thus become more able and willing to save. The additional saving involves increased financial investment. This may have an upward pull on stock market prices that continues for a long period of time. If this line of reasoning is accurate, a strong and long-lasting upward price trend may be expected.

A study by Peters (1991), which analysed S&P 500 price changes from 1928 to 1989, showed that securities markets are highly leptokurtotic. Leptokurtotic markets exhibit fat tails in their returns distributions. The probabilities of very high and very low values are greater than would be predicted by normal distributions. This is consistent with markets trending in a particular direction, that is price movements being related to previous price movements. Peters suggested that as few as three variables can accurately predict market movements. However, since these three variables frequently change, there may be no practical way of making profits from predicting market movements. Also leptokurtosis may have alternative explanations, such as the observed distribution being an amalgam of several different normal distributions (it is likely that over a prolonged period of time a stock index would have been subject to numerous different distributions of returns).

● ● ● ● Overshooting and mean reversion

Summers (1986) simulated a series of share prices which over-reacted to new information. He went on to show that the techniques used in the early tests of serial correlation were not able to discriminate between an over-reacting series and a random series. Such tests cannot therefore be used to refute the proposition that markets are prone to over-reaction.

It has often been suggested that the observed volatility of stock markets is greater than might be expected from the efficient market hypothesis. The stock market crash of October 1987 is an example of volatility that is difficult to explain in terms of new information coming into the market. Share prices are seen as being the present values of expected future dividend receipts, but dividends show much less fluctuation than share prices.

Shiller (1981) tested the hypothesis that stock price volatility exceeds what is justified on the basis of variations in dividends. The basic premise of these studies is that stock prices should be more stable than dividends since stock prices reflect expectations of dividends. To draw an analogy with tossing a coin, if a coin is tossed 100 times the expectation is that there will be 50 heads. Each time the coin is tossed 100 times the forecast would be of 50 heads. The forecast does not vary, it has zero volatility. However, on most occasions that the coin is tossed 100 times the actual number of heads will differ from 50. The observed numbers of heads will tend to form a normal distribution with a mean of 50. The observed number of heads is more volatile than the forecast number of heads. The implication of this reasoning for share prices is that they should exhibit greater stability than dividends. Share prices are based on expected dividends which should be more stable than actual dividends. The volatility of share prices should be less than the volatility of dividends. Shiller's research found that stock prices were much more volatile than dividends.

Although studies of short-term serial correlation tended to find that there was no significant correlation coefficient, investigations of longer time periods have suggested that markets over-react to new information. Tests covering periods of several years (Poterba and Summers 1988, Fama and French 1988) have found a tendency for prices to deviate from their fair values and then revert towards them (mean reversion). In other words significant negative serial correlation has been found over multiyear time horizons. This is consistent with Shiller's view that fads appear to exist in securities markets. Episodes of apparent overshooting followed by corrections give the appearance of asset prices fluctuating around their fair values. Market prices seem to exhibit excess volatility.

These studies have their critics. It has been suggested that the price fluctuations arise from variations in the required rate of return by which expected dividend streams are discounted, perhaps due to changes in the risk premiums (Cochrane 1991). It has also been suggested that the apparent serial correlation arises from small sample bias, the tests being based on a small number of observations (Cecchetti, Lam and Mark 1990).

DeBondt and Thaler (1985, 1987) have put forward an over-reaction hypothesis. The over-reaction hypothesis suggests that when investors react to unanticipated news that will benefit a company's stock, the price rise will initially be greater than it should be. There will be a subsequent price decline to the level justified by the new information. Conversely, the price fall arising from adverse news will initially be exaggerated, requiring a subsequent correction.

DeBondt and Thaler proposed a directional effect and a magnitude effect. The directional effect is the tendency for an initial over-reaction to be followed by a moderating movement in the opposite direction. The magnitude effect is the tendency for the size of the correction to be related to the extent of the initial over-reaction. A relatively large initial over-reaction will be followed by a relatively large compensating correction. Brown and Harlow (1988) added the intensity effect, which states that the shorter the duration of the initial price change, the more extreme the subsequent response will be. Brown and Harlow found that over-reaction (all three effects) was most marked in the case of short-term responses to negative news.

A related observation by DeBondt and Thaler is sometimes referred to as the winner–loser problem. Stocks that have been relatively good performers over the last three to five years will tend to underperform during the next three to five years; conversely, past underperformers become future outperformers. Jegadeesh and Titman (1993) found evidence consistent with this observation.

Serial correlation in volatility

ARCH and GARCH models allow price changes to be serially uncorrelated but not independent. Predictability comes not through being able to forecast price changes but by being able to forecast the variance of the changes. Although the best forecast of a price change may be zero, the variance of possible price changes will depend upon past volatility. Al-Loughani and Chappell (1997) found that the FTSE 100 index between 1983 and 1989 did not follow a random walk but demonstrated significant heteroscedaticity (variances were serially correlated). Their results provide evidence against the random walk hypothesis. The results do not necessarily provide evidence against the weak form of the EMH since they did not test whether the predictability of volatility provided the opportunity to earn excess profits. However, it has been suggested that the serial correlation in variance arises from the inappropriateness of the asset pricing model used rather than from market inefficiency (e.g. Schwaiger 1995).

Momentum and contrarian strategies

There is evidence that technical trading rules based on momentum and contrarian strategies might produce opportunities for profit. A number of studies have divided stocks into 'winner' and 'loser' portfolios. The winner portfolios contain those stocks that have performed well in the recent past, the loser portfolios those that have shown poor recent returns. The studies have then investigated whether there is a significant difference in their subsequent performances. If markets are weak form efficient there should be no significant difference between the returns (price movements) of the two portfolios.

Research has shown there to be significant differences between the returns to winner and loser portfolios. Some studies have found that winner and loser portfolios chosen on the basis of the returns (price changes) during one week exhibit contrarian behaviour in the following week. A relatively good performance one week tends to be followed by a relatively bad performance the next week, and vice versa (Lehmann 1990). Similar findings have arisen from consideration of returns over one month and the following month (Jegadeesh 1990). However, when the period used has been six months or a year momentum strategies appear to have been successful, winner portfolios continue to significantly outperform loser portfolios (Jegadeesh 1990, Jegadeesh and Titman 1993). Paradoxically tests using three and five-year periods have found contrarian strategies to work, the losers from one period become the winners in the next period, and vice versa (DeBondt and Thaler 1985, 1987).

Research on relative strength has also produced conflicting findings. Proponents of relative strength strategies look at the ratio between a stock price and the level of a stock index. A change in this ratio may signal a trade. Momentum traders see an increase in the ratio as indicative of a buying opportunity (and a decline as a sell signal). Levy (1966) produced findings that suggested that a strategy based on relative strength could outperform a buy-and-hold strategy (a strategy of simply buying stocks and holding them without indulging in any further transactions). Arnott (1979) found that a stock that has been strong in the past will tend to be weak in the future. Brush (1986) found that relative strength models cannot be used to predict which stocks would achieve superior performance after adjusting for risk and transaction costs.

Chapter 23

Market efficiency:
semi-strong and strong forms

After studying this chapter readers should be able to evaluate prospects for investment analysis in the light of:

● *The evidence relating to semi-strong form efficiency*

● *The apparent existence of market anomalies*

● *Evidence relating to the strong form of the efficient market hypothesis*

● *Behavioural finance.*

Evidence supporting semi-strong form efficiency

Much of the evidence supporting the semi-strong form of the efficient market hypothesis comes from event studies. These studies aim to establish whether it is possible to make profits from a publicly available item of news, particularly financial news relating to a specific company. If stock prices adjust very quickly to news, the market is efficient and there is no scope for trading profits following the news. If stock prices adjust slowly there is an opportunity for ascertaining, and trading upon, the direction of price change. Slow price changes indicate market inefficiency.

Ball and Brown (1968) investigated the usefulness of earnings published in company accounts from the point of view of making trading profits. Their sample of companies was divided into two groups, one with earnings that exceeded expectations and the other with disappointing earnings. In both cases most of the share price adjustment occurred during the 12 months leading up to the earnings announcement as information became gradually available through interim reports, brokers' analyses and newspaper articles. The information not previously known was found to be incorporated into the share price almost immediately after the earnings announcement.

Excess returns on stocks subject to revisions, in the consensus of analysts' estimates of earnings, have been found to be available for up to 12 months. The market appears not to immediately react to changes in the consensus forecast. Furthermore studies have shown that revisions in the consensus of analysts' estimates of earnings tend to have momentum, that is an increase in the consensus forecast one month is often followed by another increase in the next month (Givoly and Lakonishok (1980).

Fama, Fisher, Jensen and Roll (1969) investigated the potential for making profits from news about stock splits (for example replacing one old share with two new shares). A stock split adds nothing to the value of a company, and should have no effect on the total value of shares outstanding. However, the split might convey information about future cash flows. The study hypothesised that announcements of forthcoming stock splits generated expectations of higher future dividends. After the split the firms that raised dividends experienced stock price rises whereas those that failed to meet the expectation of higher dividends underwent share price falls. The interpretation was that stock prices adjusted to the expectation of higher dividends very quickly after the announcements of the stock splits, and the price rise was subsequently added to or removed dependent upon whether the dividend expectations were realised.

Takeover and merger announcements can raise stock prices substantially, especially where premiums are being paid to the shareholders of an acquired firm. Dodd (1981) found no evidence of abnormal price changes subsequent to the immediate reaction. Firth (1975) studied the effects of a firm having 10% of its shares bought by a single entity (which may be seen as an indicator of a pending takeover bid) and found that most of the increase in share value occurred between the last trade before the announcement and the next trade. Only those with inside information (prior knowledge) could earn excess returns net of transaction costs.

Sunder (1973) investigated the effects on the stock market values of firms arising from a change to LIFO (last in first out) stock valuation. The benefit from the reduced tax liability showed up in higher share prices prior to (due to the change being anticipated) or immediately after the announcement of the change. Once the information about the change was public there was no scope for making trading profits from knowledge of the change. It also seems likely that the stock price rises resulted from the changes in the net of tax cash flows rather than the accounting changes as such. Research on the effects of alterations to accounting practices such as the treatment of depreciation has indicated that share prices do not react to changes that have no impact on expected net of tax cash flows (Kaplan and Roll 1972). The reaction of the market to dividend announcements has also been investigated. Pettit (1972) found that the information content of dividend announcements was immediately reflected in share prices.

Initial public offerings of shares are often made at prices below fair value in order to ensure that the offering is fully subscribed. This tends to provide the initial buyers with a capital gain. The profits appear to be limited to those investors allocated shares in the initial sale. Purchases in the secondary market soon after issue do not provide profits. It seems that prices reach their fair values very quickly. All relevant information is quickly incorporated into prices (Ibbotson, Sindelar, and Ritter 1988, 1994). Results from Miller and Reilly (1987), Chalk and Peavy (1987) and Hanley (1993) show that the price adjustment takes place within one day of the offering. Research into the effects of sales of large blocks of shares in the secondary market has found that any resulting price change is corrected within a day so that after the day of the sale there is no scope for making profits from knowledge of the disposal (Kraus and Stoll 1972).

A study of announcements relating to economic news (such as news concerning money supply, inflation and interest rates) found no impact on stock prices beyond the day of the announcement (Pearce and Roley 1985). One study has even found that stock price reactions to economic news are completed within an hour (Jain 1988).

Evidence against semi-strong form efficiency – market anomalies

An anomaly is an exception to a rule, in this case an observation that appears to contradict the view that markets are informationally efficient. One anomaly relates to the market response to earnings announcements. Although some early studies of price reactions to earnings announcements concluded that the price changes were completed very quickly, later research has suggested that part of the price response is subject to a significant time lag. If a lag occurs, investors will have the opportunity to make profits from knowledge of the earnings announcement. They will have time to undertake trades that take advantage of the resulting price trends.

Latane, Jones and Rieke (1974) developed the concept of standardized unexpected earnings which could be defined as:

(Actual earnings − Predicted earnings) / (Standard deviation of earnings).

The division by the standard deviation of earnings (or standard error of the estimate) reflects the fact that the element of surprise or news in a particular difference between actual and predicted earnings depends upon its relationship to previous differences. The surprise element in a particular difference is greater for a firm whose earnings are typically small or normally stable.

Jones, Rendleman and Latane (1984) found that a substantial part of the price adjustment to unexpected earnings occurred after the day of the earnings announcement. Indeed price adjustments were still occurring more than 60 days after the announcement. In an efficient market, prices should adjust very quickly to earnings announcements, rather than with a lag. Other researchers, using different samples and different methods, have found similar results.

Size and ratio effects

Another anomaly has been referred to as the size effect. Banz (1981) found that small firms in terms of market capitalisation had provided much greater investment returns than large firms. Other researchers have confirmed the size effect. Fortune

(1991) calculated the cumulative value of investments made in January 1926, one being in an S&P 500 portfolio and the other in a portfolio of small firms' stocks. He found that the latter significantly outperformed the former. Hulbert (1993, 1997) confirmed the outperformance of small capitalisation stocks, but concluded that there was no relative advantage from small company stocks when account is taken of commissions.

Banz suggested that the higher returns could be due to higher betas (greater systematic risk) and that the apparent excess of returns over what was expected on the basis of betas arose from underestimating beta. More generally Banz suggested that the apparent size effect could be due to inadequacies of the capital asset pricing model. The expected rate of return is calculated by means of the CAPM. A deviation between the observed and expected rates of return could be due to the CAPM providing incorrect estimates. Tests of market efficiency tend simultaneously to be tests of the CAPM and the efficient market hypothesis. Differences between expected and observed rates of return could be the result of market inefficiency or defects of the CAPM (or both). Evidence indicating that the size effect arises from problems with the CAPM rather market inefficiency is provided by Chan, Chen and Hsieh (1985). They showed that, when another pricing model (the arbitrage pricing model) was used to measure expected return, the size effect disappeared.

The shares of small companies are often traded infrequently. The absence of trades could mean that their prices do not move while the market as a whole is moving. In consequence their betas are underestimated. Also small firms would include those that have recently encountered difficulties and borrowed heavily as a result. The increased gearing might have raised their betas so that the betas based on past data are underestimates. If the estimated betas are too low, then expected returns will be too low. The observed high returns on small company stocks, relative to expected returns, could be the result of low expectations rather than high returns on the small company stocks.

The issue of whether the apparent abnormally high returns from smaller company stocks are explicable in terms of market inefficiency or problems with the capital asset pricing model remains unresolved. However, the size effect appears to be related to two other anomalies: the price-earnings ratio effect and the January effect.

The price-earnings ratio (P/E) effect has been investigated by Basu (1977) and Reinganum (1981), among others. They both found that the shares of firms with low P/E ratios tended to yield abnormally high returns. However, Reinganum concluded that the P/E effect was a proxy for the size effect, whereas Basu took the view that the size effect was a proxy for the P/E effect. Since companies with low P/E ratios tend to be small, it is difficult to judge whether the high returns are the result of size or the P/E ratio. Levy and Lerman (1985) found that after adjusting for transaction costs necessary to rebalance a portfolio in order to maintain the low P/E ratio as prices and earnings change over time, the superior performance of portfolios of low P/E ratio stocks no longer holds.

Owners' equity is the excess of the assets of a firm over its liabilities. The price to book value ratio is the stock price divided by owners' equity. There is evidence that shares of firms with low ratios tend to outperform those of firms with high ratios. Rosenberg, Reid and Lanstein (1985) found that stocks with low price to book ratios significantly outperformed the average stock. Fama and French (1992) found that two variables, firm size and the price to book ratio, between them captured the cross sectional variation in average stock returns during the period 1963–90. Furthermore, the price to book ratio had a consistently stronger role.

Calendar effects

The January effect was demonstrated by Rozeff and Kinney (1976), who found that average stock market returns in January tended to be much higher than in other months. Guletkin and Guletkin (1983) studied stock markets in 15 countries and discovered a January effect in all of them. This implies that the January effect is not explicable in terms of the specific tax (or other institutional) arrangements in a country. Keim (1983) found that about half of the size effect occurred in January. In fact about a quarter of the size effect for the year was typically accomplished during the first five trading days in January.

Kato and Shallheim (1985) studied the Tokyo Stock Exchange and found excess returns for January and a strong relationship between size and returns (small firms substantially outperforming large firms). Fama (1991) reported results from the United States for the period 1941 to 1981. Stocks of small firms averaged returns of 8.06% in January, whereas the stocks of large firms averaged January returns of 1.342% (in both cases the January returns exceeded the average return in the other months). For the period 1982 to 1991 the January returns were 5.32% and 3.2% for the stocks of small and large firms respectively.

One possible explanation for the January effect is window dressing by fund managers. They are often required to publish the details of the portfolios that they hold at the end of the year. It has been suggested that they prefer to show large, well-known companies in their published portfolios. So they sell small company shares and buy large company shares in December and then do the opposite in January. Thus the prices of small company shares rise in January. Although this may explain the relative outperformance of smaller company shares in January, it does not explain the general January effect (unless the window dressing entails a relative move to bonds and cash in December).

Cross (1973), French (1980) and others have documented a weekend effect. They found that the average returns to stocks were negative between the close of trading on Friday and the close of trading on Monday. Gibbons and Hess (1983) examined a 17-year period between 1962 and 1978 and found that on average Monday returns were negative on an annualised basis (−33.5% p.a.). Keim and Stambaugh (1984) investigated the daily returns on the S&P 500 from 1928 to 1982 and found that, on average, Monday returns were negative. Kohers and Kohers (1995) also found a weekend effect, suggesting that there would be an advantage from buying on Mondays and selling on Fridays.

Calendar effects, such as the January effect and the weeekend effect, have been brought into doubt by Sullivan, Timmermann and White (1998). They claim to have shown that the calendar effects can be completely explained by what they refer to as data snooping. They found that the same data that was used to identify a calendar effect was also used to test for the existence of the effect. They also demonstrated that, although the small number of calendar effects that have been reported are statistically significant, there are about 9,500 conceivable calendar effects. From 9,500 some can be expected to be statistically significant through chance.

Other anomalies

The efficient market hypothesis implies that publicly available information in the form of analyses published by investment advisory firms should not provide means of obtaining rates of return in excess of what would normally be expected on the basis of the risk of the investments. However, stock rankings provided by *The Value Line Investment Survey* appear to offer information that could be used to enhance investors' returns (Huberman and Kandel 1990). Yet there is evidence that the market adjusts to this information within two trading days (Stickel 1985).

DeBondt and Thaler (1985) have argued that stocks that have performed poorly in recent years are likely to be underpriced, whereas those with strong performance in the recent past are prone to be overvalued. This could be explained in terms of particular shares (or types of share) being subject to swings in fashion amongst investors. DeBondt and Thaler provided empirical evidence in support of their proposition. Of note is their finding that the extra returns available, from investing in stocks that had recently performed poorly, occurred mainly in January. Bremer and Sweeney (1988) found similar results in that stocks were mean reverting. Loser portfolios (whose prices had performed poorly in the past) tend to become winners whilst the winners in the past become losers. A trading strategy based on selling winner portfolios (portfolios of stocks that have performed relatively well) and buying loser portfolios could have earned profits in excess of risk adjusted expectations.

Another apparent anomaly is the deviation between the prices of investment trust shares and the net asset values. It is not clear why a portfolio of securities within an investment trust should have a different price to the same portfolio outside the investment trust.

An anomaly that is consistent with the belief that markets in the shares of large firms are more likely to be efficient than the markets for small company shares is the neglected firm effect. Neglect means that few analysts follow the stock, or that few institutional investors hold it. So fewer market participants put new information into the market. Neglected stocks are more likely to be mispriced, and hence more prone to offer profit opportunities. Arbel and Strebel (1983) found that an investment strategy based on changes in the level of attention devoted by security analysts to different stocks may lead to positive abnormal returns.

Some commentators take the view that the evidence relating to anomalies implies that the efficient market hypothesis should be rejected (e.g. Fortune 1991). Others take the view that rather than the anomalies providing evidence against market efficiency they provide evidence of the inability of the capital asset pricing model to adequately incorporate risk (e.g. Clare, Priestly and Thomas 1997). Williams (1994) posed the question as to whether a systematically higher return by certain stocks or at certain times simply compensates for greater risk or less information or the need to make more complex or more time-consuming decisions.

The semi-strong form of the efficient market hypothesis has been brought into doubt by econometric studies that suggest that it is possible to forecast stock market movements to some extent. Pesaran and Timmermann (1994) looked at excess returns on the S&P 500 and the Dow Jones measured over one year, one quarter and one month for the period 1954–71. For annual excess returns a small set of variables, including dividend yield, inflation, interest rate changes and the term premium, explain about 60% of the variation in excess returns. For quarterly and monthly data, similar variables explain about 18% and 10% of excess returns respectively.

Evidence relating to the strong form of the efficient market hypothesis (EMH)

According to the strong form of the EMH even non-public information is quickly reflected in asset prices, so the limited number of investors with that information are unable to profit from it. Non-public information can be divided into two categories. There is the information held by corporate insiders on matters such as forthcoming earnings announcements or takeover bids. The other arises from stock analyses that have not been made public (arguably this should include only analyses that use research methods that are not public, since publicly known techniques of security analysis could be regarded as publicly available information).

Corporate insiders include directors and senior executives of the company. Insiders have access to privileged information and could use the information to profit from trading in securities markets before the information becomes public. Several studies of corporate insiders found that they consistently obtained abnormally high rates of return on their stock transactions (Jaffe 1974, Finnerty 1976, Nunn, Madden, and Gombola 1983, Nejat and Seyhun 1986). A later study by Peers (1992) confirmed these results but indicated that the opportunities for trading profits were limited to the most senior insiders. Niederhoffer and Osborne (1966) found that specialists on the New York Stock Exchange, who have privileged knowledge of advance buy and sell orders (limit orders), can consistently obtain abnormally high rates of return.

A related issue concerns the potential for earning excess returns by following the trading behaviour of insiders. Studies by Lee and Solt (1986), Rozeff and Zaman

(1988), Seyhun (1988) and Chowdhury, Howe and Lin (1993) showed that it was not possible to earn excess returns in this way. However, Trivoi (1980) argued that it is possible to increase returns by combining observations of insider trading with financial ratios.

The enormous illegal profits made by insider traders such as Ivan Boesky are suggestive that the market is not strong form efficient. Since a strong form efficient market is one in which profits could not be made on the basis of privileged information, prosecutions of insider traders who have made fortunes from using inside knowledge is evidence against strong form efficiency.

Using non-public analysis

There have been a number of studies of the ability to profit from non-public security analyses. Friend, Brown, Herman and Vickers (1962) studied the performance of US mutual funds and found that, on average, they did not outperform stock indices. Jensen (1968) concluded that mutual funds earned, on average, about 1% p.a. less than would be expected on the basis of their betas (systematic risk). In aggregate they were not able to predict stock price movements well enough to outperform a buy and hold strategy. Also past performance of funds could not be used to predict future performance, suggesting that not even star fund managers possessed knowledge or expertise that would enable them to consistently outperform the market. Firth (1978) studied the performance of UK unit trusts. He found that, on a risk adjusted basis, their performance tended to match that of the market as a whole. Also the past performance of individual trusts gave no guide to future performance. Cowles (1983) failed to find any evidence that professional investors achieved a performance that was superior to the results of a market tracking strategy. Grossman and Stiglitz (1980) and Cornell and Roll (1981) suggested that market equilibrium should provide some incentive for analysis. Those who acquire and process information should receive superior gross returns, but only average returns net of costs. A study undertaken by Malkiel (1988) showed that during the 20 years to 1987, over 70% of pension fund managers were outperformed by the S&P 500 index. The majority of the evidence on the performance of professional fund managers is that returns, net of costs, are at best average.

Rhodes (2000), in producing a report for the UK Financial Services Authority based on both a review of existing literature and original research, concluded that:

> The literature on the performance of UK funds has failed to find evidence that information on past investment performance can be used to good effect by retail investors in choosing funds. The general pattern is one in which investment performance does not persist. Small groups of funds may show some repeat performance over a short period of time, particularly poorly performing funds. However, the size of this effect and the fact that it is only very short lived means that there is no investment strategy for retail investors that could usefully be employed. The results from the US literature are similar.

The results concurred with the earlier analyses in finding that there was no persistency in the performance of managed funds after 1987. There was evidence of repeat performance before this point but it would be misleading to suggest that retail investors could use this finding in the present day.

The weight of evidence is that information on past performance cannot be exploited usefully by retail investors.

Ambachtsheer (1974) found a correlation of 0.16 between forecast and actual outcomes. Even the low forecasting ability indicated by this correlation coefficient is useful in achieving better than average returns. Dimson and Marsh (1984) examined the ability of analysts to forecast returns on the shares of over 200 of the largest UK quoted companies. They found a coefficient of correlation of 0.08 between forecasts and outcomes. Although the correlation was extremely small, transactions carried out in the light of the forecasts appeared to result in a 2.2% outperformance of the market over the following year. Over half of the informational content of the forecasts was reflected in share prices within one month of the forecast.

Studies on American, British and Canadian analysts have shown that excess returns are available to investors who follow the published recommendations of analysts employed by stockbrokers. These studies show that analysts' stock recommendations have a positive information coefficient (IC), where information coefficient is defined as the correlation between predicted and actual stock returns. The mean analyst IC appears to be about 0.1 (Davies and Canes (1978), Stanley, Lewellen and Schlarbaum (1981), Bjerring, Lakonishok and Vermaelen (1983), Dimson and Marsh (1984), Elton, Gruber and Grossman (1986)).

Dimson and Marsh (1984) and Elton, Gruber and Grossman (1986) found that there was little advantage from acting on the advice of a single firm of stockbrokers. However, they suggest that by combining the advice of a number of brokerage firms the resulting information can lead to excess returns. Womack (1996) concluded that analysts seem to have good ability in both market timing and stock selection.

Some studies have concluded that there are no differences between analysts in their ability to forecast stock returns (Coggin and Hunter (1983), Dimson and Marsh (1984)). Another study found that there was no evidence that one U.S. brokerage firm was consistently better than another in recommending stocks (Elton, Gruber and Grossman (1986)). These results might be interpreted as evidence that the informational value of analysts reports arises from the usefulness of commonly used analytical techniques rather than individual talent.

Can apparently irrational behaviour be expected?

There are lines of reasoning that suggest that irrational behaviour can have significant impacts on financial markets. One concerns noise trading. A noise trader uses irrelevant, or inaccurate, information when making investment decisions. The errant price movements caused by noise traders might be expected to be corrected by rational investors. Unjustified falls would be countered by purchases on the part of rational investors; conversely, unwarranted rises would tend to cause rational investors to sell and thereby eliminate the inappropriate price movement.

Sheifer and Summers (1990) suggested that rational investors face two forms of uncertainty that could result in them not correcting the effects of noise traders. First, their own rational valuations may be wrong. This possibility could make them reluctant to pursue the more modest profit opportunities, so small deviations from fair value may remain uncorrected. Second, rational investors face uncertainty as to how long the stock prices will stay away from their fundamental values. The effects of uncertainty on the trading behaviour of rational investors allow noise traders to move prices away from the values that would accurately reflect the available information.

Behavioural finance

Behavioural finance applies the findings of psychological research on decision making to investment decisions. There is evidence from psychological studies that there are systematic biases in the way people think. One such bias is the tendency to give too much emphasis to the most recent information. Another bias, suggested by prospects theory, is the tendency for people to weigh prospective losses about twice as heavily as prospective gains. Financial economics treats upside and downside risk as being equally weighted, prospects theory suggests that people are more concerned with the downside.

Research has found a number of other systematic biases that affect investors. These include overconfidence, representativeness, conservatism, narrow framing, and ambiguity aversion. All of these biases interfere with the process of rational decision making that is assumed by the efficient market hypothesis.

Overconfidence arises partly from self-attribution bias. This is a tendency on the part of investors to regard successes as arising from their expertise while failures are due to bad luck or the actions of others. This leads to excessive confidence in one's own powers of forecasting. It is capable of explaining a number of types of apparently irrational behaviour. For example, it can explain why some investors hold undiversified portfolios. If investors are highly confident about their stock selection abilities, they will not feel the need to reduce risk by means of diversification. It could also explain why some investors trade very frequently, to the point where transactions costs cause their investment behaviour to be loss making.

To the extent that some investors attribute their profits from rising markets to their own talents, rising markets could be self perpetuating. Overconfident investors may be encouraged to invest further and thereby reinforce an upward movement in stock prices. Conversely a falling market reduces confidence and investing. This is consistent with the view that markets exhibit over-reaction.

Representativeness helps to explain why many investors seem to extrapolate price movements. Many investors appear to believe that if prices have been rising in the past then they will continue to rise, and conversely with falling prices. The concept of representativeness suggests that this is because those investors see an investment with recent price increases as representative of longer-term successful investments, conversely with price falls.

The concept of conservatism suggests that investors are slow to change their views following the receipt of new information. This is consistent with the research findings that, following unexpected earnings announcements, it can take several weeks for the resulting stock price movement to be completed. Investors take time to change their views about a stock following news of unexpectedly high or low company profits.

Narrow framing refers to the tendency of investors to focus too narrowly. One aspect is focus on the constituents of a portfolio rather than the portfolio as a whole. This may help to explain the disposition effect. The disposition effect is the inclination, when selling part of a portfolio, to sell assets that have risen in price relative to their purchase prices rather than assets that have fallen in price.

Another dimension of narrow framing is the focus on the short term even when the investment horizon is long term. It is not rational for an investor accumulating assets for retirement 25 years hence to be concerned about the week-by-week performance of the portfolio. Yet long-term investors do focus on short-term volatility. Studies have shown that when, in experimental situations, people have been presented with monthly distributions of returns they are less likely to invest than when they are shown annual distributions (with the annualised volatility being the same in both cases). The implication is that focus on short-term volatility deters investment. It appears that people do not appreciate the effects of time diversification. By time diversification is meant the tendency for good periods to offset bad periods with the effect that the dispersion of investment returns does not increase proportionately with the period of the investment. Investors who focus too much on short-term fluctuations overestimate stock market risk and allocate too little of their money to investment in shares.

This has been suggested as a possible explanation of what is called 'The Equity Premium Puzzle'. The puzzle is why the excess of equity returns over returns on bonds and deposits is so high (when averaged over long periods of time). Although additional return is appropriate in order to compensate for the extra risk, it is generally thought that the additional return actually received is much more than is justified by the extra risk. However, if investors focus too strongly on the short term they may overestimate equity risk and hence require an excessive premium on the expected rate of return in order to induce them to invest in shares. Focus on individual stocks, rather than the portfolio as a whole, would also cause investors to overestimate stock market risk since the risk of individual shares exceeds the risk of portfolios.

Ambiguity aversion suggests that investors prefer to invest in companies that they feel they understand. Over 90% of the equity investments of investors in the USA,

UK and Japan is in companies in their own countries. This home bias exists despite the demonstrated benefits of international diversification. Likewise there are biases towards the investor's local region and the firm that employs them. This preference for the familiar results in the holding of portfolios that are insufficiently diversified. In consequence investors bear more risk than is necessary.

According to prospect theory, people in a position of gain become increasingly risk-averse and unwilling to accept gambles. When people are in a position of loss they become more inclined to accept risk. Other biases include retrievability, which suggests that more attention is given to the most easily recalled information. Retrievability is consistent with the over-reaction hypothesis, one dimension of which is the over-emphasis on recent information and recent events when making investment decisions.

Some other biases have similarities to the concept of overconfidence. According to the confirmation bias, investors pay more attention to evidence that supports their opinions than to evidence that contradicts them. This can cause investors to persist with unsuccessful investment strategies. Another cognitive bias is the illusion of control. In some circumstances people behave as if they were able to exert control where this is impossible or unlikely. The illusion of control is associated with the under-estimation of risk.

Investors seek lessons in thinking

The dominant framework used by academics to study stock movements used to be the efficient markets hypothesis. This was developed at the University of Chicago in the mid-1960s and says that price reflects fundamental value, defined as the best possible forecast, given available information, of a security's future cash flows, discounted at a rate that is appropriate for the risk of those cash flows.

Over the past decade, another view of financial markets known broadly as 'behavioural finance' has emerged. Proponents argue that investors can make systematic errors in forecasting cash flows or in setting the discount rate and these errors can push stock prices away from fundamental value for extended periods of time.

The stratospheric rise in the value of US equities and of the technology sector in particular during the late 1990s has shaken many observers' belief in efficient markets, and drawn many to the behavioural finance view. This raises the possibility that behavioural finance will replace the efficient markets hypothesis as the dominant model, a prospect that strikes fear into the hearts of financial economists who have built careers on the efficient markets hypothesis.

Researchers in behavioural finance spend a good deal of time studying work by psychologists trying to understand the biases that affect decision-making. Some of these ideas can provide a useful way of looking at financial markets. This article summarises the more important cognitive errors, as well as the insights they may offer investors.

Overconfidence
In general, people significantly overestimate the accuracy of their forecasts. For example, we might ask an investor to forecast a company's earnings a year from now and to provide a range, such that he is 95 per cent certain that earnings will fall within that

range. Studies have found that the ranges people give are far too narrow: actual earnings fall into the range only 60 per cent of the time.

Overconfidence may be due, at least in part, to an error known as self-attribution bias. This refers to investors' tendency to ascribe any success they have picking stocks to their own insight and any disasters to bad luck. Persistent application of such a rule will lead an investor to the pleasing but inaccurate conclusion that he is a genius; put differently, he will become overconfident about his ability.

Overconfidence may also be related to optimism. For example, in one study 80 per cent of drivers believed themselves to be above-average in ability. About half of my MBA students believe they will be among the 20 per cent to receive a top grade.

One manifestation of overconfidence in financial markets may be excessive trading, for which there is much evidence. A recent study by researchers Brad Barber and Terrance Odean found that after taking trading costs into account, the average return of the individual investor client base of a large US discount brokerage firm was significantly below market benchmarks. (See the second article in this issue on overconfidence.)

Put simply, these investors would have been better off if they had traded less. The behavioural finance interpretation of these findings is that investors are overconfident about the value of information they uncover: they believe they have information worth trading on, whereas in fact they do not. They trade too much and the trading costs lower their average return.

Overconfidence may also explain investors' love affair with actively managed funds, in spite of overwhelming evidence that such funds do not, on average, beat market indices. Many investors appear to believe they can pick money managers who are going to beat the index, even though only a few investors will actually be able to do this.

Representativeness

When evaluating the probability that an object A comes from a class B, people typically base their judgment on the extent to which A is representative of B, in other words, the extent to which A reflects the essential characteristics of B. For example, con-sider the following: 'Steve is very shy and withdrawn, invariably helpful, but with little interest in people or in the world of reality. A meek and tidy soul, he has a need for order and structure, and a passion for detail.'

Studies find that when asked to guess whether Steve is a librarian or a lawyer, people are much more likely to guess librarian, because, with apologies to librarians, Steve 'sounds' more like a librarian; put differently, he is representative of librarians.

Representativeness can be a good rule of thumb but it can also lead people astray. In the above example, Steve is in fact more likely to be a lawyer. Although he sounds like a librarian, there are far fewer librarians than there are lawyers, making it unlikely that Steve is a librarian, the description notwithstanding.

One possible consequence of representativeness in financial markets is that investors may be too quick to detect patterns in data that are in fact random. If a company reports increased earnings several quarters in a row, representativeness may lead investors to conclude that the company has a high long-term earnings growth rate: after all, past earnings are representative of a high growth rate. However, this conclusion is likely to be premature: investors are forgetting that even though the company 'looks' as if it has a high growth rate, even a mediocre company can produce several good quarters of earnings, simply by chance.

Representativeness can therefore explain numerous episodes in which investors appeared keen to buy stocks with impressive earnings histories or simply high past returns, even though these stocks had been declared overvalued by market observers. It can also explain why mutual funds with good past performance attract large inflows of funds, even though past performance is a poor predictor of future returns. Investors may be drawn to funds with a good track record because such funds are representative of funds with skilled managers. However, investors are forgetting that even unskilled managers can post periods of high returns by chance.

Conservatism

Once they have formed an opinion, people are often unwilling to change it, even when they receive

▶

pertinent new information. Suppose that, based on its past performance, investors have decided that company A has merely average long-term earnings prospects. Suddenly, A posts much higher earnings than expected. Conservatism predicts that investors will persist in their belief that the company is only average and will not react sufficiently to the good news. The stock price should therefore move too little on the day of the announcement but should gradually drift upward in later weeks as investors shed their initial conservatism.

This prediction has been confirmed in a phenomenon known as 'post-earnings announcement drift' that forms the basis of many investment strategies popular with money managers. Companies that report unexpectedly good (bad) earnings news typically have unusually high (low) returns after the announcement.

Narrow framing

When monitoring their economic well-being, investors should pay attention to changes in their total wealth, because it is this – the value of stock market investments, home and capitalised future salary – that determines how much they can afford to spend on goods and services, which is, ultimately, all they should care about.

In spite of this, many investors appear to engage in 'narrow framing', namely an excessive focus on changes in wealth that are narrowly defined, both in a temporal and in a cross-sectional sense. Even if they are saving for retirement and so have a long investment horizon, they often pay too much attention to short-term gains and losses. Moreover, they become obsessive about price changes in a single stock they own, even if it represents only a small fraction of their total wealth.

Narrow framing is dangerous because it can lead people to overestimate the risk they are taking, especially when they are loss-averse, that is, more sensitive to losses than to gains. This is because the more narrowly an investor frames, the more likely he is to see losses: the stock market often has short-term losses, but these are less frequent in the long term. Similarly, individual stocks are more likely to trade at a loss relative to purchase price than a diversified portfolio. If people are loss-averse, narrow

framing can make risky investments seem riskier than they are.

This effect has been demonstrated in experiments. Some studies ask people how they would split their money between a riskless investment and a risky investment. The latter is actually stocks, although participants are not told this. Crucially, some subjects are shown the distribution of monthly returns on the risky investment, while others are shown annual returns.

The way data are presented should not matter, but it does. Those shown monthly returns are much less keen to invest in the risky asset. The most plausible explanation for this is that at a monthly horizon, losses are more frequent, scaring anyone who is loss averse. The broader implication is that investors who focus too much on short-term fluctuations will overestimate stock market risk and allocate too little of their money to equities.

Another undesirable consequence of narrow framing is the disposition effect, the finding that when investors sell stocks, they typically sell stocks that have gone up in value relative to their purchase price, rather than stocks that have gone down. This is not a sensible practice, because on average, stocks display short-term momentum: a stock that has recently gone down in value will, on average, continue to go down even further over the next six months. It is not hard to guess at the underlying cause of the disposition effect: if investors pay too much attention to the gains and losses of individual stocks that they own, it is probably difficult for them to close out their investment in a specific stock at a loss.

Ambiguity aversion

People are excessively fearful of situations of ambiguity where they feel they have little information about the financial gambles they are considering. In experiments, people are much more willing to bet that a ball drawn at random from an urn containing 100 balls is blue when they know the distribution of black and blue balls to be 50:50, than when they know only that the urn contains 100 black and blue balls, but not the proportion of each. In a financial setting, ambiguity aversion suggests that investors will be more wary of stocks that they feel they don't

▶

'understand'. The flip-side of such aversion is a preference for the familiar, or an excessive liking for gambles about which investors feel they have good information.

Preference for the familiar is a leading explanation of the dramatic under-diversification displayed by many investors. First, there is extensive home bias: over 90 per cent of the equity allocation of investors in the US, UK and Japan is to domestic equities, in spite of the amply demonstrated benefits of international diversification. Other studies have found home bias within countries: investors often hold a disproportionate number of shares in local companies. Finally, studies in the US have found that in their defined contribution pension plans, investors allocate heavily to their own company stock, leaving themselves dangerously under-diversified.

Researchers have tried to find rational explanations of these effects, but with limited success. One explanation, but certainly not a justification, is that an investor's home country, his local region and the company he works for are familiar settings, and he prefers familiar investments.

Exploiting psychology

There are at least two ways that knowing about such bias can be helpful. First, knowing that these mistakes are common will alert investors to the possibility of making them. When about to trade a stock based on some research, investors should stop to consider whether, like so many others, they are overconfident about the analysis. When investors see a string of good earnings announcements from a company, they should be careful not to jump too quickly to the conclusion that this is a company with a high long-term growth rate. Investors with a long investment horizon should avoid worrying too much about short-term fluctuations in the stock market.

Once investors have tried to purge decision-making of such bias, they can take a more aggressive approach and try to design strategies that exploit the hapless investors who are still subject to them. Of course, some care is required here: the more people cure themselves of bias, the less profitable such strategies will be. Nonetheless, some bias is so deep-seated that it may be a long time before investors cure it completely.

As a simple example, consider narrow framing. If people engage in this, they will overestimate the risk of stocks and insist on a high rate of return to compensate for the risk. Specifically, they will lower their demand for stocks until the price falls sufficiently for them to be able to expect a high rate of return. In fact, the historic rate of return on equities has been much higher than can be explained by standard measures of risk – the so-called equity premium puzzle – and increasingly people believe narrow framing may be the cause. If we believe in narrow framing, we must also believe the future equity premium will be high. For an investor who does not engage in narrow framing, and who therefore does not find stocks to be so risky, this higher premium is effectively a free lunch, and one that can be captured by investing more aggressively in equities.

Representativeness, meanwhile, suggests that value strategies will be profitable. Such strategies direct investors towards stocks that trade at low multiples of price to fundamentals such as earnings. If a company reports a series of disappointing earnings, investors who overuse representativeness will come to the premature conclusion that the company is a long-term dud and will push the stock price too far down. Since the stock is now undervalued, a value strategy may earn high returns as the stock eventually corrects to a more reasonable level. In fact, over the past three decades, value strategies have, on average, been highly profitable. An investor who believes this is partly caused by representativeness, and also believes that representativeness is a deep-seated bias, will want to continue pursuing such strategies.

As discussed earlier, conservatism can lead to a post-earnings announcement drift, an effect that can be exploited by investors. Conservatism predicts that prices will not react sufficiently to other kinds of corporate news, such as dividend initiations or announcements of share repurchases, so there should also be a price drift after these announcements that can be exploited. This prediction has been confirmed by US data: dividend initiations and repurchase announcements are, on average, followed by unusually high returns.

A final word of caution. This article has taken the view that many investors suffer from the same kind of psychological bias and that their ill-informed demand pushes prices away from fundamental value, presenting savvy investors with potentially free lunches. There is however, a significant fraction of academics who, in spite of mounting evidence, believe that prices always reflect fundamental value and that the efficient markets hypothesis holds. These academics often concede that many of the phenomena discussed in this article – the high level of trading, historic profitability of value strategies, the disposition effect and the equity premium puzzle – cannot easily be explained in a world of rational investors.

However, they believe that the right way forward is to redouble their efforts within the rational model, rather than give in to the potentially undisciplined alternative of behavioural finance where, it is said, it may be all too easy to think up stories that can explain any historical fact.

This academic conflict has important implications for investors. Efficient markets devotees argue that value strategies earn high returns not because they exploit investor bias, but because they are riskier. If this is correct, there is no free lunch in value strategies and no reason to favour them over any other strategy. The difficulty with this view is that economists have been unable to find a plausible measure of risk under which value strategies are indeed riskier; nonetheless, it is a possibility that cannot be ruled out.

Ultimately, the battle between efficient markets theory and behavioural finance theory will be decided by each theory's ability to predict phenomena not previously known. Researchers are now working on understanding and testing the broader predictions of the two models. If behavioural finance comes through this process successfully, its place in financial economics will be secure.

Source: Nicholas Barberis, *Financial Times*, *Mastering Investment Supplement*, Part 6, June 18 2001, pp. 2–4. Reprinted with permission.

CAPM and problems with testing the efficient market hypothesis

Tests of the efficient market hypothesis tend to compare experienced returns with expected returns. The expected returns are typically based on the CAPM. The security market line, shown by equation 1, summarises the CAPM.

$$E(R_i) = r_f + \beta \, [E(R_m) - r_f] \tag{1}$$

$E(R_i)$ is the expected return on security i, r_f is the risk-free rate of return (normally proxied by the Treasury bill rate), β is the beta of the security and $E(R_m)$ is the expected return on the market portfolio (normally proxied by a stock index). Informational efficiency is tested by ascertaining whether $E(R_i)$ can be consistently bettered. If it can then abnormal profits can be made and the market is not informationally efficient.

Such tests are dependent upon the capital asset pricing model providing a reliable estimate of the expected return on the security. However, the usefulness of the security market line has been questioned. For example, Fama and French (1992) found that long-term equity returns do not depend on beta. Roll (1977) has argued that the market portfolio should contain every available asset and that it is impossible to measure the expected return on such a broadly based portfolio. If these lines of reasoning are correct, many of the tests of the efficient market hypothesis may be seen as invalid.

Even if it were conclusively demonstrated that it is impossible to consistently earn abnormal returns using available information, this may not remove all rationale for active portfolio management. Normal returns, as indicated by $E(R_i)$ in equation 1, may be variable as a result of changes in the term $[E(R_m) - r_f]$. If it were possible to forecast such changes, a guide for asset allocation would be provided. A relatively high expected value for $[E(R_m) - r_f]$ would suggest that the proportion of the portfolio invested in stocks should be increased at the expense of low risk assets such as bills and deposits. Vice versa for a relatively low value. In this context it is interesting to observe the figures in Table 23.1, which were found for the United States markets by DuBois (1992).

The premium range shows the value of $[E(R_m) - r_f]$ for a month. The next column shows the value of $[R_m - r_f]$ over the following year. The third column shows the probability of the return on stocks exceeding the return on Treasury bills during that year. The figures suggest that high returns on stocks relative to Treasury bills are indicative of future high relative returns on stocks. Tests of market efficiency have focused on abnormal returns and their predictability. The figures in Table 23.1 (and others produced by DuBois) suggest that normal returns may follow patterns that might be used by fund managers in deciding upon the allocation of their portfolios between asset classes such as stocks, bonds, and risk free securities.

● ● ● ● Conclusions

The issue is not whether a market is or is not efficient. The issue is how efficient a particular market is. Market efficiency could be seen to parallel the perfectly competitive market of economic theory. They are rarely, if ever, achieved in reality. Nonetheless they both constitute a useful benchmark against which to compare actual markets. They also serve to provide models that are useful for the interpretation and understanding of the real world.

It is interesting to reflect on some views expressed by Fisher Black (1986). He argued that traders can be divided into information traders and noise traders. Noise is irrelevant or meaningless information. Noise trading puts noise into market prices, causing them to depart from their true values. The deviations caused by

Table 23.1 Stocks/bills premium and subsequent performance of stocks versus bills, 1951–89

Premium range	Average subsequent one-year excess return	Probability of positive excess return
>10%	26.1%	100%
8–9.9%	16.7%	89%
6–7.9%	6.1%	63%
5–5.9%	4.8%	67%
4–4.9%	2.7%	62%
2–3.9%	2.8%	60%
<2%	−6.9%	40%

noise trading can be cumulative. As a stock price diverges further from its true value, the scope for profits from information trading becomes greater. Although information trading tends to pull prices towards their true values, it can be difficult to distinguish noise from relevant and accurate information. Black argued that a market may be efficient even if a share price differs from its fundamental value by a factor of as much as two.

Discussion question

If the efficient market hypothesis is valid, are investment analysis and active fund management worthwhile?

Chapter 24

Styles of portfolio construction

After studying this chapter readers should be able to:

- *Understand the difference between active and passive fund management.*

- *appreciate stages of portfolio construction*

- *distinguish between value stocks and growth stocks*

- *understand the nature of index (tracker) funds*

- *appreciate the varied nature of hedge funds*

- *understand the basic principles of 'socially responsible investing'.*

A portfolio manager faces a number of choices in relation to portfolio construction. In particular there is the choice between active and passive management. This choice may be made in relation to each of a number of stages of portfolio construction.

Active and passive management

Active portfolio management attempts to outperform the market by choosing investments that are likely to show high returns. The market is often proxied by a broad based stock index, such as the S&P 500 or the FT All Share index. Active portfolio managers believe that they have the ability to identify the individual securities, sectors or asset classes that will perform relatively well. In effect this involves the belief that the fund manager has superior knowledge or understanding that provides a forecasting ability that is better than that of other market participants. Asset prices reflect the market consensus forecasts, active portfolio managers believe that they have the ability to produce forecasts that are better than the market consensus. Active portfolio managers take the view that they can identify situations in which the consensus of other investors is incorrect as to what the price of a security should be. Active fund managers operate as if they do not believe that markets are informationally efficient.

Portfolio managers who employ a passive style behave as if they do believe that markets are informationally efficient. They do not seek to outperform the market by carrying out investment analysis that is superior to that of other investors. They operate as if assets are fairly priced. Passive management can take one of the following three forms.

One type of passive management is the buy and hold strategy. The fund manager buys a portfolio of securities and holds them for the duration of the investment horizon. While they hold the portfolio, they make no attempt to change its composition. There may be a dimension of active management in the original construction of the portfolio, but thereafter the portfolio is left unaltered.

A second type of passive management entails the attempt to track the performance of a stock index. This may be achieved by holding all the stocks in the index in the proportions that they occur in the index. Whereas this could be feasible for indices covering a small number of individual stocks, more broadly based indices are difficult to replicate in this way. The tracking of a broad index involves constructing a portfolio with characteristics similar to those of the index portfolio. Tracking a narrow index by full replication will be accurate and will involve few portfolio changes (which will occur only when the composition of the index changes). However, a narrow index may not be a balanced portfolio (for example at the time of writing oils, pharmaceuticals, telecoms and financials constituted about 60% of the value of the FTSE 100 index portfolio). Tracking a broad index will involve more frequent portfolio changes and less accuracy (there will be some tracking error) since perfect replication of the index is unlikely. On the positive side a broad index is likely to provide a more balanced portfolio, and one that more faithfully represents the overall market.

A third form of passive management potentially involves a greater frequency of portfolio changes, but not as a result of the fund manager taking views that differ from the market consensus. This type of passive management entails adjusting the composition of the portfolio in response to three types of change. The three factors whose variations can lead to alterations in the portfolio are the risk-free interest rate, the consensus view on the risk and return characteristics of the market portfolio, and the degree of risk aversion exhibited by the investors on whose behalf the fund is managed. This form of passive fund management entails holding a combination of a risk-free investment (such as a bank deposit) and a portfolio of risky securities (which is likely to be the portfolio corresponding to a stock index). A rise in the risk-free interest rate would cause an increase in the proportion of the fund held on deposit. A rise in the (market consensus) expected return on the portfolio of securities, or a fall in the consensus expectation of risk, would cause the fund manager to switch money from deposits into the portfolio of securities. Increased risk aversion on the part of the investors in the fund would lead to the manager increasing deposits as a proportion of the fund. The relative proportions of risk-free and risky investments within the fund are subject to frequent change, but not as a result of the portfolio manager trying to outperform the market by forecasting asset price movements.

Stages of portfolio construction

The construction of a portfolio may involve one stage, two stages, three stages, or possibly even more. The fund manager must decide on the number of stages and their nature. There is also a choice between active and passive management at each stage (and if passive, which type of passive management).

A one-stage process involves the portfolio manager seeking the optimum portfolio from the entire range of securities available (or under consideration). This could be achieved by employing the Markowitz optimisation procedure or Sharpe's single index model. Alternatively a stock index portfolio might be used. In reality many fund managers would employ less formal procedures. If the optimum portfolio is amended in the light of the manager's market forecasts, or is affected by such forecasts, the strategy would be an active one. The strategy would be an active one if the manager takes bets on individual securities (or sectors or asset classes). A passive strategy would be uninfluenced by any forecasts that the fund manager may make.

A two-stage process might involve the optimisation process being divided into separate stock selection (and bond selection) and asset allocation stages. In the first stage a stock portfolio is decided upon and a bond portfolio is established simultaneously. These two separate portfolios can be derived using the types of approach indicated for the one-stage process (Markowitz diversification, index portfolios, etc.). In the second (asset allocation) stage the fund manager seeks an optimum combination of the stock and bond portfolios. This could be based on Markowitz optimisation or a less formal procedure. The operation could additionally involve portfolios of investments in asset classes other than stocks and bonds, for example real estate and money market instruments. The fund manager has the choice between active and passive styles at each of the two stages.

A three-stage process might introduce a sector allocation (sector rotation) decision between the stock selection and asset allocation stages. Stocks may be divided into sectors such as oils, financials, pharmaceuticals, utilities and so on. Bonds may be divided according to types of issuer, maturity and credit rating. The fund manager might seek an optimum portfolio for each sector or division. An optimum portfolio of the sector portfolios would then constitute the stock portfolio. Likewise a portfolio of various bond portfolios (one for each chosen category of bond) would be constructed. The stock and bond portfolios would then be combined to form the portfolio of risky assets. The fund manager might then choose to combine this with a holding of risk-free assets (such as deposits or Treasury bills). An active manager would then deviate from such a base portfolio by increasing the proportion held in some assets and decreasing the weighting in others, according to the manager's forecasts of relative performance.

If the fund manager includes foreign securities in the portfolio, there will be more stages. They might create separate portfolios for each country. There would then be a portfolio of country portfolios.

Value stocks and growth stocks

There is a widespread belief that there are groups of shares that have common features in terms of characteristics and behaviour. The most favoured grouping is between value stocks and growth stocks. Value stocks are shares that appear to be relatively under-priced in terms of criteria such as price-earnings ratios and the fair prices determined by dividend discount models. Growth stocks are identified by an expectation of rapid growth in earnings.

Probably the most frequently used measure to classify shares into the value and growth categories is the price to book ratio. The book value of a firm is its net value (assets minus liabilities) as shown on its balance sheet. Division of this book value by the number of shares in issue gives the book value per share. The price to book ratio is the share price divided by the book value per share.

Stocks of companies with a low price to book ratio are generally classified as value stocks, whereas a high ratio indicates a growth stock. The total number of stocks under consideration is referred to as the universe of stocks. Sometimes this universe of stocks is divided into value and growth stocks such that half the total market capitalisation is classified as value and the other half as growth. Allocating the whole universe in this way creates style jitter. Style jitter is the term given to the tendency for stocks to move from one category to the other. An alternative procedure, that reduces style jitter, is to divide the universe of stocks three ways. One third of the market capitalisation is seen as consisting of value stocks, one third as growth and one third as not readily classifiable as either.

Style investing involves the concentration of a portfolio on either value or growth stocks. Passive style investing keeps the portfolio to one of the two styles (or keeps the emphasis on one). Active style investment entails switching between styles in the light of forecasts of the relative performance of the two styles. Active style investment might take the form of moving the whole portfolio from one style to the other or of changing the relative emphasis from one to the other.

Often the value-growth classification is further refined by allocating stocks along other dimensions. A popular additional dimension is the size of firms as measured by market capitalisation. The simplest of these divides companies into large and small so that half of the market capitalisation falls into each of the two groups. The addition of this refinement produces four styles: large value, small value, large growth, small growth.

Index (tracker) funds

An index fund, alternatively known as a tracker fund, aims to replicate the performance of a stock index. The emergence of index funds arose from the observation that actively managed funds fail, on average, to outperform stock indices. This is related to the issue of market efficiency. Active fund management is predicated on the view that portfolio managers can forecast market movements and the performance of individual stocks relative to the market. If the efficient market hypothesis is correct, it is not possible to consistently forecast either overall market movements or the relative performance of individual stocks. If this is the case, investors should avoid the transaction and management costs associated with actively managed funds by investing in index funds whose aim is merely to move in line with the stock market.

Index funds are one form of passive investment. Another is a buy and hold strategy. One advantage of index funds over a buy and hold strategy is that the index fund may provide an optimal level of diversification whereas a buy and hold strategy is less likely to do so. However, this argument does rest on the use of a suitable index. Some stock indices do not provide optimal diversification. For example, at the time of writing a stock index fund reflecting the Finnish stock market would hold more than half of the portfolio in one stock (Nokia). The market portfolio of the capital asset pricing model is the ultimate perfectly diversified portfolio. When using a broad stock index as the benchmark to track, an index fund could be seen as seeking to approximate the market portfolio of the capital asset pricing model. To the extent that this is the case, the CAPM might be seen as providing a theoretical justification for index funds.

One advantage of index funds to the individual investor in collective investments is that they avoid management risk. The performance of actively managed funds can, during any period of time, vary considerably. Some will outperform the index and others will underperform it. The variation between the best and the worst can be considerable. If the direction and size of the deviations from the index occur by chance, as empirical evidence seems to suggest, the individual investor faces a management risk. Individual investors run the risk that their chosen funds will be relatively poor performers. By investing in index funds they avoid this management risk.

Another advantage of index funds, relative to actively managed funds, is that they ensure that the portfolio remains well diversified. Actively managed funds, in their attempts to outperform the market, may hold poorly diversified portfolios. For example, they may tilt the portfolio towards particular industries. To the extent that actively managed funds hold inadequately diversified portfolios, they sacrifice part of the risk reduction benefit of diversification.

Probably the greatest advantage of index funds is that they are much cheaper to run than actively managed funds. For example, many actively managed UK unit trusts and OEICs have a 6% initial charge, an annual 1.5% management charge and transaction costs of around 1% per year. This compares with index tracker funds which typically have a zero initial charge a 0.5% annual charge, and minimal transaction costs.

A drawback of index funds is that they tend to omit the shares of very small firms. Even broad indices have a cut-off in terms of company size. For example, in the UK the FT All Share index covers about 800 stocks. This eliminates more than 1,000 firms whose capitalisation is not sufficient. Actively managed funds are able to include any stocks, including those with very small capitalisations.

Tracking error

Portfolios constructed to replicate an index rarely succeed in precisely tracking the index. The tracking error is the difference between the total return on the replicating portfolio and the total return on the index. The total return consists of both dividends and capital gains (or losses).

The portfolio may hold all the stocks in the index, with weights corresponding to those of the index. This involves little tracking error but can involve significant transaction costs. Alternatively a subset of the index might be used. This approach reduces transaction costs but increases tracking error.

Even if the portfolio contains all the stocks in the index, appropriately weighted, there are sources of tracking error. The constituent stocks of an index are subject to change and replacing stocks involves transaction costs. Furthermore the replacement is not instantaneous. Tracking is imperfect during the time taken to replace stocks.

Changes in the composition of an index can also affect stock prices. If index funds are widely used, stocks leaving the index will be sold in large numbers by index funds. As a result their prices fall and the funds receive unfavourable prices. Conversely, stocks entering the index will be bought by index funds with the effect that their prices rise. The funds thus buy these stocks at raised prices. So the marginal stocks, those prone to move in and out of an index, are sold at low prices and bought at high prices. This weakens the performance of index portfolios.

Hedge funds

Although hedge funds have existed since 1949, it is only since the mid-1980s that they have achieved a significant role among investment vehicles. There is no generally accepted definition of hedge funds. They are characterised by their flexibility of investment style and strategy. They often use short selling, leverage and derivatives. Although early hedge funds were hedged in the sense that they held offsetting long and short positions, nowadays many hedge funds do not follow such a strategy. Arguably the term hedge fund is a misnomer for those funds that do not adopt the style of offsetting long and short positions.

Short selling means the practice of borrowing shares and selling the borrowed shares. This means that stock is owed and needs to be returned to the lender in the future. Such a short position in stock benefits from a falling price. If stock prices fall it costs less to buy the shares for the purpose of returning them to the lender. A fund that has a long position in (that is owns) some stocks and a short position in others is hedged against general market movements. The fund manager short sells over-priced stocks and buys under-priced stocks with a view to profiting when the prices move to their appropriate values while being immune from movements in the stock market as a whole.

This is risk arbitrage rather than pure arbitrage. The fund is exposed to the specific (non-systematic) risks of the individual securities that arise from firm or sector specific events. In the case of shares there is the risk that the fund manager has not correctly discerned which are over-priced and which are under-priced. There is no certainty as to how long it will take for relative mispricing between shares to be corrected. It is also unlikely that exposure to overall market movements is completely avoided (particularly since stock betas cannot be precisely ascertained and are liable to change).

The process of short selling entails additional risk in that the borrower of stock must pay a deposit, known as margin, and more must be paid if the stock price rises. It is possible that the mispricing worsens before it improves, in particular the price of the short sold stock could rise before it falls. There could come a point where the fund is unable to meet the calls for additional margin payments and is forced to close out the short position by buying shares at a high price, which would result in losses.

Other characteristics of hedge funds are that they are largely exempt from regulation, typically prevent investors from withdrawing their money early, and levy fees that are related to fund performance. One attraction of hedge funds to other fund managers is that their returns show low correlation with the returns on other investments, such as shares and bonds. So the inclusion of hedge fund investments in a portfolio is useful for the purpose of reducing portfolio risk by diversification. This arises from the wide variety of investments and strategies available to hedge fund managers. A downside of the flexibility is that such a high degree of discretion by hedge fund managers means that there is a considerable risk of mistakes on the part of managers. In other words there is a high level of management risk. This is not helped by the high degree of secrecy employed by many hedge fund managers concerning their investments and strategies.

Hedge funds can be categorised according to their investment strategy. A broad division is between directional and non-directional funds. Directional funds take a position on the direction of movement of a market; the market could be a stock market, a bond market, a currency market or a commodity market. Non-directional funds aim to make arbitrage profits. The arbitrage profits would be sought from buying under-priced assets and taking short positions in over-priced assets. The long and short positions tend to hedge each other, thus removing any net exposure to general market movements.

Hedge funds following directional strategies can be subdivided into a number of categories according to the type of strategy. Those that follow macro strategies seek to make profits from economic changes at the country or regional level. Some funds take the strategy of focusing on emerging markets, such as those of countries with new or small stock markets. Another strategy is to take long positions in equities, that is buying shares. Other hedge funds concentrate on the opposite strategy, that is short selling securities which they consider to be over-priced.

Hedge funds pursuing non-directional strategies can also be subdivided into more specific categories. There are funds that use fixed income arbitrage, which entails long and short positions in bonds. Event-driven hedge funds seek to take positions in stocks so as to profit from events such as mergers, takeovers or restructuring. Equity hedge is an investment style that uses long and short positions in equities, buying under-priced and short selling over-priced shares. Distressed securities hedge funds focus on companies that are in financial difficulties. Merger arbitrage hedge funds buy the securities of a company that is being acquired and short sell the securities of the acquiring company. Hedge funds that specialise in convertible arbitrage buy and sell securities of the same company thereby profiting from relative mispricing, for example between convertible bonds on the one hand and combinations of shares and non-convertible bonds on the other.

Socially responsible investing

There is an investment style, or family of styles, that considers more than the return and risk characteristics of portfolios. These styles also encompass an ethical dimension. The funds following a socially responsible investing (SRI) approach would avoid investments in companies that fail certain ethical criteria.

SRI funds vary as to what type of investment is avoided. Those which they commonly avoid include the securities of companies involved in armaments, alcoholic drinks, tobacco products or gambling. SRI funds might also avoid investments in companies that are seen as having poor records in terms of environmental pollution, exploitation of labour or cruelty to animals.

It might be thought that SRI funds would, on average, underperform other funds since they are more restricted in their investment choices. Funds able to choose any investment might be expected to outperform those with a more restricted range from which to select. However, there is no evidence to support this view. On the contrary SRI funds appear to have enjoyed higher returns than the average.

This is reflected in the relative performance of stock indices that are based on the types of stock used in SRI funds. The Goodmoney Industrial Average is a stock index designed to cover the same industries as the stocks used to calculate the Dow Jones Industrial Average but screened according to ethical criteria. The Goodmoney has outperformed the Dow Jones. Likewise another index of ethically acceptable stocks, the Dow Jones Sustainability Index, has outperformed its corresponding general index, the Standard & Poor's 500.

Of the explanations for the relatively good performance of ethically acceptable stocks, one concerns management and another relates to consumer behaviour. The management based argument suggests that attention to ethical dimensions and strong profitability are two aspects of high-quality management. Managers who succeed in the ethical dimension are seen as being generally aware and capable, and their abilities also show through in the achievement of high profits. The consumer based argument suggests that the companies shunned by SRI funds are also boycotted by socially concerned consumers. Such consumer boycotts undermine the profitability of companies that fail SRI criteria and cause the relative underperformance of their stocks.

The bottom line to a social conscience

Socially responsible investors hope to do well by doing good. They seek to harness their influence in capital markets to social goals that transcend return on investments, so strengthening incentives for ethical fund management. Socially responsible investing (SRI) is widespread and growing in the US and trends appear to be similar in other markets. According to criteria set out by the Social Investment Forum, in 1999 one dollar in every eight under professional management in the US was invested in an SRI fund, a total of $2,160bn, up more than 80 per cent from $1,185bn only two years earlier. Already large enough to be influential, SRI funds could soon become a major factor in capital markets at anything like recent growth rates.

The growth of these funds raises two major issues. How well are they doing and are they doing good? This article addresses these issues.

Socially responsible investing

Socially responsible investors have diverse goals and correspondingly varied definitions of social responsibility. Although the movement originated in the campaign to divest from South Africa, where the anti-apartheid campaign emerged as the first political movement to enlist investors ideologically, current targets of SRI funds typically go beyond a single issue.

Most SRI funds do not invest in companies that make or sell armaments, alcoholic drinks or tobacco products. Many funds avoid companies with a poor environmental record or those thought to exploit labour in developing countries. Funds with investors of a religious persuasion eschew companies promoting gambling or running casinos. Animal rights also affect the targets to be avoided. Indeed, it is safe to say that each ethical viewpoint championed by an active non-governmental organisation has an investment fund to support its aims.

This is a new and growing source of business and of competitive advantage. It has reached the point where a management company without an SRI fund is at a disadvantage in the US pension fund market.

The best employers have traditionally offered staff a choice of methods for investing defined contribution funds and understand that many value the ability to choose an SRI fund. A fund manager whose product line includes growth, income, international and large-cap but no SRI fund is unable to offer the full range, so we see a proliferation of offerings. This is a business move and does not imply that the management companies sympathise with the social aims of the funds. To most of them, social goals are just constraints placed on their portfolio choices. Indeed, a management company may run funds with contradictory goals.

The growth of SRI is a natural extension of a phenomenon already well established in retail markets to capital markets – the use of consumer buying power to attain social goals. Anita Roddick popularised this trend in the UK with the Body Shop and the US outdoor clothing brand Patagonia has had similar success. McDonald's and Nike have suffered from it and learned to come to terms with it. This movement is particularly influential in the human rights and environmental fields, where major clothing and shoe brands, Nike prominent among them, have been boycotted for their use of sweatshop labour and oil companies such as Shell have been punished for their alleged environmental transgressions.

Companies selling to highly educated and socially aware customers with a global viewpoint can expect this to continue and indeed become more widespread: it is natural for these customers to link consumption choices to political beliefs and actions.

In 1994, *The Economist* spoke of 'the era of the corporate image, in which consumers will increasingly make purchases on the basis of a firm's role in society: how it treats its employees, shareholders, and local neighbourhoods...' In many respects SRI is simply an extension of this process to capital markets: aware investors are looking at all dimensions of their choices.

These developments have led to the growth of a closely linked industry providing the data on which

▶

socially responsible funds base their choices. Until recently a manager could not look up a company's environmental or human rights record online in the same way as its credit rating or its earnings forecasts. Now this is possible through companies that specialise in providing the data for managers to screen investments and assess their consistency with a fund's goals. Some go beyond this and compile lists of companies rated by financial and environmental performance, for example, the Innovest group. Dow Jones, the doyen of financial indices, joined this trend several years ago by introducing its Sustainability Index. This ranks companies according to criteria believed to assess the sustainability of their contributions to society. The *Financial Times* has recently announced that the FTSE will introduce a range of indices covering corporate performance on environmental issues, human rights, social issues and relations with stakeholders. Even for managers not running SRI funds, this extra information adds value. It provides a broader picture of a company and its relationship to the outside world than is available through conventional financial indices.

The cost of virtue

Economists might think that there would be a cost to the limitations imposed by an SRI approach. After all, they believe there is no free lunch – everything good comes at a cost. So SRI funds should in principle offer lower returns than those without any constraints on their portfolio choices. Surprisingly, this does not seem to be the case.

Several studies claim to show that SRI funds offer returns as good as those on other funds and, indeed, that performance on environmental and human rights criteria is a good predictor of the overall financial performance of companies. The studies supporting the stronger of these claims leave something to be desired in terms of statistical rigour, but the basic data do, to a considerable extent, speak for themselves.

For example, the Dow Jones Sustainability Index outperformed the Standard & Poor's 500 over the 1990s by about 15 per cent. Innovest's website reviews performance data and concludes that, 'depending upon the sector, companies with above average EcoValue '21 ratings have consistently out-

performed lower-rated companies by 300 to 2,500 basis points per year'. Data from Morningstar, a company that rates mutual funds, show that SRI funds on average have earned higher returns than others.

Figure 1 shows the Goodmoney Industrial Average and the Dow Jones Industrial Average since 1977. Goodmoney is an index of 30 shares chosen to cover the same industries as the shares in the DJIA but screened according to ethical criteria. The picture here is similar.

Each of these numbers refers to averages. They suggest there is no cost to socially responsible investing. On average, there may even be a gain. But few investors or managers aim for average performance, whatever they eventually attain. And the very top performers are usually not SRI funds, so there may possibly be some cost in terms of a reduced probability of a very high return.

The performance of SRI funds is a puzzle. While they are not among the top performers, they do perform above average. Given the constraints on stock selection posed by ethical guidelines, this is surprising. As noted, several recent studies report that environmental and human rights performance is a good predictor of overall performance. This is an interesting and suggestive point. There are several possible reasons for the performance edge that SRI funds appear to provide.

One is that technology stocks meet their screening criteria – the likes of Intel and Microsoft are free from association with pollution, exploitation, alcohol and tobacco – so SRI managers have inadvertently been steered towards the sector that has performed best in the recent bull market.

If this were the entire explanation, it would imply that the superior performance is a coincidence that

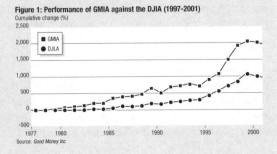

Figure 1: Performance of GMIA against the DJIA (1997-2001)
Cumulative change (%)

Source: *Good Money Inc*

may not be repeated. However, data indicate that there is more than an accident at work here. Even on a sector-by-sector basis, shares of companies with a superior environmental or human rights record appear to outperform. Clean chemical companies will outperform dirty ones, clean oil companies will outperform dirty oil companies.

This type of finding suggests a deeper and more intrinsic connection between responsible management and superior returns. In the case of the environment, academic Geoffrey Heal has pointed to evidence that superior performance is indeed linked to higher profits. Pollution is waste, and cutting back on or finding ways to reuse waste feeds back to reduced inputs and higher profits. Dow Chemicals, DuPont and Anheuser-Busch have all found improved environmental performance to be a source of profits.

A similar effect may be at work with human rights: paying workers a living wage and protecting them from harassment may cost a little more in the short run, but if it improves morale and reduces turnover then it may still be good for profits after a few years. So socially responsible management practices may contribute directly to profits.

A recent statistical study by academics Glen Dowell, Stuart Hart and Bernard Yeung is consistent with this interpretation. They looked at the environmental performance of US companies operating in developing countries, where environmental standards are lower than in the US. They divided the companies into three groups that: use US standards in their home operations and lower standards in developing countries; use US standards worldwide; adopt a standard worldwide higher than that mandated in the US.

If environmental compliance were a cost, other things being equal, one would expect the first group to be the most profitable and the third the least. In fact the authors found the opposite to be true.

This and similar findings lead them to suggest that capital market valuations incorporate the negative social costs of a company's operations. To Dowell, Hart and Yeung, higher environmental standards are a sign of state-of-the-art equipment and of alert management, all presumably contributing to financial performance.

A rather different argument for superior performance of SRI funds stems from consumer behaviour, suggests academic Peter Singer. The increasing use of consumer buying power to attain social goals has already been mentioned. The obvious implication for profits is that companies boycotted by consumers will lose market share to competitors who enjoy a better image.

Socially responsible buying is thus able to lay the foundations for successful socially responsible investing. Companies failing ethical screens will lose sales and at the same time, and for the same reason, SRI funds will stay away from them. Socially responsible investors reaping what they have sown as socially responsible consumers produce a self-reinforcing process.

This makes sense from another perspective. Standard advice to individual investors is to invest in companies whose products you know and like. It is a simple step from this sound and sensible advice to saying 'Don't invest in companies that people like you will shun'.

The impact of SRI

Socially responsible investors appear to be attaining their goal of doing well. The performance of SRI funds seems to be at least above-average. But are they also doing good? Are they attaining their ethical goals? What may seem like a rhetorical question in fact requires examination. Assume that SRI funds attained their above-average returns simply by investing substantially in technology stocks. In this case their ethical leverage has been minimal. They have run with a successful sector, delivering no specific ethical message to managers.

If we adopt another of the theories, that superior environmental and human rights performance pays off financially, and that ethical investors have benefited from this, it is again not clear that the success of SRI funds has given an ethical message to managers. In this case, manager's incentives to act ethically have been primarily conventional, not linked to the behaviour of SRI funds.

Finally, assume that ethical investors are reaping what they have sown as ethical consumers and that the behaviour of consumers in favouring retail companies with superior ethical records has contributed to the superior financial performance of these companies. In this case, there is an argument that the combined operations of ethical consumers and investors have had an impact on corporate behaviour. The truth probably contains some of each of the last two arguments, so that ethical investors have had an impact, possibly small, on corporate behaviour.

There are in fact two ways in which SRI might influence company behaviour. The most obvious, alluded to in the previous paragraph, is through the cost of capital. A company that is out of favour with investors will have to pay more for capital, either by issuing more shares or by paying higher interest rates. Over and above this is the mechanism of shareholder advocacy. Corporate law in the US, and indeed in most countries, allows shareholders with a minimal stake in a company ($2,000 in the US) to place items on the agenda of shareholder meetings and require that a vote be taken on these matters at meetings. This is a powerful mechanism for embarrassing management about alleged ethical failures. The annual meetings of large corporations receive wide press coverage and these critical resolutions produce negative publicity, possibly leading to boycotts and diminished retail sales.

Shareholder advocacy has been used to great effect by large institutional investors, such as the College Retirement Equities Fund in the US, as a route to more open corporate governance. Large investors have influenced corporate policies on such matters as chief executive succession, board membership and poison pills. Ethical investors can use the same route. According to a report by the Interfaith Center on Corporate Responsibility, in 1999 SRI managers filed about 220 resolutions with more than 150 US companies. The largest number covered environmental issues, with equity and corporate responsibility taking the next two places.

A notable success was the decision by Home Depot, a major US DIY outlet, to stop buying mature wood from endangered forests. In this case, shareholder activism was accompanied by a consumer boycott organised by rainforest-related NGOs. Baxter International, a maker of health care products, also agreed to stop using polyvinyl chloride in some of its products. PVC releases carcinogens when it is burnt. Chevron and Exxon are facing similar actions intended to force them to abandon plans to drill in the Alaskan Arctic wildlife refuge.

Through these and other examples, SRI funds do seem to be influencing corporate policies through shareholder advocacy, although the effect of shareholder advocacy alone is perhaps limited: it appears to be most effective when accompanied by a credible threat of consumer responses. The responsible consumer and the responsible investor form a team that is more than the sum of its parts.

Conclusions

Socially responsible investors are a significant presence in capital markets. The amounts in SRI funds are large and growing. What are SRI funds seeking, over and above a competitive return? What returns are they actually achieving? What impact have they had to date, and how might this change if the practice spreads?

The aims of SRI funds are as diverse as the aims of political pressure groups and non-governmental organisations. There are funds for all persuasions. A company might appeal to some but be anathema to others. There does seem to be general agreement among funds on a set of criteria that are used to define social responsibility. Weapons, pollution and abuse of human rights are all seen as unethical as, often, is gambling. Executives who want to court socially responsible investors should place their corporations strategically on these issues.

On average, socially responsible funds have performed well. There are several possible explanations for this and whether this is likely to continue depends on which are valid. An interesting possibility is that socially responsible behaviour proxies for general managerial competence and several studies seem to confirm this. There is also the fact that socially responsible investing interacts with similar behaviour by consumers, each reinforcing the other. This is part of the process of consumers thinking about all dimensions of their choices.

It is not clear yet what effect SRI is having. Certainly shareholder activism by socially responsible investors, along with consumer activism, has affected the choices of influential corporations. However, socially responsible funds adopting a passive role towards their shareholdings may have little influence beyond a minor reduction in the cost of capital to favoured companies.

Source: Geoffrey Heal, *Financial Times*, *Mastering Investment Supplement*, Part 8, July 2 2001, pp. 2–4. Reprinted with permission.

Room for improvement in protecting investors

Investors in emerging financial markets were filled with enthusiasm in the early 1990s. Later in the decade, despair predominated. What does the future hold? Many people imagine that investors have fled emerging markets and capital flows have reversed, but Figure 1 shows this is not true. The flow has slowed and for 1998–99 was negative in Asia, but investors have continued to make net investments. Foreign direct investors (that is, companies buying plants and businesses) show an even stronger pattern of continuing investment.

Developing countries typically have excellent growth opportunities but weak institutions: imperfect rule of law, poor financial regulation, banks saddled with non-performing loans and so on. Investors enter these markets with expectations of high returns but often with little understanding of the problems. As a result, prices are bid up to unrealistic levels in good times, often followed by financial crisis and institutional collapse.

A great deal has been learned in the 1990s, and investors have become more selective. It is no longer appropriate, if it ever was, to buy a cross-section of the whole emerging market asset class. Rather, one must select particular countries. In particular, for

investments in shares and bonds to be rewarding, three things must hold: selected countries and companies must be growing at strong, sustainable rates; growth must be profitable; profits must be shared with outside investors.

In a perfect world, these issues would be reflected in the prices of securities. Investors, however, have great difficulty in understanding and assessing the sources of sustainable growth and the risk from weak institutions. Only when that risk has become obvious, as now, are emerging market securities priced at levels that can provide high future returns.

Sustainable growth

Investment in emerging financial markets is based on a simple idea: that developing countries have better growth opportunities than industrialised countries. For this theory to work, there must be real, sustainable growth in the economy. Unless citizens are getting richer, it is unlikely that outside investors will get richer either, at least over the long term. Indeed, if investors got rich while citizens got poorer, it is likely that institutional rules would be changed.

Table 1 shows that real gross domestic product per head is growing more rapidly in most emerging markets than in the industrial world, even in the crisis-laden period 1995–99. Of course, many experienced negative growth in the 1990s, particularly in Africa and eastern Europe. But some developing countries have grown very rapidly over an extended period of time. A good example is Korea.

Just 30 years ago Korea had the same standard of living as many countries in Africa. In 1970 Korea had a GDP per head of $267, a figure similar to Ghana ($257) and Ivory Coast ($271). However, by 1980 it was $1,512, comparable with Poland's $1,533 and Syria's $1,501. By 1990 it had reached $4,422, pressing close to Portugal ($5,318) and Greece ($5,794). Meanwhile, in 1990 Ghana stood at $216 and Syria at $1,462.

How did Korea do it? Fundamentally, the country set out to join the global economy, committing itself

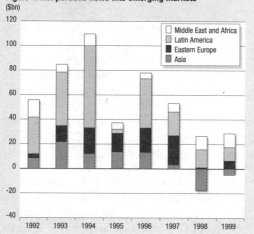

Figure 1: Net portfolio flows into emerging markets
($bn)

Legend:
- Middle East and Africa
- Latin America
- Eastern Europe
- Asia

▶

Table 1: Data on 25 emerging markets (with US, UK and Japan for comparison)

Country	Real growth of GDP/head 1995-99 (%)	Freedom from corruption	New business procedures	Private ownership of banks (%)	Financial disclosure	Rule of law	Shareholder rights	Creditor rights	Quality of financial regulation	Stock market capitalisation /GDP	Private credit /GDP	Bond market capitalisation /GDP
China	9.4	3.1	7	1	3.7	4.9	n.a.	n.a.	3.8	0.18	0.93	*
Poland	5.2	4.1	10	16	5.2	6.1	n.a.	n.a.	4.3	0.07	0.16	0.19
Taiwan	n.a.	5.5	8	23	5.4	6.9	6.0	5.0	4.8	1.04	1.55	*
Greece	3.1	4.9	13	22	5.2	6.0	2.0	2.5	3.9	0.24	0.34	0.82
Brazil	3.1	3.9	15	68	5.1	4.6	6.0	7.5	4.1	0.30	0.30	0.35
India	3.1	2.8	10	15	4.9	5.3	4.0	5.0	4.3	n.a.	n.a.	n.a.
Korea	3.0	4.0	11	75	4.7	6.9	4.0	2.5	3.9	0.22	1.43	0.42
Malaysia	2.4	4.8	6	90	5.2	6.7	6.0	5.0	3.9	2.08	1.45	0.67
Chile	2.4	7.4	12	80	6.0	7.2	6.0	10.0	5.4	0.92	0.68	*
Singapore	2.2	9.1	10	78	5.6	8.9	6.0	5.0	5.9	1.34	1.14	0.37
Philippines	2.2	2.8	10	73	4.8	4.8	8.0	5.0	4.6	0.70	0.56	*
Israel	2.1	6.6	5	35	5.4	6.9	6.0	5.0	4.9	0.41	0.71	*
Hungary	2.0	5.2	11	63	5.0	6.4	n.a.	n.a.	3.9	n.a.	n.a.	*
Median	**1.9**	**4.0**	**11**	**63**	**5.0**	**5.6**	**5.0**	**5.0**	**4.0**	**0.30**	**0.56**	**0.36**
Peru	1.9	4.4	14	74	5.0	4.0	4.0	5.0	5.0	0.23	0.20	*
Indonesia	1.6	1.7	7	57	3.9	3.2	4.0	5.0	2.4	0.30	n.a.	*
Czech Republic	1.5	4.3	11	48	4.3	6.1	n.a.	n.a.	3.1	0.29	0.60	*
South Africa	0.9	5.0	15	100	5.5	4.3	8.0	7.5	5.2	1.92	1.39	*
Egypt	0.8	3.1	10	11	4.7	5.3	4.0	5.0	4.1	0.23	0.42	*
Mexico	0.3	3.3	15	64	5.3	4.1	0.0	5.0	3.6	0.33	0.16	*
Argentina	0.0	3.5	13	40	5.1	5.6	8.0	7.5	4.4	0.16	0.18	0.19
Turkey	-0.5	3.8	15	44	5.0	5.0	4.0	10.0	3.5	0.24	0.18	*
Thailand	-0.5	3.2	12	83	4.7	5.8	6.0	2.5	3.0	0.39	1.50	*
Jordan	-2.1	4.6	11	74	n.a.	6.4	2.0	0.0	n.a.	0.70	0.75	*
Venezuela	-4.2	2.7	16	42	4.1	3.7	2.0	2.5	3.6	0.14	0.10	*
Russia	-8.7	2.1	15	67	3.6	3.6	n.a.	n.a.	2.3	0.19	0.08	0.11
For comparison												n.a.: data not available; *too small
United States	1.3	7.8	4	100	6.4	7.5	10.0	7.5	6.4	1.22	1.89	1.57
United Kingdom	1.7	8.7	7	100	6.3	8.4	8.0	5.0	6.3	1.47	1.20	0.59
Japan	0.7	6.4	11	100	5.3	7.8	6.0	5.0	5.3	0.63	2.04	1.10

Sources: International Financial Statistics *(IMF)*, Transparency International website (www.transparency.org), *"The regulation of entry" (NBER working paper 7892), "Government ownership of banks" (NBER working paper 7620)*, Global Competitiveness Report *(World Economic Forum), "Law and finance" (Journal of Political Economy, 1998, 106, 2, 1113-1155)*, A New Database on Financial Structure and Development *(World Bank)*

to improve technical knowledge and grow exports through products of increasing complexity. By competing, Koreans forced themselves to perform at ever-higher levels and achieved a far higher standard of living.

A contrasting case is Argentina. In the 1930s it had a European standard of living, but since then it has tended to coast. In the 1990s Argentina made great strides in reforming its monetary and financial system, but it still relies on commodities such as wheat, beef and hides, and has not modernised the sources of its wealth.

Embracing the world economy tends to accelerate growth because of convergence: when people, ideas, goods, services and money can flow easily across borders, and companies from all countries compete in a global marketplace, countries become more like each other. This means that countries with lower GDP per capita are likely to catch up with others by growing more rapidly.

Convergence works very well when borders are fully open. For example, the US in the late 1880s showed large internal differences in wealth: southern states were the poorest and western states the richest. But with wide-open internal borders, the southern states grew more rapidly than the average and western states more slowly, so they converged.

Those who demonstrate loudly about the supposed evils of globalisation would do well to ponder this fact. In the modern era no country has grown richer except by embracing the outside world. Those that have tried to isolate themselves from global ideas and influences have stagnated or become poorer.

Investors, then, should begin with a country's openness to global markets and global ideas. This quickly shows up in its real growth rate. Of the eight top-growth countries for 1995–99, four represent the export-driven 'East Asian model'. A fifth (India) has been more tentative about openness and reform, but starts from such a low base that even moderate reforms plus great strength in technical education have made it one of the fastest-growing markets in the set.

Greece is enjoying the fruits of convergence within the European Union. Poland represents the most thoughtful and successful transition from communism to capitalism; its superior growth in the late 1990s reflects its commitment to strong legal and financial infrastructure as well as convergence with the neighbouring EU. Brazil is a unique country that has aggressively embraced technology. Also, it has the most sophisticated financial markets in Latin America and promotes exports.

Is growth profitable?

The next requirement is that the growth be profitable. GDP is a top-line concept: a company's contribution to its country's GDP is, roughly, its sales (less its purchases of intermediate goods from other companies). To say that a country's GDP is growing is to say that most companies' revenues are growing. However, investors know (or should have learned from the dotcom mania) that a growing top line does not necessarily guarantee a growing bottom line.

A growing bottom line requires efficiency and productivity – getting the most output possible per unit of input. Economist Paul Krugman once observed that productivity is not everything, but in the long term it is almost everything. This is because inputs are invariably limited. Only by constantly upgrading ideas, technology and processes can companies and their owners get richer, and economies keep growing. What gets in the way of this process?

Sadly, the answer is often government. In developing countries, government is much more intrusive in the economy than is the case in Europe or the US and this typically damages profitability and efficiency.

The first issue is corruption, in which government officials seek private enrichment from the private sector for permits, contracts and so on. Bribery acts like a substantial tax, reducing the profitability of companies and altering their incentives in highly unproductive ways. Corruption is a problem almost everywhere, but seems to be especially acute in much of the developing world.

Corruption is now being measured, mainly by survey data, and studied by economists to document its effects. Table 1 shows how these measures compare in a number of developing countries, in this case documented by Transparency International, a German non-profit organisation.

A related issue is the bureaucracy that governments impose. India, for example, was burdened for decades by the 'licence raj', which meant companies could not make even minor changes in assets or business without a licence. The resulting cost, delay and inefficiency held back growth.

The Peruvian writer Hernando de Soto raised the difficulty of legally starting a business, even a simple one, in developing countries such as Peru. The process can drag on for years, serves no evident social purpose and is highly correlated with corruption.

Table 1 shows the result from a study into the number of procedures required to start a new business.

More broadly, governments often like to allocate capital directly rather than allowing this to be done by markets. Government is about power and the ability to allocate capital resources is a major component of such power. It may do this directly by owning banks, or indirectly by giving 'guidance' to banks and companies.

A good example is the Korean government's push, in the late 1970s, toward heavy and chemical industries, which resulted in over-investment, excess capacity and losses. Government officials probably believed they knew better than companies what would be good for the economy. Unfortunately, government choices are more often driven more by politics – favouring certain individuals, regions or companies – than by concern for economic performance. The consequence is usually growth of the top line but losses on the bottom line.

The table also shows the fraction of bank assets directly controlled by the private sector, as a proxy for the extent of private allocation of capital. Where this measure is 100 per cent or nearly so, financial markets are most fully trusted to make capital allocation decisions, which should result in the greatest efficiency.

Investors need to look not just at top-line growth but also at bottom-line productivity and efficiency. They will do well to avoid countries where the government is too intrusive. Table 1 gives an indication of where such problems are particularly severe.

Are profits shared?

Table 1 shows that the Chinese economy has grown very quickly, thanks largely to an export-driven growth policy and a burgeoning private sector.

Capital has been provided by wealthy Chinese businessmen in Hong Kong and throughout southeast Asia. However none of this guarantees that outside investors will do well in China.

In the industrial world it is taken for granted that profits are shared by outside providers of capital, but in many countries this cannot be assumed. Things can go wrong on two levels: managers may steal from owners and inside investors may steal from outside investors.

Managerial theft was most obvious in the transition of formerly communist countries in central and eastern Europe. Enterprises were controlled by state-appointed managers who saw the transition from communism as a golden opportunity to appropriate wealth. They did this most readily by selling assets of established enterprises, which they controlled, to smaller ones that they actually owned, at prices far from fair market value. This practice, called 'tunnelling', was blatant in Russia and widespread in many other transition countries.

In most developing countries, however, companies are controlled by individuals and families playing active managerial roles, so that abuse of owners by hired managers is less common. The greater temptation is for inside owners/managers to abuse outside owners and lenders. This is often done through complex conglomerate structures, making it hard for outside investors to understand exactly who has how much interest in which assets. These structures are deliberately opaque and are often used to divert profits from outside investors.

It is said that sunlight is the best disinfectant and investors should put their funds only in countries and companies where financial disclosure meets certain standards. Since most businesses do not want to reveal their affairs, government must require some level of disclosure. There must also be a decent respect for the rule of law, so insiders feel an obligation to share profits appropriately with outside suppliers of capital.

Table 1 has a column on financial disclosure and another column that ranks countries' respect for the rule of law. When a country such as China grows rapidly but has very weak financial disclosure and very weak rule of law, someone will get rich but it is unlikely to be foreign investors.

If a government wants to strengthen capital markets, it will pass laws giving rights to outside owners and lenders. Research has focused on the quality of shareholder and creditor rights. It shows these rights are generally strongest in countries whose legal systems derive from the Anglo-Saxon tradition and weakest in those following the French tradition.

Shareholder rights include measures such as the right to have one vote for each share, the right to cast such votes with a mailed-in proxy, freedom from the need to deposit shares before voting and so forth. These rights are used for Table 1.

Creditor rights mainly concern bankruptcy procedures. Can lenders force a company into bankruptcy or are there severe restrictions? In bankruptcy, are secured interests protected by the value of their collateral? Does secured debt get paid first? Do managers remain in control during bankruptcy or does a court take over?

Moreover, investors need more than laws. They also need a regulatory agency to enforce the laws. Foreign investors are uniquely vulnerable. Their interests are likely to be ignored unless a local securities commission looks after them.

One indicator for external investors is the size of internal financial markets relative to GDP. It is no accident that stock markets are large relative to GDP in countries such as Taiwan and the Philippines, which score 6–8 on shareholder rights. Where internal investors seem well treated, external investors should be safer.

The future

There will not be any euphoria over emerging markets for some time, but we can expect progress in some countries. Developing countries need external capital, so as investors become more demanding countries will have incentives to reform.

Many developing countries will undoubtedly grow faster than the economies of Europe and the US, particularly if their growth strategies are export-driven and their private sector is vigorous and competitive. But investors need to see more than rapid growth. In addition they need a good infrastructure of law, information, regulation and governance. This is hard to build, but the need for capital will be an enduring incentive and we have reason to hope for some solid success stories.

Source: David Beim, *Financial Times*, *Mastering Investment Supplement*, Part 8, July 2 2001, pp. 12–13. Reprinted with permission.

Chapter 25

Hedging with stock index futures

After studying this chapter readers should be able to:

- *hedge with stock index futures*
- *calculate a hedge ratio*
- *use futures to isolate stock selection.*

Stock index futures are contracts for notional purchases or sales of portfolios of shares on future dates. The word 'notional' is significant because stock index futures provide no facility for delivery and receipt of stock via exercise of the contract. Stock prices to be paid or received in the future are guaranteed to approximate predetermined prices because stock price movements are matched by compensatory cash flows.

Futures contracts are available on many stock indices. Stock indices on which futures are traded include the S&P 100, S&P 500, Nikkei 225, FTSE 100, DAX, CAC 40 and the Hang Seng. There are contracts relating to all the major stock markets. Contract sizes are based on sums of money per index point. So if an S&P 500 contract is based on $500 per index point and the index (in the futures market) stands at 1200, then each futures contract relates to 1200 × $500 = $600,000 of stock. Similarly, at £10 per index point, a FTSE 100 futures price of 6000 indicates that each futures contract relates to 6000 × £10 = £60,000 worth of shares.

Hedging is the reduction of an existing risk. When using stock index futures to reduce stock market risk, the anticipation is that any losses arising from movements in stock prices are offset by gains from parallel movements in futures prices. An investor might be anxious about the possibility that the prices of his or her stocks might fall. He or she could reduce the risk of a reduction in the value of the portfolio by taking a position in the futures market that would provide a gain in the event of a fall in stock prices. In such a case the investor would take a short position in stock index futures contracts. By taking a short position, he or she guarantees a notional selling price of a quantity of stock for a specific date in the future. Should stock prices fall and stock index futures behave in a corresponding fashion, the notional buying price for that date would be less than the predetermined notional selling price. The investor could close out his or her position in futures by taking a long position in the same number of contracts (i.e. by buying futures). The excess of the selling price over the buying price is paid to the investor in cash in the form of variation margin. This gain on the futures contracts is received on a daily basis as the futures price moves (the daily settlement is known as marking to market). Had the prices of stocks risen, the investor would have gained from his or her portfolio of equities but lost on futures dealings. In either case, the investor would have succeeded in reducing the extent to which the value of the portfolio fluctuates.

The use of futures to hedge the risk of a fall in stock prices does not require any alteration of the original portfolio. It is thus preferable to any form of hedging that involves changing the composition of the portfolio, such as liquidating part of the portfolio. The transaction costs of hedging with futures are also much lower than those of selling, and subsequently buying back, shares.

Example 25.1

A portfolio holder fears a generalised fall in equity prices and wishes to avoid a fall in the value of his or her portfolio.

5 April
An investor holds a balanced portfolio of shares valued at £1,000,000, but fears a fall in its value. The current FTSE 100 index is 5000.

The investor hedges by selling twenty June FTSE 100 contracts at a price of 5000 each. The investor is thus committed to the notional sale of £1 million of stock on the June delivery date at the level of equity prices implied by the futures price on 5 April. (£1,000,000 = 20 × 5000 × £10, where each futures contract relates to stock worth £10 per index point, hence 5000 × £10.)

10 May
The FTSE 100 index has fallen to 4500. Correspondingly, the value of the portfolio has declined to £900,000.

The investor closes out the futures position by buying twenty June FTSE 100 contracts at a price of 4500. The notional buying price of each contract is thus 500 below the notional selling price.

Loss on the portfolio
= £100,000
Gain from futures trading
= £100,000 (20 × 500 × £10)

By 10 May the portfolio holder feels that the fall in share prices is complete and chooses to close out his or her futures position. Of course, this strategy is one that reduces variations in the value of the portfolio holder's assets. If the FTSE 100 index had risen, there would have been a cash market gain offset by a futures market loss.

● ● ● ● Hedge ratios

Hedge ratios become necessary when the price behaviour of the futures contract is likely to differ from that of the portfolio to be hedged. If the portfolio to be hedged

Example 25.2

Example 25.2 shows how a long position in futures can be used as a hedge. In this case, a fund manager anticipates receipt of £1 million on 10 January and intends to use it to buy a balanced portfolio of UK equities. The fund manager fears, one month earlier, that stock prices will rise before the money is received.

10 December

An investor anticipates the receipt of £1 million on 10 January. The current FTSE 100 index is 5500. The investor fears a rise in the index.

The investor buys eighteen March FTSE futures contracts at a price of 5500. The investor is thereby notionally committed to paying £990,000 (18 × 5500 × £10) for stock on a future date.

10 January

The new FTSE 100 index is 5750.

The investor closes out by selling eighteen March FTSE 100 futures contracts at a price of 5700. The investor notionally guarantees a receipt of £1,026,000 (18 × 5700 × £10) upon maturity of the contracts.

The investor requires an additional £45,455 in order to buy the quantity of stock that £1 million would have bought on 10 December (£1,000,000 × [5750/5500] = £1,045,455).

There is a profit from the futures of £36,000.

Futures prices did not move precisely in line with the FTSE 100 index and, as a result, the hedge was imperfect. Basis is the difference between the spot and futures indices. A change in basis will render a hedge imperfect. The possibility of a change in basis is known as basis risk. Another source of hedge imperfection might be differences in the percentage price changes between the hedged portfolio and the FTSE 100 index arising from the portfolio having a beta different from that of the index. This latter source of imperfection can be dealt with by the use of hedge ratios.

shows relatively large variations, it is appropriate to use more futures contracts than in the case of a more stable portfolio. It is unlikely that a portfolio of stocks, for which hedging is required, precisely corresponds to the composition of a stock index. It is thus probable that it will show more or less volatility than the index.

The beta factor of a stock is a measure of the extent to which it moves in line with stock prices in general. A balanced portfolio is likely to have a beta of about 1. A stock with only half the movement of the market as a whole would have a beta of 0.5, while one with double the degree of change has a beta of 2. The beta of a portfolio of stocks is the weighted average of the betas of the stocks that constitute the portfolio.

If a calculation indicates a beta of 1.2, the portfolio tends to change by 20% more than the stock index. Hedging the portfolio would require the value of the stock index futures contracts to exceed the portfolio value by 20%. The relatively large losses (or profits) arising from the high volatility require correspondingly large offsetting profits (or losses) from futures contracts and this necessitates a relatively large number of futures contracts.

The calculation of the appropriate number of futures contracts to trade will involve ascertaining the market exposure of the stock portfolio. The market exposure of the stock portfolio is not the same as its market value. Market value needs to be adjusted by the stock betas. Table 25.1 shows hypothetical stock betas and the corresponding market exposures, which are calculated by multiplying the market values of the stocks by the betas.

Having ascertained that the market exposure of the portfolio is $2,097,875, it is necessary to find the market exposure of a stock index futures contract. If the S&P 500 futures are to be used and the S&P 500 index stands at 1350, then each futures contract would relate to $1350 \times \$500 = \$675,000$ of stock. The requisite number of futures contracts would be $\$2,097,875/\$675,000 = 3.1$ contracts (the beta of a stock index futures contract is being assumed to equal 1). This rounds down to 3 contracts. Although this technique of selling stock index futures in order to neutralise the general market exposure of a specific stock portfolio is not perfect (due to the imperfect reliability of betas and the inability to trade fractions of futures contracts), it can remove most of the market exposure of a portfolio and thereby allow an investor to take positions on the performance of individual stocks or sectors relative to the market as a whole.

Exercise 25.1

A fund manager anticipates the receipt of £3 million in two months. The intention is to invest the money equally between the three stocks X, Y and Z. These stocks have betas of 0.9, 1.1 and 1.4 respectively. The FTSE 100 stands at 6800. How can the fund manager hedge against a rise in stock prices using futures?

Answer
The market exposure of the proposed portfolio is the sum of:

X £1,000,000 × 0.9 = £900,000
Y £1,000,000 × 1.1 = £1,100,000
Z £1,000,000 × 1.4 = £1,400,000

Market exposure = £900,000 + £1,100,000 + £1,400,000 = £3,400,000

At £10 per index point, the market exposure of a futures contract is approximately 6800 × £10 = £68,000. Hedging a prospective portfolio with a market exposure of £3,400,000 requires the purchase of £3,400,000 / £68,000 = 50 futures contracts.

Table 25.1 Hypothetical stock betas and the corresponding market exposures

Stock	Value of shares ($)	Stock beta	Market exposure ($)
Aetna Life	531,250	1.1	584,375
American Express	600,000	1.2	720,000
Bethlehem Steel	432,500	1.0	432,500
Boeing	451,250	0.8	361,000
			2,097,875

Exercise 25.2

On the basis of FTSE 100 futures contracts being priced at £10 per index point, how could a fund manager hedge the following portfolio against price falls when the index is 6000?

Stock	Stock price	Number of shares held	Stock beta
Cherwell Water	100p	200,000	0.6
Cave Construction	150p	100,000	1.4
St. Clements Inns	50p	500,000	0.8
ESP Services	200p	100,000	1.2

Answer

Calculate the market exposure of the portfolio by adding the market exposures of the individual stocks (market exposure = share price × number of shares × beta).

The market exposure of the portfolio is calculated as follows:

$$£1 \quad × \ 200,000 × 0.6 \ = \ £120,000$$
$$£1.50 \ × \ 100,000 × 1.4 \ = \ £210,000$$
$$£0.5 \quad × \ 500,000 × 0.8 \ = \ £200,000$$
$$£2 \quad × \ 100,000 × 1.2 \ = \ \underline{£240,000}$$
$$£770,000$$

The market exposure of a futures contract is calculated as:

$$6,000 × £10 = £60,000$$

The fund manager should sell:

£770,000/£60,000 = 12.83 futures contracts.

Since contracts are indivisible, the number to be sold would be 12 or 13.

Exercise 25.3

An investor has the following portfolio.

	Number of shares	Share price	Share beta
Bank of Coventry	20,000	300p	0.9
Coventry Motors	30,000	100p	1.5
Nuneaton Manufacturing	10,000	600p	1.3
Cheylesmore Stores	25,000	300p	0.8

It is 15 November and the FTSE 100 index is 4700. How can the investor hedge the portfolio with futures? What factors could reduce the effectiveness of the hedge?

Answer
Calculate the market exposure of the portfolio by adding the market exposures of the individual stocks (market exposure = number of shares × share price × beta).

$20,000 \times 300p \times 0.9 = 5.4m$
$30,000 \times 100p \times 1.5 = 4.5m$
$10,000 \times 600p \times 1.3 = 7.8m$
$25,000 \times 300p \times 0.8 = 6.0m$
$$\overline{\hspace{3cm}}$$
$$23.7m$$

The total market exposure is 23,700,000p, i.e. £237,000. The market exposure provided by one futures contract is:

$4,700 \times £10 = £47,000$

Hedging the portfolio with futures would involve selling:

$£237,000/£47,000 = 5.04$ contracts.

Since it is not possible to trade fractions of contracts, the investor would sell five of them.
   Factors that could reduce hedge effectiveness include basis risk, the indivisibility of contracts, instability of beta and non-systematic risk.

Discussion questions

1 'Diversification reduces non-systematic risk. Stock index futures can reduce systematic risk. Therefore share price risk can be eliminated completely.' Do you agree?

2 How are stock index futures used? Why might they be less than perfect in their uses?

Chapter 26

Hedging with options

After studying this chapter readers should be able to:

- *hedge a stockholding with options*
- *evaluate the relative merits of long and short option positions for hedging*
- *hedge anticipated purchases of stock.*

Call options provide the right to buy shares at a particular price (the strike price) and put options give the right to sell at a strike price. Someone who is at risk from a price change can use options to offset that risk. A call option can be seen as a means of ensuring a maximum purchase price (if the market price exceeds the strike price, then the option may be exercised in order to buy at the strike price). A put option provides a minimum selling price (exercise of the right to sell, at the strike price, might occur in the event of the market price being below the strike price). So options can be regarded as means of insurance against adverse price movements.

Hedging the value of a stockholding

Consider a holder of stock who seeks protection from a fall in the stock price. The protection can be obtained by buying a put option. Profits from the option offset losses on the stock. However, profits from the rise in the stock price are not offset by losses from the option (apart from the premium paid for the option). So gains are made from a rise in the stock price.

A put option guarantees a minimum selling price for a block of 1,000 shares. Table 26.1 shows the premiums of BP Amoco put options at the close of trading on 30 March 2001, at which time the price of BP Amoco shares was 568p. A holder of 1,000 BP Amoco shares would be able to ensure that the value of the stockholding could not fall below £5,500 (1,000 × £5.50) by buying a 550p put option. The option would provide the right to sell 1,000 BP Amoco shares at 550p. If the investor chose an option that expired in April, the cost of providing such protection until the April expiry date would be £70 (1,000 × 7p). Of course, should the stock price remain in excess of 550p, the shareholder would not exercise the right to sell at 550p.

Table 26.1 Premiums of BP Amoco options at close of trading on 30 March 2001

Strike price	Calls			Puts		
	April	July	October	April	July	October
550p	27p	49p	64p	7p	27.5p	36p
600p	5p	26.5p	41p	35p	55p	63p

The BP Amoco share price was 568p.

Although the stockholder has the right to exercise the option and thereby sell stock at 550p, he or she is more likely to sell rather than exercise the option. This can be understood by considering the elements that make up an option premium. The premium (i.e. the price) of an option can be subdivided into its intrinsic value and its time value. The intrinsic value represents the pay-off that could be obtained by immediately exercising the option. For example, an April 600p put option has an intrinsic value of 32p when the stock price is 568p since, by exercising the option, shares can be sold at 32p more than the price at which they can be bought. The difference between the option premium and the intrinsic value is termed time value, which is 3p in the case of the April 600p put options. Time value can be regarded as a payment for the possibility that intrinsic value will increase prior to the date on which the option expires, i.e. the date beyond which it cannot be exercised. If a stockholder exercises an option, only the intrinsic value is received, whereas if the option is sold, both the intrinsic and time values are obtained. It thus makes sense to sell an option in preference to exercising it.

In Table 26.1 the 550p puts have exercise prices below the market value of the stock. Therefore, they cannot be exercised at a profit and have zero intrinsic value. Their prices consist entirely of time value. Put options with exercise prices below the market price of the stock are said to be out-of-the-money. When the stock price is equal to the exercise price, the option is said to be at-the-money. Put options with exercise prices above the stock price (the only ones with intrinsic value) are termed in-the-money.

Long versus short option positions

Hedging against a price fall can be carried out by buying a put option, and protection against a price rise can be obtained from the purchase of a call option. Alternatively, a call option might be written (sold) as a means of protection from a price fall or a put option written as a means of hedging against a price rise. Writing options is the better approach if the price change is relatively modest, whereas buying options is the more effective strategy in the event of a substantial movement in the price of the stock. Figure 26.1 compares the purchase of a put option with the sale of a call option.

In the example illustrated by Figure 26.1, the two options have the same exercise price of 100p. The put is priced at 5p and the call at 6p. The long (i.e. purchased) put provides protection against a fall in the stock price below 100p but, considering the premium of 5p, the put option does not confer a net advantage over an unhedged position until the stock price has fallen below 95p. So the long put is beneficial only in the event of a substantial price fall.

By writing the call for 6p, a premium receipt is obtained and that receipt can be seen as providing downside protection. A stock price fall from 100p to 94p would leave the hedger no worse off since the loss of 6p on the stock would be offset by the premium receipt. However, the downside protection is constant in money terms and stock prices below 94p would entail a net loss. Of course, stock prices above 94p would entail a net profit. So the short call is advantageous in the case of a modest stock price fall.

The short call is superior to the long put down to a stock price of 89p. This is demonstrated by Figure 26.1. The net profit from the put option does not exceed that of the call option until the stock price has fallen sufficiently to generate an intrinsic value for the put option of 5p (to offset the put premium) plus 6p (to match the call premium). So the short option position is superior to the long option position until the stock price has moved by the sum of the two option premiums. In this case, a hedger seeking protection from a price fall but anticipating a fall of less than 11p would prefer the short call, whereas a hedger fearing a greater fall would buy a put option.

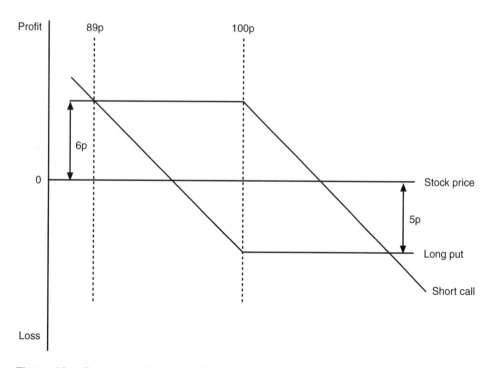

Figure 26.1 Purchase of a put option vs sale of a call option

Hedging anticipated purchases

Options can be used to hedge intended purchases of stocks. Suppose it is 30 March 2001 and that a portfolio manager intends to buy BP Amoco stock with funds expected to become available in early April. The current price of BP Amoco stock is 568p per share and the portfolio manager wishes to avoid the risk of having to pay a much higher price. The prices of BP Amoco call options are shown in Table 26.1.

The portfolio manager could buy April 600p call options at 5p. Each option contract provides the right, but not the obligation, to buy 1,000 BP Amoco shares at a price of 600p per share. The price of the option is 5p per share, which amounts to £50 (5p x 1,000) per option contract. If when the stock was purchased in April the price were 650p, the portfolio manager could exercise the options and thereby buy stock at 600p. This represents a saving of 50p per share at a premium cost of 5p per share: a net benefit of 45p per share. The effective purchase price would be 605p (strike price plus premium paid).

By exercising an option the hedger obtains its intrinsic value, which is the difference between the stock price and the option's strike price. However, the price of an option includes time value in addition to the intrinsic value. If the hedger sold the option, the time value as well as the intrinsic value would be received. The time value might be 2p and hence the sale price of the option would be 52p. The portfolio manager would have bought options for 5p and sold them for 52p. There would have been a net profit of 47p per share rather than the 45p profit (intrinsic value minus premium) obtained from exercising the options. The 47p per share profit from the options partially offsets the increased price of the stock, whose effective price becomes 603p (650p − 47p).

If the stock price were 600p or less at the time the stock was purchased, the options held would have no intrinsic value and therefore could not be profitably exercised. However, they would still have time value. For example, if the share price were still 568p, the April 600p call options might be selling at 2p. The options would have been bought for 5p and could be sold for 2p. The net cost of 3p (i.e. £30 per contract covering 1,000 shares) compares favourably with the net cost of 5p (£50) incurred if the option is allowed to expire unexercised.

Discussion questions

1 How can options be used in fund management?

2 (a) What factors affect the prices of stock options? (b) How do investors use options?

Exercise 26.1

The shares of Big Con plc stand at 110p. Put options with a strike price of 120p are priced at 14p.

(a) What is the intrinsic value of the options?

(b) What is the time value of the options?

(c) If the share price fell to 50p by the expiry date, what would be the profit/loss for the holder and writer of the options?

(d) What is the maximum loss for the writer of the options?

(e) Why might an investor buy such a put option?

Answers

(a) 10p (120p − 110p, strike price minus stock price).

(b) 4p (14p − 10p, option premium minus intrinsic value).

(c) The holder makes a profit of 56p, which equals the loss of the writer (70p − 14p, the new value of the option minus the premium paid).

(d) 106p (120p − 14p, the loss if the stock price falls to zero which amounts to the intrinsic value minus the premium received).

(e) Possibilities include (a) seeking a speculative profit from a forecast of a stock price fall and (b) hedging a shareholding against a possible stock price fall.

Exercise 26.2

It is June 10th and shares in Covuni Plc are 98p. Option prices are:

Strike price	Calls		Puts	
	Sept.	Dec.	Sept.	Dec.
90p	9p	9½p	1p	1½p
100p	2p	3p	4p	5p
110p	1p	1½p	13p	13½p

(a) Why are the 100p put options more expensive than the 100p call options?

(b) Suggest two alternative strategies for hedging a holding of 1,000 shares (one strategy should use calls and the other puts). Under what circumstances would one be preferred over the other?

(c) How might a speculator make a profit from a 2p rise in the share price?

(d) If the September 90p options are held to expiry and the share price remains at 98p, what would you expect the option prices to be at expiry?

Answers

(a) The put options have an intrinsic value of 100p − 98p = 2p. The call options have no intrinsic value; they are out-of-the-money.

(b) (i) Buy a 100p put option. Best when a large price fall is expected.

(ii) Write a 100p call option. Best when a small price fall is expected.

(c) Write a 100p put option.

(d) The 90p call would have an intrinsic value of 98p − 90p = 8p. At expiry time value is zero. So the option price should be 8p. The 90p put would have expired out of the money and hence would have zero value at expiry.

Chapter 27

Bond prices

After studying this chapter readers should:

- *be able to estimate the fair price of a bond*
- *be able to demonstrate an understanding of consols and permanent interest-bearing shares (PIBs)*
- *appreciate the significance of bond price convexity.*

Discount models

As with other financial investments, bond prices are based on the present value of expected future cash flows. The general formula for calculating a bond price is:

$$P = C/(1+r) + C/(1+r)^2 + C/(1+r)^3 + \ldots + C/(1+r)^n + B/(1+r)^n \qquad (1)$$

or

$$P = C\sum_{k=1}^{n} 1/(1+r)^k + B/(1+r)^n \qquad (2)$$

P is the fair market price of the bond (its dirty price, which includes accrued interest), C is the regular coupon payment each period, B is the money value to be paid to the bondholder at redemption, r is the rate of discount per period, and n is the number of periods remaining to redemption.

An important simplification that has been made in equations (1) and (2) is the use of the same rate of discount for all the future cash flows. This assumes that interest rates are the same irrespective of the term of the investment (i.e. that the yield curve is flat). When valuing a bond an investment analyst could use a different rate of discount for each cash flow in order to take account of the fact that there are different interest rates for different maturities. However, typically in practice a single rate, the redemption yield or yield to maturity, is applied to all future cash flows. The redemption yield (yield to maturity) of a bond could be looked upon as an average of discount rates applicable to the various future cash flows. The redemption yield indicates the average annual return to be received by an investor holding a bond to maturity.

Interest rates (in the sense of yields on risk-free bonds) are not the only determinants of discount rates. Bonds with relatively high default risk need to yield a high expected rate of return to compensate for the risk. The rate of discount is the required rate of return from a bond. The required rate of return can be regarded as the sum of the yield on bonds that are free of default risk (government bonds) and a risk premium to reflect the default risk of the bond being valued. High default risk entails a high required rate of return and hence a high discount rate. It follows that, for any particular stream of future cash flows, high-risk bonds would have higher rates of discount and hence lower prices than low-risk bonds.

Two conclusions that can be drawn from this account of bond pricing are, first, that bond prices have an inverse relationship to interest rates, and second, that they have an inverse relationship to the risk of default. High interest rates and high risk are associated with low prices.

An important distinction to be made when considering bond prices is between the clean and dirty prices. When a bond is purchased, the buyer must include in the purchase price a sum corresponding to the seller's share of the next coupon. If the coupon is paid six monthly, and the bond is sold three months after the last coupon payment date, the seller will require the price to include half the next coupon so that holding the bond for the previous three months provides an interest yield. The rights, to the coupon, accumulated by the seller are referred to as accrued interest. The clean price of a bond excludes accrued interest whereas the dirty price includes it. Quoted prices are usually clean prices whereas the price to be paid is the dirty price.

Exercise 27.1

A bond pays a coupon of £4 every six months, and £100 will be repaid at redemption. There are two years to redemption and the next coupon is due in six months. The redemption yield on similar bonds is 6% p.a. Estimate the fair price of the bond.

Answer

$$P = C/(1+r) + C/(1+r)^2 + C/(1+r)^3 + C/(1+r)^4 + 100/(1+r)^4$$

where P is the fair price of the bond, C is the periodic coupon, and r is the redemption yield on a six-month basis.

$$P = £4/(1.03) + £4/(1.03)^2 + £4/(1.03)^3 + £4/(1.03)^4 + £100/(1.03)^4$$
$$P = £3.88 + £3.77 + £3.66 + £3.55 + £88.85$$
$$P = £103.71$$

●●●● Valuing coupon streams as annuities

An annuity is a stream of future payments, typically a fixed sum of money each period. The stream of coupon payments on a bond can be seen as equivalent to an annuity. Correspondingly the prospective series of coupon receipts can be valued as an annuity. The equation for valuing an annuity is:

$$AV = \{C - [C/(1 + r)^n]\}/r \tag{3}$$

Exercise 27.2

(a) It is 22 November 1994. Treasury 10% 1996 matures on 21 November 1996.
Calculate the fair price of this bond when the redemption yield is:
(i) 10% p.a. and (ii) 5% p.a.

(b) It is 22 November 1994. Treasury 5% 1996 matures on 21 November 1996.
Calculate the fair price of this bond when the redemption yield is:
(i) 10% p.a. and (ii) 5% p.a.

(c) It is 22 November 1994. A zero coupon bond matures on 21 November 1996.
Calculate the fair price of this bond when the redemption yield is:
(i) 10% p.a. and (ii) 5% p.a.

Answers

(a) (i) $£5/(1.05) + £5/(1.05)^2 + £5/(1.05)^3 + £105/(1.05)^4$
$= £4.76 + £4.54 + £4.32 + £86.38 = £100$

(ii) $£5/(1.025) + £5/(1.025)^2 + £5/(1.025)^3 + £105/(1.025)^4$
$= £4.88 + £4.76 + £4.64 + £95.12 = £109.40$
(Treasury 10% pays £10 per year, i.e. £5 every six months)

(b) (i) $£2.5/(1.05) + £2.5/(1.05)^2 + £2.5/(1.05)^3 + £102.5/(1.05)^4$
$= £2.38 + £2.27 + £2.16 + £84.33 = £91.14$

(ii) $£2.5/(1.025) + £2.5/(1.025)^2 + £2.5/(1.025)^3 + £102.5/(1.025)^4$
$= £2.44 + £2.38 + £2.32 + £92.86 = £100$
(Treasury 5% pays £5 per year, i.e. £2.50 every six months)

(c) (i) $£100/(1.1)^2 = £82.64$ or $£100/(1.05)^4 = £82.27$

(ii) $£100/(1.05)^2 = £90.70$ or $£100/(1.025)^4 = £90.60$

It is to be noted that when the redemption yield equals the coupon rate the bond trades at par (i.e. its price equals its nominal value of £100). Also sensitivity to interest rate changes rises as the coupon rate falls. A fall in the interest rate from 10% p.a. to 5% p.a. causes a 9.4% rise in the price of the 10% coupon bond, a 9.72% [(100 − 91.14)/91.14 = 0.0972] rise in the price of the 5% coupon bond, and a 9.75% rise in the price of the zero coupon bond using annual discounting or a 10.13% rise in the price of the zero coupon bond when six-monthly discounting is used.

It can thus be seen that when the discounting is carried out in a consistent way across the three cases the relationship between coupon rate and sensitivity to interest rate changes is as follows:

Coupon rate	% Bond price change
10%	9.4%
5%	9.72%
0%	10.13%

Lower coupon bonds have the greater sensitivity to interest rate changes.

where AV is the value of the annuity (the present value of the expected coupons), C is the coupon, n is the number of periods for which the coupon will be paid (typically six month periods) and r is the periodic interest rate (which is half the per

Exercise 27.3

Two years ago, an investor bought a five-year zero coupon bond with a par value of £100 when interest rates were 7% p.a. The investor sold it recently when interest rates were 5% p.a.
  What was the realised compound yield?

Answer
The price of the bond, two years ago, was £100/[1.07]^5 = £71.30.
  The current fair price would be £100/[1.05]^3 = £86.38.
  The realised compound yield was [£86.38/£71.30]$^{0.5}$ − 1 = 1.1007 − 1 = 0.1007 i.e. 10.07% p.a.

annum rate in the case of six-monthly payments). The equation shown is applicable when the next coupon receipt is a full period away.

The value of the bond can be estimated as being equal to the value of the annuity plus the present value of the sum payable at maturity.

$$BV = AV + M/(1 + r)^n \tag{4}$$

where BV is the value of the bond and M is the sum to be received by the bondholder at maturity. Despite the appearance of precision, this remains merely an estimate of the fair price. This is partly because r is a proxy for a series of separate interest rates, each applicable to a particular future cash flow.

Consols and PIBs

Consols are undated government bonds; the government may choose to pay the fixed periodic coupon in perpetuity, there is no obligation to ever redeem the bond. PIBs (permanent interest-bearing shares) are issued by building societies. Like consols PIBs pay a fixed annual sum in perpetuity, the building society need never repay the original investment. Preference shares are issued by firms and (usually) pay a fixed annual dividend in perpetuity, with no obligation to repay the initial sum paid for the shares. The factor that consols, PIBs and preference shares have in common is the perpetual nature of the coupon or dividend payments. When cash flows are perpetual equation (1) or (2) can be simplified to equation (5).

$$P = C/r \tag{5}$$

P is the fair price of the security, C is the periodic coupon, and r is the rate of discount (required rate of return). It can be noted that equation (5) implies inverse proportionality between interest rates and asset prices. If the rate of discount halves the fair price doubles, if the rate of discount doubles the fair price halves.

Bond price convexity

Bond prices are inversely related to interest rates, but the relationship is not symmetrical. A particular percentage point interest rate change will have asymmetrical effects on the bond price dependent upon whether rates rise or fall. The proportionate fall in the bond price resulting from a rise in interest rates is less than the proportionate rise in the bond price caused by a fall when the percentage point change in interest rates is the same in the two cases.

This can be illustrated by reference to the case of an irredeemable bond (a bond with no maturity date). The price of an irredeemable bond is given by equation 6.

$$P = C/r \tag{6}$$

In equation 6, P represents the fair price of the bond, C the coupon and r is the interest rate (required rate of return). Consider the case of a £5 annual coupon and an initial interest rate of 10% p.a. The fair price of the bond would be estimated as:

£5 / 0.1 = £50.

If the interest rate falls by 2 percentage points to 8% p.a., the price of the bond is expected to rise to

£5 / 0.08 = £62.50.

If the interest rate rises by 2 percentage points to 12% p.a., the fair price of the bond falls to

£5 / 0.12 = £41.67.

Whereas the interest rate fall results in a 25% price rise, the equivalent interest rate increase causes a 16.67% price decline. This asymmetry of price response is referred to as convexity.

Chapter 28

The risks of investing in bonds

After studying this chapter readers should be able to:

• *calculate and interpret Macaulay's duration*

• *calculate and interpret modified duration*

• *calculate and interpret money duration*

• *appreciate the characteristics and behaviour of Macaulay's duration*

• *immunise a bond portfolio against interest rate risk using a dedicated portfolio, maturity matching or duration matching.*

There are two types of risk encountered by investors in bonds: price (or capital) risk and reinvestment (or income) risk. Price risk is the risk that bond prices can change. For example, a general rise in interest rates, or a fall in the credit rating of a particular bond, would reduce the price of a bond. A capital loss would result. Reinvestment risk refers to the uncertainty as to the interest rate at which coupons and redemption sums can be invested. This causes uncertainty as to the final sum that will be available at the end of an investment horizon.

Capital risk is measured by duration. The duration measures are useful for the purposes of predicting the effects of interest rate changes and protecting bond portfolios against the effects of such changes. Duration measures can also be used to design portfolios such that price risk and reinvestment risk tend to cancel each other out.

The measurement of bond price volatility

Bond price volatility is measured by duration. The duration measures include Macaulay's duration, modified duration and money duration. Macaulay's duration is the average period of time to the receipt of cash flows. Each time period (to the receipt of a cash flow) is weighted by the proportionate contribution of that cash flow to the fair price of the bond. Macaulay's duration is transformed into modified duration by means of dividing it by $(1 + r/n)$ where r is the redemption yield (which approximates an interest rate) and n is the number of coupon payments per year.

Macaulay's duration has another meaning. It is the proportionate change in the bond price arising from a unit proportional change in (1 + redemption yield). That is:

$$\text{Macaulay's duration} = \frac{\Delta P/P}{\Delta(1+r)/(1+r)} \qquad (1)$$

(The symbol Δ signifies 'change in'.)

The corresponding interpretation of modified duration is:

$$\text{Modified duration} = \frac{\Delta P/P}{\Delta r} \qquad (2)$$

Equation (2) is derived from equation (1) by means of dividing by (1 + r) and observing that $\Delta(1 + r) = \Delta r$.

Equations (1) and (2) assume annual coupon payments. When coupons are paid more frequently, r is replaced by r/n (the annual redemption yield divided by the number of coupon payments per year). This is consistent with treating the redemption yield on a per period basis. For example, UK and US government bonds typically pay coupons six-monthly. In those cases n = 2, and r/2 is the redemption yield per six-month period.

The calculation of duration can be demonstrated by an example. Suppose that a bond has just paid a coupon, matures in two years and pays a coupon of £6 six-monthly. The interest rate is 10% p.a. for all maturities. The fair price of the bond is:

$$P = £6/(1.05) + £6/(1.05)^2 + £6/(1.05)^3 + £106/(1.05)^4$$

$$= £5.71 + £5.44 + £5.18 + £87.21 = £103.54$$

(Note that an interest rate of 10% p.a. is 5% per six-month period.)

Macaulay's duration is calculated as the weighted average of the periods to the receipt of cash flows. The weighting is based on the contribution, of the period's cash flow, to the fair value of the bond. The periods are 0.5, 1, 1.5 and 2 years.

$$\text{Macaulay's duration} = (5.71/103.54)0.5 + (5.44/103.54)1.0 +$$
$$(5.18/103.54)1.5 + (87.21/103.54)2.0$$

$$= 0.028 + 0.053 + 0.075 + 1.685 = 1.841 \text{ years}$$

Conversion of Macaulay's duration to modified duration entails division by (1 + r/n).

$$\text{Modified duration} = 1.841/(1 + 0.1/2) = 1.841/(1.05) = 1.753$$

Exercise 28.1

Treasury 10% 1999 will reach final maturity on 10 June 1999. It is now 11 June 1997. One and two-year interest rates are both 7% p.a. Calculate (a) the fair price, (b) Macaulay's duration and (c) the modified duration of the bond.

Answers

(a) Fair price = £5/1.035 + £5/(1.035)^2 + £5/(1.035)^3 + £105/(1.035)^4 = £4.83 + £4.67 + £4.51 + £91.50 = £105.51

(The '10%' following 'Treasury' implies that £10 a year is paid i.e. the coupon is £5 per six month period).

(b) Macaulay's duration = (4.83/105.51)0.5 + (4.67/105.51)1.0 + (4.51/105.51)1.5 + (91.5/105.51)2.0 = 0.02 + 0.04 + 0.06 + 1.73 = 1.85 years

(c) Modified duration = 1.85/(1.035) = 1.79 (On the assumption that coupons are paid twice a year.)

Money duration

Modified duration multiplied by the change in bond yield (multiplied by −1) shows the approximate proportionate change in the bond price resulting from the yield change.

$$\Delta P/P = - \text{MD} \times \Delta r \tag{1}$$

where $\Delta P/P$ is the proportionate change in the bond price, −MD is the negative of modified duration, and Δr is the change in the bond yield. (The bond yield is the redemption yield, which closely approximates the interest rate relating to the duration of the bond.)

Multiplying both sides of equation (1) by the initial bond price, P, gives equation 2.

$$\Delta P = (\Delta P/P) \times P = -\text{MD} \times \Delta r \times P \tag{2}$$

The term (MD × P) might be called money duration. It shows the price change resulting from a yield change. It should be noted that yields are here expressed as decimals rather than percentages, so for example 1% would be expressed as 0.01 and a basis point (0.01%) as 0.0001. Alternative names for money duration are perturbation and, where the yield change is 0.01%, the price value of a basis point (PVBP).

For small changes in yield (e.g. 0.1%), equation (2) provides a reasonably good approximation to the actual change in the bond price. However, for large changes (e.g. 1%), the approximation is less satisfactory. As the change in the yield (or interest rate) increases, equation (2) becomes less accurate as a means of estimating bond price movements. This is because of convexity.

Exercise 28.2

It is 27 January 1998. Treasury 15% 2000 matures on 26 January 2000. The interest rate is 6% p.a. In relation to this bond calculate the:

(a) Fair price.
(b) Macaulay's duration.
(c) Modified duration.
(d) A fund manager holds Treasury 15% 2000 and is considering replacing it with either three-month Treasury bills or Treasury 12% 2002. What should the fund manager do if he/she expects (i) a rise, and (ii) a fall, in interest rates? Explain your answer.

Answers
(a) Let P = fair price.
   $P = £7.50/(1.03) + £7.50/(1.03)^2 + £7.50/(1.03)^3 + £107.50/(1.03)^4$
   $P = £7.28 + £7.07 + £6.86 + £95.51 = £116.72$

(b) Let D = Macaulay's duration.
   $D = (£7.28/£116.72)0.5 + (£7.07/£116.72)1.0 + (£6.86/£116.72)1.5 +$
   $(£95.51/£116.72)2.0$
   $D = 0.031 + 0.061 + 0.088 + 1.637 = 1.817$ years

(c) Modified duration $= D/(1 + r/n) = 1.817/(1.03) = 1.764$
   (It is assumed that coupons are paid twice a year. Most UK government bonds pay coupons twice a year.)

(d) (i) If the fund manager expects a rise in interest rates, bond prices are expected to fall. The fund manager should shorten duration by replacing Treasury 15% 2000 with three-month Treasury bills. This will reduce the extent of the loss since Treasury bills, having lower duration, are less sensitive to interest rate changes than the bonds.
   (ii) If the fund manager expects interest rates to fall, the expectation is that bond prices will rise. Higher duration provides greater sensitivity to interest rate changes. By replacing Treasury 15% 2000 with Treasury 12% 2002, the fund manager raises duration and hence increases the profit to be made from a fall in interest rates. (Since duration increases with greater maturity and lower coupons, Treasury 12% 2002 will have a longer duration than Treasury 15% 2000.)

The behaviour of Macaulay's duration

The duration (Macaulay's duration) of a bond is systematically affected by certain characteristics of that bond. This can be summarised by a set of rules.

Rule 1: The duration of a zero coupon bond equals its time to maturity.

Since a zero coupon bond generates only one cash flow, the payment of principal at maturity, the average time to the receipt of cash flows equals the time to that payment.

Rule 2: Holding time to maturity and redemption yield (yield to maturity) constant, duration is inversely related to the coupon.

Exercise 28.3

An investor has two bonds. Bond A pays a 5% annual coupon and matures in five years. Bond B pays an 8% coupon semi-annually and matures in three years. The investor needs to sell one bond immediately and hold the other for two years. The current rate of interest is 6% p.a.

(a) Which bond would the investor sell if that investor expected interest rates to:
   (i) increase?
   (ii) decrease?

(b) The investor expects interest rates to rise and acts accordingly. Soon after, interest rates increase to 7% p.a. and remain constant for the following two years. What would be the realised compound yield on the bond the investor decided to hold?

Answers

(a) The fair price of bond A is:

£5/(1.06) + £5/(1.06)^2 + £5/(1.06)^3 + £5/(1.06)^4 + £105/(1.06)^5
=£4.72 + £4.45 + £4.20 + £3.96 + £78.46 = £95.79

The Macaulay's duration of bond A is:

(£4.72/£95.79)1.0 + (£4.45/£95.79)2.0 + (£4.2/£95.79)3.0 + (£3.96/£95.79)4.0 + (£78.46/£95.79)5.0

= 0.049 + 0.093 + 0.132 + 0.165 + 4.095 = 4.534 years

Modified duration is:

4.534/(1.06) = 4.277

The fair price of bond B is:

£4/(1.03) + £4/(1.03)^2 + £4/(1.03)^3 + £4/(1.03)^4 + £4/(1.03)^5 + £104/(1.03)^6 = £3.88 + £3.77 + £3.66 + £3.55 + £3.45 + £87.10 = £105.41

The Macaulay's duration of bond B is:

(£3.88/£105.41)0.5 + (£3.77/£105.41)1.0 + (£3.66/£105.41)1.5 + (£3.55/£105.41)2.0 + (£3.45/£105.41)2.5 + (£87.1/£105.41)3.0

= 0.018 + 0.036 + 0.052 + 0.067 + 0.082 + 2.479 = 2.734 years

Modified duration is:

2.734/(1.03) = 2.654

If the investor expects interest rates to increase, bond prices are expected to fall. The bond with the higher modified duration should show the greatest fall. The investor would therefore choose to sell bond A because it has the higher modified duration.

If the investor expects interest rates to decrease, bond prices are expected to rise. The bond with the higher modified duration would show the greater price rise. The investor should choose to hold bond A and sell bond B since bond A has the higher modified duration.

(b) The investor holds bond B for two years. At the end of the two years bond B should sell for:

£4/(1.035) + £104/(1.035)^2 = £3.86 + £97.09 = £100.95

The value of reinvested coupons after two years would be:

£4(1.035)^3 + £4(1.035)^2 + £4(1.035) + £4 = £4.43 + £4.28 + £4.14 + £4 = £16.85

So the total value at the end of two years is £100.95 + £16.85 = £117.80.

£117.80/£105.41 = 1.1175

1.1175$^{0.25}$ = 1.0282

The six-month rate of return is 2.82%, which is 5.64% p.a. This is the realised compound yield.

Duration is the weighted average time to the receipt of cash flows, and the weighting of each time period is related to the cash flow at the end of that time period. Low coupon bonds involve low weightings attached to time periods other than the period to final maturity. The period to the repayment of principal will dominate the earlier periods in the determination of duration.

Rule 3: Holding the coupon rate constant, duration generally increases with time to maturity.

As maturity increases, the time periods to the receipt of cash flows will increase. This will tend to increase duration. However, for bonds trading at a very deep discount (bonds whose coupon rates are far below their redemption yields) increases in maturity may eventually be associated with reductions in duration.

Duration increases by less than a year for each year that maturity increases (unless the bond has a zero coupon). Furthermore duration increases at a decreasing rate as time to maturity increases. Doubling the time to maturity tends to increase duration, but by less than double.

Rule 4: Holding coupon and maturity constant, duration is inversely related to redemption yield (yield to maturity).

Higher redemption yields imply higher discount rates. Higher discount rates reduce the relative importance of distant cash flows. Distant time periods receive lower weightings, and hence duration falls. This rule does not apply to zero coupon bonds.

Rule 5: The duration of an irredeemable bond is given by $(1 + r)/r$, where r is the redemption yield.

If a bond pays the same coupon each period forever without the principal ever being repaid, the duration equals $(1 + r)/r$. It is illustrative to consider some examples. Table 28.1 shows the duration relating to various redemption yields.

In the case of high redemption yields, the cash flows occurring early in the life of the bond dominate the calculation of duration. The distant cash flows are so heavily discounted that they provide very low weightings for the longer periods. Finally it might be noted that as the maturity of a bond increases, its duration will eventually converge towards that of an irredeemable bond.

Table 28.1 Duration relating to various redemption yields

Redemption yield (% p.a.)	Duration (in years)
21	5.76
16	7.25
11	10.09
6	17.67
1	101.00

Portfolio immunisation

A portfolio of bonds may be held with a view to the provision of a known flow of income in the future. The investor could be an individual or an institution such as an insurance company making annuity payments. Immunisation of a bond portfolio aims to protect the investor against the future cash flows falling below the levels required. Shortfalls could occur as a result of either capital losses or a decline in the interest rates at which proceeds can be reinvested.

One approach to portfolio immunisation is the construction of a dedicated portfolio. A dedicated portfolio entails future cash flow receipts, both of coupons and repayments of principal at redemption, that precisely match the cash flows required. For example, the future payments to pensioners from an annuity fund might be synchronised with the coupon and redemption receipts from the bonds that comprise the fund. The matching of receipts with requirements must relate to both amount and timing. Although dedicated portfolios achieve immunisation they are very difficult to construct.

An alternative approach to immunisation is maturity matching. The required cash flows from the portfolio, in terms of both amount and timing, are used as the basis for choosing the bonds for the portfolio. By ensuring that bond maturities coincide with cash withdrawals from the portfolio, the risk of interest rate changes depressing the market values of bonds is avoided. In this way the portfolio manager would be sure of receiving the redemption value of a bond. One element of uncertainty does remain when such a strategy is used. Since interest rates vary over time, there is uncertainty as to the rate of return to be obtained from investing coupon receipts. This is reinvestment risk. Changes in the rates of return on reinvested income can have a substantial impact on subsequent values of the portfolio. This risk can be reduced by using duration matching instead of maturity matching.

Duration matching involves matching the Macaulay's duration of the bond portfolio to the time at which the cash flow will be required. Bond price changes tend to offset variations in returns from reinvested coupons. The capital risk of bond price changes and the income risk from reinvestment of coupons tend to cancel each other out.

Since there would normally be more than one cash outflow to be funded from a bond portfolio, duration matching becomes a matter of matching the Macaulay's duration of the portfolio with the Macaulay's duration of the cash outflows.

A bond portfolio immunised by duration matching will require frequent rebalancing in order to maintain the matching. In other words, it will be necessary to frequently make changes to the composition of the portfolio. This is because Macaulay's duration changes as a result of interest rate movements, and in consequence of the passage of time. These factors are likely to affect the duration of the cash outflow commitments differently from the duration of the bond portfolio. In consequence, the composition of the portfolio would need to be changed in order to keep its duration in line with that of the cash outflow commitments.

Exercise 28.4

(a) Find the duration of a bond with a four-year maturity, a £6 annual coupon and a redemption yield of 8% p.a.

(b) Show numerically how this bond will provide protection from interest rate risk if the holding period is equal to the duration of the bond. For the calculation assume that interest rates increase by 1%.

Answer

$P = £6/(1.08) + £6/(1.08)^2 + £6/(1.08)^3 + £106/(1.08)^4$

$P = £5.56 + £5.14 + £4.76 + £77.91 = £93.37.$

Macaulay's duration = (5.56 /93.37)1.0 + (5.14 /93.37)2.0 + (4.76 /93.37)3.0 +
(77.91/93.37)4.0

= 0.06 + 0.11 + 0.15 + 3.34 = 3.66 years

(a) The holding period is 3.66 years. At the end of the holding period, the Macaulay's duration of the bond will be 0.34 years (i.e. the remaining period to maturity).

Modified duration = 0.34 /1.08 = 0.315

$\%\Delta P = -0.315 \times 1 = -0.315\%$ (−0.00315 as a decimal)

$£93.37 \times -0.00315 = -£0.294$

The prospective capital loss is £0.294.

$£6[(1.01)^{2.66} + (1.01)^{1.66} + (1.01)^{0.66} - 3] = £0.300.$

The additional interest from the reinvestment of coupons is £0.300.

It can be seen that the capital loss from the 1% rise in interest rates is approximately matched by the increase in interest receipts.

Duration matching is probably the easiest means of immunising a portfolio because of the facility of using bond futures to achieve the requisite adjustments. Any discrepancy between the duration of the liabilities (prospective cash outflows) and the duration of the bond portfolio can be removed by taking an offsetting position in bond futures.

Bond futures are commitments to trade bonds during a future month at a price agreed when taking the futures position. Futures positions make profits and losses as bond prices change. Futures thus have durations. Buying futures adds to a portfolio's duration, and selling futures reduces the portfolio's duration. Since futures positions cost nothing to establish (the only initial cash outlay is a returnable deposit known as initial margin), they provide an easy and cash efficient means of altering the duration of a portfolio.

Discussion questions

How can bond price volatility be measured? What is the purpose of making such measurements?

Chapter 29

Bond price convexity

After studying this chapter readers should be able to:

- *appreciate the nature and significance of convexity*
- *understand why convexity has value.*

The problem of convexity

Money duration merely provides an approximation to the relationship between yield changes and bond price movements. This is illustrated by Figure 29.1 which shows the price/yield relationship for a bond together with a straight line representing money duration.

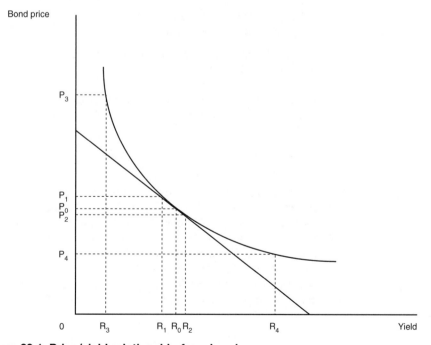

Figure 29.1 Price/yield relationship for a bond

It can be seen from Figure 29.1 that for small changes in yield, such as R_0 to R_1 or R_0 to R_2, the price change indicated by money duration along the straight line is a fair approximation to the actual price change as shown by the curved price/yield relationship. However, for large yield changes, such as R_0 to R_3 or R_0 to R_4, the money duration line provides a poor estimate of the actual price change. Money duration underestimates price rises and overestimates falls. In both cases the new bond price is underestimated. The inaccuracies arise because money duration fails to take account of the convexity (curvature) of the actual price/yield relationship of a bond.

Exercise 29.1

It is 24 November 1992. Treasury 12% 1994 (which has just paid a coupon) has a final maturity date of 24 May 1994. The interest rate is 8% p.a.

Calculate (a) the Macaulay's duration, and (b) the modified duration of the gilt. (c) What capital gain or loss would arise from a holding of £1 million nominal of this gilt in the event of a ¼% p.a. fall in interest rates? Comment on the accuracy of this estimate of capital gain or loss.

Answers

The fair price of the bond would be:
$$P = £6/(1.04) + £6/(1.04)^2 + £106/(1.04)^3$$
$$= £5.77 + £5.55 + £94.23 = £105.55$$

(a) The Macaulay's duration of the bond would be:
$$D = (£5.77/£105.55)\,0.5 + (£5.55/£105.55)\,1.0 + (£94.23/£105.55)1.5$$
$$= 0.0273 + 0.0526 + 1.3391 = 1.419$$
$$= 1.42 \text{ years (to 2 decimal places)}$$

(b) The modified duration (on the assumption that coupons are paid twice a year) would be:
$$M = 1.419/1.04 = 1.3644$$
$$= 1.36 \text{ (to 2 decimal places)}$$
The value of £1 million nominal of the gilt would be:
$$£1,000,000 \times £105.55/£100 = £1,055,500$$

(c) The capital gain would be calculated from:
% change in bond price $= -$modified duration $\times$ change in redemption yield
$$= -1.36 \times -0.25 = 0.34\%$$

So the capital gain would be 0.0034 × £1,055,500 = £3,588.7. Hence the new value of the bonds should be £1,055,500 + £3,588.7 = £1,059,088.7.

It is to be noted that £6/(1.03875) + £6/(1.03875)² + £106/(1.03875)³ = £5.7762 + £5.5607 + £94.5742 = £105.9111. Hence, according to the discount model, the new value of the bonds should be £1,059,111. So the modified duration approach predicts the new value of the bonds very closely – the error is less than £23.

Modified duration does not provide a precisely accurate answer since it assumes a linear price-yield relationship, whereas the relationship is actually convex.

Exercise 29.2

A bond has just paid a six-monthly coupon of £4. There are four more coupons to be paid by maturity. How accurate is modified duration for the purpose of estimating the effect of an (a) 0.2% p.a., and (b) 1% p.a., decrease in the redemption yield on the bond price, when redemption yields are initially 2% p.a? Comment on the results of the calculations.

Answers

(a) With a redemption yield of 2% p.a., the fair price of the bond would be:

£4/(1.01) + £4/(1.01)^2 + £4/(1.01)^3 + £104/(1.01)^4 = £3.96 + £3.92 + £3.88 + £99.94 = £111.70

Macaulay's duration is:

(3.96/111.7)0.5 + (3.92/111.7)1.0 + (3.88/111.7)1.5 + (99.94/111.7)2.0 = 0.018 + 0.035 + 0.052 + 1.789 = 1.894

Modified duration is:

1.894/(1.01) = 1.875

A fall in the redemption yield of 0.2% implies a price rise of 0.375%. (%ΔP= −1.875 × −0.2% = 0.375%)

The new bond price is estimated to be £111.70 × 1.00375 = £112.12

The dividend discount model predicts a new price of:

£4/(1.009) + £4/(1.009)^2 + £4/(1.009)^3 + £104/(1.009)^4 = £3.96 + £3.93 + £3.89 + £100.34 = £112.12

(0.009 is based on a six-month interest rate of 2% − 0.2% = 1.8% p.a.)

The estimate based on modified duration is very accurate.

(b) A fall in the redemption yield of 1% implies an estimated price rise of:

−1.875 × −1% = 1.875%

Therefore modified duration indicates a new price of £111.70 × 1.01875 = £113.79.

The dividend discount model shows a new price of:

£4/(1.005) + £4/(1.005)^2 + £4/(1.005)^3 + £104/(1.005)^4 = £3.98 + £3.96 + £3.94 + £101.95 = £113.83.

(0.005 is based on a six-month interest rate of 2% − 1% = 1% p.a.)

Modified duration underestimates the extent of the bond price rise when the interest rate (redemption yield) change is large. This error arises because of convexity.

The value of convexity

Two bonds with identical durations, prices and yields may have different convexities. In Figure 29.2 the curve A shows the price/yield relationship for bond A and curve B does so for bond B. It can be seen that bond B has greater convexity (curvature) than bond A. This gives bond B an advantage over bond A. Changes in yield from R_0, in either direction, raise the price of B relative to that of A. This renders B preferable to A, especially if high volatility is expected. This should entail B selling at a higher price, and hence lower yield, compared with A. It is unlikely that a situation, in which the bonds have identical prices and yields, will persist.

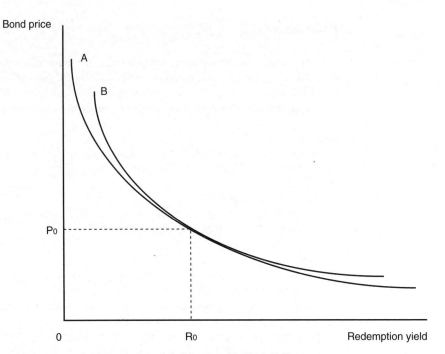

Figure 29.2 Price/yield relationships for bonds A and B

Chapter 30

Yield curves, bond portfolios and mortgages

After studying this chapter readers should be able to:

- *understand the principles of bond portfolio construction*

- *appreciate the nature of yield curves*

- *use yield curves to ascertain market expectations of future interest rates*

- *understand the nature of bond index (tracker) funds.*

The construction of bond portfolios

The construction of a bond portfolio is frequently based on taking a view with respect to interest rates. If interest rates are expected to fall, so that bond prices are expected to rise, a portfolio with a relatively high duration would be constructed. Conversely, an expectation of a rise in interest rates would entail a portfolio with low duration so that potential losses are reduced.

It is not just duration that a bond portfolio manager needs to be concerned with. Convexity has value in that it leads to higher bond prices following interest rate movements (when compared with an investment with zero convexity). High convexity bonds provide this benefit to a greater extent than low convexity bonds. The benefits of convexity are greater when interest changes are relatively large. This implies that the portfolio manager needs to consider the prospective size of interest rate movement as well as the direction.

A bond with high convexity will tend to have a relatively low redemption yield. The advantage bestowed by high convexity would be offset by a lower prospective yield. If interest rate movements are small, the gains from convexity would not compensate for the low yield. So if a portfolio manager expects a small interest rate change, bonds with low convexity should be chosen. If the expectation is that there will be a substantial interest rate movement, high convexity bonds should be chosen.

The portfolio manager also needs to take account of any change in the slope of the yield curve that will accompany a change in the level of interest rates. The yield curve is the relationship between redemption yield and the maturity of a bond. The most common shape is an upward slope depicting a tendency for yields to rise as maturity increases. If a portfolio manager expects the slope to change, the portfolio should be adjusted accordingly.

The effects of a change in slope can be seen by considering two possible portfolio constructions. These constructions are known as a bullet portfolio and a barbell portfolio. A bullet portfolio uses bonds of a single maturity, for example ten years. A barbell portfolio focuses on two maturities, for example five years and twenty years. The two portfolios may have identical money durations but exhibit very different responses to a change in the slope of the yield curve. A steepening of the yield curve would be to the disadvantage of the barbell portfolio relative to the bullet portfolio.

A steepening of the yield curve involves yields on distant maturity bonds rising relative to those on short term bonds. For a barbell portfolio, the interest rate rise impacts (negatively) on the bonds that are most sensitive to interest rate changes whereas the interest rate fall (positively) affects the bonds that are less sensitive to interest rate movements. So a steepening of the yield curve tends to disadvantage barbell portfolios. Conversely, a flattening of the yield curve (long-term yields falling and short-term yields rising) is to the advantage of a barbell portfolio.

Yield curves

A yield curve shows the relationship between the redemption yields of (interest rates on) bonds and the maturities of those bonds. Figure 30.1 illustrates three possible shapes of the yield curve. These are not the only possible shapes. The number of possible yield curve patterns (alternatively known as the term structure of interest rates) is infinite.

On the far left of the yield curve the investments are very short-term deposits that can be withdrawn without notice, or with just a few days' notice. On the far right the investments have very distant maturities, for example 25-year government bonds.

The most common yield curve pattern is for yields (interest rates) to rise with increasing maturity but for the rate of increase to diminish. The diminishing rate of increase implies that, for distant maturities, increases in maturity entail little or no increment to yields. The yield curve labelled 'normal' illustrates this pattern.

The yield curve sometimes exhibits a downward slope, as illustrated by the curve labelled 'inverted'. The flat yield curve shows a situation in which interest rates are the same irrespective of the length of time for which money is invested, such a situation is extremely unusual.

Explanations of the term structure of interest rates, and hence the shape of the yield curve, can be divided into three theories: pure expectations, expectations with risk premium and market segmentation. According to the pure expectations approach, long-term interest rates can be seen as averages (geometric means) of spot and expected future short-term interest rates. So, for example, the 12-month interest rate would be an average of the current three-month rate and the expected

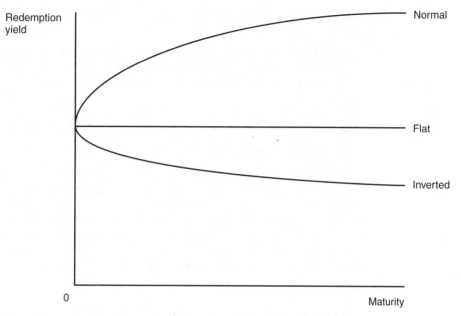

Figure 30.1 Three possible shapes of the yield curve

rates for each of the subsequent three three-month periods. Likewise the five-year interest rate would be an average of the current one-year rate and the expected rates for each of the subsequent four years.

Suppose that the spot (current) one-year interest rate is 10% p.a. and the expected rate for the following year is 12% p.a. The current two-year interest rate should be the geometric mean of these two rates.

$$\sqrt{(1.1)(1.12)} = \sqrt{1.232} = 1.11 \tag{1}$$

The two-year rate is $1.11 - 1 = 0.11$ as a decimal, which is 11% p.a. as a percentage. The two-year rate is the rate which when compounded over two years gives the same final value as 10% in one year compounded with 12% in the following year. According to the pure expectations theory, investors should have no preference between the alternative of investing at 11% p.a. for two years and the other alternative of investing for one year at 10% p.a. while anticipating investment of the proceeds for a further year at 12% p.a.

If the pure expectations theory is an accurate explanation of the level of long-term interest rates, it is possible to infer market expectations of future interest rates from the yield curve. The implied future interest rates are referred to as forward interest rates.

In the previous example, an investor knowing that the one-year rate is 10% p.a. and the two-year rate is 11% p.a. could deduce that the one-year rate expected to be available one year from now is 12% p.a. The forward interest rate is the rate which, when compounded on the one-year rate of 10% p.a., produces the same sum as 11% p.a. compounded over two years.

Exercise 30.1

The current three-month interest rate is 11% p.a. and the market expectations of the next seven three-month rates are 11%, 11%, 10%, 10%, 10%, 9% and 9% p.a. What, according to the pure expectations theory, should the current two-year rate be?

Answer
$\sqrt{(1.0275)^3(1.025)^3(1.0225)^2} - 1 = \sqrt{1.22136} - 1 = 1.1052 - 1 = 0.1052$

As a percentage this is 10.52% p.a.

Since the interest rates are three-month rates, the annual rates need to be divided by four (three-months being treated as a quarter of a year). So, for example, 11% p.a. is 2.75% over three months. The eight three-month returns are compounded on one another to obtain the value of the investment at the end of the two years, which is 1.22136. Since interest rates are always expressed on a per annum (per year) basis, the square root of the final sum is taken. The square root shows the per annum rate which when compounded over two years produces the final sum of 1.22136.

Exercise 30.2

If the two-year interest rate is 10.5% p.a. and the one-year rate is 9.5% p.a., what does the market expect the one-year interest rate to be a year from now?

Answer
$(1.105)^2/1.095 = 1.1151$

$(1.1151 - 1) \times 100 = 11.51\%$ p.a.

The pure expectations approach assumes that investors are indifferent between investing for a long period on the one hand and investing for a shorter period with a view to reinvesting the principal plus interest on the other hand. For example, an investor would have no preference between making a 12-month deposit and making a 6-month deposit with a view to reinvesting the proceeds for a further six months so long as the expected interest receipts are the same. This is equivalent to saying that the pure expectations approach assumes that investors treat alternative maturities as perfect substitutes for one another.

The pure expectations model assumes that investors are risk neutral. A risk neutral investor is not concerned about the possibility that interest rate expectations will not prove to be correct so long as potential favourable deviations from expectations are as likely as unfavourable ones. Risk in itself is not regarded negatively. Most people are not risk neutral, they are risk averse – they dislike risk. Risk averse investors are prepared to forgo some investment return in order to achieve greater certainty in regard to the value of investments and the income from them. As a result of risk aversion, investors may not be indifferent between alternative maturities. Attitudes to risk may generate preferences for either short or long maturities.

If such is the case, the term structure of interest rates (the yield curve) will reflect risk premiums.

If an investment is close to maturity, there is little risk of capital loss arising from interest rate changes. A bond with a distant maturity (long duration) would suffer considerable capital loss in the event of a large rise in interest rates. The risk of such losses is known as capital risk. To compensate for the risk that capital losses might be realised on long-term investments, investors may require a risk premium on such investments. A risk premium is an addition to the interest or yield to compensate investors for accepting risk. This tends to impart an upward slope to a yield curve. This tendency towards an upward slope is likely to be reinforced by the preference of many borrowers to borrow for long periods (rather than borrowing for a succession of short periods). Such borrowers may be willing to pay an interest premium for the facility of borrowing long term.

There is a form of risk that would tend to have the opposite effect on the slope of a yield curve: this is known as income risk. Some investors may prefer long maturity investments because they provide greater certainty of income flows. For example, a conventional UK government bond pays a constant coupon every six months until the bond reaches its redemption date. On the other hand, interest receipts from bank deposits can change frequently. Income flows from a bank deposit are very uncertain. This uncertainty is income risk.

If investors have a preference for predictability of interest receipts, they may require a higher rate of interest on short-term investments to compensate for income risk. This would tend to cause the yield curve to be inverted (downward sloping).

The effects on the slope of the yield curve from factors such as capital risk and income risk are in addition to the effect of expectations of future short-term interest rates. If money market participants expect short-term interest rates to rise, the yield curve would tend to be upward sloping. If the effect of capital risk is greater than the effect of income risk, the upward slope would be steeper as a result. If market expectations are that short-term interest rates will fall in the future, the yield curve would tend to be downward sloping. A dominance of capital risk aversion over income risk aversion would render the downward slope less steep (or possibly turn a downward slope into an upward slope).

The third theory of the term structure of interest rates is the market segmentation approach, according to which interest rates for different maturities are determined independently of one another. That is, investors (and borrowers) do not consider successions of short-term investments (or borrowings) as substitutes for long-term ones. The interest rate for short maturities is determined by the supply of and demand for short-term funds. Long-term interest rates are those that equate the sums that investors wish to lend long term with the amount that borrowers are seeking.

A variation on the market segmentation theme is the preferred habitat hypothesis. This is less extreme than the market segmentation theory since it allows for some substitutability between maturities. However, the preferred habitat view sees substitutability as being less than perfect so that interest premiums are needed to entice investors from their preferred maturities to other maturities.

Forward interest rates and expected future interest rates

The manager of a portfolio of bonds may make changes to the portfolio in the light of that manager's expectations of future interest rates. The expectations that are relevant to investment decisions are expectations relative to market expectations. An active portfolio manager bases investment decisions on attempts to forecast interest rates more accurately than the average participant in the money market. For this reason the manager of an actively managed bond portfolio needs to be able to ascertain the market consensus forecast. Such market expectations can be deduced from forward interest rates.

Forward interest rates are rates for periods commencing at points of time in the future. They are implied by current rates for differing maturities. For example, the current three-month interest rate and the current six-month interest rate between them imply a rate for a three-month period which runs from a point in time three months from the present until a point in time six months hence.

The forward three-month rate for a period commencing three months from the present is the rate that would yield the same return as the current six-month rate, when compounded on the current three-month rate. For example, if the three-month rate is 9% p.a. and the six-month rate 10% p.a., the forward rate is shown as x in equation 2.

$$(1.0225)(1 + x) = 1.05 \qquad\qquad (2)$$

0.0225 is the decimal rate for three months based on 9% p.a. (2.25% over a quarter of a year is obtained by taking a quarter of 9%) and 0.05 is the decimal rate for six months based on 10% p.a. The forward rate is calculated as:

$$x = (1.05/1.0225) - 1 = 0.0269$$

which is 2.69% over three months and hence 10.76% p.a. (multiplying 2.69% by four).

The forward rate can be interpreted as the market expectation of the future interest rate under specific circumstances. These circumstances are (i) the expectations theory of the yield curve is correct and (ii) there is no risk premium. If the expectations theory is seen as a good model but a risk premium is thought to be present, an adjustment is required to remove the effects of the risk premium before the result can be interpreted as the market forecast of the future interest rate. This is illustrated in Exercise 30.3.

Exercise 30.3

The one-year interest rate is 6.5% p.a. and the six-month interest rate is 6% p.a. What is the forward six-month interest rate for the period between six months and one year from now? Can this forward interest rate be taken to be the interest rate expected by money market participants?

Answer
Let x be the forward interest rate.
$(1.03)(1 + x/2) = (1.065)$
$1 + x/2 = (1.065)/(1.03)$
$x = 2\{ [(1.065)/(1.03)] - 1\}$
Therefore $x = 0.068 = 6.8\%$ p.a.

The forward interest rate of 6.8% p.a. can be taken to be the market expectation if (i) the expectations theory of the yield curve is correct and (ii) there is no risk premium. If the expectations theory is correct but there is a risk premium, the risk premium must be removed before carrying out the calculation. Suppose that the six-month rate contains no risk premium but the one-year rate contains a risk premium of 0.1% p.a. The one-year interest rate, net of the risk premium, is 6.4% p.a. The new calculation would be as follows:

$(1.03)(1 + x/2) = (1.064)$
$x = 2\{[(1.064)/(1.03)] - 1\}$
Therefore $x = 0.066 = 6.6\%$ p.a.

Bond index (tracker) funds

Bond index funds attempt to construct portfolios that replicate the performance of a bond index. The performance to be tracked is total return which comprises coupons, capital gains (or losses) and interest on reinvested coupons. Differences between the performance of an index and that of an index portfolio are referred to as tracking error.

Tracking error has three sources. First, there is tracking error resulting from a mismatch between the bonds in the portfolio and the bonds in the index. Second, there may be differences between the bond prices used for calculating an index and those available to a portfolio manager. Third, a portfolio manager faces transaction costs whereas the constructor of an index does not.

The first two sources of deviation can be either advantageous or disadvantageous to a portfolio manager. Transaction costs are always disadvantageous. There is a trade-off between tracking error arising from mismatches and the error from transaction costs. Attempts to precisely replicate the contents of an index may entail a large number of relatively small transactions. This is expensive in terms of transaction costs. On the other hand, use of a smaller sample of bonds to represent an index increases deviations arising from mismatches between the index and the index portfolio. The reduction in transaction costs incurs increased mismatch error.

Exercise 30.4

Zero coupon bonds with maturities one, two and three years from the present have prices of £95, £88 and £80 respectively.

(a) What are the spot one, two and three-year interest rates?

(b) Draw the yield curve.

(c) What is the two-year forward interest rate for the period from one year hence to three years from the present?

Answers

(a) £100/£95 = 1.0526 which implies a spot one-year interest rate of 5.26%.

£100/£88 = 1.13636

$\sqrt{1.13636}$ = 1.0660 which implies a spot two-year interest rate of 6.60% p.a.

£100/£80 = 1.25

$1.25^{0.33}$ = 1.0772 which implies a spot three-year interest rate of 7.72% p.a.

(b) This is known as the spot (or zero coupon) yield curve (Figure 30.2). It is regarded as more informative than a yield curve that relates redemption yields to bond maturities because it is unambiguous. Yield curves that relate redemption yields of coupon bearing bonds to maturities involve ambiguities since each coupon represents a maturity, so the redemption date is not the only maturity date. Coupon bearing bonds may have differing redemption yields, despite having common redemption dates, because of differences in the coupon payments.

(c) 1.25/1.0526 = 1.18754

$\sqrt{1.18754}$ = 1.0897

1.0897 − 1 = 0.0897 i.e. 8.97% p.a.

The expected two-year rate for the period beginning one year from the present is 8.97% p.a.

Since it is unlikely that perfect replication of an index in terms of specific bonds and precise proportions is practical in terms of transaction costs, a representative sample of bonds would normally be used. One approach to obtaining a representative sample is the cell, or stratified sampling, approach. Each cell contains its own combination of characteristics, and the portfolio manager ensures that all the important cells are reflected in the chosen sample.

For example, the relevant characteristics might be duration (e.g. above five years versus below five years), coupon (e.g. above 5% versus below 5%) and sector (e.g. government versus corporate). This produces eight cells (one would be short duration, low coupon, government and another would be long duration, low coupon, corporate and so on). The portfolio manager might attempt to hold at least one bond with the characteristics of each cell. The relative importance of each cell in the index would be reflected in the value of bonds allocated to the cell.

There are hybrid funds that have characteristics of both index funds and actively managed funds. Enhanced index funds allow limited deviation from the index in an attempt to outperform the index. Closet trackers are actively managed funds that use part of the fund to track an index. Managers of closet trackers seek to avoid

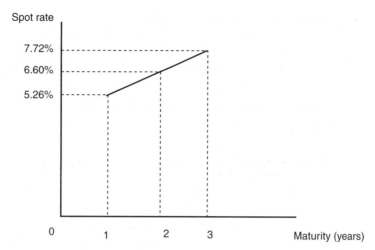

Figure 30.2 Spot yield curve

the risk of substantially underperforming the index and of thereby being low in league tables of fund managers.

Mortgages

Mortgages are debts secured by property. They are often used for the purchase of homes. The borrower borrows for a period, such as twenty-five years. The borrower undertakes to make periodic, typically monthly, repayments to the lender. If the borrower fails to maintain the payments, the lender has the legal right to take the property by which the mortgage is secured.

Mortgages in the United Kingdom can be financed on either a repayment or an endowment basis. Repayment mortgages entail monthly payments that cover both interest and debt reduction. If the interest rate were constant for the full period of the mortgage, the monthly payments would also be constant. With variable-rate mortgages the monthly payment will change as interest rates change. In the UK most mortgages are variable rate.

In the early years of a mortgage term most of the monthly payment reflects interest on the debt, with relatively little being left over for reducing the size of the debt. In later years, when part of the debt has been repaid by means of these monthly sums and interest costs have thereby been reduced, more of the monthly payment is available for reducing the debt. Towards the end of the mortgage term, the outstanding debt will have been significantly reduced with the result that interest is a smaller portion of the payments. As a mortgage term nears its end, most of the monthly sum is used for debt reduction (capital repayment).

Endowment mortgages entail none of the debt being repaid until the mortgage matures. The borrower pays interest on the entire sum borrowed throughout the period of the mortgage. In addition the borrower makes monthly contributions to an endowment fund operated by an insurance company. The intention is that, at maturity, the accumulated endowment fund will be sufficient to pay off the mortgage debt. However there is a risk that the accumulated sum will not be sufficient (there is also the possibility that it will be more than sufficient with the effect that there is a lump sum available to the borrower in addition to what is required to repay the mortgage).

Characteristics of repayment mortgages

The nature of repayment mortgages has implications for the pattern of interest and principal payments on the part of the borrower. The characteristics of the repayment process can be seen by demonstrating the effects of differing interest rates and terms to maturity on the monthly payments, the total interest paid and the rate at which the mortgage debt is reduced.

Characteristic 1. The monthly repayments increase as the interest rate rises, but not proportionately. For example, at 5% p.a. a £100,000 15-year mortgage will cost £790 per month. At 10% p.a. the same mortgage would cost £1,075 per month. A doubling of the interest rate entails a 36% increase in the monthly payment. The absence of proportionality can be explained in terms of the higher monthly payments reducing the mortgage debt more rapidly in the later years. In consequence less of the debt needs to be paid off in the early years. Also the total debt repayment is not affected by interest rates.

Characteristic 2. A reduction in the term of a mortgage increases the monthly payments, but not proportionately. For example, a £100,000 30-year mortgage at 5% p.a. entails a monthly payment of £536 whereas an equivalent 15-year mortgage involves payments of £790 a month. Halving the period of the mortgage causes a 47% increase in the monthly payments. The absence of proportionality can be explained in terms of the reduced cumulative interest payment resulting from the faster repayment of the mortgage debt.

Characteristic 3. The cumulative interest payments increase more than proportionately with the term of the mortgage. For example, with an interest rate of 5% p.a. a £100,000 15-year mortgage would entail cumulative interest payments of £42,342 whereas an equivalent 30-year mortgage involves total interest costs of £89,493. Raising the term of the mortgage by 100% increases the total interest payments by 111%. This can be explained in terms of the lower debt repayments in the early years, in the case of the 30-year mortgage, and the resulting higher interest costs together with the longer period over which interest is payable.

Characteristic 4. The cumulative interest payments are larger with higher interest rates and they rise more than proportionately. A 25-year £100,000 mortgage at 5% p.a. entails total interest payments of £75,377. An equivalent mortgage with a 10% p.a. interest rate would involve total interest payments of £172,610. This can be explained in terms of less of the capital being paid off in the early years when the interest rate is higher. Not only is the interest rate higher, so is the average size of the mortgage debt.

Characteristic 5. The time taken to repay half the mortgage debt will here be referred to as the half-life of the mortgage. The relationship between interest rates and the half-life of a mortgage is that the half-life rises with increases in the interest rate, but the rise is less than proportional. At 5% p.a. a 25-year £100,000 mortgage has a half-life of 16 years, 2 months (i.e. 194 months). At 10% p.a. the half-life is 18 years, 10 months (i.e. 226 months). With the higher interest rate less of the debt is repaid in the early years.

Characteristic 6. The half-life of a mortgage rises with increases in the term of the mortgage and the increase in the half-life is more than proportional to the increase in the term of the mortgage. A 15-year £100,000 mortgage at 5% p.a. will have a half-life of 8 years, 10 months (i.e. 106 months). An equivalent mortgage with a term of 30 years would have a half-life of 20 years, 2 months (i.e. 242 months).

Fixed-rate mortgages

It is often possible to obtain mortgages on which the interest rate is fixed for a period of time, for example five years. Theories of the term structure of interest rates throw light on such products, including the advantages and disadvantages.

The starting point is the pure expectations theory of the term structure. This suggests that long-term interest rates are averages of expected future short-term interest rates. For example, the interest rate for a five-year loan would be the average of the next five one-year rates. There would be no expected difference between (a) borrowing for five years and (b) borrowing for one year with a view to renewing the borrowing at the end of the year (and renewing on the next three anniversaries). The word *expected* is important here since future interest rates are uncertain.

On this view the advantage of the fixed-rate mortgage is that it provides certainty of interest rate costs over the period of the loan, not that it entails an advantageous interest rate. The interest rate payable matches the expected average rate to be paid on a variable-rate mortgage. At the end of the five years the fixed rate would have proven to be either higher or lower than the corresponding average variable rate. However, at the beginning of the period there is no way of knowing which would be the case. The expected rate is in the middle of a range of possibilities.

The expected future interest rates are those that are anticipated by money market participants (for example banks). The likelihood of an individual borrower (or adviser) being able to produce a superior forecast of future interest rates is, at best, very remote. Interest rates are notoriously difficult to forecast, and the best advice is not to try. The choice between fixed- and variable-rate mortgages should not be made on the basis of whether the borrower believes that interest rates will be higher or lower than the fixed rate. The borrower should also be aware that making the choice on the basis of whether the fixed rate is higher or lower than the current variable rate involves an implicit forecast of interest rates. The implicit forecast is that interest rates will remain unchanged.

A decision to take out a fixed-rate mortgage should be based on the value of the certainty that the fixed rate provides. The borrower with a fixed rate avoids the risk that interest rates will rise to the extent that repayments cease to be affordable. Unfortunately nothing in financial markets is free, and that is true for the avoidance of risk. The borrower must expect to pay for the reduction of risk. This relates to an extension of the pure expectations theory of the term structure of interest rates. The principle of expectations with risk premium says that long-term interest rates equal the average of the expected future short-term rates plus a risk premium. The risk premium is an addition to the interest rate to reflect the higher risk (and lower liquidity) faced by the lender.

This point can be elaborated by considering how the lender (bank or building society) obtains the money to be lent to the borrower. The bank might borrow money for five years by selling five-year bonds in the money markets. The rate of interest payable on the bonds will determine the fixed rate that the bank will charge its customers. Investors in five-year bonds face more risk than investors in shorter-term assets; an increase in interest rates would reduce the market value of the bonds. To compensate for this extra risk the investors would require extra interest, that is a risk premium. So the bank has to pay a risk premium and this will be passed on to borrowers in the form of higher interest rates. So fixed-rate borrowers should expect to pay extra interest for the increased certainty about the interest rates payable. Fixed-rate borrowers should expect to pay the average of expected future variable interest rates plus a risk premium.

Consideration of how banks and building societies raise funds for the provision of fixed-rate mortgages also explains why early redemption penalties are often imposed. Often borrowers with fixed-rate mortgages want to change to a variable rate when interest rates fall. However, the provider has borrowed on a fixed-rate basis and is committed to continue to pay the fixed rate. Early termination of the mortgage would leave the bank or building society paying the high rate of interest, and making a loss in doing so since the money must now be lent at the lower interest rate. The mortgage provider would therefore expect compensation for this loss from the borrower. A borrower needs to realise that the interest rate certainty provided by a fixed-rate mortgage involves a guarantee that precludes advantageous interest rate movements as well as adverse ones. A cost of avoiding rises is the loss of potential falls.

A mortgage that protects against interest rate rises while allowing rates to fall is known as a capped mortgage. Capped mortgages contain an interest rate option that must be paid for (in the same way that insurance policies have to be paid for).

Capped-rate mortgages

A capped mortgage sets an upper limit to the variable interest rate to be paid without setting a lower limit. The borrower avoids very high interest rates but is not committed to a fixed rate. The bank or building society offering such a mortgage buys an interest rate option from an options dealer.

An interest rate option (or cap) will compensate for an interest rise above a particular level. The seller of the option undertakes to pay the interest difference if the rate goes above a particular level. The bank or building society thus has an upper limit to its interest payments, and is thus able to pass an upper limit on to its customers.

The seller of the option takes on a risk. If interest rates rise the bank or building society receives payments from the provider of the option, but if rates fall there are no payments to the option dealer. The seller of the option has potential losses but no prospective gains. The dealer will therefore require payment for the option. This payment will reflect the potential for loss.

So the bank or building society must pay for the option. It will pass the cost on to the ultimate beneficiary of the interest rate cap, that is the borrower. This cost will be reflected in an addition to the interest rate that the borrower pays. If the borrower makes an early withdrawal from the mortgage agreement, the lender may not have fully recouped the price of the option from the additional interest payments. The bank or building society may seek a cash payment from the borrower to compensate for the unpaid portion of the cost of the option. If a borrower insures against interest rate rises, the insurance has to be paid for irrespective of whether the insurance subsequently turns out to be required.

Other forms of mortgage

Discounted-rate mortgages allow a percentage deduction from the standard variable interest rate during the first few years of the mortgage. This appears to be a marketing device aimed at attracting business to the mortgage provider.

A related product is the Graduated-payment mortgage. This differs from the Discounted-rate mortgage in that the low rates of the early years are combined with higher than normal rates in later years. When Graduated-payment mortgages were introduced in the UK there were protests (supported by sections of the media) from mortgage holders who found that they had signed contracts that allowed them out of relatively high interest rates only at the cost of financial penalties. Graduated-payment mortgages were effectively abandoned in the UK as a result of the adverse publicity surrounding them. The fact that some people could not understand them resulted in no one having access to them. This lack of borrower (and media) sophistication in the UK may be the reason why other types of mortgage popular in North America have not been introduced in the UK.

Two of these other types are balloon mortgages and shared-appreciation mortgages. Balloon mortgages may allow interest-only payments for a few years, after which the Balloon mortgage is repaid by taking out a conventional mortgage. Shared-appreciation mortgages entail the lender charging reduced interest rates in return for a share of any capital gains arising from increases in the value of the property.

The mortgage and endowment equations

A repayment mortgage entails an initial sum (debt) which is paid off over a succession of ensuing time periods. The equation showing the periodic (e.g. monthly) payments to be made under a repayment mortgage agreement is:

$$p = \frac{M \times r}{1 - [1/(1+r)^T]}$$

where
$\begin{aligned} p &= \text{periodic payment} \\ M &= \text{initial size of mortgage} \\ r &= \text{periodic interest rate (annual interest rate/number of payments per year)} \\ T &= \text{number of payments (e.g. number of months to maturity).} \end{aligned}$

An endowment is the reverse of a mortgage: it involves a series of payments into a fund that result in a sum at the end of the term. An endowment mortgage involves paying interest only on the mortgage debt, which is paid off at maturity from the proceeds of an endowment policy. The equation for an endowment is:

$$M = p[(1+y)^T - 1]/y$$

where
$\begin{aligned} M &= \text{sum to be accumulated} \\ p &= \text{periodic payment} \\ y &= \text{rate of return on the endowment fund.} \end{aligned}$

The question as to whether an endowment policy will produce a sufficient sum to repay a mortgage rests on the rate of return on the endowment fund. If the rate of return on the endowment equals the rate of interest on the mortgage, the endowment and repayment mortgages will be identical in terms of the size of the periodic payments. This is illustrated by Example 30.1. If the rate of return on the endowment is higher than the mortgage interest rate, the endowment mortgage will be the cheaper (or will provide more than enough to pay off the mortgage). If the rate of return on the endowment is lower than the mortgage interest rate, the endowment mortgage will entail the higher monthly payments (or will provide insufficient funds to redeem the mortgage at maturity). Since endowment policies are typically based on stock market investments the relative performance of the two types of mortgage depends upon whether stock market returns (net of the charges on an endowment policy) exceed, or fall short of, mortgage interest rates. History suggests that holders of endowment mortgages would normally be better off, but they bear more risk.

Example 30.1(a): Endowment mortgage

An endowment policy can be used to pay off a mortgage debt. For example if returns on an endowment are 10% p.a., an annual payment of £16,380 into an endowment will be worth £100,000 in five years. This can be used to repay a £100,000 debt. An endowment mortgage involves paying interest on the £100,000 debt each year. If interest rates are 10% p.a., this amounts to £10,000 p.a. So the total annual payment is £16,380 + £10,000 = £26,380.

Example 30.1(b): Repayment mortgage

Repayment mortgages involve amortising the debt (gradually paying it off).

Table 30.1 Mortgage repayment schedule on a £100,000 five-year debt with interest fixed at 10% p.a.

Year	Interest	Repayment	Remaining debt
1	£10,000	£16,380	£83,620
2	£8,362	£18,018	£65,602
3	£6,560	£19,820	£45,782
4	£4,578	£21,802	£23,980
5	£2,398	£23,982	−£2

There is a constant payment of £26,380 each year. The £2 surplus arises because of rounding to the nearest pound.

Exercise 30.5

(a) A repayment mortgage of £100,000 is to be paid off in equal monthly instalments over 25 years. What are the monthly mortgage payments at a constant interest rate of 6% p.a.?

(b) Someone is planning to accumulate £250,000 over 40 years. What is the required annual contribution to the endowment fund if the rate of return on the fund is 5% p.a.?

Answers

(a) $p = M/ [\{1 - (1+r)^{-T}\} / r]$
$p = 100{,}000/ [\{1 - (1.005)^{-300}\} / 0.005]$
$p = £644.30$

(b) $M = p [(1+y)^{T} - 1] / y$
$250{,}000 = p [(1.05)^{40} - 1] / 0.05$
$250{,}000 = p \times 120.8$
$p = 250{,}000 / 120.8 = 2069.54$

The required annual contribution is £2,069.54

Glossary

Acceptance By accepting a bill issued by a company a bank guarantees that it will be honoured.

Accrued interest The interest earned since the last payment on a bond. This amount is paid to a seller of a bond.

Accumulation unit/share Units in a unit trust (or shares in an OEIC) where the income is automatically re-invested.

Active investment management Fund management that entails stock selection and/or market timing in an attempt to outperform the market.

Additional voluntary contributions (AVCs) Pension contributions by an individual that are additional to the main scheme contributions.

ADR (American depository receipt) When dealing in many of the big UK shares, American investors need not deal in London. Instead shares are left with US banks, while investors trade in ADRs which effectively give them the right to those shares should they want them.

Aggressive stocks High expected return/high risk stocks. They have betas greater than one.

American-style options Options that can be exercised prior to expiration.

Annual charge The annual management charge made by an investment manager.

Annuity A fund that provides an annual income, generally for retirement and most often for the life of the annuitant (the person who owns the annuity). Typically nothing accrues to the estate of the annuitant at death.

Arbitrage The exploitation of price anomalies for profit. For example, if prices for the same item differ between locations, the item may be bought relatively cheaply and sold at a higher price. Pure arbitrage involves no risk and no use of the arbitrager's own capital.

Ask price The price at which an investor can buy (also known as offer price).

Asset allocation The attempt to find a mix of asset classes (stocks, bonds, real estate, etc.) that best meets the needs of the investor.

At best An order to a stockbroker to deal at the best possible price rather than at a limit, getting the highest selling price or finding the lowest buying price.

Attainable set All possible portfolios that can be constructed from a given universe of securities.

Back-end load Also called a redemption charge, an exit fee or deferred sales charge, refers to a fee paid upon the redemption of unit trusts or OEICs.

Bank bill A bill of exchange accepted by a bank.

Basis point 1/100th of 1%.

Basket trade The trade of an entire portfolio of securities at one time.

Bear Someone who expects a fall in the prices of instruments such as stocks and bonds.

Bearer bond A bond that is not registered in a name. The rights to coupons and principal accrue to the holder.

Bed and breakfast Market practice of selling securities and buying them back to establish a profit or loss for capital gains tax purposes.

Beta A measure of the responsiveness of the price of an individual stock or portfolio to movements in stock prices as a whole.

Bid/offer spread Also known as bid/ask spread. The difference between the selling and buying prices of an investment.

Bid price The price at which an investor can sell to a market-maker.

Bid rate The rate of interest at which an investor can deposit money.

Big Bang The deregulation of London capital markets in 1986 which, among other things, permitted foreign ownership of British brokerage firms.

Bill of exchange A document which commits one company to pay a specific sum of money to another on a particular date.

Blue chip Blue chip companies are high-quality, financially strong companies that are leaders in industries that have been viable over some years.

Bond A security sold in order to raise capital. Bonds normally provide the buyer with a fixed income flow plus the return of the initial capital on the maturity date of the bond. Bonds are debts of the issuer.

Broker An intermediary that buys or sells on behalf of an investor.

Broker-dealer A broker that can deal on their own account as well as acting as an agent for clients.

Bull Someone who expects a rise in the price of an investment.

Bulldog bonds Sterling-denominated bonds issued in the United Kingdom by non-UK borrowers.

Call money A bank loan repayable on demand.

Call option The right to buy a financial instrument at a specific price during a period of time (or at a point in time).

Call provision A bond with a call provision allows the issuer to redeem the bond prior to maturity.

Capital gain (or loss) The change in value of an investment.

Capital gains tax Tax on the increase in the value of an investment.

Capital growth Increase in the value of an investment.

Capitalisation issue Also known as a scrip issue. A free issue of shares to shareholders in proportion to their existing holding. They should become no richer as a result, since the share price should fall proportionately.

Certificate of deposit (CD) A tradable instrument issued by a bank in return for a deposit. The maturity is normally short, for example three months.

Chartists Technical analysts who believe they can predict future price movements by analysing trends in past movements, hence their reliance upon charts.

Circuit breaker A price change limit and trading halt aimed at curbing the extent of price fluctuation.

Clearing house An institution that settles mutual indebtedness between organisations and which records trades (in the case of futures and options the clearing house also becomes the counter-party to contract holders).

Closely held shares Insider-owned shares that are not likely to be sold.

Closing price The price at the close of the market.

Commercial bill A bill issued by an organisation other than a government.

Commercial paper Unsecured bills or notes issued by companies for short-term borrowing.

Commission The fee charged by brokers, or financial advisers, for security transactions. Investors pay brokers' commissions directly, but normally pay financial advisers' commissions indirectly via the management fees charged by the investment management company.

Compound rate of return The average rate of return on an investment held for more than one period. It involves interest on interest. It is calculated as a geometric mean.

Conflicts of interest The potential that actions taken on one's own behalf are at the expense of a customer, as when an account executive owns a sizeable position in a particular security and issues an advisory to customers to buy that security.

Constant growth model Also known as the Gordon growth model. A special case of the dividend discount model in which expected growth in dividends is assumed to be constant.

Contrarian An approach to investing which is to buy into a market decline and sell into a market advance.

Conversion premium The price of a convertible security minus the conversion value. Frequently expressed as a percentage of the latter.

Conversion price The face value of a convertible security divided by the conversion ratio.

Conversion ratio The number of shares of stock for each convertible security.

Conversion value The value of a convertible security if converted now. The conversion value equals the conversion ratio times the market price of the stock (share price).

Convertible (bond) A bond that can be converted into a specified number of shares of stock at a point, or points, in time.

Convexity The difference between the actual percentage change in bond value due to a yield change and the approximate percentage change in bond value as measured by modified duration.

Corporate bond A bond issued by a company rather than by a government.

Coupon An interest payment on a bond or note.

Covered call Writing a call option on shares that are already held.

Cross-hedging The use of a futures on one underlying as a 'near substitute' for the asset that one really wishes to hedge.

Cum Latin for 'with'. A share quoted as 'cum' something will carry with it the rights to the forthcoming dividend, scrip issue, rights issue or whatever. If quoted 'ex' it will not carry those rights.

Cumulative preference shares Preference shares for which, if a dividend payment is missed, it must be made up before dividends may be paid to ordinary shareholders.

Currency account Bank account in a foreign currency.

Custodian A custodian, which is frequently a bank, looks after the assets of a fund.

Cyclical stocks Shares of companies whose earnings fluctuate with the business cycle.

Day order A limit order that is good only for the day on which it is placed.

Debenture Bond issued by a UK company and secured against assets of the company.

Debt ratio The ratio of long-term debt to the total capital of a company.

Default risk The risk that the issuer of a bond will not make its fixed payments.

Defined benefit Also known as final salary. A pension scheme in which the pension is based on final salary and number of years worked.

Defined contribution Also known as money purchase. A pension scheme in which contributions are paid into a fund whose eventual value determines the amount of the pension paid.

Delta The change in the price of an option due to a one pence change in the price of the stock underlying the option.

Deregulation Reduction in government control.

Derivatives For example, options, futures, swaps. Instruments whose prices are based upon, or derived from, the prices of other instruments, such as stocks, stock indices or bonds.

Direct quotation Quotation of an exchange rate in terms of a number of units of the domestic currency per unit of the foreign currency.

Discount Amount by which the current price falls below the redemption value of a security.

Discount rate The rate of interest used to convert a future value into a present value.

Discretionary management An investment service where the client gives an investment manager control over the management of the client's portfolio.

Disintermediation Flows of funds between borrowers and lenders (e.g. by bond sales) that do not involve the money passing through financial intermediaries such as banks.

Diversifiable risk Non-market or non-systematic risk that can be reduced through portfolio diversification.

Dividend The six-monthly or annual distribution to shareholders of part of the company's profits.

Dividend cover The number of times that the dividend could have been paid from a company's profits (i.e. profits/dividends).

Dividend discount model (DDM) A share price valuation model in which the value of a share is estimated as the present value of the dividends that can be expected from the share over the share's lifetime or horizon, which may be assumed to be infinite.

Dividend yield The annual dividend divided by the current price of the stock.

Dow Jones Industrial Average An American stock index covering 30 stocks.

Drop-lock bond A floating rate bond which automatically becomes a fixed rate bond in the event of interest rates falling below a particular level.

Dual-currency bonds Bonds that pay coupons in one currency and repay principal in another.

Dual-listed stocks Stocks listed on more than one stock exchange.

Duration Also known as Macaulay's duration. A measure of bond price volatility. Measured as the average time to the receipt of cash flows.

Dynamic portfolio insurance A strategy that attempts to protect the return on a portfolio by quickly pulling money out of asset markets that are performing poorly.

Earnings Net profit after tax due to holders of ordinary shares but not necessarily paid out to them. Earnings are usually expressed as so many pence per share.

Earnings yield A company's annual earnings per share, expressed as a percentage of the share's market price.

Efficient frontier All Markowitz-efficient portfolios shown in expected return/risk space.

Efficient market hypothesis (EMH) A view that asset prices respond quickly to new information and that all relevant information is incorporated into security prices by the time it reaches the investing public.

Enterprise investment scheme (EIS) EISs offer a range of tax reliefs to investors in small, mainly unquoted, companies.

Equities Ordinary shares (common stock) whose owners take the main risks and who are entitled to those profits left over after all prior charges have been met. They represent part ownership of a company.

Equity Represents ownership in a business.

Eurobonds Bonds issued in countries other than the country whose currency is being borrowed.

Eurocurrency Deposits and loans denominated in a currency other than that of the country in which the deposit is held or the loan is made.

Eurodollars US dollars held on deposit in a bank or bank branch outside of the United States.

European-style options Options that cannot be exercised prior to the expiration date.

Ex The opposite to cum, ex means 'without'. A price quoted 'ex dividend' will not carry the right to the next dividend. Similarly shares which are ex rights or ex scrip will exclude the rights to such distributions.

Exchange rate risk Also known as currency risk. It is the risk associated with a foreign investment in that the exchange rate may move against the investor.

Ex-dividend Anyone who acquires an ex-dividend stock will not receive the declared dividend.

Execution The implementation of an order to purchase or sell a security.

Execution-only With this type of service a stockbroker simply buys or sells at the investor's request, without offering any advice.

Exercise price Also known as the strike or striking price. The price at which the holder of an option has the right to buy or sell stock.

Exit charge A charge made if an investor sells an investment before holding it for a specified period.

Expected rate of return Also known as the required rate of return. It is the rate of return on an asset expected or required by investors.

Expiry date The last day on which an option can be exercised.

Extendible bond A bond that may be extended for a longer period at the holder's option, possibly at a higher interest rate.

Fee-based adviser A financial adviser who does not receive commission but charges the client a fee. Any commission is transferred to the client.

Fill-or-kill order A limit order for immediate execution. If it cannot be executed immediately, it is withdrawn.

Final salary scheme Also known as defined benefit scheme. A pension scheme that relates the pension received to the final salary and number of years worked for the employer providing the pension.

Financial future The notional right to buy or sell a standard quantity of a financial instrument on a specific future date at a price determined at the time of buying or selling the futures contract.

Fixed annuities Annuities that pay a constant amount of money each year and, as such, are subject to erosion by inflation.

Fixed income investment An investment, such as a bond, that pays a stated amount of money per period.

Floating rate notes (FRNs) Relatively long-dated securities on which the coupon payment is determined periodically at a prevailing money market interest rate.

Flotation The issue of shares of stock in a company for the first time.

Forward Agreement to exchange financial instruments on a future date at a price determined in the present, e.g. forward currency.

Forward-forward Agreement on the future exchange of financial instruments that will mature on a more distant date, e.g. forward-forward interest rates.

Forward rate agreement (FRA) Notional agreement to deposit or borrow on a specific future date at an interest rate determined in the present (a form of interest rate future).

Front-end load Also known as initial charge. A sales fee paid for the purchase of mutual fund shares (or unit trusts).

FT-SE-A All Share Index Value weighted index of approximately 800 stocks traded on the London Stock Exchange.

FT-SE Eurotrack 100 Value weighted index of 100 European stocks (excluding UK stocks).

FT-SE Mid 250 Value weighted index of 250 UK stocks (the 101st to the 350th in terms of size).

FT-SE 100 Financial Times – Stock Exchange 100. A value weighted index of the top 100 UK stocks.

Fund of funds A unit trust (or OEIC) that invests solely in other unit trusts (or OEICs).

Fundamental analysis Ascertaining the appropriate prices of securities by analysing economic data.

Futures contract A notional obligation to buy or sell an investment or commodity at a given price on a specified future date.

Gearing Expressed as a percentage, gearing refers to the extent of a company's indebtedness, being the ratio of all its borrowings to its assets. A geared investment is one in which the exposure to the stock market exceeds the investor's money outlay; gearing can be obtained by using futures or options.

Gilt Gilt-edged security. A British government bond.

Good-till-cancelled order An order to buy or sell shares that remains on the books until it is cancelled.

Guaranteed equity funds Funds that limit exposure to falls in the stock market while providing a proportion of the gains. They are usually constructed using options.

Hard currency A currency that is fully convertible into major currencies such as the US dollar through the currency markets.

Hedge A transaction undertaken in order to reduce an existing risk.

Immunisation The elimination of interest rate risk in a fixed income portfolio.

In-the-money Options that provide a pay-off from immediate exercise.

Income drawdown As opposed to buying an annuity at retirement, income drawdown involves taking an income from the pension fund which otherwise remains intact.

Income unit Income units of a unit trust pay the dividends to the investor rather than automatically investing them.

Index-linked gilts UK government bonds on which both the level of the coupon paid and the final redemption payment are linked to the retail price index.

Index trackers Funds that aim to track a stock index by replicating or simulating the index. The value of the fund should move in line with the index.

Indirect quotation Quotation of an exchange rate in terms of the number of units of foreign currency per unit of domestic currency.

Industry risk Stock price risk associated with a particular industry.

Inflation risk Also known as purchasing power risk. It is the risk that inflation will erode the value of an investment.

Information risk The risk that other investors may not recognise an investment's true worth.

Information trade A trade based upon information concerning the security.

Initial charge The charge made by the investment manager when a unit trust or OEIC share is purchased.

Inside information Information about a company that is not available to the general public.

Insider trading Trading on inside information.

Institutional investor An institution that invests money on behalf of a number of smaller investors, e.g. pension fund, insurance fund, unit trust, OEIC, investment trust.

Inter-bank market The market in which banks lend to, and borrow from, one another.

Interest rate parity The equilibrium relationship between the spot and forward exchange rates and the interest rates associated with the two currencies.

Interest rate risk The risk of price change in fixed income investments due to changes in market interest rates.

Intermediary An institution that takes deposits and uses the receipts to make loans.

Intrinsic value The gross profit available from the immediate exercise of an option.

Investment trust A quoted company whose business is to invest, mainly in other shares, for the benefit of its own shareholders. It differs from a unit trust in being a 'closed-end fund' and in having its own shares quoted on the stock exchange (a type of mutual fund).

Junk bond Corporate bond with high risk of default and corresponding high yield.

Kerb market Unofficial market, often operating outside the normal trading hours of the official market.

LIBOR (London Interbank Offered Rate) The rate of interest at which major banks in London will lend to each other. (It is the borrowing rate as opposed to the deposit rate, which is LIBID.)

Life office A life assurance company authorised to sell life assurance products and pensions.

Limit order An order to a stockbroker which permits a deal to be done only if it is possible to execute at a certain price or better.

Liquidation The sale of assets.

Liquidity Assets that are either in the form of money or can be easily converted into money.

Liquidity premium The additional return paid to investors for sacrificing the liquidity of their investments.

Liquidity risk The risk that an investment may not be easily convertible into cash at the full current market value.

Listed share A share that is authorised to be traded on a formal stock exchange.

Loan stock An unsecured bond issued by a UK company.

Long Someone holding shares is said to be long of them. A long position gains from price rises and loses from price falls.

Manipulation The activity of a person or a pool of people that is designed to make the price of a security behave in a manner that is different from that caused by normal supply and demand forces.

Manipulation risk The risk that the price of an investment could be affected by manipulation.

Market efficiency The tendency for security prices to reflect economic information fully.

Market-maker A dealer who publishes bid and offer prices on certain securities and is committed to trade at those prices. It is thus ensured that a market always exists in those securities.

Market order An order placed at the market price.

Market portfolio A portfolio of all securities in proportion to their relative market values.

Market price The price at which a security currently trades.

Market risk Non-diversifiable or systematic risk that affects the entire market.

Market timing Attempts to move capital in and out of various markets to maximise participation in bullish movements and minimise exposure to bear markets.

Markowitz-efficient A portfolio that has the highest expected return for a particular level of risk.

Maturity Period to the redemption of a financial claim.

Momentum Of, for example earnings, measures the 'growth in the growth rate' of earnings.

Money broker As a broker in the inter-bank market, a money broker brings together banks wishing to lend and those wishing to borrow. There are also money brokers in currencies and eurobonds.

Money purchase Also known as defined contribution. A pension scheme that accumulates a fund for the individual, with a view to using the fund to buy an annuity at retirement.

Mutual life office A life office that is formally owned by its policyholders rather than by shareholders.

Negative yield curve Short-term interest rates higher than long-term ones.

Net asset value (NAV) The value of all assets held by an investment trust divided by the number of investment trust shares outstanding.

New York Stock Exchange (NYSE) composite index A value-weighted stock index based on all the stocks listed on the NYSE.

Noise trading The trading activity of those without sound fundamental information.

Nominal rate of return The rate of return that is not adjusted for inflation.

Nominal value The face value or par value of a security as opposed to its market value.

Nominee Shares can be registered in a nominee name rather than the real one if they are being managed on behalf of someone else (also known as street name).

Normal distribution The distribution of the probabilities of alternative values of a variable (e.g. a price). It has a bell-shaped form indicating high probabilities of values near the average and low probability of extreme values.

Note An instrument recording a promise to pay sums of money in the future. Similar to bonds but typically of shorter maturity.

Occupational pension scheme Pension scheme sponsored by an employer.

OEICs Open-ended investment companies. Similar to unit trusts but in the form of shares.

Offer price The price at which an investor can buy.

Offer rate The rate of interest at which money can be borrowed.

Offshore banking Banking facilities in locations that offer a very favourable tax environment. Typically the country in which the bank is registered is not that in which the actual banking operations are undertaken.

Open interest The number of outstanding contracts in a futures market.

Open market operations Dealings in the financial markets by a central bank (e.g. the Bank of England) for the purpose of influencing the liquidity of financial institutions and/or controlling interest rates.

Option The right to buy or sell at a specific price during a time period (or at a point in time). Can also be a right to borrow or lend at a particular interest rate.

Out-of-the-money Options for which there is no pay-off from immediate exercise.

Over the counter (OTC) Tailor-made instruments, as opposed to the standardised exchange-traded ones.

Oversubscription An offer of shares or other securities to the investing public is oversubscribed when the number of shares applied for exceeds the number available. This can lead to the scaling down of applications, their placing in a ballot or even their rejection.

P/E (price/earnings) ratio The share price divided by the company's annual earnings per share.

Par value The value of a bond at maturity, also known as face value or nominal value.

Partly paid Securities on which only part of the full cost has been paid, with a further call or calls due to be paid by holders at a future date.

Political risk The risk associated with foreign investments due to political uncertainty in the country or region.

Portfolio An investor's collection of assets.

Portfolio insurance Strategies used to protect a portfolio in the event of a market downturn.

Portfolio rate of return Rate of return on an entire portfolio of investments.

Positive yield curve Long-term interest rates higher than short-term ones.

Preference shares Shares on which a constant level of dividend is paid, providing the money is available. The dividends must be paid before holders of ordinary shares get any money.

Premium 1. Price of an option. 2. Amount by which the forward price of a currency exceeds its spot price. 3. Excess of a futures value over the spot value.

Primary market Market for newly raised capital.

Principal 1. Someone buying or selling on their own account rather than as an agent for a client. 2. The sum of money repayable at the maturity of a bond or other debt instrument.

Private placement The sale of an entire issue of securities to one or a few investors.

Programme trading Trading of entire portfolios or baskets of stock at one time, often in conjunction with derivatives.

Purchasing power risk The risk that inflation may diminish the purchasing power of funds.

Put bonds Limit buyer risk by obligating the issuer to buy the bond if the price falls below a certain level.

Put option The right to sell an instrument at a particular price during a time period (or on a specific date).

Random walk hypothesis The theory that price changes will be random if they rationally reflect available economic information.

Rate of return The return on an investment stated as a percentage of the amount invested.

Real rate of return The inflation-adjusted rate of return.

Redemption date The date when fixed interest stocks, such as gilts and debentures, are redeemed, usually at their nominal value.

Redemption yield The yield on a fixed interest stock (e.g. a bond) which takes into account the annual benefit to be gained as the stock climbs towards its redemption price. If the stock stands above its redemption price, the redemption yield will be lower than the coupon yield.

Repo Sale and repurchase agreement. The sale of securities with a simultaneous commitment to buy them back at a later date. A means of short-term borrowing.

Retractable bonds Bonds that may be redeemed, at the holder's option, on a specified date prior to expiration.

Return on equity (ROE) Net income (earnings) divided by equity.

Return on investment (ROI) Net income divided by total capital, where total capital is debt plus equity.

Return to volatility ratio Also known as the Treynor measure. Measures the ratio of excess return to portfolio beta.

Reward to variability ratio Also known as the Sharpe measure. Measures the return to the investor above the riskless rate due to taking on the uncertainty of a portfolio of risky securities rather than Treasury bills. It is calculated as the ratio of excess return to portfolio standard deviation, where excess return is the difference between portfolio return and Treasury bill yields or riskless returns.

Rights issue An issue of new shares to shareholders, generally at a discount to the current market price, with the number of shares offered being in proportion to the shareholder's existing holding.

Risk-free investment An investment that is virtually free of risk, such as a short-term Treasury bill.

Risk management Controlling the level of financial risk to which an investment is exposed, e.g. by hedging.

Round-trip commission Often used in commodities and futures, involves paying the purchase and sales commissions up front.

Running yield Alternatively known as the coupon yield, dividend yield, flat yield, interest yield or current yield. The annual rate of return offered by the coupon or dividend on a bond or stock.

Samurai bonds Yen-denominated bonds issued in Japan by non-Japanese issuers.

Scrip issue The issue of free shares to investors in proportion to their existing shareholdings. There should be a proportionate fall in the share price leaving investors no better off.

Secondary market A market in which already existing securities are bought and sold. Distinct from the primary market in which newly issued securities are sold.

Securitisation 1. The aggregation of existing assets such as mortgages so as to use them as backing for bond issues, effectively selling a bundle of existing assets. 2. Sale of bills or bonds as an alternative to borrowing from banks.

Security A medium of investment, e.g. stocks, bonds, bills.

Security Market Line (SML) Arising from the Capital Asset Pricing Model, it is a line relating the required rate of return on a stock to the beta of the stock.

Semi-strong form The form of the efficient market hypothesis that maintains that all publicly available information is reflected in share prices.

Settlement The actual transfer of the security from seller to buyer.

Share Instrument denoting part ownership of the equity of a company. Alternatively known as a stock.

Short position A position that profits from price falls and loses from price rises. It entails a commitment to deliver a financial instrument.

Short selling Selling borrowed stock.

SICAV The French equivalent of an OEIC.

Signalling theory Says that companies may signal information through the use of dividends etc. rather than announce it, partly because a signal has greater credibility.

Sinking fund Provisions in a bond's indenture that help to guarantee that the bond will be repaid at maturity. The indenture specifies that a certain amount of the firm's earnings is put aside each year to fund the repayment.

Small firm effect Findings that the shares of smaller capitalisation companies produce relatively strong performance.

Sovereign risk Risk that a government will default on its debt.

Specialist Market-maker on the New York Stock Exchange.

Specific risk Risk beyond market and industry risk that relates to the specific investment being undertaken.

Speculation Buying or selling with a view to making profits from price changes.

Split-capital trust An investment trust that splits its share capital into different types, for example income shares that receive the income and capital shares that benefit from any capital growth.

Spot price Current price as opposed to forward or futures price.

Spread The excess of the ask (offer) price or interest rate over the bid price or interest rate. It is the market-maker's or banker's margin.

Stag Someone who applies for a new issue of shares, intending to sell them almost immediately in order to make a quick profit.

Stamp duty A tax on the purchase of shares.

Standard deviation A measure of the extent to which a set of possible values (forming a normal distribution) is dispersed around their average (mean). Often used as a measure of price volatility.

Stock Most commonly used to denote shares representing ownership of the equity of a firm (common stock, ordinary shares). However, it is sometimes treated as synonymous with bonds.

Stock dividends Extra shares of stock, based upon the number already owned.

Stock exchange Market for the trading of stocks and bonds.

Stock index A measure of the average value of stock prices at a point in time (e.g. S&P 500, FTSE 100, Nikkei 225, DAX, CAC 40, Hang Seng).

Stock split Similar to a scrip issue in that the shareholder is given a certain number of new shares for every share owned.

Stop loss order An order to sell shares once the price of the stock falls to a certain level.

Straddle The simultaneous long position of a put and call option on the same stock with the same expiry date and strike price. (A short straddle involves short positions in both put and call options.)

Strangle A put and a call option on the same stock with different strike prices but the same expiry date (the options are either both long or both short).

Strap The purchase of two calls and a put option.

Street name Also known as a nominee account. The registration of customers' securities in the name of the brokerage firm.

Strike price Also known as exercise price. The stock price at which the holder of an option has the right to buy or sell shares.

Strong form The form of the efficient market hypothesis that maintains that all information of any kind, including non-public inside information, is already reflected in security prices.

Swap 1. An agreement by two parties to exchange future cash flows on terms agreed in the present. 2. A simultaneous spot purchase (or sale) and forward sale (or purchase), i.e. buying for one point in time and selling for another.

Tap stock Government securities of which only part of the issue has so far been sold to the public, the rest being let out on to the market as the government, through its agents, sees fit.

Tax rate risk The risk that tax rates may change, resulting in a loss of after-tax return.

Tax shelter An investment whose purposes include the reduction of taxes.

Technical analysis Prediction of price movements based on the proposition that markets have their own internal momentum, independent of economic events. Chartism is a form of technical analysis that uses charts and graphs of past price movements to forecast future price behaviour.

Tender An issue of securities in which investors must bid a maximum price at which they are willing to subscribe. When the striking price is fixed, all those tendering at that level or above will receive shares.

Time value The amount by which the price of an option exceeds its intrinsic value.

Tombstone An advertisement for a public issue of bonds that contains the names of all the members of the selling syndicate.

Tracker fund Also known as index fund. The fund manager aims to mirror the performance of a stock index.

Transfer value The sum of money that is available to be taken from a pension scheme when moving to a new one.

Treasury bill A debt instrument issued by the central government for raising short-term finance. It is seen as a risk-free investment and the return on it is regarded as being risk free.

Treasury bond A debt instrument issued by the US government for raising long-term finance.

Trustee Legal owner of a fund. Looks after the assets of the fund on behalf of investors.

Turnover In the brokerage business turnover is the volume of buying and selling.

Undated Government bonds which have no fixed date set for repayment.

Underwriter Someone who undertakes to subscribe for all or part of an issue of securities if it is not wholly taken up by the public, in return for which an underwriting commission is paid. The underwriter will pass on this commitment to sub-underwriters such as banks, insurance companies and pension funds, and they will also receive commission.

Unit trust A trust formed to manage a portfolio on behalf of the holders of its units. Each unitholder's stake in that trust is in direct proportion to the number of units he/she holds. The value of units depends upon the value of the portfolio. A unit trust is an open-ended mutual fund.

Unsecured loan stock A bond issued by a company but which is not secured by any of the company's assets.

Value-weighted A stock index whose components are weighted by the market capitalisations of the companies.

Variable annuities Annuities that each year pay a sum of money that is determined by the market performance of funds invested.

Venture capital trusts (VCTs) Collective investments for shares in small and new enterprises.

Volatility The degree of price, or return, fluctuation over time. It is often measured by standard deviation.

Warrant A long-term call option giving the holder the right to subscribe for a stock at a specific price during a period of time.

Weak form The form of the efficient market hypothesis according to which share prices fully reflect all information contained in past share prices.

White knight A friendly acquirer of a company faced with a hostile takeover.

White squires Prevent hostile takeovers by holding large blocks of a company's shares in their friendly hands.

Wholesale market The market for deposits and loans in which each transaction involves a large sum of money. It is largely an inter-bank market.

With-profits fund A form of investment fund for pensions and life assurance-related investments. There is a guaranteed minimum sum payable at maturity. The minimum sum is added to each year by means of reversionary bonuses that cannot be taken away. At maturity a terminal bonus is added.

Yankee bond A dollar-denominated bond issued in the United States by a borrower outside the United States.

Yield The annual return on an investment divided by its price, measured as a percentage.

Yield curve Relationship between the time to maturity of bonds (strictly speaking zero coupon bonds) and their redemption yields.

Yield gap The difference between the average coupon yield on long-dated gilts and the average dividend yield on equities.

Zero coupon bond A bond that pays no coupon. The return to the holder arises from the bond being sold at a discount to its redemption value at maturity.

Zero dividend preference shares Sometimes called 'zeros', they are often sold by investment trusts. They pay no dividends but provide a capital sum to the investor when the investment trust is wound up.

Suggested answers to discussion questions

Chapter 3

1 Distinguish between unit trusts and investment trusts.

Answer

(a) Unit trusts are funds operated by fund managers such as stockbrokers, banks or insurance companies. Investment trusts are companies whose business is to invest in other companies.

(b) Unit trusts are open-ended investments. Purchases and sales of units are from, and to, the fund manager and entail expansions/contractions in the size of the fund. Investment trusts are closed-end. Investment trust shares are traded on stock markets. Purchases and sales are from, and to, other investors and have no effect on the size of the fund.

(c) The value of unit trusts is directly related to the value of the shares held by the fund. The value of a unit equals the value of the fund divided by the number of units in existence. The values of investment trust shares are determined by supply and demand and as a result are not precisely related to the value of the fund. If the value of investment trust shares is below the value of the fund, the shares are said to be at a discount to net asset value.

(d) Investment trusts have much greater scope for borrowing in order to increase the exposure of the fund to stock markets.

(e) Investment trusts may have winding-up dates, may issue warrants and may have split-capital structures. These are not possible for unit trusts.

2 What are the relative merits of unit trusts, OEICs, investment trusts, investment bonds and endowment policies from the point of view of individual investors?

Answer

There are common features, e.g. diversification to reduce risk, administration to save the investor time and effort, professional management to meet the investor's objectives, and economies of scale in transactions to reduce the costs of buying and selling shares.

There are differences, e.g. most are open-ended but investment trusts are closed-end funds, investment trusts have premiums/discounts whereas the others do not, investment trusts can be more highly geared than the others, there is a life assurance component with investment bonds and endowment policies, there can be differences with regard to choices of underlying funds, endowment policies are typically the least flexible as to patterns of investment and withdrawal, there are variations in tax treatment and differing levels of charges. Investment bonds and endowment policies tend to entail the highest charges and be the least tax efficient for most potential investors. Investment trusts tend to have relatively low charges, as do unit trusts (and OEICs) that track stock indices. Unit trusts, OEICs and investment trusts can benefit from increased tax efficiency by being held in ISAs (individual savings accounts) or pension plans.

3 What might an investor consider when choosing between unit trusts, OEICs, investment trusts and investment bonds?

Answer

(a) Do they provide the required level of portfolio diversification?
(b) Do they provide with-profits as well as unit-linked investments?
(c) Do they provide the sector, style or geographic focus required?
(d) Do they provide an adequate income flow, if required?
(e) How do they differ in terms of tax efficiency? Can they be incorporated into ISAs? Can they be included in pension plans?
(f) How do they differ in terms of charges?
(g) Are they flexible in relation to patterns of investment and withdrawal?
(h) Are there differences in relation to prospective risks and returns? (The discounts and gearing of investment trusts is relevant here.)
(i) Is the investment philosophy and history acceptable? Do they satisfy any ethical requirements of the investor?

● ● ● ● Chapter 4

How would you explain the popularity of with-profits pension funds?

Answer

People need to fund retirement and the demographic timebomb makes this even more important. The increasing ratio of pensioners to workers reduces the ability of the state to meet pension needs. With-profits pension funds, like many other funds, provide the advantages of collective investments. These advantages include risk reduction by diversification, administration, professional management, and economies of scale in the buying and selling of investments. Pension funds also attract generous tax concessions.

With-profits funds also provide specific advantages such as the smoothing of returns that aims to even out the effects of stock market fluctuations. They guarantee minimum values so as to provide protection against substantial stock market falls. So with-profits funds provide the prospective high returns of stock market investment but with reduced risk. However, part of the returns are held back as reserves by the fund managers and this reduces returns to the personal investor. Also, with-profits funds tend to be opaque in that the reasons for the allocation of returns to investors are often not clear.

Chapter 7

How do bonds differ from shares? Why is there such a large variety of bonds?

Answer

(a) Most bonds pay fixed coupons that the issuer is legally obliged to pay. Ordinary shares pay variable dividends, which are at the discretion of the issuer. Preference shares typically pay fixed dividends, but without a legal obligation on the issuer to make payments. Bonds are debt of the issuer, shares denote part ownership of the firm.

(b) The conventional bond pays a fixed stream of coupons and redeems the nominal value at maturity. There are also bonds with variable coupons, some have deferred coupons, others pay no coupons. Some bonds have no redemption date, other bonds have flexible redemption dates. Some are convertible into shares, some have option features that allow the issuer or holder to force redemption. There are also eurobonds and foreign bonds; such bonds raise money in foreign currencies. Some bonds are secured against the property of the issuer, some are not. Bonds differ in terms of their credit ratings, in particular between investment grade and speculative grade. Index-linked bonds relate both coupons and redemption values to a price index.

(c) The large variety arises from the desire to meet the precise needs of issuers and investors, and those needs are very varied.

Chapter 8

1 What are the functions of stock markets? How do stock market trading systems differ?

Answer

(a) Stock markets transfer money from savers to those needing to obtain capital. They thereby provide both investment opportunities and sources of finance. As secondary markets they increase investors' willingness to invest in primary markets. They also provide price information, which is useful for the valuation of firms.

(b) The trading systems are order-driven, quote-driven, or a hybrid of the two systems. Trading systems may be floor-based or computer-based.

2 What are the various types of share and bond? Why is there such a large variety?

Answer

Ordinary shares (common stock) provide part ownership of the firm and the right to vote at general meetings. The dividends are at the discretion of the board of directors and there is no legal obligation to pay dividends. In the event of bankruptcy, the owners of ordinary shares are the last to receive anything from the sale of the firm's assets. Preference shares (and preferred shares) also provide part ownership of the firm but normally without voting rights. The dividends are typically fixed, but there is no legal obligation on the firm to pay dividends. Preference shares come in a wide variety of forms: cumulative, convertible, redeemable and participating are characteristics that preference shares may or may not possess.

Bonds do not represent part ownership of the firm, instead they are debts of the firm. The firm is legally obliged to pay the coupons (dividends) and to redeem the bond at maturity. Bonds are available in a vast variety. There are domestic, foreign and eurobonds. There are government and corporate bonds. Bonds may be convertible into shares or other bonds. Patterns of coupon payment also vary; coupons may be fixed, variable, index-linked or deferred. The sum to be repaid at maturity may be index-linked. Some bonds have embedded options giving issuers or holders the right to redeem the bonds before maturity. In the event of bankruptcy, bondholders must be paid proceeds from the sale of the firm's assets before any money can be paid to shareholders.

There is a large variety of shares and bonds because the needs of different issuers and investors vary. Issuers may be prepared to pay more to investors in order to issue the shares or bonds that suit them best. Likewise investors may accept a lower return in order to get the investments that best suit their needs.

Chapter 9

Can behavioural finance help to explain stock market bubbles and crashes?

Answer

Relevant behavioural finance theories include representativeness, narrow framing and overconfidence. These may be particularly important for explaining the behaviour of the naïve investors who invest in response to stock price rises. Other relevant factors include the role of borrowing to finance investment, and the resulting potential for virtuous and vicious circles. Also of significance are the events and circumstances that lead to upturns and downturns: interest rate changes, technological developments, changes in levels of prosperity, statements by influential people, sensationalised newspaper and television reporting, investors running out of sources of finance or shares to sell.

● ● ● ● Chapter 12

1 What is a stock index? What are the different approaches to the calculation of a stock index? Are the various approaches equally useful with respect to satisfying the purposes of stock indices?

Answer

(a) A stock index is an indicator of the total value of shares on a stock exchange.
(b) Stock indices differ in terms of how many stocks are included in the calculation, the weightings of the stocks (unweighted, price weighted, value weighted) and the method of averaging (arithmetic means, geometric means).
(c) Purposes include monitoring a stock market and aggregate wealth. They provide a basis for tracker funds, derivatives and fund performance evaluation. Stock indices are leading economic indicators. They are used in applications of the capital asset pricing model.

Arithmetically averaged, value weighted indices provide the most accurate indicators of the overall value of a stock market. In consequence such measures fulfil the functions of indices to a greater extent than other indices.

2 Is it possible that two different stock indices, both measuring movements of the same stock market, can move in opposite directions?

Answer

Stock indices can differ in terms of sample sizes, weighting and averaging. In relation to sample sizes, it is possible that the FTSE 100 (which covers the top 100 UK stocks) can differ in direction to the FT All-Share index (which covers about 800 stocks) if the rest of the market has a different direction to that of the top 100. Such a possibility is plausible since the FTSE 100 is dominated by a small number of sectors (telecommunications, banking, pharmaceuticals, oil).

Stock indices may be unweighted, price weighted or value weighted. Value weighted indices give greatest importance to large companies whereas unweighted indices give equal importance to all companies. If small company shares perform differently to large company shares, indices calculated on the two different bases could move in opposite directions. Indices that use geometric averaging are effectively unweighted indices. Geometric averaging also distorts the relative influence of high growth and low growth companies.

● ● ● ● Chapter 16

What is a security market line? How useful is a security market line as a guide to choosing which shares to buy or sell?

Answer

(a) A linear function that relates the required rate of return on an investment to the beta of that investment.

(b) If a share is fairly priced, it will be on the security market line (the anticipated return on the share equals the required rate of return).

(c) A share that is above the security market line has an anticipated rate of return that exceeds the required rate of return. Such a share is a potential purchase.

(d) A share that is below the security market line offers an anticipated rate of return that is below the required rate of return. Such a share should be sold.

● ● ● ● Chapter 19

1 How can the constant dividend discount model be rendered more realistic as a method for estimating the fair prices of shares?

Answer

(a) The constant dividend discount model obtains a fair price for a share by discounted a stream of future dividends, which are assumed to remain unchanged.

(b) The Gordon growth model (constant growth model) allows for dividend growth at a constant rate.

(c) Stochastic dividend discount models allow for the possibility that in some years dividends do not grow.

(d) Multi-period models (e.g. two-period models) allow for different time periods to exhibit different rates of dividend growth.

2 How reliable are dividend discount models as means of estimating the fair prices of shares? How can two-period dividend discount models be used for ascertaining fair prices of shares?

Answer

(a) The constant dividend model is highly unrealistic. The Gordon Growth model (constant growth model), the stochastic model and the multi-period model make more realistic assumptions. The reliability of the models depends on the accuracy of the forecasts of dividend growth and of the appropriateness of the required rate of return employed.

(b) The share price, for the point in time at which dividend growth is expected to change, is estimated using the Gordon growth model (or the stochastic version). The discounted value of the estimated future share price is added to the discounted value of the dividends expected (during the period up to the expected date of the change in the dividend growth rate).

Chapter 23

If the efficient market hypothesis is valid, are investment analysis and active fund management worthwhile?

Answer

The efficient market hypothesis suggests that all relevant information is quickly incorporated into security prices. This implies that there is no scope for making profits from forecasting stock prices. Investment analysis is concerned with stock selection and/or market timing. Stock selection entails trying to ascertain mispriced investments with a view to buying under-priced securities and selling over-priced securities. Market timing attempts to forecast the points in time at which markets turn upwards or downwards. The efficient market hypothesis suggests that investment analysis is pointless on the grounds that available information is already reflected in asset prices and therefore cannot be used to make forecasts of price changes.

Active fund management seeks to use the results of investment analysis to manage portfolios of stocks in such a way that the portfolios outperform benchmarks, such as stock indices. If investment analysis is ineffective, active fund management is pointless. Investors would do better to invest in funds that aim to track stock indices and thereby avoid the expense of investment analysis and active fund management.

However, there is a paradox. For new information to become incorporated into security prices, there may need to be buying or selling based on that information. Investors who undertake those trades could make profits. Those who are first to receive, or react to, new information will make profits. Investment analysis and active fund management on the part of those who act quickest would be profitable. The absence of any profitable opportunities would require all investors, both buyers and sellers, to instantly adjust their price expectations in the light of new information.

 Chapter 25

1 'Diversification reduces non-systematic risk. Stock index futures can reduce systematic risk. Therefore share price risk can be eliminated completely.' Do you agree?

Answer

It is the case that a well-diversified portfolio should have no non-systematic risk. It is also the case that hedging a portfolio with stock index futures reduces systematic risk. However, hedging with stock index futures cannot eliminate systematic risk completely. There are a number of reasons for this.

First, the index to which a futures contract relates may not be fully representative of the market as a whole. For example, futures based on the FTSE 100 cannot perfectly eliminate the systematic risk of the whole market since the top 100 companies are not fully representative of the whole stock market. Second, there are reasons for expecting hedging to be imperfect. These include basis risk and the indivisibility of contracts. Also hedge ratios are based on portfolio betas, and betas may be unstable in that future betas are unlikely to be precisely equal to the past betas on which the hedge ratios are based.

2 How are stock index futures used? Why might they be less than perfect in their uses?

Answer

(a) They may be used in hedging (i.e. risk reduction). The existing risk should be balanced by a beta-weighted offsetting position in futures. Imperfections arise because of basis risk, the instability of beta, the indivisibility of contracts and non-systematic risk (futures cover only systematic risk).
(b) Futures may be used in futures funds. Futures funds may replicate tracker funds or may be geared. Changes in basis can reduce the accuracy of replication.
(c) Futures may be used for the purpose of speculation. Problems could arise from market impact effects, illiquidity, changes in basis and the possibility that forecasts may be wrong.
(d) Futures can be used to make arbitrage profits. Imperfections could arise because apparent arbitrage opportunities may not be real ones because of transaction costs, non-synchronous trading, market impact effects and the possibility of adverse market movements while the arbitrage is being constructed.

● ● ● ● Chapter 26

1 How can options be used in fund management?

Answer

Options can be used to hedge against falls in share prices. Protection against a fall in share prices can be obtained by buying put options or by writing call options. Anticipatory hedges protect future purchases from price rises by the purchase of calls or the sale of puts.

Written options can be used to augment the income of a portfolio. Some high-income funds pay high dividends to investors partly as a result of the premium receipts from writing options.

Options are used in the construction of guaranteed investment funds. These funds provide profits from a rising stock market while guaranteeing that the sum invested cannot be lost. The alternative strategies are fiduciary calls and protective puts.

Call options can be used to gain exposure to share prices at a fraction of the cost of the shares. This allows fund managers to take geared positions on stocks.

2 (a) What factors affect the prices of stock options? (b) How do investors use options?

Answer

(a) Moneyness (the extent to which the option is in- or out-of-the-money), expected stock price volatility, time to expiry, interest rates and expected dividend yields.

(b) Options can be used to hedge against price falls (buying puts or writing calls). They can be used to hedge against price rises (buying calls or writing puts). They can be used to speculate on stock price changes; the gearing effect may be attractive to speculators. They can be used in the construction of guaranteed investment funds.

● ● ● ● Chapter 28

How can bond price volatility be measured? What is the purpose of making such measurements?

Answer

Bond price volatility is measured by duration. Macaulay's duration is calculated as the average period of time to cash flows. Each period to a cash flow is weighted by the contribution of that cash flow to the fair price of the bond (for example the present value of a coupon is divided by the fair price of the bond and the result is multiplied by the time period between the present and the receipt of that coupon).

Related measures are modified duration and money duration. Modified duration is calculated as Macaulay's duration divided by [1 + (redemption yield)/(number of coupon payments per year)]. Money duration is modified duration multiplied by the bond price. Money duration measures the change in the bond price resulting from an interest rate change and is alternatively known as perturbation or the price value of a basis point.

The purposes of making such volatility calculations include the desire to forecast the bond price changes that would result from interest rate movements. Modified duration and money duration enable prediction of the effects of interest rate changes on bond prices.

Duration is also used in bond portfolio management. If the duration of a fund manager's assets is matched to the duration of the liabilities, the portfolio is protected against unexpected interest rate fluctuations. Matching the durations is known as immunisation and is based on price risk and reinvestment risk offsetting each other.

Chapter 30

1 (a) What is a yield curve? (b) What could cause a yield curve to change shape?

Answer

(a) The relationship between yield and maturity for bonds and money market investments.
(b) (i) According to the pure expectations theory, changes in relative interest rate expectations for different future periods. (ii) According to expectations with risk premiums, changes in capital risk aversion and income risk aversion (in addition to changes in relative expectations). (iii) According to the market segmentation hypothesis, changes in the relative demand and supply pressures for different maturities.

2 What can be deduced from the position and shape of a yield curve?

Answer

If the expectations theory is valid, implications can be drawn about market expectations of future interest rates. Observed interest rates (strictly speaking zero coupon rates) for differing maturities can be used to deduce expected future interest rates for the periods between those maturities. Forward interest rate calculations are used. If risk premiums are seen as being present, the forward interest rate calculations need to be adjusted to take account of the risk premiums when drawing implications about interest rate expectations.

It may also be possible to draw implications about perceived risks and the levels of risk aversion. In particular an upward sloping yield curve is consistent with capital risk and capital risk aversion. A downward sloping yield curve is consistent with income risk and income risk aversion.

Index